PROPHETS OF THE WEST

An Introduction to the
Philosophy of History

JOHN EDWARD SULLIVAN
Doctor of Theology

HOLT, RINEHART AND WINSTON, INC.
New York Chicago San Francisco Atlanta Dallas
Montreal Toronto London Sydney

Acknowledgments

Croce, B., *History as the Story of Liberty* (London: George Allen & Unwin Ltd., 1941).

Huxley, J., *The Humanist Frame* (London: George Allen & Unwin Ltd., 1962).

Rickman, H. P. (ed.), *Meaning in History* (London: George Allen & Unwin Ltd., 1961).

Spengler, O., *The Decline of the West* (London: George Allen & Unwin Ltd., 1926).

From Pitirim, Sorokin, *Social and Cultural Dynamics*, The Bedminster Press, New York, 1962. Copyright, 1937, 1941 by the Bedminster Press. Reprinted by permission.

From Immanuel Kant: *On History*, translated by Lewis White Beck, copyright, © 1963, by the Liberal Arts Press, Inc., reprinted by permission of the Liberal Arts Press Division of the Bobbs-Merrill Company, Inc.

Kroeber, A. L., *An Anthropologist Looks at History* (Berkeley, Calif.: University of California Press, 1963). Reprinted by permission of The Regents of the University of California.

Kroeber, A. L., *The Nature of Culture* (Chicago: University of Chicago Press, 1952).

Collingwood, R., *The Idea of History*, by permission of the Clarendon Press, Oxford.

Collingwood, R., *An Autobiography*, by permission of the Clarendon Press, Oxford.

Collingwood, R., *An Essay on Philosophical Method*, by permission of the Clarendon Press, Oxford.

Reprinted from *The New Science of Giambattista Vico*, translated by Thomas Goddard Bergin and Max Harold Fisch. Copyright © 1968 by Cornell University, copyright © 1961 by Thomas Goddard Bergin and Max Harold Fisch, copyright 1948 by Cornell University. Used by permission of Cornell University Press.

From *Modern Historical and Social Philosophies* by Pitirim Sorokin. Dover Publications, Inc., New York, 1963. Reprinted through the permission of the publisher.

From the book *The Crisis of Our Age* by Pitirim A. Sorokin. Copyright, 1941, by E. P. Dutton & Co., Inc. Reprinted by permission of the publishers.

ii

Dedicated to
Robert B. Perry
with whom I have been learning
the meaning of friendship.

foreword

Some books are regarded by their editors as more or less routine and others as a publishing *event*. As academic editor of John Edward Sullivan's *Prophets of the West*, I am happy to regard this book as a publishing event. Lest the reader mistake this for a purely subjective opinion, I invite him to survey the sweep of this book, covering as it does, a wide range of philosophies of history from Augustine to De Chardin. Nor is the coverage, even where it is brief, superficial, as the author has given ample evidence both in text and in footnotes that he has thoroughly examined the sources for himself. As a matter of fact, this book represents a distillation of six years of research in the philosophy of history, giving witness on each page to the author's competence both as a teacher and as a scholar of the fascinating material which he has chosen to present.

Although philosophy of history is an intellectual discipline that dates back to the early Greeks, it is a subject which, through the influence of such scholars as Toynbee, has come into prominence only in recent times. Even more recently has it acquired a foothold as an academic subject in our schools. The present volume, however, is one that should have a variety of uses—both for the general reader and the student. For academic purposes it should have a cross-disciplinary appeal to philosophers and historians alike, and beyond this its appeal should extend to an ever-widening circle of professors of religion who wish to provide for themselves and their students a dimension of understanding that is not available in their specialized area of research. Best of all, whether to the student of philosophy, history, religion, or even of the social sciences, Sullivan's *Prophets* will provide an integrated view of Western civilization and culture that few books have even attempted to achieve.

Further, this book will serve a purpose that ordinary courses in history, philosophy, or religion will not, namely, that of providing for the reader a perspective in which to view history itself. Particularly in this part of the Western world is it the case that modern man has very little sense of the meaning or meanings of history—whether in his individual life or in his social life. The evidence for this deficiency is the present iconoclastic tendency to reject—without adequate study or understanding—the whole of one's social and religious traditions. For example, the recent death-of-God movement, as well as the secular city debate it entails, give evidence of the near total ignorance of the Augustian distinction between the City of God and the City of Man. A careful and penetrating analysis of this distinction might well give rise to a re-examination of the relevance of the Christian revelation of the dilemmas of modern man. Yet, in the midst of present-day turmoil, little more than lip tribute is given to the sense of direction that the Augustinian synthesis provides.

I do not wish, however, to create the impression that the author confines himself to the Christian viewpoint alone. As a matter of fact, the bulk of this volume is devoted to various secular philosophies of history which have flourished in the last two or three hundred years and which have been placed (some of them at least) in direct opposition to the idea of a providential God who rules the course of human events. Take, for example, the philosophies of progress of the Enlightenment period which were, as the author points out, an extension of the Christian hope that mankind could be saved or redeemed, not by an all-beneficent Provider, but by purely human efforts and, in more recent views, by exclusively technological means. As the author observes: "A belief in the perfectibility and the indefinite progress of the human race on earth tended to take the place of the Christian faith in the life of the world to come as the final goal of all human effort."

Indeed, one of the great turning points in man's view of himself and of human history came about at a time (that of the deists) which marked, not a total rejection of the Judaeo-Christian viewpoint, but a re-interpretation of it which led to its modern decline. To the deist of the sixteenth and seventeenth centuries the dominant view of the universe was a mechanistic one which held that all things are governed by a minimal number but also by a rigid set of laws. To interfere with these laws is to interfere with the order of nature itself. For example, it was held that the laws of economics were so rigid that any interference with them on the part of government would lead to a state of havoc in society. Hence the policy of an economic determinism, a *laissez-faire* system that prepared the way for quite a different type of determinism in the nineteenth century, that of Karl Marx. In the Marxian interpretation of history economics itself was the sole or at least the chief determinant in the shaping of human civilization and culture, which is to say, that everything else, government and religion included, is a by-product of the economic drive.

In connection with deism the point I wish to stress is the fact that it provided modern man, *classical* modern man, with a halfway house to the various forms of naturalism and materialism that are discussed in this text. Indeed, it was only over a period of time that the dominantly religious view of man and of human history gave way to the various facets of secular humanism as we know it today. Worthy of note also is the fact that men are different today because they are under the influence (whether they recognize it or not) of different world views. Thus a person who has been placed under the spell of the rather pessimistic outlook of a Spengler will respond far differently to the future of mankind than will a person, let us say, who is influenced by the Christian optimism of a Teilhard de Chardin. In any event, the situation as we know it today, that is, in terms of the ultimates that shape human lives and institutions, is mixed, and not even a philosopher of history can forebode with any degree of certainty what the outcome will be. One thing, however, is clear: it is hardly a foregone conclusion that the once dominantly religious view of history will return. It may, of course, return, and, if it does, it will exist under a far different form, probably in a more secular form. The point is this: there exists to this day (in a considerably different context) a City of Man–City of God dispute that has not been finally resolved, and perhaps will not be resolved until the end of the historical process.

Be all of this as it may, my point in writing this foreword is not to provide a hasty review of the leading currents of thought traced out by the author in this book. (That would indeed be a formidable task.) My main concern is to show (relative to the values of this book) that if modern man is to acquire a profound understanding of himself, he can do so only in the light of the different philosophies of history that have made him what he is today. As I see it, men have a profound need to overcome the historical myopia which it is the aim of this book to cure. More specifically, if contemporary man wishes to understand why the dominant mood today is against human reason, let him study in this volume the presuppositions of an earlier era which held that reason itself, like a god, is both absolute and supreme. Further, if he wishes to know why a reaction is developing against the all-pervasive influence of science, let him also discover in this volume how certain philosophies of history, like Comte's, envisioned the positive sciences as the central key to the happiness of man. Finally, let him keep in mind that most of the currents of thought which have pervaded our present-day society have been anticipated at least by one or another of the philosophies of history treated in this book.

The story of these different philosophies is, as I have said, a fascinating one, but it is one that must be patiently read and studied in the mines of this compact volume, footnotes and all. Consider, for example, the hidden treasure of wisdom in the footnote from Hegel's *Philosophy of History*: "A nation is moral, virtuous, vigorous, while it is engaged in realizing its grand objects, and defends its work against external violence . . . interest is present only where there is opposition . . . . Mere customary life . . . is that which brings on natural death. Custom is activity without opposition . . . a political nullity and tedium."

In conclusion, the strength of this work is the vision it encompasses throughout the whole range of history from Augustine to Teilhard de Chardin. Its value, apart from the large measure of speculative insights it affords, is the degree of wisdom it can provide in learning the lessons of history for the problems of modern man. Indeed, the future of man will largely depend on what man can discover about his past, and the present volume is no small tool for examining the possibilities of what that future might be.

Robert J. Kreyche
University of Arizona
Tucson
January 1970

preface

The origin of this book goes back to my first teaching post in which I was asked to provide a survey course in the history of the Christian church. Though I had made a historical study of one of the key theological ideas of the great Saint Augustine, I was little prepared for teaching history. Moreover, my intellectual leaning is not toward the amassing or retention of historical materials, but rather in the direction of reflection on this data. Something had to be done and done quickly.

Any historical survey worthy of the name is one man's synthesis of the available historical data. Selective in the extreme, it arranges and organizes the materials around certain leading themes thought to be of overriding significance for its subject, all the while devouring huge tracts of time, space, and historical humanity. In my case two millenia or so of Christian history had to be compressed, summarized, and synthesized. That history is quite complex. It not only runs alongside of but runs through the history of the western world, to say nothing of its many openings towards other lands and cultures. Happily I came across what I came to consider a masterful synthetic reconstruction of much of the past of Christianity. Christopher Dawson's *The Making of Europe* ties together thousands of historical data into an organic whole, illuminating the receding corridors of Christianity with a very brilliant light and hypothesis. But was it true?

Whether I could answer this question to my complete satisfaction, whether indeed it was even a proper question to ask, teaching had to go on. My experience as a student in historical courses, along with my recent foray into Augustinian studies, made me wary. Undoubtedly I had heard some wonderfully interesting and informative lectures about the human past as a student, but unification of massive stretches of data covering continents, centuries, and peoples had not been their outstanding feature.

The grand movements of history seemed to have been lost to sight behind the billowing clouds thrown up by the dusty historical materials. Or were there any grand movements in human history? And if so, how could they ever be known at all? The very raising of questions such as these was enough to delight the heart of one given over to philosophical reflection, and from this point on I was led inevitably to a wide range of associated problems such as the engrossing question as to whether there are such things as historical facts. In short, I found myself in a new land, in one of the youngest provinces of philosophy, in the philosophy of history, or, as some prefer, in metahistory.

Exploration of the new territory began, and as I was led into reading a seemingly endless variety of materials, I found that taking notes was a matter of survival in this vast, strange land. While reading continued, one day this ambitious thought came to mind: Why not put the results of this reading at the disposal of others, for if there is one thing to equal the joys of intellectual discovery, it is that of sharing the adventure with others. And thus the idea of this book was born.

Born, it is true, but, as it turned out, soon sorely in need of disciplining and dieting. As my reading continued for some years, the notes grew in size, and the idea for a book became heavy with complications, indeed outsized. Eventually I had projected a work which would exhaustively and tidily report on the historical development of metahistory. Once this ambition had been exposed to the critical gaze of others, particularly to that of my graduate students, it became painfully evident that the idea of a philosophy of history—such as I had originally conceived it—was too large for a single volume. Grudgingly I admitted that it had to be put on a strict diet, that it had to be slenderized and stylized to meet the reading public. And so the idea of this book reached a more mature age.

As for the intent of this book—given now in its final form—let me say quite simply that it is not meant to serve as an exhaustive historical study of the philosophy of history. Nor, on the other hand, is it intended as a tidy, neatly logical abstraction of the problems from metahistory. It is intended as a guide to the province of metahistory, a selective guide through the philosophy of history. One does not expect a guided tour to visit every monument or ruin, nor demand that it stop at every battlefield or town. What can be expected is sufficient exposure to works of genius and art, time for acquaintance with the great figures, controversies, and crises of the past. Necessarily there is emphasis on the history of the territory, as in every tour, but history is never related for itself. It is given that we might understand how the philosophy of history came to be in its present condition as well as enable us to transcend the inevitable narrowness of its contemporary limits. This is the idea behind this book.

Our tour through the province of metahistory proceeds in four stages (or parts). Each stage is broken up into stops (or chapters) for intimate and leisurely viewing of points of interest. Stage one, the metamorphoses of the city of God, begins with their theological ancestor, Augustine's *City of God*, but proceeds forthwith to the eighteenth century philosophies of progress and the nineteenth century classic western philosophies of history from Hegel and Marx to Comte and Spencer. Stage two, historicism complete and incomplete, takes us through the later nineteenth century into the twentieth. Critical historians, such as Ranke, and especially the critical philosophers of history such as Dilthey, Croce, and Collingwood, are the focal points.

With stage three, designated as the rhythms of history, we are completely within the twentieth century. Professional philosophers are left behind in favor of such historians as Spengler and Toynbee and social scientists such as Sorokin and Kroeber who have been staking out their claims to apparently abandoned sections of the philosophy of history. Stage four, the ascent of history, brings our tour to a close. Natural scientists such as Julian Huxley and Teilhard de Chardin now occupy the center of attention. Only a sophisticated twentieth century science could hope to support these interpretations of history. What is surprising is that a Christian dimension could be thought compatible with this version of history. With the final chapter on Teilhard our tour ends, as it begins, with a Christian interpretation of history, but with one that seeks a close integration between the sacred and the secular.

John Edward Sullivan

Tuscon, Arizona
February 1970

contents

The Metamorphoses of Augustine's City of God

PART ONE

1

THE CITY OF GOD
AND THE CITY OF MAN:

Augustine and Vico

Although the designation philosophy of history dates from the Enlightenment, the classic development of its theme was left to Western thinkers of the early nineteenth century. By this time the concept implied that the course of human history is rational and intelligible. Once this has been said, however, there are some ambiguities in the conception of the rationality of the historical process. It was not a discovery of the modern philosophers of history that the course of history is rational in the sense that it is intelligible, or largely so, in reference to historical and immanent causes. One can go back easily to the ancient Greek historians for such a view. Nor was it left to the modern era to consider the course of history as rational and orderly in the sense that it was driving or being driven toward a preordained goal and fulfilling a preordained plan. This view is implicated in the biblical providential conception of history. The novelty of the classical philosophies of history consisted in a unique combination of the two ancient themes. Rejecting all transcendence, nineteenth-century philosophers claimed that the course of history is fully rational and completely intelligible solely in reference to historical causes which forced events along the path and in the direction of desirable earthly goals. Laws governing the course of history were discovered, or so it was claimed, and history as a self-enclosed system began to join a like conception of nature. The final step was taken when history was reduced to nature and one comprehensive law was postulated for the whole of reality.

3

Not all philosophers went this far, nor did this development take place all at once. Some previous steps needed to be taken before the final synthesis could become intellectually respectable. Before Hegel and Marx or Comte and Spencer conceived their philosophies of history, philosophies of progress were displacing a perennial Christian providential view of history among European intellectuals. Before the philosophies of progress became socially acceptable there was Voltaire. Before Voltaire there was Vico, and before Vico, Bossuet. Bossuet's *Discourse on Universal History* of 1681 owed its best elements to Augustine's *City of God*.

The City of God: Augustine

Augustine's theological interpretation of history was occasioned by the sack of Rome in 410 by Alaric and his Arian Christian Goths. This disaster shocked the ancient civilized world, Christian as well as non-Christian. A question concerning the event was put to Augustine. Why did the Empire decline so rapidly once its rulers had embraced Christianity and abandoned paganism? Could the decline perhaps be attributed to peculiar Christian virtues which extolled tolerance for offenses and submission to injury? Augustine's initial answer to this large problem was brief. Rome declined from within, as evidenced by its increasingly corroded morals, long before it fell outwardly to an invading force. Further, Christianity is not only the true religion, but also, when it is sincerely practiced, the best religion for the city of man. Not completely satisfied himself with this brief answer, Augustine found it necessary to deal with this question in a number of books (or chapters).[1] *The City of God* is Augustine's detailed answer.

Before explaining how the course of history should be interpreted positively in the light of biblical revelation, Augustine repudiates several pagan views of the course of time. He first rejects the traditional pagan notion of fate or fortune. According to this doctrine, everything in the course of history, as in the course of a man's life, is dictated by blind necessity or destiny. In place of this fatalistic notion Augustine offered a Christian view of divine providence. Everything in nature and in history, including the sack of Rome, falls within the plan of divine providence and under divine governance; nothing escapes divine foreknowledge or the divine will. Providence is a divine art which orders everything in an all-embracing harmony, from inorganic matter through living things to the events of human history. Not only are the rise and fall of kingdoms contained in this wise order but sin and evil as well. Death and the struggle for existence, physical evil, are necessary among subrational living things, since the infinite perfections of the creator God can be only approximately represented on this level of being by a succession of seasons and generations. Among men, on the other hand, death and suffering in the present order of things are the result ultimately of sin, the true evil in the universe. Moral evil, or sin, has no part in the reflection of the divine beauty among creatures. The possibility of sin, however,. that is, creaturely freedom, is necessary, since it is inextricably bound up·with the rational nature of God's image in the universe, at least this side of eternity.[2]

This is not to say that man's free will, the cause of moral evil, is lost in the harmonious ordering of all events in the divine plan. Man's freedom, or his causality, blunted as it may well be due to original sin, is a necessary part of the order of created causes willed by God. But God is able to bring about his purposes in and through and despite the limited and often evil goals of man. Free to sin, or free to adhere to God, granted his omnipresent grace, man in either case remains free and responsible. This freedom not only does not escape the divine harmony but is a necessary element in it. Nor does sin itself reduce the divine plan to chaos and disorder. Along with physical evils it can be compared to the shadows blended into a portrait or to antitheses that set off a poem or to discordant notes harmonized in a new song of creation and re-creation. Nothing is able to frustrate the divine artist.[3]

One should also understand that divine justice is not compromised by the events of human history. Certain goods and certain evils are the common lot of good men and sinners in this life. This apparent lack of discrimination in the distribution of good and evil does not offend divine justice. If the good received only blessings in this life, one might well question their motives, while the miseries they undergo not only have a penal aspect about them, because of the sins of the good, but also play the role of proving and improving their goodness. If sinners, on the other hand, received only misery in this life, they might think that they have a complaint against divine justice, but they receive a reward in the form of temporal blessings. True as this may be on the level of general principle, Augustine is quick to observe that it does not mean that we can infallibly recognize the justice of divine providence at the level of human events and history. One should realize that the blessings of eternal happiness are reserved for good men who have persevered even as the miseries of eternal punishment belong exclusively to unrepentant sinners. Divine justice and the plan of divine providence achieve their final harmony only at the last judgment when man will understand the justice of divine providence in human events as well as in history.[4]

Augustine also rejects another pagan view of history which was variously proposed in the ancient world, the theory of eternal cycles. Biblical revelation is radically incompatible with this estimate of history. Time began with the creation of the world. Hence, any theory of eternal cycles that postulates an eternity of worlds succeeding one another in the past must be discarded. Furthermore, the eternal happiness of the saints in the state of blessedness militates directly against any theory that projects a succession of worlds in the future in which the same events and same persons would reappear. Finally, every theory of eternal cycles must be flatly repudiated because of the once-for-all death of Christ, the "Straight Way." Summing up in his person a long and progressively clearer line of divine promises and prefigurations in sacred history, Christ died once for all men and lives glorified with the Father, making intercession for them. In his life, death, and resurrection lies the direct route to blessedness in eternity, offered to all men.[5]

A third estimate of the course of history prominent among the ancients must also be discarded if the biblical revelation is to be taken seriously. Founded in a radical dualism, this view sees history as the theater in which an eternal conflict of two ultimate principles, or beings, one good, the other evil, takes place. Man is only a puppet in this dramatic conflict. Augustine is quick to denounce this notion. God alone is the supreme principle of creation and being, and he is supremely good. God has no contrary from eternity, since he is the eternal affirmation of good and being. Evil is not an ultimate principle but only a derived one, defective in operation and will. Evil can exist only in a created nature that was created good but became evil through an evil choice. No doubt, the Bible speaks of a spiritual world of angels, good and bad. But they are creatures of the good God, vastly inferior to him, and have become better or evil because of their free choice. Even this notion should be more carefully stated, since it is not the natures of sinful demons that are totally evil but their wills. The Bible also speaks of the influence of the demons in the events of human lives and history, but this influence is under divine governance and is effective only when it coincides with the evil inclinations of the will of sinners. History is a conflict of good and evil, undoubtedly, but not a conflict of eternal and co-equal principles of good and evil. Sin is possible only to a defective will, the will of a creature, be he angel or man. Nor is the conflict of good and evil the whole of the story, since final victory for good is already assured in Christ.[6]

Some major features of the Augustinian view of history are already clear. Governed in all of its details by divine providence, though not to the exclusion of human freedom, history bears within itself a certain segment of mankind in which a steady progress toward a final victory of good over evil is assured in Christ. Then only will man fully realize and understand in detail the plan and purpose of providence. Augustine associates the segment of historical humanity that bears the burden and promise of the final purpose of providence with the notion of the city of God. Balancing the historical force for good is another association of men representing the forces for evil in history. This human association is connected with what Augustine calls the city of the devil. The theme of the two cities dominates Augustine's positive interpretation of the course of history.[7]

Neither city should be understood as if it were to be simply identified with any historical association of men. Both cities have their origins outside of history proper, among the angels, good and evil. Neither has its final end within the borders of history proper, eternal happiness or eternal punishment. Both cities are associations of angels and men: the city of God includes the faithful angels and good men who persevere; the city of the devil embraces demons and unrepentant sinners. Thus Augustine refers to the two cities as "mystical" cities, that is, societies that transcend the visible and perceptible outlines of historical communities and the limits of history proper. His two cities are associations based on that which angels and men can have in common, on two radically different kinds of love. The city of God loves God in many ways but always with contempt for disordered self-love, while the city of the devil loves self in an infinite variety of forms but always despising God as a rival. It is on this foundation of two loves that Augustine erects his two cities.[8]

No doubt the city of God or the city of the devil cannot be equated with any historical society of man, yet there are representatives of both cities in history. Mankind is one, not only by reason of similarity of nature but by reason of common descent from a single pair of ancestors. Man is sinful, not by reason of nature but because of the free and sinful choice of Adam, which places him and his descendants in association with the city of the devil. Since the fall of Adam each man necessarily has been born a member of that city which depises God and loves self in a radically disordered way. Yet God's grace and favor, in view of Christ's incarnation to come, was offered in some way to each man from the beginning. Some men spurn this offer, becoming deliberate members of the city of the devil on earth; these make up the earthly city, the city of man. Other men accept God's favor, becoming members of the city of God on earth; these form the heavenly city on earth, the people of God.[9]

History is the story of the courses of the historical representatives of the two cities on earth. Since the plan of providence is bound up in a special way with the course of the pilgrim people of God, turning points in its history are the turning points of all history. Three ages, perhaps, best represent the course of this sacred history: the period before the Mosaic Law, that under the Mosaic Law, and that after the Law, that is, under Christ, the fulfillment of the Law.[10] These ages are not only linked through genealogical descent but also are progressive phases in the revelation of God's purpose as well as of his increasingly active role in history. The earlier stages not only announce the later stages in divine promises but also prefigure the later stages through the medium of certain events and persons. Sacred history is a prophetic history, prophesying not only by word but also by historical event. Under divine guidance, the history of the city of God on earth moves progressively toward a predetermined goal, in which earlier stages prepare for later stages.[11]

The history of the city of God on earth begins with Abel and after his murder is taken up by Seth and some of his descendants. During this primitive phase of sacred history, the members of the people of God did not form an organized community, nor did the grace of God intervene in history in favor of this "people" very perceptibly, excepting the events accompanying the flood. The call of Abraham initiated the second stage in the history of the pilgrim city of God. This phase continued among Abraham's descendants, who were formed into an historical community under Moses, the chosen people of God, ancient Israel. During this stage of sacred history, the representative of the city of God in history became an organized community which established the holy city of Jerusalem, while the interventions by God in history to form and preserve this people became more striking. The third and final phase of this history began and, in a sense, ended with Christ. At once the culmination of all the prophecies and prefigurations of the earlier phases of sacred history, Christ was also the intervention of God himself in the form of man in the very course of the history of mankind. From this point of view sacred history has reached its term. Yet the offering of the grace and salvation of Christ to all men in and through a visible community, the church of Christ, continues in history until the community of the elect is filled and the "mystical" Christ attains full measure. In its final phase on earth the city of God is the Catholic Church, a visible, organized community meant for all men. It will endure in history until Christ returns again for the last judgment and to announce the absolute end of all history.[12]

Parallel to the course of the city of God on earth runs another course of events, the course of the earthly city or the city of man, the historical representative of the city of the devil. This history is also under divine providence, but it is a history of man left to his own devices, loving himself to the positive exclusion of God and his grace. Its course impinges on the course of the pilgrim people of God in many instances, and it displays three grand phases which match the course of sacred history. Cain, the murderer of Abel and the founder of a temporal city, initiates this story. The first deliberate and unrepentant representative of the city of the devil in history, Cain manifested his disordered self-love and envy in the killing of his brother, who worshipped the true God. This fratricide, in a way, is an archetype of the relations between the two cities in history.[13] Cain's foundation of a temporal city also epitomizes the earthbound horizon of the members of the city of man. At the center of the second age of "profane" history stands proud Babylon. The story of Cain and Abel is repeated here, though it varies greatly in details. In their plan to erect an earthly city that would reach the sky, members of the original city of Babylon expressed their impious pride and rejection of the true God. Later, as the capital of a great empire, Babylon became a place of captivity for the ancient chosen people of God. Rome, the second Babylon, is the focal point of the third age of profane history. More of a universal empire than any other kingdom in history, Rome appeared just in time to confront a universal people of God in the making, the church of Christ. Once again the essentials of the story of Cain and Abel are repeated. Rome rejected worship of the one true God, all the while perverting religion by using a syncretistic polytheism as a sort of social cement for the unity of the empire. Rome also authorized the killing of thousands of worshippers of the true God, the army of Christian martyrs. The sack of Rome in 410 by foreign invaders was only an external certification of what had happened inwardly in the morals of Rome a long time before. It was not the end of the world, but it may well have been the end of Rome.

The elder Augustine was not inclined to speculate about the time of the end of the world and the final victory of Christ. He was even prepared to think in terms of six hundred thousand years ahead. He was inclined to believe that citizens from all nations must first be enrolled in the pilgrim city of God before the end was to come. He did not doubt for a moment that a final conflict would take place in which the full power of the devil and his city, gathered from all nations, would be unleashed against the city of God on earth. Then the glorious Christ would intervene in history for judgment and the final victory of good.

All of this is perhaps a bit too neat. Augustine was aware of the simplicity of his theological estimate of the course of history. Profane history appears doomed to a perpetual repetition of the Cain and Abel syndrome, while progress is found only in sacred history, which, after all, is due principally to the interventions of God and not to purely human endeavor. Augustine was prepared to recognize some progress in the achievement of the "relative goods" proper to the city of man in history. The civic virtues of the early Romans, the truths discovered by the Greek philosophers, above all by Plato, the emergence of monotheistic worship among the pagans, all were advances in secular history. Yet, as history witnesses, these were not permanent gains of mankind nor were they well used even at the time of acquisition, being referred ultimately to man and his selfish interests. Augustine was also ready to admit that better relations could exist between a Christian empire and the city of God on earth than could be allowed for in the archetypal relationship of Cain and Abel. But even this prospect called forth no blind attachment of Augustine to Christian Rome such as was evidenced among his Christian contemporaries in the East. Only an unwary optimism would place much reliance even on a Christian state.

History is the story of two loves, eros and agape. Since charity is not restricted to the visible communion of the Christian church, so selfish love is not confined to the borders of the historical communities of the city of man. Even if the whole world should one day become Christian in name, the conflict between the two loves on earth would not cease. In that unlikely event, the pilgrim city of God would find all of its enemies within its own visible communion.[14]

The City of Man: Vico

It has frequently been observed that a change of note was taking place in the historical consciousness of Europe between the generation of Bossuet and Voltaire.[15] Whether this is entirely accurate or not, it seems true enough that Bossuet's *Discourse on Universal History* was the last formidable theological interpretation of history in the traditional Christian pattern. Bossuet's interpretation of history placed him squarely on the side of Augustine's *City of God*.[16] Free thinkers of Bossuet's generation were pointing to the "disorder in human affairs" as evidence against any providential ordering of human history. The distribution of good and evil seemed irrational and unjust, since it did not discriminate between the good and the wicked. "If you knew how to fix the point from which these things have to be viewed," Bossuet answered, "you will see only wisdom where before you saw disorder." From the viewpoint of divine providence, there is order in the history of man, even in the distribution of evil. "God works out his fearsome judgments according to the rules of his ever-infallible justice. It is he who prepares effects in their far-distant causes."[17]

For Bossuet the "key" or "thread" to universal history is to be found in the interplay of religion and civil government. On this point biblical revelation is clear: the paramount reason for successive empires and civilizations in the secular process of history is "subservience" to God's designs for his chosen people. No earthly empire or kingdom could possibly be the ultimate goal of the historical process, because this is reserved for the city of God. Unity and meaning are given to the course of history as a whole because of this divine goal, which is the "key" to universal history.

> There is no human power which does not minister, whether it will or not, to other designs than its own. God alone knows how to bring everything about according to his will; and therefore, everything is surprising to consider only particular causes, and yet everything goes on with a regular progression.[18]

It is one thing to hold to this belief and quite another to suggest that historical evidence might be plainly in support of it. Strong opposition to Bossuet's "busy" and "transparent" divine providence was not long in coming from his contemporaries.[19] Within a generation or two leading figures of the Enlightenment proposed a secularized version of Bossuet's "regular progression" in human affairs, the philosophies of progress. Taking into account "only particular causes," they find nothing "surprising" in the course of events, but rather that all flow according to rational design, one to which they were privy.

Before this view became common, however, an earlier development must be taken into account, the "new science" of Vico.

Giambattista Vico (1668–1744) was born of a poor family in Naples but managed to acquire a broadly based education. After studying law for a time, he turned to the study of language and history. Eventually he was given a professorship of rhetoric in the University of Naples, a position that required him to teach literature, philosophy, and history. *The New Science* appeared in its first form in 1725, the fruit of some twenty years of tireless research. Almost brutally ignored in its own generation, *The New Science* anticipated so much of the work of the classical modern philosophers of history that today it is recognized as the most original contribution in the transition from theology to the philosophy of history.[20] Undoubtedly this is so, yet three quarters of a century passed before Vico's work began to have notable influence. By this time the classic philosophies of history were beginning to take form, and many of Vico's insights were incorporated in these. Hence we can confine ourselves to a much more modest summary of *The New Science* than, in truth, it deserves.

Vico meant his masterpiece to be a science of the "civil world," the historical human world, which should accomplish for the "world of nations" what others had done for the "world of nature." This meant that Vico challenged the conception prevalent at the beginning of the eighteenth century that the only true science was the new science of nature, of mathematical physics, especially as it was understood according to the method and principles of Descartes. As is well known, Descartes attempted to reform philosophy and all of the sciences on the model of mathematical science and certainty. The historical disciplines, for Descartes, were not sciences at all, resting as they did on probable traditions and authority rather than on intuition and certain knowledge. Coming from the study of law and literature to history and philosophy, Vico could be expected to dispute the Cartesian criteria of science and truth. True scientific knowledge is a knowledge through causes, and we can know perfectly and intimately only that which we have caused or made. On the basis of this principle Vico claimed that his study of the historical world of human creations and causation is scientific.

By implication, Vico denies the perfect scientific character of natural science even if it is translated into mathematics, "the language of nature," according to Descartes. "Whoever reflects on this," Vico wrote, "cannot but marvel that the philosophers should have spent all their energies on the study of nature, which, since God made it, He alone knows." Not man but God created the physical world, and consequently only God, and not man, can have perfect and intimate knowledge of this world. Moreover, while admitting that perfect knowledge is attainable within mathematics, which involves the creativity of man, Vico held that the resulting mathematic fictions were unreal abstractions. A science of nature, which is largely unknowable, built on unreal mathematical constructs was not to be compared with Vico's new science. From darkest and earliest antiquity an eternal truth of unquestionable certainty is manifested throughout history: "that the world of civil society has certainly been made by man, and that its principles are therefore to be found within the modifications of our own mind."[21] This did not mean that the historical world and its course could be deduced from the nature of the human mind, as someone like Fichte attempted later. It did mean that the creations of man in profane history—laws, myths, religions, customs, languages, institutions— could be understood with a certitude all its own by man the historian.

Vico's masterpiece was new not only in its scientific claims, but compared with the traditional theology of history from Augustine to Bossuet it had a new focus, the providential ordering of the city of man. "This Science must . . . be a rational civil theology of divine providence which seems hitherto to have been lacking." Before his time, Vico claims, philosophers were either altogether ignorant of divine providence in human affairs, such as the Stoics and Epicureans with their doctrines of chance or fate, or considered it solely in the order of nature, as all recent philosophers. Theologians like Bossuet, on the other hand, Vico implies, considered divine providence principally in relation to the chosen people of God and sacred history. Divine providence is effective not only in sacred history but also in profane history, in the "civil world" of man and in the "economy of civil institutions."

> Our new Science must be a demonstration, so to speak, of what providence has wrought in history, for it must be a history of the institutions by which, without human discernment or counsel, and often against the designs of men, providence has ordered this great city of the human race.[22]

As a convinced Catholic, Vico admits a special and transcending divine providence which was the privilege of the people of God and recognizes special interventions in their favor, but his interests lie in the "gentile" world and the city of man.[23] Divine providence governing profane history and its development is an immanent and not a transcending providence, operating according to uniform methods and using means as natural and as easy as human customs themselves.

> Since divine providence has omnipotence as minister, it develops its orders by means as easy as the natural customs of men. Since it has

infinite wisdom as counselor, whatever it establishes is order. Since it has for its end its own immeasurable goodness, whatever it ordains must be directed to a good always superior to that which men have proposed to themselves.[24]

As many have observed, divine providence, with Vico, is well on its way to becoming as secular and as natural as historical development itself. It is not altogether clear, but it seems since the time of Christ and the establishment of his church that the special and transcending divine providence conceded to biblical times and history has been largely superseded by or become one with Vico's general and immanent divine governance.

Whatever is the truth here, providence in *The New Science* is best understood as an hypothesis to account for the uniform ways in which men, while freely and intentionally pursuing their own limited and often selfish ends, unconsciously served wider ends.

> It is true that men themselves have made this world of nations . . . but this world without doubt has issued from a mind often diverse, at times quite contrary, and always superior to the particular ends that men had proposed to themselves; which narrow ends, made means to serve wider ends, it has always employed to preserve the human race upon the earth.

From the tension displayed here between the particular ends willed by man and the more universal goals accomplished in history, it is not too long a step to the Hegelian dialectic and "cunning of reason." Divine providence makes use of human passion, avarice, ambition, and private vices as well as human virtues, customs, and institutions to preserve man from himself and ensure his continuing historical existence.

> Men mean to gratify their bestial lust and abandon their offspring, and they inaugurate the chastity of marriage from which families arise. The fathers mean to exercise without restraint their paternal power over their clients, and they subject them to the civil powers from which the cities arise. The reigning orders of nobles mean to abuse their lordly freedom over the plebeians, and they are obliged to submit to the laws which establish popular liberty. The free peoples mean to shake off the yoke of their laws, and they become subject to monarchs. The monarchs mean to strengthen their own positions by debasing their subjects with all the vices of dissoluteness, and they dispose them to endure slavery at the hands of stronger nations. The nations mean to dissolve themselves, and their remnants flee for safety to the wilderness, whence, like the phoenix, they rise again. That which did all this was mind, for men did it with intelligence; it was not fate, for they did it by choice; not chance, for the results of their always so acting are perpetually the same.[25]

Vico believes that a clear pattern and order operative in and through the activities of man can be discerned in the history of the gentile world.

Beginning with Noah's gentile descendants after the flood rather than with Adam, Vico distinguishes three ages of historical man.

> (1) The *age of gods*, in which the gentiles believed they lived under divine government and everything was commanded them by auspices and oracles, which are the oldest institutions in profane history. (2) The *age of heroes*, in which they reigned everywhere supreme in aristocratic communities, on account of a certain superiority of nature which they held themselves to have over the plebs. (3) The *age of men*, in which all men recognized themselves as equal in human nature, and there were established the popular commonwealths first and then the monarchies, both of which are forms of human governments.[26]

Corresponding to these successive stages in the development of historical humanity are three kinds of customs, laws, languages, authorities, reasonings, economies, and even natures; in short, what can be called three types of cultures.[27]

In each of the stages, one of the human faculties tends to prevail over the others: sensation, imagination, and intellect. "What Aristotle said of the individual man is therefore true of the race in general: *"Nihil est in intellectu quin prius fuerit in sensu."*[28] In the age of gods men were dominated by fear and emotions, which impelled them to fashion a world peopled by spirits and gods. This was the age of myths and of theocratic government as well. From a condition of promiscuity arose the institution of the family, and from the family developed the patriarchal or family-state. The later developments of the age of gods contain the seeds of the age of heroes, which followed upon it. The second age of humanity still attributes deeds done by many to one, the deified hero, but the hero is more human and hence more divine than the forces of the natural world. Men of this era may be brutal and savage, yet they are more civilized than those of the divine epoch. Certain tribes conquer others and reduce them to slavery, but the institution of slavery is a step up from the earlier practice of sacrificing captives to the gods. With the formation of aristocratic government under tribal leaders in cities, class struggles begin between the patricians and plebeians, with property a central issue. From these seeds develops the third age, the age of men, in which historical records begin to appear. The deification of great men ceases, and human affairs or natural events are no longer explained by the will of the gods. Religion now becomes the basis of morals rather than being isolated from them, as was the case in the earlier stages. Popular governments or democracies open the age and concern for rights and liberties appears. Myths fade and reason begins to dominate. Eventually monarchies appear, "the form of government best adapted to human nature when reason is fully developed."[29]

What should be said about the immanent and worldly goal of this serial order in profane history? No doubt this regular and typical course of humanity shows progress from anarchy to order, from the primitive savage and heroic customs to more rational and civilized ones, but Vico's principle of *corso* and *ricorso* tends to leave the answer unclear. After the whole course of the three ages just summarized has been traversed (*corso*), a new course begins which is at the same time a resurgence (*ricorso*). The *ricorso* is not like a cosmic cycle, a mere repetition of the previous process, but a historical process bearing the legal overtones of a retrial or judgment and appeal. Providential history as a whole is the highest court of justice, and since the historical *corso* has not received justice due to the corrosive character of man and his works, an age of dissolution, disintegration, and oversophistication, a "barbarism of reflection," is required in order to return to a "creative barbarism of sense" when the cycle begins anew.[30]

Such a recurrence or *ricorso* occurred when after the fall of Rome, due to a sophisticated and reflective barbarism, a creative barbarism appeared in the early Middle Ages. At this crucial turning point in profane history divine providence intervening in sacred history merges with divine providence operating through human affairs and profane history.

> When, working in superhuman ways, God had revealed and confirmed the truth of the Christian religion . . . and when armed nations were about to arise on every hand destined to combat the true divinity of its Founder, he permitted a new order of humanity to be born among the nations in order that [the true religion] might be firmly established according to the natural course of human institutions themselves.[31]

The Dark Ages represented another divine period, the feudal or medieval period being another heroic age; our present age is a new human age, and it appears that a term of sorts has been reached in the course of "ideal history."

> Today a complete humanity seems to be spread abroad through all nations, for a few monarchs rule over this world of peoples. If there are some barbarous peoples still surviving, it is because their monarchies have persisted in the vulgar wisdom of imaginative and cruel religions, in some cases with the less balanced nature of their subjects as an added factor.[32]

Yet Vico hints at a sort of spiral progress from the pagan *corso* to the Christian *ricorso*. The cycles are not purely monotonous repetitions of previous periods; rather, a more fruitful flowering of humanity as a result of the Christian religion with its "infinitely pure and perfect idea of God and commanding charity to all nations" can be expected in the *ricorso* in which we live.[33]

> Christian Europe is everywhere radiant with such humanity that it abounds in all the good things that make for the happiness of human

life, ministering to the comforts of the body as well as to the pleasures of mind and spirit. And all this in virtue of the Christian religion which teaches truths so sublime that it receives into its service the most learned philosophies of the gentiles and cultivates three languages as its own: Hebrew, the most ancient in the world; Greek, the most delicate; and Latin, the grandest. *Thus even for human ends, the Christian religion is the best in the world. . . .*[34]

Vico does not speculate about the future, but he was convinced that he had perceived the order of human events under divine providence in his new science.

Since these orders were established by divine providence, the course of the nations had to be, must now be, and will have to be such as our Science demonstrates . . . an ideal eternal history traversed in time by . . . every nation in its rise, development, maturity, decline and fall.[35]

NOTES

1.   See Letter #138 (to Marcellinus), nn. 46–50. Some works useful for understanding the Augustinian view of history can be cited here: J. N. Figgis, *The Political Aspects of St. Augustine's City of God* (London: Longmans, 1921), esp. ch. III; C. Dawson, "The City of God," in *A Monument to Augustine* (New York: Meridian, 1957), pp. 43–77, reprinted in C. Dawson, *The Dynamics of World History* (New York: New American Library, 1962), pp. 288–318; J. O'Meara, *Charter of Christendom: The Significance of the City of God* (New York: Macmillan, 1961); G. L. Keyes, *Christian Faith and the Interpretation of History; A Study of St. Augustine's Philosophy of History* (Lincoln, Nebr.: University of Nebraska Press, 1966).

     For patristic views generally of history see R. L. P. Milburn, *Early Christian Interpretations of History* (London: A. & C. Black, 1954), and A. Luneau, *L'Histoire du Salut chez les Pères de l'Eglise* (Paris: Editions du Cerf, 1964).

2.   See Augustine, *The City of God*, e.g., Book V, nn. 1–10; Book XII, nn. 4–5; Book XIII, nn. 1–3, 15, 20; Book XIV, n. 11.

3.   See Augustine, *The City of God*, Book V, nn. 9–10; Book XI, nn. 18, 22–23.

4.   See, e.g., Augustine, *The City of God*, Book XX, nn. 1–3. Providence, in relation to the recent disaster at Rome, is treated in detail in Book I, esp. nn. 8–16.

5.   See, e.g., Augustine, *The City of God*, Book XII, nn. 13, 17, 19–20.

6.   See, e.g., Augustine, *The City of God*, Book XI, n. 15; Book XII, nn. 2–8.

7.   Augustine derived his notion of the city of God from the Bible; see *The City of God*, Book XI, n. 1. This theme was not first elaborated in *The City of God*, as it appears in earlier works of Augustine; see O'Meara, pp. 12–19.

8.   "Two cities have been formed by two loves: the earthly by the love of self, even to the contempt of God; the heavenly by the love of God, even to the

contempt of self. The former, in a word, glories in itself, the latter in God. For the one seeks glory from men; but the greatest glory of the other is God, the witness of conscience." Augustine, *The City of God*, Book XIV, n. 28 (New York: Random House, 1950), trans. M. Dods; see Book XV, n. 1.

Since self-love ultimately divides rather than joins, Augustine was convinced that the city of the devil never truly formed a lasting association. Eternal punishment simply confirms this, as each member of the city of the devil in eternity will be forever isolated from everyone else. Hence the name city can no longer be given to the group of the condemned. See Book XV, n. 4.

9. See, Augustine, *The City of God*, Book XII, nn. 21, 27; Book XV, n. 1. Augustine was inclined to believe that it was not yet 6000 years since the time of creation, but he was not prepared to be dogmatic about this, allowing even for the possibility of 600,000 years since the beginning of time. See Book XII, nn. 10, 12.

10. We prefer the simpler division of three ages to that of the six ages, paralleling the six days of creation and the six turning points in the life of the individual, which is prominent in the thought of Augustine and terminates *The City of God* itself (Book XXII, n. 30). The six-age outline of history has the advantage of pointing to the union of the beginning and end in the seventh age. Nevertheless, Augustine also used the three-age theme; see, e.g., Letter #55 (to Januarius); *The City of God*, Book VIII, n. 32, and Book X, n. 25.

11. See, e.g., Augustine, *The City of God*, Book XVII, nn. 3, 5, 8.

12. When Augustine speaks of sacred or secular history he refers primarily to the record of events made either by human authors under the inspiration of the Spirit or by purely human authors. We have taken the liberty of a more modern usage of the term history, speaking of sacred history and profane history in the sense of the events themselves. This is in full accord with Augustine's understanding of divine providence.

13. See, e.g., Augustine, *The City of God*, Book XV, nn. 5, 15.

14. See, e.g., Augustine, *The City of God*, Book XVIII, n. 51. Despite the fact that Augustine considered earthly peace, secured, at least negatively, through the offices of the state, as the highest of purely earthly goods, there does not appear to be any room in his view for a third city between the earthly city and the heavenly city. See O'Meara, pp. 42–49.

15. J. H. Brumfitt, *Voltaire: Historian* (London: Oxford University Press, 1958), claims that Voltaire brought about a "Copernican revolution in history" (p. 165). Both G. P. Gooch, *History and Historians in the Nineteenth Century*, 2d ed., rev. (Boston: Beacon, 1962), pp. 6–7, and H. E. Barnes, *A History of Historical Writing*, 2d ed., rev. (New York: Dover, 1962), pp. 152–154, appear to have a similar opinion. E. Cassirer, on the other hand, in *The Philosophy of the Enlightenment* (Boston: Beacon, 1955), p. 207, claims that "the Copernican revolution in the realm of historical science" was initiated two generations before Voltaire by Bayle's *Historical and Critical Dictionary*. G. H. Nadel, "Philosophy of History before Historicism," in *Studies in the Philosophy of History* (selected essays from *History and Theory*) (New York: Harper & Row, 1965), p. 50, believes Cassirer mistaken on this issue, assigning novelty to the Renaissance rather than to Bayle.

16. Bossuet's *Universal History* fits well enough into the traditional Augustinian tradition of interpreting the course of history in terms of the city of God. Otto of Freising's *Historia de duabus Civitatibus* (1147) is usually considered to be

typical of the medieval conception of history which continued the Augustinian tradition; see F. Fellner, "The 'Two Cities' of Otto of Freising," in P. Guilday (ed.), *The Catholic Philosophies of History* (New York: Kenedy, 1936), pp. 45–82. Yet the Augustinian tradition does not represent the whole of the medieval conception of history. Joachim of Fiore (d. 1202), for example, made the Trinity and not Christology the focal point of his theology of history, distinguishing three ages of the world to correspond with the three persons of the Trinity; see K. Löwith, *Meaning in History* (Chicago: University of Chicago Press, 1949), pp. 145–159. An account of the whole medieval millennial movement is given by N. Cohn, *The Pursuit of the Millennium* (New York: Harper & Row, 1961).

As is well known, the Renaissance had considerable impact on both historical scholarship and the traditional medieval conception of the course of history. The Italian Renaissance (for example, Machiavelli) revived older cyclical theories about the course of history along with the role of fortune as derived principally from Polybius' *History*; see H. Weisinger, "Ideas of History during the Renaissance," *Journal of the History of Ideas* (1945), Vol. VI, p. 426 f. The French humanist Jean Bodin is perhaps most typical of the later Renaissance, and the Polybian cycles appear once again in his *Method for the Easy Understanding of History* (1566). P. E. Tillinghast, *Approaches to History* (Englewood Cliffs, N.J.: Prentice-Hall, 1963), pp. 84–116, gives a useful introduction to Bodin and selections from his *Method*. Nadel, pp. 49–73, surveys the period from 1550 to 1750, finding "exemplar history" to be the dominant theme of the period, that is, history as philosophy teaching by examples, or history as part of moral philosophy. Echoes of this classical conception of history can be found in Bossuet and Voltaire as well. Exemplar history is intimately related to a cyclical view of the events of history; see H. Butterfield, *The Statecraft of Machiavelli* (London: Cambridge University Press, 1960), p. 28 f.

The Reformation had an even greater impact on the more traditional medieval conception of the course of history. For the view of Luther, the recent work of J. M. Headley, *Luther's View of Church History* (New Haven, Conn.: Yale University Press, 1963), is valuable. E. L. Tuveson, *Millennium and Utopia* (Berkeley, Calif.: University of California Press, 1949), speaks of "a Protestant interpretation" of history which derived from Luther's conception and dominated Protestant thought for almost two centuries. Tuveson labels this interpretation "the doctrine of universal decline," which was based on a view of the Apocalypse that identified anti-Christ with the papacy, and concluded that the "last days" had already set in. The millennium was in the past, and there was nothing for the true believers to do but steel themselves for the steadily worsening tribulations to come before the return of Christ. See Tuveson, pp. 22–56, and Headley, pp. 156–265.

17.   *Oeuvres de Bossuet* (Paris, 1858), Vol. II, *Sermon sur la Providence*, pp. 411–412, and Vol. I, *Discours sur l'histoire universelle*, p. 397.

18.   Bossuet, *Discours*, p. 298; see pp. 264, 126. A fuller discussion of Bossuet as historian is given in P. Barry, "Bossuet's Discourse in Universal History," in Guilday, pp. 149–186.

19.   See the excellent work of P. Hazard, *The European Mind, 1680–1715* (Cleveland: World Publishing, 1963) [reprint], especially the chapter entitled "Bossuet at Bay," pp. 198–216.

20.   Löwith, p. 115: "It [The New Science of Vico] anticipated not only

fundamental ideas of Herder and Hegel, Dilthey and Spengler, but also the more particular discoveries of Roman history by Niebuhr and Mommsen, the theory of Homer by Wolf, the interpretation of mythology by Bachofen, the reconstruction of ancient life through etymology by Grimm, the historical understanding of laws by Savigny, of the ancient city and of feudalism by Fustel de Coulanges, and of the class struggles by Marx and Sorel."

Short expositions of Vico's philosophy of history are given by Löwith, pp. 115–136; P. C. Perrotta, "Giambattista Vico: Philosopher-Historian," in Guilday, pp. 189–236; and R. G. Collingwood, *The Idea of History*, pp. 63–71. An extended treatment is given by A. R. Caponigri, *Time and Idea—The Theory of History in Giambattista Vico* (Chicago: Regnery, 1953), and in B. Croce, *The Philosophy of Giambattista Vico* (London: 1913), trans. R. G. Collingwood.

21.   *The New Science of Giambattista Vico*, trans. T. G. Bergin and M. H. Fisch (New York: Cornell University Press, 1961), sec. 331, pp. 52–53; see sec. 349, pp. 62–63. The Introduction to this translation, pp. xxi–liii, contains an excellent analysis of the key notions of Vico. For the relation between philosophy and history (philology), as Vico understood it, see sec. 138, p. 21; sec. 163, pp. 25–26; sec. 359, p. 65. Vico claimed to be following "Bacon's method of philosophizing," though he was very well aware that he had extended its application from the world of nature to "the civil institutions of mankind."

22.   *The New Science*, sec. 342, pp. 59–60.

23.   See *The New Science*, e.g., secs. 165–167, p. 26; sec. 310, sec. 313, p. 48, "For besides the ordinary help from providence which was all that the gentiles had, the Hebrews had extraordinary help from the true God."

24.   *The New Science*, sec. 344, p. 60.

25.   *The New Science*, sec. 1108, pp. 382–383. As a Catholic Vico believed in the "fall of Adam" and that human nature consequently was "fallen and weak"; see sec. 310, p. 48. Hence he held that "self-love" and "private utility" were decisive factors in the development of human society and institutions; see sec. 341, pp. 58–59. For the "dialectic" of history, see, e.g., sec. 677, p. 206, "This heroism is now by civil nature impossible, since its causes, just enumerated, have given place to their contraries, which have produced the other two kinds of civil states, free popular commonwealths and monarchies."

26.   *The New Science*, sec. 31, p. 3.

27.   See the whole of Book IV, pp. 283–347. Book Two, "Poetic Wisdom," contains the most original work of Vico and constitutes about one half of *The New Science*; see sec. 34, p. 5: "We find that the principle of these origins both of languages and letters lies in the fact that the early gentile peoples . . . were poets who spoke in poetic characters. This discovery, which is the master key of this Science, has cost us the persistent research of almost all our literary life, because with our civilized natures we cannot at all imagine and can understand only by great toil the poetic nature of these first men." Vico was very conscious that he could not rely on the works of historians and philosophers for an understanding of the nature of primitive man, as the philosophers spoke as if all they knew was understood from the beginning of history, while the historians were committed to the principle that their nations were the first in the world; see sec. 330, p. 52.

28.   *The New Science*, sec. 363, p. 70.

29.   *The New Science*, sec. 1008, p. 334.

30.   The whole of Book V of *The New Science*, pp. 349–373, treats of the *ricorso*. One passage describing the transitional period is worth quoting in full because of similarities with very recent views of the course of history:

"If the peoples are rotting in that ultimate civil disease and cannot agree on a monarch from within, and are not conquered and preserved by better nations from without, then providence for their extreme ill has its extreme remedy at hand. For such peoples, like so many beasts, have fallen into the custom of each man thinking only of his own private interests and have reached the extreme of delicacy, or better of pride . . . they live like wild beasts in a deep solitude of spirit and will, scarcely any two being able to agree since each follows his own pleasure or caprice. By reason of all this, providence decrees that, through obstinate factions and desperate civil wars, they shall turn their cities into forests and the forests into dens and lairs of men. In this way, through long centuries of barbarism, rust will consume the misbegotten subtleties of malicious wits that have turned them into beasts made more inhuman by the barbarism of reflection than the first men had been made by the barbarism of sense . . . . Hence peoples who have reached this point of premeditated malice, when they receive this last remedy of providence and are thereby stunned and brutalized, are sensible no longer of comforts, delicacies, pleasures, and pomp, but only of the sheer necessities of life. And the few survivors in the midst of an abundance of the things necessary for life naturally become sociable, and returning to the primitive simplicity of the first world of peoples, are again religious, truthful, and faithful," sec. 1106, p. 381.

The pattern of the cycle is most succinctly expressed in this way: "Men first feel necessity, then look for utility, next attend to comfort, still later amuse themselves with pleasure, thence grow dissolute in luxury, and finally go mad and waste their substance. The nature of peoples is first crude, then severe, then benign, then delicate, finally dissolute," secs. 241–242, p. 37.

31.   *The New Science*, sec. 1047, p. 352.

32.   *The New Science*, sec. 1089, p. 370.

33.   See *The New Science*, sec. 1092, p. 371.

34.   *The New Science*, sec. 1094, p. 372.

35.   *The New Science*, secs. 348–349, p. 62. Exceptions due to "extraordinary causes" are explicitly referred to by Vico, e.g., sec. 1092, p. 371. Hence the "ideal history" is not an ironclad law.

2

THE PHILOSOPHIES
OF PROGRESS:

Turgot to Herder

One of the most striking contributions of the modern age to historical consciousness was the gradual development of the theory of human progress in history. Many seventeenth-century writers played a role in the development of the idea of continuous and successive human perfectibility, but its greatest champions belonged to the eighteenth century, where the notion found a most receptive audience. The naturalistic rationalism of the Enlightenment had no place for the supernaturalism of traditional Christian eschatology, and yet it could not divest itself altogether of the Christian teleological conception of life and history. A belief in the perfectibility and the indefinite progress of the human race on earth tended to take the place of the Christian faith in the life of the world to come as the final goal of human effort.[1] Diderot made the point plain: "Posterity is for the philosopher what the next life is for the man of religious beliefs." As the century wore on, a marriage was arranged between the idea of progress and the Newtonian laws of the physical universe, with laws of society and history geared to inevitable progress hopefully awaited. It was left to the nineteenth century, however, to produce something more than still-born progeny.

Voltaire

Before moving on to a survey of the philosophies of progress, it may be well to consider Voltaire's contribution to this theme. Voltaire was no advocate of the idea of progress. "After being extricated from one slough for a time, mankind is soon plunged into another. To ages of civilization succeed ages of barbarism; that barbarism is again expelled and again reappears; it is the regular alternation of day and night."[2] Monsieur Arouet de Voltaire was the perfect representative of the age of the Enlightenment. Witty, ironic, sarcastic, subtle, and brutal in turn, as a propagandist he has few equals. Poet, playwright, a teller of tales, historian, philosopher, biblical critic, he even dabbled in scientific experiment. To each of his literary endeavors he brought a masterly incisive style, and for all of his work he found an increasingly congenial program. "Ecrasez l'infâme"— the infamy and darkness of Christianity must be exposed to the "gradually expanding light" of reason and truth. To this project Voltaire dedicated his many talents and energies.

Fundamental to the Christian belief is the biblical conception of providential history in which interventions of God in the natural course of events in favor of a chosen people were a central theme. Bossuet's *Universal History* represented a traditional interpretation of this theme. Voltaire engaged in a continuing scathing commentary on Bossuet's view of history and in the process coined a new expression, the philosophy of history. He was the first, it seems, to author a work expressly entitled *Philosophy of History* (1765), in which he claimed to be composing history "as a philosopher."[3]

One of Voltaire's more professional attacks on Bossuet's *Universal History* is found in his *Essay on the Customs and Spirit of Nations*. Bossuet had described the course of history from creation to the time of Charlemagne, drawing on the Bible and standard classical authorities. He confined his attention, however, to the Near East and Europe. Such a universal history did not sit well with Voltaire, who considered it necessary "to go back to a more remote period." Despite his avowed intention of beginning with the time of Charlemagne, Voltaire devoted the first two chapters of the *Essay* to the history of China and India. Indeed, throughout his work he gave much space to these two civilizations as well as to the Islamic, and referred as well to even more distant lands. Plainly the *Essay* was intended as a corrective for the limited "universal history" envisioned by Bossuet.

In addition, Voltaire's *Essay* implied that the entire providential view of history must be replaced by explanations according to natural, historical causes, "reasoning only according to natural notions." Divine interventions in the historical order, especially exclusively in favor of the Jews, had no

place in a "philosophy of history." Consequently, in the *Essay* and elsewhere Voltaire eliminated providence from consideration in his estimate
of the forces operative in the historical process and appealed only to particular causes in the historical order. It may be true that God so arranged
things that the empire of Asia was given to the Babylonians to punish
the Jews, that Cyrus was established on the throne to avenge the Jews,
that the Romans emerged in world history to chastise the Jews, as Bossuet
intimated, but "the splendors of Cyrus and the Romans have still other
causes." Only the latter would find room in a history composed by the
philosopher.[4]

Voltaire's incessant satire and burning wit were as responsible as any
element of the Enlightenment for changing the historical consciousness
of Europe. No doubt, Voltaire was not the first to explain events in history by particular historical causes. Even Bossuet did not overlook this
feature of human history. But Voltaire's sustained attack on the "busy"
and "transparent" divine providence of Bossuet helped to place historical
studies more firmly on the foundations of immanent causes, where an
appeal to providence came to be considered out of place, if not naive.
Clearly Voltaire was not a "philosopher of history" in the grand manner
of Hegel, yet a move in that direction was already underway among his
contemporaries in France who were promoting the idea of historical
progress.

Turgot-Condorcet

France was the home of the first clamorous exponents of the idea of
progress, and we can pick up the theory as it appeared in some suggestive
lectures by Jacques Turgot in 1755.[5] Like Voltaire, Turgot was tilting with
Bossuet, but his weapons were not exactly the same.

As a very young man Turgot had planned a universal history which
was to have challenged Bossuet's idea of history. Although never finished,
the general outline appeared in the two discourses of 1750, which together
constituted a conception of world history from antiquity to the present.
The two lectures were tied together by one overarching theme, a theory
of the progressive perfection of man in history. Delivered before the Sor-
bonne, a traditional stronghold of the Catholic faith, it was to be expected
that Turgot, then a cleric, would have to take into account the role of
Christianity in the progress of historical humanity. His first discourse was
aimed precisely at this goal, bearing the title, "Advantages Which the
Establishment of Christianity Secured for Mankind." Turgot marshaled
an array of historical data to prove that Christianity had been a significant
agent in the progress of mankind since the fall of the Roman Empire.

It was Christianity, he noted, that had civilized reasonably well the northern barbarians, abolished slavery, protected the weak, the sick, and the poor, and preached love and brotherhood to all. Undoubtedly, Turgot's lecture was well received by the clerical audience, among whom was the Cardinal-Archbishop of Paris.

History does not record the reception accorded Turgot's second discourse, "A Philosophical View of the Successive Advances of the Human Mind," which traced the fortunes of man in the light of a theory of progress, with occasional deferences made in the direction of divine providence.[6] The historical world of man has a much different shape than the world of physical nature, Turgot believed. "The phenomena of nature, subject to constant laws, are enclosed in a circle of revolutions which are always the same." Constancy, repetition, the eternal return of the same, these are features of the natural world. "The succession of men, however, presents a changing spectacle from century to century." Innovation, novelty, eternal change and progress, these are or should be the shapes of the world of history. "All ages are linked to each other by a series of causes and effects which binds the present state of the world with all those which have preceded it." Language and writing are the bonds linking age to age, thus making possible the transmission of accumulated knowledge. To this legacy of the ages the discoveries of each generation continue to be added. "Thus the human race, considered from its beginnings," Turgot said, "appears to the eyes of a philosopher to be one immense whole which, like every individual, has its infancy and its progress."[7]

Progress in knowledge, particularly in the natural sciences, was denied by few of Turgot's generation, and if this accumulation were all that Turgot intended, then his idea of progress was scarcely new. But this was by no means the extent of Turgot's notion of progress toward perfection. Progress in laws and forms of government, in the arts and sciences, in morals and enlightenment, and in the unity of mankind, this was the range of Turgot's idea of the growing perfection of man.[8]

Turgot's view of universal history differed from that of Voltaire in several important ways. Human reason struggling against ignorance and passion was the exclusive agent of progress in history, in the estimation of Voltaire, and the greatest brake on the movement of history was Christianity. Turgot, on the other hand, believed that Christianity had been a powerful civilizing and moralizing force in the progress of historical humanity and also allowed a significant role for passions, emotions, and ambition in the development of human history. "The passions multiplied ideas, extended knowledge, perfected minds, in default of the reason whose day had not yet dawned, and which would have been less potent if it had reigned earlier."[9] Much of the difference between Voltaire and Turgot rests on their conceptions of human nature. The static and ahistorical concept of human nature by which Voltaire measured man in history does not match Turgot's more delicate concept of a developing humanity in which the nature of man passed from a primitive condition of reliance on imagination and sense through intermediate stages to the civilized condition of reasoned and reasonable activity.[10] Turgot's views at this point were closer to those of Vico than to those of Voltaire. In the evolution of rational humanity it was to be expected that reason would attain its majority only after long intervening steps of subrational and near-rational humanity. Both Turgot and Vico held that a rational design was thus secured in the history of man, but Vico identified this pattern with that of divine providence while Turgot only nodded in the direction of providence. When Turgot pushed on to the idea of continuous progress being realized in the unfolding of this design, he parted company with Vico and Voltaire at once. Vico's cyclical conception of the historical process did not lend itself to any notion of continuous progress, and the pessimism of Voltaire held him back from the acceptance of inevitable progress.

The Marquis de Condorcet, a friend and biographer of Turgot, took up the idea of progress where Turgot left off. The "apostle of progress," Condorcet spoke with the passion of a prophet and revolutionary who was living under the shadow of death. His *Sketch for a Historical Picture of the Progress of the Human Mind* was finished in 1793 when he was a fugitive from the French Revolution he had earlier served. Shortly thereafter he died of unexplained causes, having been captured by sans-culottes in the outskirts of Paris. Condorcet may have written his *Outline* without the benefit of library or notes, yet he had learned well from Turgot how to view the history of mankind in the light of the idea of progress. Condorcet rejected the rather shadowy divine providence that still lurked behind Turgot's perception of developing perfection in the history of man, and he appealed to "reason and fact" for his belief in progress. With a purely empirical and philosophical starting point it is possible to show that

> nature has set no term to the perfection of human faculties; that the perfectibility of man is truly indefinite; and that the progress of this perfectibility, from now onwards independent of any power that might wish to halt it, has no other limit than the duration of the globe upon which nature has cast us. This progress will doubtless vary in speed, but it will never be reversed as long as the earth occupies its present place in the system of the universe, and as long as the general laws of this system produce neither a general cataclysm nor such changes as will deprive the human race of its present faculties and present resources. . . .[11]

Condorcet's historical sketch was aimed at demonstrating how the past of man had brought off the possibility of indefinite progress as well as the prospects for future progress. Looking back through the corridors of history, Condorcet saw nine distinct periods, each of which represented a definite stage in the development of civilization. Nine of these stages had already passed into the record, while the tenth stage was inaugurated by the French Revolution. There is no need to delay over the details of Condorcet's assessment of history, which began with primitive man in the hunting and fishing stage, passed rapidly through the pastoral and agricultural stages, paused for classical Greek civilization and the Roman Empire, picked up speed again for the Dark Ages and the high Middle Ages, and settled into a steady pace with the age of printing and the age of Descartes. What is significant in Condorcet's view of the past is the unevenness of the pace of progress. The forces of darkness had persistently cloaked the light of reason after every advance, though with greater success in some periods. False and useless religious ideas had confused man and diverted him from his natural pursuits. It is not difficult to imagine which religion Condorcet had particularly in mind. Christianity for Condorcet, as well as for Voltaire, was *l'infâme*. Almost the only contribution to progress made during ten centuries of Christianity, from the fall of Rome to the invention of printing, was the mitigation of ancient slavery through the development of serfdom. With the invention of printing, which ensured the diffusion of knowledge and the growth of science, progress gained an insurmountable advantage over its ancient foes of prejudice and religion. The age of Descartes, sparked by Newton, Locke, and Rousseau, confirmed this advantage and made the victory of progress certain. The final stage in the development of human perfectibility began with the French Revolution.

At this point Condorcet took on a new role, that of prophet. "Why," he questioned, "should it be regarded as a fantastic undertaking to sketch, with some pretense to truth, the future destiny of man on the basis of his history?" The question was not entirely unreasonable, to be sure, but Condorcet's answer left little room for any distinction between the operations of nature and the progressive development of humanity in history.

> The sole foundation for belief in the natural sciences is this idea, that the general laws directing the phenomena of the universe, known or unknown, are necessary and constant. Why should this principle be any less true for the development of the intellectual and moral faculties of man than for the other operations of nature?

Prediction on the basis of general laws is possible in natural science, and the same possibility should not be ruled out in history or social science. If one accepted Hume's critique of causality, as it seems that Condorcet did, then the laws of natural science were only probabilities and on this score did not differ appreciably from generalizations derived from man's experience of the past. Hence history and nature were assimilated, and both were reduced to a science of probabilities, to the calculus of probabilities then undergoing significant development. As an accomplished mathematician, Condorcet was not unaware of the implications of his view.

Condorcet had no noteworthy success in deriving "laws" of social development from the human past, but he had little doubt about the direction that future progress should take. He believed that equality, the ideal of the French Revolution, is the goal of mankind. "Our hopes for the future condition of the human race can be subsumed under three important heads: the abolition of inequality among nations, the progress of equality within each nation, and the true perfection of mankind."[12] Within time all nations must be converted to the ideals of the revolution and reach the level of civilization and enlightenment attained among the French and Anglo-American nations. Within each nation equality was to be attained by everyone becoming an enlightened citizen in a free society. Finally, true perfection on the biological level was within reach of future generations through progress in knowledge; death would not be conquered, but disease and biological imperfections could be eliminated, thus assuring man an indefinite span of life.

Condorcet had no such hopes for himself as he wrote his masterpiece. Condemned as an enemy of the republic, he had few illusions about his survival, but the idea of progress offered its consolations:

In the contemplation of this vision he receives the reward of his efforts for the progress of reason, for the defense of liberty. He then dares to join his exertions to the eternal chain of human destinies. There he finds the true recompense of virtue; it lies in the pleasure of having accomplished an enduring good, which fate will never again destroy by an unfortunate reversal restoring prejudice and slavery. This contemplation is for him an asylum where the memory of his persecutors cannot pursue him. Living in thought with man re-established in his rights as well as in the dignity of his nature, he forgets the man whom avarice, fear or envy torments and corrupts. Then he truly is with his equals in an Elysium which his reason has been able to create and which his love for humanity embellishes with purest joys.[13]

British Exponents of Progress

Divested of theological trappings as in Condorcet, the idea of progress was not immediately welcomed by eighteenth-century English writers. Hume, for example, had much the same attitude toward progress as Voltaire. While he was convinced of the superiority of the civilization of his own day over that of earlier ages, he was rather skeptical about the prospects for progress in the future. Adam Smith, on the other hand, in *The Wealth of Nations* gave a history of the gradual economic progress of man in society and strongly suggested that it would continue with an indefinite increase of wealth and prosperity if the "natural order" in economic matters were not obstructed by government regulation. In a well-known passage he noted that (Book IV, ch. 2) the secularization of divine providence was also well underway:

> [The individual] intends his own security . . . his own gain, and he is in this as in many other cases led by an invisible hand 'to promote an end which was no part of it. Nor is it always the worse for the society that it was no part of it. By pursuing his own interest he frequently promotes that of the society more effectually than when he really intends to promote it.

Even the skeptical author of the *Decline and Fall of the Roman Empire*, Edward Gibbon, was not unaffected by the theory of progress then in the air:

> Man's progress . . . has been irregular . . . infinitely slow in the beginning, and increasing by degrees with redoubled velocity; ages of laborious ascent have been followed by a movement of rapid downfall. . . . Yet the experience of four thousand years should enlarge our hopes and diminish our apprehensions . . . [and] it may safely be presumed that no people, unless the face of nature is changed, will relapse into their original barbarism.

Thus a "pleasing conclusion" suggested itself to Gibbon: "every age of the world has increased and still increases the real wealth, the happiness, the knowledge, and perhaps the virtue of the human race" (ch. xxxviii). How this view was to be reconciled with Gibbon's high regard for the Roman Empire and his low estimate of Christianity is not clear.

The theory of progress was proclaimed in a much more startling fashion by revolutionary idealists and socialists. Among these prophets it is difficult to distinguish descriptions of the social millennium from those of a purely religious apocalyptic. A leading exponent of this trend, William Godwin, gave this picture of the millennium:

> In that blessed day there will be no wars, no crimes, no administration of justice, as it is called, and no government. Besides this, there will be neither disease, anguish, melancholy, nor resentment. Every man will seek with ineffable ardor the good of all. Mind will be active and eager, and yet never disappointed.[14]

Thus the Christian hope in the heavenly and eternal city of God was brought down to earth and situated within history as its goal. God may be left out of the picture, or conveniently ignored when not denied, but little else seems to have been lost from Christian eschatology in this vision of paradise on earth.

Kant-Herder

The idea of progress made an appearance in the Germanies also, though accents vary from writer to writer. Immanuel Kant devoted no major work to the philosophy of history and progress, yet his brief excursions into the field present in fairly sharp focus the project of the classic modern philosophers of history. An essay entitled "Idea for a Universal History from a Cosmopolitan Point of View" (1784) is the best single source for the Kantian view. Kant's approach to universal history was plainly that of the philosopher with certain presuppositions. Among these was the familiar idea of progress in history: "what seems complex and chaotic in the single individual may be seen from the viewpoint of the human race as a whole to be a steady and progressive though slow evolution of its original endowment." Behind this assumption of the age stood a fundamental Kantian principle, a teleological conception of nature; though it may not be prodigal in its gifts, even functioning with the "strictest parsimony," "nature does nothing in vain."[15] Purpose was written not only in subhuman nature but also in the nature of man and his history; slowly but inexorably progressing behind the back and over the head of man, nature should be assumed to be attaining its goal just as surely in history as in the world of subhuman phenomena.

> The history of mankind can be seen, in the large, as the realization of Nature's secret plan to bring forth a perfectly constituted state as the only condition in which the capacities of mankind can be fully developed and also bring forth that external relation among states which is perfectly adequate to this end.[16]

Kant arrived at this conclusion through an analysis of the nature of man as he understood it. He held, in accord with his teleological concept of nature, that all of the natural capacities of a creature are destined to evolve completely to their natural end. In man, then, the natural capacities associated with reason must be fully developed also, but only in the race as a whole and not in the individual. Such a short period has been set for the life of the individual that the purpose of nature can be brought about only with an almost limitless series of generations. Nature clearly indicates its purpose for man in endowing him with reason and freedom, implying that man must produce everything beyond his bare existence for himself from his own resources.

> Securing his own food, shelter, safety, and defense (for which Nature gave him neither the horns of the bull, nor the claws of the lion, nor the fangs of the dog, but hands only), all amusement which can make life pleasant, insight and intelligence, finally even goodness of heart— all this should be wholly his own work.[17]

It may appear strange that earlier generations should toil and labor only for the sake of the later, but this condition is necessary, Kant believed, if one adverts to the mortality of that rational animal that is man.

The driving force behind the development of all human capacities is man's "antagonism in society," or his "unsocial sociability." Man is at once inclined to associate with others and to isolate himself from others, and from the opposition between these two drives arises eventually all culture, art, and social order.

> This opposition it is which awakens all his powers, brings him to conquer his inclination to laziness and, propelled by vainglory, lust for power, and avarice, to achieve a rank among his fellows whom he cannot tolerate but from whom he cannot withdraw. Thus are taken the first true steps from barbarism to culture, which consists in the social worth of man; then gradually develop all talents, and taste is refined; through continued enlightenment the beginnings are laid for a way of thought which can in time convert the coarse, natural disposition for moral discrimination into definite practical principles, and thereby change a society of men driven together by their natural feelings into a moral whole.[18]

Nature uses human social unsociability as the means to effect its purpose of developing to the full the potentialities of mankind. These capacities can be developed only in a society that offers the greatest freedom commensurate with order and freedom of all. "Such a society is one in which there is mutual opposition among the members, together with the most exact definition of freedom and fixing of its limits so that it may be consistent with the freedom of others."[19] The achievement of a lawful civic constitution of this exalted type is a most difficult problem, Kant believed, and the last to be solved by mankind. One reason for this assertion is the necessity in the ideal commonwealth of free men of a government that is itself composed of men. "From such crooked wood as man is made of, nothing perfectly straight can be built." Another even more compelling reason is the unsociability and opposition between states and commonwealths. The same tension that drives man to the formation of a commonwealth drives individual states into competition and wars. Nature uses these antagonisms as before, and eventually man will learn to form a league of nations.[20] This is nature's secret plan, for it is the only condition in which mankind can fully develop its potentialities.

Kant was not of the opinion that a union of states was the end of history but rather the necessary condition at which nature aimed so that mankind could develop fully, a "halfway mark in the development of mankind." As yet, in the estimation made by Kant of his own age, Western man was only partially cultured through art and science, though it was true that a state of "mere" civilization had been reached in which social graces and love of honor passed for true morality. Man had not yet reached the fullness of culture that necessarily includes a true moral order in which morally good dispositions displaced the pretense and glitter of mere civilization.[21] Hence, mankind had not yet reached even the halfway house on the road to full development. A long interval of time would be needed, it seems, before the citizens within societies could be educated to the point of seeking a true commonwealth and before the chaotic conditions of international relations could be resolved by a league of nations. One condition demanded the other, and both were demanded as the springboard from which mankind could launch into the realization of its fullest potential and bring about perfectly the secret design of nature.

Kant did not claim that evidence from man's past fully supported or manifested his estimate of universal history. He presented "an Idea of how the course of the world must be if it is to lead to certain rational ends." The Idea could serve as a "guiding thread" to history for which there was some evidence, but more so to present "a consoling view of the future . . . a justification of Nature—or better, of Providence. . . ." Even more, the philosophical attempt to systematize universal history from the viewpoint of the achievement of rational ends pursued by nature by its very existence would contribute to the attainment of these ends. "Philosophy can have her belief in a millennium, but her millennium is not Utopian, since the Idea can help, though only from afar, to bring the millennium to pass."[22] If not yet rational, the course of history could become rational.

With the *Outlines of a Philosophy of the History of Man* of Johann G. Herder, published in four volumes between 1784 and 1791, we enter into a different world of thought. Herder, in his earlier years, had been a student of Kant, but his interest in the philosophy of history antedated that of Kant and seemed to have aroused a taste for philosophical history in his former master. Herder's masterpiece represents a view more characteristic of Romanticism than of the Enlightenment, relying more on intuition and feeling than on discursive reason and ending with an esthetic rather than a coldly rational assessment of the human past. As one of the principal movers of *Sturm und Drang*, Herder could no longer tolerate academic philosophy or Kantian rationalism. Kant, for his part, was equally repelled by Herder's heavy reliance on poetic imagination and analogies without end. Called upon to review the first volume of Herder's *Ideas*, Kant concluded his review with these words:

> It is to be hoped that philosophy, whose concern consists more in the pruning than the sprouting of superfluous growth, may guide him [Herder] to the consummation of his enterprise, not with hints, but precise concepts, not through supposed, but through observed laws, not through the intervention of flighty imagination, whether metaphysical or sentimental, but rather through the exercise of careful reason. . . .[23]

Herder was incensed by this review and manifested his pique in his second volume, in which he roundly criticized several principles from Kant's essay on universal history.

Herder began his philosophical history of mankind by placing man in the context of the history of the cosmos, thus anticipating the work of Herbert Spencer and of Teilhard de Chardin of our own generation. Beginning with the physical qualities of the earth and its relations to other planets, he surveys plant and lower animal life, finally arriving at man the microcosm, the crowning glory of earthly creation. In the midst of this exposition, Herder propounds the hypothesis that the whole visible universe is animated by a single spiritual force, or a unified set of forces, which organizes everything in such a way that eventually "spirit" and man freely emerge. Man is the highest product of this life force on earth, where everything exists to serve his development.

> Everything in nature is connected: one state pushes forward and prepares another. If then man is the last and highest link, closing the chain of earthly organization, he must begin the chain of a higher order of creatures as its lower link. . . . This view, which is supported by all the laws of nature, gives the key to the wonderful phenomenon of man, and at the same time to the only philosophy of history.[24]

Herder's philosophy of history is intertwined with narrative description and consists principally of a number of insights which are neither fully developed nor completely consistent with one another. This, of course, may bother us, as it did Kant, but it could not touch the romantic spirit of Herder. He was convinced not only of the chain of being linking man to all of nature but also of the chain of tradition and history linking individuals to each other and to the whole of mankind. "The history of mankind is necessarily a whole, i.e., a chain of sociability and plastic tradition, from the first link to the last." If man had drawn everything from his own individual resources, and independently of all external circumstance, there would be no history of mankind but only histories of individuals. "No one of us became man by himself."[25] Hence, Herder argued, "the natural state of man is society," but it was only those social forms built on "natural government" that claimed his allegiance. In and through the natural forms of society the individual attained to humanity, but this did not entail the view that man was made for the state. Herder believed that he had sighted this reprehensible concept in Kant's essay on universal history and was quick to denounce it.[26] "There appears to me to be an education of our species, and a philosophy of the history of man, as certainly and as truly as there is a human nature, i.e., a cooperation of individuals, which alone makes us man. . . ."[27]

Though a Christian minister who believed in divine providence, Herder approached the history of mankind as a philosopher who did not "count on miracles" but observed "laws." "The whole history of mankind is a pure natural history of human powers, actions and aptitudes, modified by time and place." A sound philosophy, such as that which is operative in natural history and mathematics, cannot attribute the facts of history to "hidden purposes" or "magic influences" but to the causes displayed in the course of history itself.

> In the narration of history, it [the mind] will seek the strictest truth, and in forming its conceptions and judgments, the most complete connection; it should never attempt to explain a thing which is, or happens, by a thing which is not. With this rigorous principle, everything ideal, all the phantoms of a magic creation, will vanish. It will try to see simply what is, and as soon as this is seen, the causes why it could not be otherwise will usually appear.[28]

Human history should be investigated through the genetic, causal concept as a purely natural phenomenon governed by laws. From Herder's investigations one leading law emerged: "everywhere on our earth whatever could be has been, according to the situation and wants of the place, the circumstances and occasions of the times, and the native or generated character of the people." The key to any historical occurrence of note lies in the circumstances of the age, the conditions of soil and climate, and the national character (*Volksgeist*), for given this specific concurrence, whatever could take place actually did take place. The impartial historian, having enumerated the external circumstances at work in an historical event and having penetrated into the "spirit" of the people involved, comes to see that things could have happened only in the way they did. "Time, place, and national character alone, in short the general cooperation of active powers in their most definite individuality, govern all the events that happen among mankind, as well as the occurrences in nature."[29] Herder notes, if the question is asked, Why did the enlightened Greeks appear in the world, the answer is amazingly simple: "Because Greeks existed and existed under such circumstances that they could not be otherwise than enlightened."[30]

Herder believed that the history of Greece could serve as the pure exemplar for a philosophy of history according to which the histories of all nations could be measured. The Greeks were not only a pure stock biologically but their progress and passage through every stage of civilization resulted exclusively from their own efforts. "Greece . . . enjoyed its full time; it formed everything it was capable of forming, and a lucky combination of circumstances aided it in its progress to perfection." Such an exemplary history as that of the Greeks could be described only by the analogy of a growing organism: "As the botanist cannot obtain a complete knowledge of a plant unless he follows it from the seed through its germination, blossoming and decay, such is Greek history to us." The national "plant" of Greece had completed its life cycle in perfect style, and this is why for Herder its history was exemplary.

Herder must be taken seriously in his botanical analogies, convinced as he was that the history of Greece displayed a life cycle. This concept applies with special force to Greek culture and civilization, which, after all, was nothing but the living expression of the Greek national soul.

> Every kind of human knowledge has its particular circle, that is its nature, time, place, period of life. The cultivation of Greece . . . grew with time, place, and circumstances, and declined with them. . . . All kinds of human knowledge have one thing in common: each aims at a point of perfection, but when it is attained by a chain of fortunate circumstances, it can neither preserve it forever, nor can it instantly return, without a decreasing series starting . . . nothing can possibly succeed it, except mere imitations. . . .[31]

Each historical form of humanity, each generation, each civilization and culture, each national group is unique. Each is not merely a stage on the way to something better but an end in itself, having realized the potential of humanity in that time, place, and circumstance. In the end, the different national cultures are not even comparable because of their uniqueness.

Herder's philosophy of history does not fit easily into the pattern of the philosophies of progress. His approach recalls that of Vico more than of any of his predecessors. He rejected the usual notion of progress in which earlier generations of mankind were building for later.[32] He also ridiculed the favored European prejudice that more perfect civilizations succeed one another, beginning with the Orient, passing through Greece and Rome, and ending with a European nation or complex of nations.

> We must also disapprove the opinion that the Romans came on the stage in the succession of ages, to form a more perfect link in the chain of cultivation than the Greeks . . . . In whatever the Greeks excelled, there the Romans never went beyond them; on the other hand, in what was properly their own, they learned nothing from the Greeks.[33]

Despite his high regard for the German nations, which he viewed as the historical successor to Rome, Herder did not rank them higher than their predecessor peoples, though he was sorely tempted. There is considerable tension between this view and another equally plain characteristic of history, as Herder saw it. He stressed the unbroken chain of tradition and history which made a philosophical history of mankind possible. If continuity between nations and civilizations was not given, then, according to his own standards, only histories of individual nations and peoples were possible. There was continuity in the history of mankind, Herder believed, but not progress from people to people. "All the cultivation of the east, west, and north of Europe is a plant sprung from Roman, Greek, and Arabic seed."[34] A new and unique humanity could be hoped for from the developing national spirit of the young and handsome German nations with their modesty, generosity, and nobility of character. One could not consistently hope for more, even from such a people.

NOTES

1.   Works on the idea of progress are legion, but several can be noted as useful for our purposes: J. B. Bury, *The Idea of Progress* (New York: Macmillan, 1932); C. Frankel, *The Faith of Reason: The Idea of Progress in the French Enlightenment* (New York: Columbia University Press, 1948); F. J. Teggart (ed.), *The Idea of Progress: A Collection of Readings*, 2d ed. (Berkeley, Calif.: University of California Press, 1949); C. Dawson, *Progress and Religion* (New York: Doubleday, 1960) [reprint]; E. L. Tuveson, *Millennium and Utopia: A Study in the Background of the Idea of Progress* (Berkeley, Calif.: University of California Press, 1949); J. Baillie, *The Belief in Progress* (New York: Scribner, 1950); C. Van Doren, *The Idea of Progress* (New York: Praeger, 1967).

One summary of the notion of progress is given by G. H. Hildebrand in Teggart, p. 4, where it is noted that the idea includes three principles: "First, the belief that history follows a continuous, necessary, and orderly course; secondly, the belief that this course is the effect of a regularly operating causal law; and third, the belief that the course of change has brought and will continue to bring improvement in the condition of mankind."

The belief in progress was not universal, as is clear from H. Vyvenberg, *Historical Pessimism in the French Enlightenment* (Cambridge, Mass.: Harvard University Press, 1958). Neither Voltaire nor Rousseau can be considered a proponent of the idea of progress.

2.   From a section entitled, "Miscellany," *The Philosophical Dictionary*, in B. R. Redman (ed.), *The Portable Voltaire* (New York: Viking, 1949), p. 225. A useful study of Voltaire as historian is given in the excellent work of J. H. Brumfitt, *Voltaire: Historian* (London: Oxford, 1958); the chapter entitled, "Philosophy of History," pp. 95–128, is especially valuable.

3.   The originally separate work entitled "Philosophie de l'histoire" (1765) was added as an introductory section (1769) to Voltaire's *Essay on the Customs and Spirit of Nations*. Substantial portions are translated in J. H. Brumfitt (ed.), *Voltaire: The Age of Louis XIV and Other Selected Writings* (New York: Washington Square Press, 1963), pp. 240–273. It is likely that Voltaire picked up much of his notion of the "philosophy of history" from Lord Bolingbroke, with whom he was well acquainted. For the latter, history is "philosophy teaching by example," and this role of history is plain in the works of Voltaire.

4.   See the Preface to *Essay on the Customs and the Spirit of Nations* and J. B. Black, *The Art of History* (New York: Russell and Russell, 1926), pp. 29–75.

5.   Vague antecedents of the idea of progress are sighted by some in the various utopias of the sixteenth and seventeenth centuries: Thomas More's *Utopia* (1516), Francis Bacon's *The New Atlantis* (1624), T. Campanella's *The City*

of the Sun (1637). Hints at the theory can be found in the works of Bacon, Descartes, and Pascal, while clearer outlines begin to emerge with de Fontenelle's *Digression on the Ancients and Moderns* (1688) and the *Observations on the Continuous Progress of Reason* (1737) of the Abbé de Saint-Pierre.

Tuveson, especially in the chapter entitled, "Progress as Redemption: The New Paradise Regained," pp. 153–203, has demonstrated that English divines of the seventeenth century revived an early Christian belief that a period of great happiness for mankind on earth—the millennium—was yet to come as the crown and culmination of human history. This idea was developed by T. Burnet in *Archaeologiae Philosophicae; or the Ancient Doctrine concerning the Originals of Things* (1692) into an inevitable steady ascent of mankind, that is, a full-blown theory of progress, though one still allied with the millennial expectations which were based on an interpretation of the Apocalypse.

6.   Published in the same year as the delivery of Turgot's lectures was Rousseau's *Discourse on the Arts and Sciences* which had been submitted to the Academy of Dijon in the previous year. The academy had offered a prize for the best essay on the question whether progress in the arts and sciences had contributed to the improvement of morals. Rousseau's essay won first place with its negative answer: humanity is corrupted as the arts and sciences advance to perfection, since it is a law of history that morals rise or fall in inverse ratio to the rise and fall of the arts and sciences. It seemed to Rousseau that civilization is a huge mistake, having taken man further and further from the primitive state of innocence and happiness; history is the story of an infinite regress, not of progress.

7.   J. Turgot, *Oeuvres*, Vol. I, pp. 214–215, Schelle edn. (Paris: 1913–1922), as cited in F. E. Manuel, *The Prophets of Paris* (Cambridge, Mass.: Harvard University Press, 1962), p. 21. A thorough exposition of Turgot's philosophy of history appears on pages 13–51 of this excellent work.

8.   Turgot, *Oeuvres*, Vol. II, p. 598 (Paris: 1844), as cited in K. Löwith, *Meaning in History* (Chicago: University of Chicago Press, 1949), p. 100.

9.   Turgot, *Oeuvres*, Vol. I, Schelle edn., p. 283, as cited in Manuel, p. 47.

10.   Many writers have pointed out passages in Turgot's writings that anticipated Comte's law of the three stages: knowledge once had been exclusively theological, that is, the projection of divine power into natural forces and objects, then it became metaphysical, objects of knowledge being conceived and expressed as essences, and finally positive, where relations were expressed in terms of mathematics and the real nature of things was recognized. See Manuel, p. 32.

11.   Marquis de Condorcet, *Sketch for a Historical Picture of the Human Mind*, Introduction, trans. J. Barraclough (New York: 1955), in P. Gardiner, *Theories of History* (Glencoe, Ill.: Free Press, 1959), p. 52. Once again Manuel's excellent *Prophets of Paris*, on which we have relied, contains a useful section on Condorcet (pp. 55–102).

12.   Condorcet, *Sketch for a Historical Picture*, Tenth Stage, in Gardiner, p. 57.

13.   Condorcet, *Sketch for a Historical Picture*, trans. F. E. Manuel, in Manuel, p. 102.

14.   W. Godwin, *Inquiry Concerning Political Justice*, Vol. II, p. 528, cited in Dawson, p. 158. See C. L. Becker, *The Heavenly City of the Eighteenth Century Philosophers* (New Haven, Conn.: Yale University Press, 1932), for what is considered to be a classic statement of how the age of reason was simply rebuilding Augustine's city of God with secular materials.

15.   "Idea for a Universal History," trans. L. W. Beck, in *Kant on History*

(Indianapolis: Bobbs-Merrill, 1963), pp. 11, 12, 14. This very useful volume contains a collection of Kantian essays on the philosophy of history. An excellent analysis of the Kantian philosophy of history appears in the Editor's Introduction, pp. xii–xvi.

16.   Beck, p. 21.

17.   Beck, p. 14; see also pp. 12–14.

18.   Beck, p. 15; see also p. 17.

19.   Beck, p. 16.

20.   See Beck, pp. 18–19.

21.   See Beck, p. 21.

22.   See Beck, pp. 24, 25, 21–22. For the Kantian understanding of an Idea, see the Editor's Introduction, pp. xix–xxi. The last essay in this volume, "An Old Question Raised Again: Is the Human Race Constantly Progressing?" written fourteen years after the essay on universal history, is more firmly attached to the idea of progress: "Here, therefore, is a proposition valid for the most rigorous theory, in spite of all skeptics, and not just a well-meaning and practically commendable proposition: The human race has always been in progress toward the better and will continue to be so henceforth. To him who does not consider what happens in just some one nation but also has regard to the whole scope of all the peoples on earth who will gradually come to participate in progress, this reveals the prospect of an immeasurable time . . . ," pp. 147–148.

23.   Beck, p. 39.

24.   J. Herder, *Outlines of a Philosophy of the History of Man*, trans. T. Churchill (London: 1800), Book V, p. 6, as adapted in P. E. Tillinghast, *Approaches to History* (Englewood Cliffs, N.J.: Prentice-Hall, 1963), p. 156 f. In addition to Tillinghast's analysis of Herder's philosophy of history (pp. 147–156), one can consult R. T. Clark, *Herder, His Life and Thought* (Berkeley, Calif.: University of California Press, 1955), esp. pp. 308–347, and A. Lovejoy, "Herder: Progressionism without Transformism," in B. Glass (ed.), *Forerunners of Darwin* (Baltimore: The Johns Hopkins Press, 1958), pp. 207–221.

25.   Herder, IX, 1.

26.   Herder, IX, 4; see also VIII, 5.

27.   Herder, IX, 1.

28.   Herder, XIII, 7.

29.   Herder, XII, 6.

30.   Herder, XIII, 7. The same principle is applied to the Romans, "The Romans were precisely what they were capable of becoming . . . ," XIV, 6.

31.   Herder, XIII, 7.

32.   Herder, VIII, 5.

33.   Herder, XIV, 6.

34.   Herder, XVI, 6.

3

THE DIALECTIC OF HISTORY:

Hegel and Marx

Entering into the nineteenth century, one must select from a profusion of philosophies of history. No apology need be made, we believe, for presenting the views of Georg Hegel, Karl Marx, Auguste Comte, and Herbert Spencer as the most representative of the period. Most of the ingredients for the nineteenth-century philosophy of history were already in the air, especially among the philosophers of progress just reviewed. Vico's *New Science*, baptized with Voltaire's designation of the philosophy of history, so to speak, matured among the philosophies of progress. With Herder and Kant the field was still searching for an identity, which it found among nineteenth-century thinkers. Progress was to be its family name. All of the classic philosophies of history built on the philosophy of progress, but with quite different accents. One variation on the theme was supplied by Hegel in his dialectical unfolding of Spirit, which was promptly stood on its head by the "real" dialectic of Marx and Engels. Another variation was suggested by the Comtean historicosocial evolution of humanity, which was immediately subsumed under the comprehensive evolutionism of Spencer. Progress might well be the surname of the classic philosophies of history, but its pronunciation was very different among German, French, and English members of the family.

German philosophers were first on the scene. Considerations concerning progress and the history of mankind were little more than appendixes to the philosophy of Kant. Aware of his own *a priori* approach to universal history, Kant had no intention of suppressing historical research

38

or the empirical approach. Some of his successors had no such caution. "The philosopher follows the *a priori* thread of the world-plan which is clear to him without any history," Fichte wrote, "and if he makes use of history it is not to prove anything, since his theses are already proved independently of all history."[1] Consequently, Fichte claimed to know "the world-plan which can be clearly comprehended in its unity, and from which the major epochs of human life may be completely deduced and described in their origins and mutual inter-connexions."[2] We need not detain ourselves with the five historical epochs that Fichte deduced, though it should be observed that, together with Schiller and Schelling, he anticipated some of the characteristic features of the Hegelian system.[3]

The Dialectical Unfolding of Spirit: The Hegelian Synthesis

Any summary of the Hegelian philosophy of history is apt to be a distortion, for it constitutes an integral part of a monolithic philosophical system. Delivered in Berlin for the first time in the winter of 1822–1823, Hegel's lectures on the subject followed on the formulation of his final system in such works as *The Phenomenology of Spirit*, *The Science of Logic*, *The Encyclopedia of the Philosophical Sciences*, and *The Philosophy of Right and Law*. The system was supposed as proved or given by Hegel in his lectures on the philosophy of history, yet he claimed to approach world history empirically with one hypothesis only, that the development of world history has been a rational process.

> The only Thought which Philosophy brings with it to the contemplation of History, is the simple conception . . . that Reason is the Sovereign of the World; that the history of the world, therefore, presents us with a rational process. This conviction and intuition is a hypothesis in the domain of history as such. In that of Philosophy it is no hypothesis. It is there proved. . . .[4]

Hegel saw nothing unusual about this procedure. Do not the working historians, even the most impartial, come to the evidence with categories and presuppositions?

> Even the ordinary, the "impartial" historiographer, who believes and professes that he maintains a simply receptive attitude; surrendering himself only to the data supplied him—is by no means passive as regards the exercise of his thinking powers. He brings his categories with him, and sees the phenomena presented to his mental vision, exclusively through these media . . . in all that pretends to the name of science, it is indispensable that Reason should not sleep—that

reflection should be in full play. To him who looks upon the world rationally, the world in its turn presents a rational aspect. The relation is mutual.[5]

To the data of world history Hegel brought his categories and his system. Philosophical studies, for Hegel, embraced three parts: logic, the science of the Idea, the philosophy of Nature, and the philosophy of Spirit, the sciences of the concrete embodiment of the Idea. In the Hegelian system, logic not only concerns itself with the formal articulation of the concepts of pure reason but is at once a metaphysic or ontology, even a theodicy.

> Logic . . . is to be understood as the system of pure reason, as the Realm of pure thought. This realm is the truth as it is, without husk in and for itself. One may therefore express it thus: that this content shows forth God as He is in His eternal essence before the creation of nature and of a finite spirit.[6]

The whole system of categories or concepts in the Hegelian logic is a progressive definition of God or the Absolute in itself. These categories are dialectically related, having the peculiar property of giving rise one to another. The content of the concepts are of such a character that they arrange themselves in triads of thesis, antithesis, and synthesis, where the synthesizing concept of the preceding triad becomes in turn a point of departure or thesis for a new triad. Starting with the concept of being, Hegel demonstrates how this concept passes necessarily into successive concepts until the final category is reached, the Absolute Idea, the category of self-knowledge or self-consciousness.

In addition to all the triads of logic, there is a supertriad in which the Idea itself is thesis, Nature the antithesis, and Spirit the synthesis. The logical Idea is merely abstract reason, or reason that does not exist and has not manifested itself. To be fully itself, the Idea demands concrete embodiment, which is secured by externalizing or manifesting itself as Nature and returning to itself as Spirit. It is plain that the Christian notion of creation, "demythologized" as it may be, lies behind the supertriad of Hegel. God the Spirit is the absolute Idea who creates all reality by externalizing or alienating his substance in the world of nature and the world of man. After externalizing its substance in the world of reality, the absolute Idea progressively reassumes its substance into itself and so arrives at full self-consciousness or Absolute Spirit. Hence, all of reality is rational in some fashion, for the Idea or Reason is there actualized.

> The rational is actual; and the actual is rational. Upon this rests all naive consciousness, as does philosophy, and philosophy starts from it in considering the spiritual universe as well as the natural one . . . what matters is to recognize and know the substance which is im-

manent and the eternal which is present beneath the temporal and passing which appears. For the rational which is synonymous with the idea appears (by entering through its actuality into outward appearance) in a limited wealth of forms, appearance, configurations, and thus encloses its kernel with a variegated rind. Consciousness at the outset lives in this rind, but the conception permeates it in search of the inner impulse which beats in the outer configuration.[7]

In the realm of Nature, the Idea has gone over to its opposite and in doing so becomes estranged from itself, that is, idea-less and irrational in large measure. The forms in nature can be explained empirically, but they elude all logical deduction. "Nature is the development of the Idea in Space."[8] Space is sheer externality, which is the most removed of all from mind or Spirit. Yet the philosophy of Nature too exhibits a dialectical evolutionary process in which the Idea disengages itself from absolute mindlessness to return to the threshold of Spirit. From inanimate matter to animal organisms there is the gradual ascending return of the Idea from pure otherness and objectivity to itself, to an initial subjectivity in the animal. This evolution was a logical succession of concepts or stages for Hegel and not a temporal evolutionary process which he dismissed as not worthy of serious consideration. Nature brings one to the borders of Spirit, but only to the borders, since self-consciousness, the property of Spirit, is denied all of Nature.

The Absolute, as the Idea, objectifies itself in Nature but inadequately. As self-knowledge, or thought which thinks itself, the Absolute must come to exist as Spirit, that is, manifest itself in and through the consciousness of human spirit. As the philosophy of Nature, the philosophy of Spirit exhibits a dialectical evolutionary process also: subjective Spirit, objective Spirit, and absolute Spirit. Starting from the level of subjective Spirit, the finite human spirit in its inwardness and subjectivity, ascending through the sphere of objective Spirit, the objectifications or institutions of human spirit, especially the State, the Spirit finally becomes Absolute Spirit in and through the human spirit. At this level the human spirit is no longer finite and limited but knows the Absolute, which is to say that it knows itself as infinite, the totality, the Absolute. The process of the reabsorption of the absolute Idea in itself is now completed in the sphere of absolute Spirit, in the completely rational human spirit of the philosopher. Art, religion, and philosophy are three ways of apprehending the Absolute, but only in philosophy is the Absolute apprehended in a purely conceptual way, the mode proper to Idea.[9]

All of this and much more Hegel brought to his interpretation of world history.[10] History, he held, is "the development of Spirit in time," as Nature was the development of the Idea in space. The nature of Spirit and its development can be most easily understood by glancing at its direct opposite, which is Matter. "As the essence of Matter is gravity, so we may affirm that the essence or substance of Spirit is freedom." Matter is composite, seeking unity through gravity by tending toward its opposite, an indivisible point. If matter could ever attain this unity, it would be matter no longer. Hence matter has its essence or ideal unity outside of itself. "Spirit can be defined as that which has its center in itself." Spirit has its unity in itself; it is self-contained existence. This is freedom, for I am free when my existence depends on myself. The self-contained existence of Spirit is really self-consciousness or self-knowledge, which involves not only knowledge but an energy, enabling Spirit to realize and actuate itself. By this activation of itself Spirit becomes consciously and really free.

> The destiny of the spiritual World and . . . the final cause of the World at large, we allege to be the consciousness of its own freedom on the part of Spirit, and *ipso facto*, the reality of that freedom. . . . In the process before us, the essential nature of freedom—which involves in it absolute necessity—is to be displayed as coming to a consciousness of itself . . . and thereby realizing its existence. Itself is its own object of attainment, and the sole aim of Spirit. This result it is, at which the process of the World's History has been continually aiming. . . .[11]

Amid the ceaseless change of events and conditions in history, "phenomenal history," Spirit is realizing its freedom, both as the efficient principle of its activation and as the final term of the grand movement of the historical process. The means which the World-Spirit (*Weltgeist*) uses to achieve its goal are as "external and phenomenal" as the actions of men. Human "passions" are the general instruments of the World-Spirit, the "vast congeries of volitions, interests, and activities . . . of individuals and peoples, in which they seek and satisfy their own purposes," but which, at the same time, are "the means and instruments of a higher and broader purpose of which they know nothing." Once again we come across an idea that is scarcely original with Hegel: "in history an additional result is commonly produced by human actions beyond that which they aim at and obtain." "Something further is thereby accomplished, latent in the actions in question, though not present in their consciousness and not included in their design." Spirit is at work in and through this "phenomenal history."[12]

The World-Spirit is not limited to this form of human activity in working out its goal in history but also makes use of "World-Historical persons" whose vocation it was to be the agents of Spirit. These are the choice agents and instruments in the realization of the goal of world history.

> Such are all great historical men—whose own particular aims involve those larger issues which are the will of the World-Spirit. . . . Such individuals had no consciousness of the general Idea they were un-

folding . . . but at the same time they were thinking men, who had an insight into the requirements of the time—*what was ripe for development. . . .* It was theirs to know . . . the necessary, the directly sequent step in progress, which their world was to take; to make this their aim, and to expend their energy in promoting it.

These "soul-leaders" should not be judged by any ordinary moral standards. They may treat great and even sacred interests rather highhandedly, but "so mighty a form must trample down many an innocent flower—crush to pieces many an object in its path." There can be no doubt that "the claim of the World-Spirit rises above all special claims." In this inconsiderate manner the "cunning of reason" secures its goal in history.[13]

The concrete term or object of the unfolding of Spirit in time is the State, that "moral whole" in which the individual has and enjoys his freedom, the essential mark of the Spirit.

The State is the Divine Idea as it exists on earth. We have in it, therefore the object of history in a more definite shape than before; that in which Freedom obtains objectivity. For law is the objectivity of Spirit; volition its true form. Only that which obeys law is free; for it obeys itself—it is independent and so free.[14]

Underlying this view is a whole series of dialectically related concepts and categories in the Hegelian philosophy of Spirit, especially the distinction between the sphere of subjective Spirit and that of objective Spirit. Suffice it to note that as the Idea objectifies itself or expresses itself in Nature, so Spirit objectifies or externalizes itself in the realm of objective Spirit, particularly in the shape of human institutions. Only in the sphere of objective Spirit and only at the level of the State does self-consciousness rise to the level of universal self-consciousness. Only on this level, too, is there a union of subjective will or volition and universal rational will, at least ideally. In being governed by law and the State, man is governed by the universal which he has himself projected into the world, and consequently is governed by himself and is free.[15] "Society and State are the very conditions in which Freedom is realized."[16]

For Hegel the State is the embodiment of one moment in the life of the World-Spirit, the incarnation of a national spirit (*Volksgeist*). In the process of universal history, each particular national spirit must be considered as one individual only, for each is a phase in the development of the World-Spirit.

The spirit of the nation, concretely manifested, expresses every aspect of its consciousness and will—the whole cycle of its realization. Its religion, its polity, its ethics, its legislation, and even its science, art, and mechanical skill, all bear its stamp. These special peculiarities find their key in that common peculiarity—the particular principle that characterizes a people.

In this view Hegel has assimilated into his version of universal history another prominent feature of Vico's new science and Herder's philosophical history: the spirit of a people or age is expressed and objectified in the total culture of that people or age. Hegel did not wish to be dogmatic about this matter and claimed that the specific quality that characterizes a people must be derived from experience and historically proved. However, he had little doubt that such a national principle existed and was convinced that only "intimate acquaintance with the Idea" could insure success in its historical investigation.[17]

With these principles securely in hand, Hegel turned to the consideration of the actual course of world history. The first thing to do is to make certain that change and development in history are not confused with change and development in Nature. "The changes that take place in Nature . . . exhibit only a perpetually self-repeating cycle." Nature is so repetitive in its changes that it induces a feeling of boredom in the observer. "Only in those changes which take place in the region of Spirit does anything new arise." Peculiar to man is the impulse of perfectibility, which is constantly creative and limitless in scope. One should also note that development, or a capacity to realize itself, appears in natural organisms, but this development is much different from that in the realm of Spirit. Development of subhuman life "takes place in a direct, unopposed, unhindered manner." The situation is radically different for Spirit. The realization of Spirit is mediated by human consciousness and will, which, at first, are completely absorbed by merely natural appetites and goals, not altogether unlike the animals. Thus is Spirit alienated from itself, in the first instance, for it is Spirit animating these misplaced desires. Hence Spirit is at war with itself.

> That development which in the sphere of Nature is a peaceful growth, is in that of Spirit, a severe, a mighty conflict with itself . . . . Its expansion, therefore, does not present the harmless tranquillity of mere growth . . . but a stern reluctant working against itself.[18]

The conflict of Spirit with itself is the dialectic of history, and its ultimate goal and result is freedom.

Only in the light of the development of the freedom of Spirit do the external phenomena of the historical process possess "value" and receive their "meaning and importance." If one approaches universal history without this insight, it is not possible to comprehend or explain the periods of progress and the periods of decay which the external facts seem to point to. "Universal History exhibits the gradation in the development of . . . the consciousness of Freedom." This principle gives meaning to all of history, to periods of progress and periods of regress, to all of phenomenal history. The general character of the successive and dialectical process of the development of freedom in history is easily outlined.

The first step in the process presents that immersion of Spirit in Nature which has been already referred to; the second shows it as advancing to the consciousness of its freedom. But this initial separation from Nature is imperfect and partial, since it is immediately derived from the merely natural state, is consequently related to it, and is still encumbered with it as an essentially connected element. The third step is the elevation of the soul from this still limited and special form of freedom to its pure universal form; that state in which the spiritual essence attains the consciousness and feeling of itself. These grades are the ground-principles of the general process . . . constituting the links in a dialectic of transition. . . .[19]

The first steps in this process belong to prehistory, in the estimation of Hegel, and should not enter into a philosophical investigation of world history. "It is the State which first presents subject-matter that is not only adapted to the prose of History, but involves the production of such history in the very progress of its own being."[20] The philosopher must take up the course of history where Spirit or Reason has begun to actualize and realize itself in consciousness, will, and action, that is, in the State. Growth of families to clans, of clans to peoples, the development of language, the diffusion of these peoples, the whole series of interesting events attendant upon all of this, none of this is a part of world history, and, in fact, preceded it.[21] Hegel believed that his elimination of prehistory from the course of world history was confirmed by the fact that there were no historical records kept during this long period of humanity. Annals and records, subjective history, are intrinsically bound up with the real course of history, that is, objective history.

In our language the term History [*Geschichte*] unites the objective with the subjective side, and denotes quite as much the *historia rerum gestarum* as the *res gestae* themselves; on the other hand it comprehends not less what has happened, than the narration of what has happened. This union of two meanings we must regard as of a higher order than mere outward accident; we must suppose historical narrations to have appeared contemporaneously with historical deeds and events. It is an internal vital principle common to both that produces them synchronously.[22]

The unfolding of the truly historical process began in Asia and ends in Europe. "The history of the world travels from East to West, for Europe is the absolute end of history, Asia the beginning." Charted in the light of the developing freedom of Spirit, the course of history looked something like this to Hegel. "The East knew and to the present day knows only that *One* (the Despot and not the people) is free; the Greek and Roman world, that *Some* (the citizens and not the slaves) are free; the German world knows that *All* (man as man) are free." These grades in the progress of the consciousness and the reality of freedom supply us with the "natural divisions" of universal history. The reality of freedom can be easily described: "The History of the World is the discipline of the uncontrolled natural will, bringing it into obedience to a Universal principle, and conferring subjective freedom."[23] This brings us back to the concrete object of Spirit in history, which is the State. As we have seen, in the ideal State man is governed by the universal, which he has projected and concretized in the world. Governed by himself in this way, he attains subjective and conscious personal freedom. This ideal situation, Hegel believed, obtained only in the German world of his day.

We need not detain ourselves with the complicated and often brilliant analysis that Hegel gives of the course of history in the light of the developing freedom of man. It is sufficient to recall that a particular national principle or national spirit unified the Oriental, the Greek, the Roman, and the German worlds. Having run its course, this principle in each case was succeeded by another and higher national spirit which had been imbedded all the time in the earlier one. Step by dialectical step the freedom of Spirit unfolded itself in the consciousness of man and in the reality of his creations.[24] With the benefit of Christianity, the "absolute religion" for Hegel, in the German world, or more truly, in the Prussian State of Hegel's day, "freedom has found the means of realizing its Idea—its true existence. This is the ultimate result which the process of History is intended to accomplish. . . ."[25] This "extremely tame political conclusion," as Engels called it later, appears to be the end and goal of history, the end of the unfolding of Spirit and its freedom.

That may be so, but Hegel did not pretend to know the future. Philosophy always arrives too late, he held, to preach what the world ought to be like.

> As thought of the world it appears at a time when actuality has completed its developmental process and is finished. . . . When philosophy paints its gray in gray, a form of life has become old, and this gray in gray cannot rejuvenate itself, only understand it. The owl of Minerva begins its flight when dusk is falling.[26]

This is not exactly a claim to knowledge of the future, nor a very optimistic outlook on his beloved German world.

> The principles of the national spirits are . . . altogether limited. . . . From this finiteness, the universal spirit, the spirit of the world which is unlimited, creates itself; it is this world spirit which exercises its right over them . . . in world history as the world court.[27]

Hegel rejected the mantle of prophet—or did he? He did not go on to envision a world state in which the limited national principles would be transcended by a universal principle, it is true, but he did claim that the judgment of nations was immanent in history and that the "cunning of reason" accomplished its purposes in the world court.

However that may be, once again the "owl of Minerva" takes flight, leaving us in awe.

> Nothing in the past is lost . . . for the Idea is ever present; Spirit is immortal, with it nothing is past, no future, but an essential *now*. This necessarily implies that the present form of Spirit comprehends all earlier steps. These have indeed unfolded themselves in succession independently, but what Spirit is it has always been essentially. The life of the ever-present Spirit is a circle of progressive embodiments . . . [but] the grades which Spirit seems to have left behind, it still possesses in the depth of the present.[28]

The Real Dialectic of History: The Marxist Critique

Hegelianism reigned supreme among German philosophers for almost a decade after the death of Hegel in 1831. No doubt left-wing disciples were prone to point to the tension between the conservative and dynamic elements within the system, but only with the ascent of Frederick IV to the throne of Prussia in 1840 did abstract philosophical criticism turn into a philosophy of action. Fredcrick attempted to impose a strict orthodox Hegelianism on all universities, but the result was a radical critique of the whole social order in the name of the Hegelian dialectic. The Hegelian dialectic implied a continual progress and ceaseless development in history, for which no final state of affairs, or at least no set of existing conditions, could be stipulated in advance as if it were the ultimate term of the process. Yet, in the Hegelian system, the principle of dialectical progress was paired incongruously with several "absolutes" or ultimates: Christianity as the absolute religion, the Prussian State as the final incarnation of Spirit in the realm of politics, and Hegelianism itself as the absolute philosophy. One by one these conservative and static elements were rejected by Young Hegelians, and even the dialectic did not escape unscathed. It remained, but in a radically inverted position as the leading principle of a revolutionary and activistic philosophy.

Ludwig Feuerbach was responsible for some of this development. The starting point of all philosophy, he held, must be concrete, sensible reality and not the Idea as in the Hegelian system. Consciousness and thought are derived and secondary as compared to spatio-temporal Nature, which is the fundamental reality. Thus Feuerbach replaced Hegelian idealism with a materialism that reduced everything to sensual man and concrete nature. Even more characteristic of Feuerbach's philosophy was his substitution of a religion of mankind or humanity for that of Christianity. God, he thought, is a name for mankind's own idealized collective essence and attributes projected into a transcendent sphere, the fundamental alienation of mankind from itself. Not only had man externalized or alienated his essential qualities in God, thus impoverishing his own nature, but he also thereby had become an egoistic individual isolated from collective life wherein he finds his true being and fulfillment. Once this was understood, man could rid himself of the alienation and illusion involved in religion; he could recover faith in himself and in his own powers and secure the realization of his true collective being in a truly democratic republic. Freed from individualism and alienation at once, man would then enter freely into the collective life of a society in which the love of humanity reigns as the supreme law.

Feuerbach's materialistic and humanistic inversion of Hegelianism was taken several steps further in the direction of a socialistic philosophy of action by Moses Hess. Human emancipation was the task of the age, Hess believed, but this project could not be brought off by simple religious "reforms," as Feuerbach intimated. Rather, a radical social revolution was required. The alienation that Feuerbach pointed to in the field of religion was a superficial one at best, Hess held, since the real alienation of man from himself was produced by the capitalist system. Man is exploited by man in this system in which the weak are forced to create wealth by their labor for others. Having alienated their own substance and creative energies in commodities for the capitalist, the workers are in turn enslaved by their own products, for in the capitalist society wealth becomes the god in which man worships his own essence. Profit, competition, and private property must be done away with if alienation is to be overcome. A communist society must replace the capitalist system, since only in this way can human relations based on true altruism and love be operative in society and egoistic individualism surpassed.

What Feuerbach and Hess had only begun, Karl Marx brought to completion with the aid of the French Socialist Pierre Proudhon. As a student at the University of Berlin, Marx had associated with a circle of Young Hegelians, but he soon became dissatisfied with the purely theoretical approach of this left-wing group. When an academic career was closed to him because of an imprudent critique of Hegel, he turned to journalism, becoming editor of a radical journal in Cologne. There, during 1842 and early 1843, his inclination toward a practical philosophy of action was intensified by better acquaintance with the living conditions and social problems of the lower classes. When the Prussian government ordered the journal to cease publication in 1843, Marx moved to Paris with the plan of continuing publication of the paper under a new name. In Paris he came in contact with displaced Russian revolutionaries and radical French Socialists, especially Proudhon. Proudhon had conceived the idea of applying the Hegelian dialectic to society and economic problems; the real dialectic was to be found in the conflict between the higher and lower classes. Already enthused with Feuerbach's materialistic humanism and fired by the communist version of Hess, Marx found an interpretation of the Hegelian dialectic which he thought could make sense of it all. An integral view of history began to take shape in his mind, which came to be called "historical materialism." By 1846, the twenty-eight-year-old Marx and his even younger collaborator Friedrich Engels were able to put together a fairly coherent and comprehensive statement of historical materialism in *The German Ideology*. Two years later the new revolutionary creed was summarized by Marx and Engels in the *Manifesto of the Communist Party*.[29]

In *The German Ideology* Marx and Engels begin by rejecting all written history and historical theorizing before their time. "In the whole conception of history up to the present," they wrote, "the real basis of history has been totally neglected or else considered as a minor matter, quite irrelevant to the course of history." Earlier writers saw in the events of history only the political activities of princes or states, or, what was worse, religious and theoretical struggles taking place. Weakest of all the philosophers of history were the Germans, who thought that pure spirit and religious illusion were the "driving forces of history." The final consummation of illusory history was proclaimed by Hegel.

> The Hegelian philosophy of history is the last consequence . . . for which it is not a question of real, or even, of political interests, but of pure thoughts, which inevitably appear as . . . a series of "thoughts" that devour one another and are finally swallowed up in "self-consciousness."[30]

The place to begin any historical analysis, Marx and Engels believed, is with flesh and blood reality, with the "real premises" of "real history," and to go on from there to discover the "real basis" of the historical process. This statement is an exaggeration, as it is abundantly clear that Marx and Engels already thought they knew what history was all about.

> Our conception of history depends on our ability to expound the real process of production, starting out from the simple material production of life, and to comprehend the form of intercourse connected with this and created by this (i.e. civil society in its various stages) as the basis of all history . . . and so, from this starting point, to explain the whole mass of different theoretical products and forms of consciousness, religion, philosophy, ethics, etc., etc.,. . . .[31]

With this proposition as their starting point, Marx and Engels begin their analysis. Presupposed to all of human history is the existence of living human beings and the natural conditions in which they find themselves. Granted this, the first fundamental condition of all human history is the "production of material life," since it should be obvious, at least to non-Hegelians, that man must be able to live in order to be able to "make history." Included in their notion of material life are ordinary processes of life such as eating and drinking as well as other necessities such as clothing, dwellings, and so on. A second fundamental circumstance of all history is the "production of new needs," for new needs arise as soon as the basic needs of human life are satisfied. A third and equally obvious circumstance of real history is human reproduction, which gives rise to the family, the first social relationship in history.

> These three aspects of social activity are not . . . to be taken as three different stages but just as . . . three aspects . . . three "moments," which have existed simultaneously since the dawn of history and the first man, and still assert themselves in history today.[32]

One more aspect of the "fundamental historical relationships" suggested itself to Marx and Engels before one could even begin to arrive at "consciousness," a favored historical subject among German philosophers of history. This relationship is the "forces of production," and it is the most basic of all. A certain mode of production, or "industrial stage," is always combined with a certain mode of cooperation, or "social stage," and even the mode of cooperation itself is a "productive force." "The multitude of productive forces accessible to man determines the nature of society." From the very beginning of human history a "materialistic," or economic, connection of men with one another exists; determined by their needs and their mode of production, this connection is as old as man himself. "This connection is ever taking on new forms, and thus presents a 'history' independently of any political or religious nonsense which would hold men together on its own."[33] This was an understatement of the Marxist belief. Not only is economic history independent of political and religious history but the latter is dependent on and ultimately determined by the mode of production of material life. This is true because the "real" essence of man consists "in the ensemble of social relations."[34] "As individuals express their life, so they are. What they are, therefore, coincides with their production, both with what they produce and with how they produce. The nature of individuals thus depends on the material conditions determining their production."[35]

We are now on the real ground of all human history, having reached the concrete individuals in their flesh and blood reality. All that remains to do is to show how human history and its creations have sprung from this starting point. Marx and Engels have no doubt about the general features of this process.

We set out from real, active men, and on the basis of their real life-process we demonstrate the development of the ideological reflexes and echoes of this life-process. The phantoms formed in the human brain are also, necessarily, sublimates of their material life-process, which is empirically verifiable and bound to material premises. Morality, religion, metaphysics, all the rest of ideology and their corresponding forms of consciousness, thus no longer retain the semblance of independence. They have no history, no development; but men, developing their material production and their material intercourse, alter, along with their real existence, their thinking and the products of their thinking.[36]

Marx and Engels are much more successful in referring all developments in history to the economic substructure of society than they are in giving a coherent account of the history of humanity. Once the four fundamental conditions of all history have been established, one can turn to the development of consciousness. From the beginning and as long as man continues to exist, consciousness is a "social product," determined by the form of society and the stage of economic development.[37] At the outset consciousness concerns itself with the immediate sensible environment and with the individuals associated in the group. This mere "herd-consciousness," or "tribal consciousness," is still on a purely animal level in which nature appears as a "completely alien, all-powerful and unassailable force, with which men's relations are purely animal and by which they are overawed like beasts." Such a purely animal consciousness of nature is natural religion, and it rests on the fact that man at this point had not yet modified nature nor his social milieu to any notable degree by creative activity. With the increased productivity and modification of nature by man, along with the increase of needs and of population, consciousness began to emancipate itself from this animal condition, but always in dependence on the economic structure of society, and especially on the developing division of labor. Consciousness can, of course, break out of the straitjacket of the existing social relations to the formulation of "pure" theological or philosophical theory, but it would not be conceiving something "real." Consciousness of the really real advances only on the ground of true historical development, along with the successive stages of the economic development of man.

At this point we encounter the Marxist version of the Hegelian dialectic. Written in the process of economic and social development is a contradiction or conflict between social organization and the forces of production, which is the driving force of all history.

These three moments, the forces of production, the state of society, and consciousness, can and must come into contradiction with one another, because the division of labour implies the possibility, nay the fact that intellectual and material activity—enjoyment and labor, production and consumption—devolve on different individuals, and that the only possibility of their not coming into contradiction lies in the negation in its turn of the division of labour.[38]

The division of labor brings with it a number of contradictions between the general interests of all and individual interests. One of these is the unequal distribution of the products of labor, that is, of property. "Division of labour and private property are . . . identical expressions." Furthermore, an exclusive area of activity is forced on the individual by the division of labor, one from which he cannot escape. "Man's own deed becomes an alien power opposed to him, which enslaves him instead of being controlled by him." The crystallization and consolidation of what man himself produces into an "objective power above us, growing out of control" is the principal feature of all history up to the present.[39]

> The social power, i.e. the multiplied productive force, which arises through the cooperation of different individuals as it is determined within the division of labour, appears to these individuals, since their cooperation is not voluntary but natural, not as their own united power, but as an alien force existing outside them, of the origin and end of which they are ignorant, which they thus cannot control, which on the contrary passes through a peculiar series of phases and stages independent of the will and action of man, nay even being the prime governor of these.[40]

Marx and Engels arrange the map of human history according to the principal forms of the division of labor and property that have succeeded one another as a result of the opposition and conflict between the dynamic forces of production and the more stable element of social organization in classes. The first epoch of human history was characterized by a collective tribal ownership of property and an elementary division of labor rooted in the family which corresponded to an undeveloped stage of production limited to hunting and fishing, herding and agriculture. The second epoch, proceeding from tribal unions in cities, was that of communal property, which is the source of private property. During this phase of history a clear division of labor between agriculture and industry developed along with a definite class structure of citizen and slave. The formation of the city brought about concentration of private property in the hands of the citizens, while slavery became the basis of the whole productive system. The third age was that of estate property, or feudal ownership, which developed from the countryside rather than the town or city.

> The chief form of property during the feudal epoch consisted on the one hand of landed property with serf-labour chained to it, and on the other of individual labour with small capital commanding the

labour of the journeymen. The organization of both was determined
by the restricted conditions of production—the small-scale and primitive cultivation of the land, and the craft type of industry.

From the ruins of feudal society developed the fourth and final form of
the economic structure of society, the modern bourgeois society, in·which
the perennial historical combat of the classes is so concentrated and so
clear that no one except an "idealist" can possibly ignore it. Two great
and final classes, the bourgeoisie and the proletariat, directly confront one
another in the last massive conflict of history.[41]

The features of the bourgeois world and of the conflict between capital
and labor are more sharply drawn in the *Communist Manifesto*, where
"real" history is easily summarized: "The history of all hitherto existing
society is the history of class struggles."[42] The modern bourgeois society
developed dialectically from the means of production and of exchange
generated in feudal society. At a certain stage in its evolution, the feudal
organization of agriculture and manufacturing industry, or the feudal
property relations, were no longer compatible with the more advanced
productive forces. The temporary balance between the forces of production and social organization was upset once again, and feudal social organization became a brake on the movement of the productive forces. By
natural and inevitable succession the bourgeois society began to replace
the feudal epoch. "Into their places stepped free competition, accompanied by a social and political constitution adapted to it, and by the
economical and political sway of the bourgeois class."[43] During its rule of
about a century or so, since the beginnings of thc Industrial Revolution,
the bourgeoisie has created productive forces so massive and extensive
that they eclipse those of all previous generations taken together. As with
all dominant classes in previous forms of society, the bourgeoisie has succeeded in justifying its status by subjecting society as a whole to its conditions of ascendance, principally bourgeois private property. Not only
that but the whole of modern culture, the state, religion, philosophy, and
morality, is nothing but a reflection of the conditions of bourgeois society.
"The ruling ideas of each age have ever been the ideas of the ruling
class."[44] Yet eternity is not granted to the bourgeois society, and the dialectical movement of history continues behind the illusory political and
religious conflicts of the day. Once again the uneven rhythm of the productive forces and social organization is displaying itself with clear signs,
the portent of a new age.

Bourgeois society not only authored modern industry with its great
technical advances but also a number of wide-ranging, indeed, universal
contradictions. It has rendered the great mass of mankind propertyless
while at the same time being responsible for the accumulation of vast
wealth. Furthermore, it has called into existence a new class, the modern

working class or proletariat, and simplified the class antagonisms immensely. The modern worker is forced to sell himself as a "commodity,"
like every other article of commerce, and has become an "appendage of
the machine."

> It [the bourgeoisie] has resolved personal worth into exchange value,
> and in place of the numberless . . . freedoms, has set up that single,
> unconscionable freedom—Free Trade. In one word, for exploitation,
> veiled by religious and political illusion, it has substituted naked,
> shameless, direct, brutal exploitation.[45]

Finally, bourgeois society has been spreading its inhuman conditions
throughout the world, principally through the developing world market.
A universal historical change is building up as society as a whole becomes
more split up into the two final classes.

"The proletariat can exist . . . only world-historically, just as communism, its movement, can only have a world-historical existence."[46] All
previous historical movements, from the primitive communistic society to
the ancient society built on slavery, thence to the feudal society erected
on serfdom, and from there to the modern bourgeois society resting on
wage labor, have been movements of minorities, of classes. "The prole-
tarian movement is the self-conscious, independent movement of the
immense majority, in the interest of the immense majority." Only the
Communists "represent the interests of the movement as a whole," independently of all nationality, since they have the advantage of "clearly
understanding the line of march, the conditions and ultimate general
results of the proletariat movement." The Communist knows that all
history, since the primitive communistic period, has been the history of
class struggles, which has developed along with the division of labor and
private property. The issues are clearly defined in the modern epoch, and
the aim can be summed up in a single statement: "abolition of private
property." The proletariat in its universal historical contest with the
bourgeoisie may have to organize itself as a political class and "win the
battle of democracy," but its aim is ever the elimination of the old conditions of production, or bourgeois private property. In accomplishing
this revolution, the proletariat "will, along with these conditions, have
swept away the conditions for the existence of class antagonism and of
classes generally, and will thereby have abolished its own supremacy as a
class." In place of all previous societies with their classes and class antagonisms, excepting the primitive communistic society, there will be "an
association in which the free development of each is the condition for
the free development of all."[47]

In a later work, Engels is quite clear about the role of the proletariat
in the final conflict of world history. The proletariat has the mission of
eliminating "all exploitation, oppression, class distinctions, and class

struggles." This objective may be the inevitable aim of the historical process, but consciousness of the "real movement" of history can be very useful. Active social forces are exactly like natural forces; once man understands their reactions, directions, and effects, he can subject them to his own ends and transform them into "willing servants." "The proletariat seizes political power and turns the means of production into state property. But in doing so it abolishes itself as proletariat, abolishes all class distinctions and class antagonisms, abolishes the State as State." When this is brought about, man will be completely and finally marked off from the animals, and a subhuman form of existence will come to an end. Truly human conditions of existence will replace the degrading effects of the class societies. "Man . . . for the first time becomes the real conscious lord of nature because he is now master of his own social organization." Up to this final outcome of history the social organization had confronted man as a necessity imposed by nature and history; now it is to become the conscious result of his own free action. "It is the ascent of man from the kingdom of necessity to the kingdom of freedom." From this moment on there will be a fully human history, for "only from that time will man make himself . . . make his own history."[48]

This was the challenge and prospect offered to the "world-historical" individuals of Marxism, the proletariat, and their historical mission. Scientific socialism, resting on the presuppositions of historical materialism, had the task of comprehending the historical conditions for this revolutionary act. History does not end with the accomplishment of the historical mission of the proletariat, nor does the law of the "real" dialectic continue to demand interminable developments. Truly human history, history fully under the control of man and made by him, was yet to begin. Through the mission of the proletariat man was to become lord of history.[49]

All of this has the ring of a religious apocalyptic, and Engels was fully aware of the resemblance. "Both Christianity and the worker's socialism preach salvation from bondage and misery; Christianity places this salvation in a life beyond, after death, in heaven; socialism places it in this world, in a transformation of society."[50] A religion of humanity, like communism, had nothing to fear from a Christianity that preached salvation in the next life yet compromised itself by embracing a world that was to pass in the form of modern bourgeois society, or so Marx believed.[51] The grand dialectical movement of progress in history made the victory of the classless society absolutely inevitable.

NOTES

1. J. Fichte, "The Basic Features of the Present Age," cited by J. Pieper, *The End of Time* (London: Faber, 1954), p. 105.

2. Cited without reference by J. B. Bury, *The Idea of Progress* (London: Macmillan, 1932), p. 253.

3. See R. G. Collingwood, *The Idea of History* (Oxford: Clarendon Press, 1946), pp. 104–113. Bury's summary of Fichte's deduced schema of world history is useful. "The end of mankind upon earth is to reach a state in which all the relations of life shall be ordered according to reason, not instinctively but with full consciousness and deliberate purpose . . . [this] determines the necessary stages of history. It gives us at least two main periods, the earliest and the latest: the earliest in which men act by instinct, and the latest, in which they are conscious of reason and try to realize it fully. But before reaching this final stage they must pass through an epoch in which reason is conscious of itself but not regnant. And to have reached this they must have emancipated themselves from instinct, and this process of emancipation means a fourth epoch. But they could not have wanted to emancipate themselves unless they felt instinct as a servitude imposed by external authority, and therefore we have to distinguish yet another epoch in which reason is expressed in authoritarian institutions to which men blindly submit. In this way Fichte deduces five historical epochs . . . ." (Bury, pp. 251–252)

The five epochs of Fichte were (1) instinctive reason, or the age of innocence; (2) authoritarian reason, or the age of authority; (3) enfranchisement, or the age of unregulated liberty and skepticism; (4) conscious reason, or the age of science; (5) regnant reason, or the age of art. Fichte believed that his generation (1803) was in age three.

4. G. Hegel, *The Philosophy of History*, trans. J. Sibree (New York: Dover, 1956), p. 9. Sibree's translation has been reprinted many times both in paperback and hardcover. Several fine works on Hegel's complex system of thought can be listed: W. T. Stace, *The Philosophy of Hegel* (New York: Dover, 1955) (for the Hegelian system); H. Marcuse, *Reason and Revolution: Hegel and the Rise of Social Theory*, 2d ed. (New York: Humanities Press, Inc., 1954) (oriented more toward the philosophy of history); F. Copleston, *A History of Philosophy*, Vol. VII (Westminster, Md.: Newman Press, 1965), pp. 159–247 and *passim* (the Hegelian system and its historical context); and C. J. Friedrich, *The Philosophy of Hegel* (New York: Random House, 1953) (selections from the works of Hegel, along with a fine introduction to Hegelian thought by the editor). The latter volume contains (pp. 3–158) lengthy sections of Hegel's philosophy of history; the first part of this selection is a translation of a more critical edition of Hegel's introduction than Sibree had available. Nevertheless, we have used the Sibree translation, based on Karl Hegel's edition of his father's philosophy of history, because it is a complete translation and is the edition that carried the influence of Hegel outside the lecture hall. Friedrich himself seems to agree with this estimation, for which see his introduction to the New York edition of Sibree's translation, cited above.

5. Hegel, *Philosophy of History*, p. 11. See *The Encyclopedia of Philosophy*, trans. G. E. Mueller (New York: Philosophical Library, Inc., 1959), section entitled, "Philosophy of History," secs. 442–449, pp. 254–259.

6. *The Science of Logic,* in Friedrich, p. 186. "Pure science includes thought in so far as it is just as much the thing in itself as it is thought, or the thing in itself so far as it is just as much pure thought as it is the thing in itself. Truth, as science, is pure self-consciousness unfolding itself, and it has the form of self in that what exists in and for itself is the known concept, while the concept is that which exists in and for itself," in Friedrich, p. 185. "The method [dialectical] is in no way different from its object and content; for it is the content in itself, the dialectic which it has in itself, that moves it on," in Friedrich, p. 191. "That by which the concept forges ahead is the . . . negative which it carries in itself; it is this that constitutes the genuine dialectical procedure," in Friedrich, pp. 192–193. For Hegel's definition of dialectic, see *Encyclopedia of Philosophy,* sec. 13, in Mueller, p. 82.

It should be noted that Hegel distinguished "understanding" (*Verstand*) from "reason" (*Vernunft*). By the understanding is meant that stage of the development of mind at which opposites are regarded as mutually exclusive; the laws of identity, contradiction, excluded middle are its canons. At the stage of reason mind rises to the principle of the identity of opposites; the categories break up and flow into each other, filled with life and movement as they are. Static, fixed, and lifeless categories pertain to the stage of understanding. See *Encyclopedia of Philosophy,* e.g., secs. 5, 19–22, 66–71, in Mueller, pp. 69–71, 86–88, 117–120. Mueller renders *Verstand* by "reason" and *Vernunft* by "comprehensiveness."

7. G. Hegel, *Philosophy of Right and Law,* in Friedrich, pp. 224–225. "To recognize and know reason as the rose within the cross of the present, and thus to enjoy this present, this sort of rational insight is the reconciliation with actuality which philosophy provides for those who have received the inner demand to understand," in Friedrich, p. 226.

8. Hegel, *Philosophy of History,* p. 72. See *Encyclopedia of Philosophy,* "Philosophy of Nature," secs. 192–196, 273–298, in Mueller, pp. 165–167, 185–187.

9. Christianity was the "absolute" religion for Hegel, but it apprehends the absolute truth in a defective way. Art apprehends the Absolute under the sensuous form of beauty, religion in the form of pictorial or symbolic thought (*Vorstellung*), philosophy in a purely conceptual and rational mode. Elevating the truths of Christianity to the level of philosophical thought meant the elimination of the element of contingency: creation of the world becomes a necessity, as does the alienation of God and man, which is written in the nature of things. Likewise the Gospel accounts of the reconciliation of God and man through the incarnation and connected events present the real truth in the form of a story of an event. "Demythologizing," as it is called today, goes back at least as far as Hegel. Hegel conceived his "absolute" philosophy as esoteric Christianity, while Christianity, as the "absolute" religion, was esoteric Hegelianism. For all of this see *Encyclopedia of Philosophy,* "Philosophy of the Spirit," secs. 377–421, in Mueller, pp. 191–254, and "Absolute Spirit," secs. 453–477, in Mueller, pp. 269–287.

10. In the realm of the history of philosophy Hegel was quite forthright in claiming that the history of ideas followed necessarily logical sequences that could be deduced from the idea, "I am now ready to assert that the sequence of the systems of philosophy in history is the same as the sequence in the logical deduction of the concepts as determined by the idea. I assert that if

one treats the basic concepts of the systems which have appeared in history purely and stripped of what is their external configuration, their application to particular situations and the like, he arrives at the different levels of the determination of the idea in its logical outline," *The History of Philosophy*, in Friedrich, p. 165. As the "absolute" philosophy, Hegel was convinced that his system was "the result of the work of all the centuries." "In this latest philosophy all that appears at first as past must be preserved and contained: it must be a mirror of the entire history. The last form which results from such progress as a progressive explication is the most concrete," in Friedrich, pp. 170, 172.

11.   Hegel, *Philosophy of History*, pp. 17–19.

12.   Hegel, *Philosophy of History*, pp. 25, 27. Hegel was the last of the philosophers of history that we shall consider who still attempted to align his vision of history with the plan of providence. "Philosophy of history can be called a Theodicaea—a justification of the ways of God," p. 15. And, more boldly, "God governs the world; the actual workings of his government—the carrying out of his plan—is the history of the world. This plan philosophy strives to comprehend," p. 36. In the *Encyclopedia of Philosophy*, sec. 449, in Mueller, p. 256, Hegel says, "Philosophy of history must think history as a comprehensive process unfolding itself in finite and concrete teleological wholes—in religious language, as providence."

13.   Hegel, *Philosophy of History*, pp. 31, 30, 32, 33, 37. "In contemplating the fate which virtue, morality, and even piety experience in history, we must not fall into the Litany of Lamentations, that the good and pious often—or for the most part—fare ill in the world, while the evil-disposed and wicked prosper . . . that so-called well or ill-faring of these or those isolated individuals cannot be regarded as an essential element in the rational order of the universe," p. 34.

14.   Hegel, *Philosophy of History*, p. 39. "All the worth which the human being possesses—all spiritual reality, he possesses only through the State. For his spiritual reality consists in this, that his own essence—Reason—is objectively present to him, that it possesses objective immediate existence for him. Thus only is he fully conscious; thus only is he a partaker of morality—of a just and moral social and political life. For Truth is the Unity of the universal and subjective will; and the Universal is to be found in the State, in its laws, its universal and rational arrangements," p. 39. In the *Philosophy of Right and Law* Hegel refers to the State as "this actual God," and as "the course of God through the world."

15.   See Stace, pp. 422–438.

16.   See Hegel, *Philosophy of History*, pp. 40–49.

17.   Hegel, *Philosophy of History*, p. 64; see pp. 49–54. "This matured totality . . . constitutes one Being, the spirit of one People. To it the individual members belong; each unit is the Son of his Nation, and at the same time—in so far as the State to which he belongs is undergoing development—the Son of his Age. None remains behind it, still less advances beyond it. This spiritual Being (the Spirit of his Time) is his; he is a representative of it; it is that in which he originated, and in which he lives," p. 52. "The relation of the individual to the Spirit is that he appropriates to himself this substantial existence; that it becomes his character and capability, enabling him to have a definite place in the world—to be something. For he finds the being of the people to which he belongs an already established, firm world—objectively

present to him—with which he has to incorporate himself," p. 74. In view of
these statements, it is not difficult to understand the violent reaction of Kierkegaard in favor of the individual and his existence. Existentialists and personalists
of our own generation continue the conflict with Hegel, and, we might add,
with the present reality. The individual is all but swallowed up in the universal
of Hegel, whether it be the State, culture, or history, though Hegel makes an
effort to exempt facets of the individual; see, e.g., pp. 33, 34, 37, 67.

18.   Hegel, *Philosophy of History*, pp. 54–56. "Spirit—consuming the envelope
of its existence—does not merely pass into another envelope, nor rise rejuvenated
from the ashes of its previous form; it comes forth exalted, glorified, a purer
spirit. It certainly makes war upon itself—consumes its own existence; but in
this very destruction it works up that existence into a new form, and each
successive phase becomes in its turn a material, working on which it exalts
itself to a new grade."

19.   Hegel, *Philosophy of History*, p. 56.

20.   Hegel, *Philosophy of History*, p. 61.

21.   See Hegel, *Philosophy of History*, pp. 59–63. "Spirit begins with a germ
of infinite possibility, but only possibility. . . . In actual existence Progress appears as an advancing from the imperfect to the more perfect; but the former
must not be understood abstractly as only the imperfect, but as something
which involves the very opposite of itself—the so-called perfect—as a germ or
impulse. So—reflectively, at least—possibility points to something destined to
become actual. . . . Thus the imperfect as involving its opposite, is a contradiction, which certainly exists, but which is continually annulled and solved;
the instinctive movement . . . to break through the rind of mere nature, sen-
suousness, and that which is alien to it, and to attain to the light of consciousness, i.e., to itself," p. 57.

22.   Hegel, *Philosophy of History*, p. 60.

23.   Hegel, *Philosophy of History*, pp. 103–104; see pp. 18–19.

24.   "A Nation is moral, virtuous, vigorous, while it is engaged in realizing
its grand objects, and defends its work against external violence during the
process of giving to its purposes an objective existence. The contradiction
between its potential, subjective being—its inner aim and life—and its actual
being is removed; it has attained full reality, has itself objectively present to it.
But this having been attained . . . the living substantial soul itself may be said
to have ceased its activity. The essential, supreme interest has consequently
vanished from its life, for interest is present only where there is opposition. . . .
This mere customary life . . . is that which brings on natural death. Custom
is activity without opposition . . . a political nullity and tedium. In order that
a truly universal interest may arise, the Spirit of a people must advance . . .
to a transcending of its principle, but this act would involve a principle of a
new order, a new National Spirit," Hegel, *Philosophy of History*, pp. 74–75.

25.   Hegel, *Philosophy of History*, pp. 109–110.

26.   Hegel, *Philosophy of Right and Law*, in Friedrich, p. 227.

27.   Hegel, *Philosophy of Right and Law*, in Friedrich, p. 329.

28.   Hegel, *Philosophy of History*, p. 79. "In looking back and contemplating
the achievements of history and their sad limitations, mind rises in this contemplation above them and elevates itself to the truth of the absolute spirit,
which is not bound by subjective and historical minds. Stripped of its worldli-
ness objective mind becomes a knowing comprehension, free in and for itself

as united with the Absolute . . . in the forms of art, religion, and philosophy.
In each of them, free and actual intelligence grasps its identity with the
dialectical essence of the world; it exists not only as achievement of a past, but
also as the presence of the eternal Now in an educational process of self-liber-
ation and self-articulation," secs. 452, 453, in Mueller, pp. 260, 269.

29.   As can be imagined, the literature on Marxism is extensive. Several
excellent works which we have used can be cited here: S. Hook, *Towards an
Understanding of Karl Marx* (New York: John Day, 1933), and *From Hegel to
Marx* (New York: John Day, 1950); A. Cornu, *The Origins of Marxian
Thought* (Springfield, Ill.: Charles C Thomas, 1957); H. Marcuse, *Reason and
Revolution: Hegel and the Rise of Social Theory*, 2d ed. (New York: Hu-
manities Press, Inc., 1954); G. A. Wetter, *Dialectical Materialism* (New York:
Praeger, 1958); E. R. A. Seligman, *The Economic Interpretation of History*,
2d ed., rev. (New York: Columbia University Press, 1961) [reprint]; M. M.
Bober, *Karl Marx's Interpretation of History*, 2d ed., rev. (New York: W. W.
Norton, 1965) [reprint]. Our necessarily abbreviated and oversimplified account
of the intellectual backgrounds of Marx can be easily filled out by the works of
Hook and Cornu. For the most part we concentrate on historical materialism
as it was first thought out in a comprehensive fashion by Marx. Dialectical materialism, the work of Engels, it seems, is given only incidental attention in our
account.

Engels accepted the designation historical materialism as an adequate description of the Marxist view and in 1892 summarized it as follows: "I use
. . . the term 'historical materialism' to designate that view of history which
sees the ultimate cause and the great moving power of all important historical
events in the economic development of society, in the changes in the modes of
production and exchange, in the consequent division of society into distinct
classes, and in the struggle of these classes against one another." "On Historical
Materialism," Introduction to the English edition of *Socialism: Utopian and
Scientific*, 1892, in L. Feuer (ed.), *Marx and Engels, Basic Writings on Politics
and Philosophy* (New York: Doubleday, 1959), pp. 53–54.

For a characteristic statement by Engels of dialectical materialism in conjunction with historical materialism, see *Ludwig Feuerbach and the End of
Classical German Philosophy* (1888), in Feuer, pp. 195–242.

30.   K. Marx and F. Engels, *The German Ideology*, trans, and ed. R. Paschal
(New York: International Publishers, 1947) [1960 reprint], pp. 30–31. Only
the last section of *The German Ideology* was published during the lifetime of
Marx and Engels, while the whole was first published in full in 1932. In 1888,
Engels had this to say of the early work: "I have once again ferreted out and
looked over the old manuscript of 1845–46. . . . The finished portion consists
of an exposition of the materialist conception of history, which proves only
how incomplete our knowledge of economic history still was at that time."
Foreword to *Ludwig Feuerbach and the End of Classical German Philosophy*,
in Feuer, p. 196.

31.   Marx and Engels, *The German Ideology*, p. 28.

32.   See Marx and Engels, *The German Ideology*, pp. 16–18.

33.   Marx and Engels, *The German Ideology*, pp. 18–19.

34.   See K. Marx, *Theses on Feuerbach*, Thesis VI. "Feuerbach starts out
from the fact of religious self-alienation. . . . His work consists in the dissolution of the religious world into its secular basis. He overlooks the fact . . .
that the secular foundation detaches itself from itself and establishes itself in

the clouds as an independent realm is really to be explained only by the self-cleavage and self-contradictoriness of this secular basis. The latter must itself, therefore, first be understood in its contradiction and then, by the removal of the contradiction, revolutionized in practice." Thesis IV, in Feuer, p. 244.

35.   Marx and Engels, *The German Ideology*, p. 7. "Men can be distinguished from animals by consciousness, by religion or anything else you like. They themselves begin to distinguish themselves from animals as soon as they begin to *produce* their means of subsistence. . . ." See also p. 29, "This sum of productive forces, forms of capital and social forms of intercourse, which every individual and generation finds in existence as something given, as the real basis of what the philosophers have conceived as 'substance' and 'essence' of man. . . ."

36.   Marx and Engels, *The German Ideology*, p. 14.

37.   See K. Marx, Preface to *A Contribution to the Critique of Political Economy* (1859). "In the social production which men carry on they enter into definite relations that are indispensable and independent of their will; these relations of production correspond to a definite stage of development of their material powers of production. The sum total of these relations of production constitutes the economic structure of society—the real foundation, on which rise legal and political super-structures and to which correspond definite forms of social consciousness. The mode of production in material life determines the general character of the social, political, and spiritual processes of life. It is not the consciousness of men that determines their existence, but, on the contrary, their social existence determines their consciousness," in Feuer, p. 43.

38.   Marx and Engels, *The German Ideology*, p. 21; see pp. 19–21 and 27 f. "At a certain stage of their development the material forces of production in society come into conflict with the existing relations of production, or—what is but a legal expression for the same thing—with the property relations within which they had been at work before. From forms of development of the forces of production these relations turn into their fetters. Then comes the period of social revolution," Preface to Marx, *A Contribution to the Critique of Political Economy*, in Feuer, pp. 43–44. See the Second Preface to K. Marx, *Capital: A Critique of Political Economy* (1873), "The mystifying side of Hegelian dialectic I criticized nearly 30 years ago . . . working on the first volume of *Das Kapital* . . . I openly avowed myself the pupil of that mighty thinker. . . . With him it is standing on its head. It must be turned right side up again, if you would discover the rational kernel within the mystical shell," in Feuer, pp. 145–146. This critique can be found in T. B. Bottomore, *Karl Marx: Early Writings* (New York: McGraw-Hill, 1964), pp. 195–219. This useful volume contains other interesting writings of the young Marx, all published in 1844.

39.   Marx and Engels, *The German Ideology*, pp. 22–23.

40.   Marx and Engels, *The German Ideology*, p. 24. For a fuller understanding of the concept of "alienation," a term taken over from Hegel by the youthful Marx, see the *Economic and Philosophical Manuscripts*, first manuscript, section entitled "Alienated Labor," in Bottomore, pp. 120–134. The older Marx no longer used this Hegelian term.

41.   Marx and Engels, *The German Ideology*, pp. 9–13; see pp. 43–58. In the preface to *A Contribution to the Critique of Political Economy* Marx speaks of the four epochs of history in these terms: "In broad outlines we can

designate the Asiatic, the ancient, the feudal, and the modern bourgeois methods of production as so many epochs in the progress of the economic formation of society."

42.   K. Marx and F. Engels, *Manifesto of the Communist Party*, in Feuer, p. 7. In a note added to the English edition of 1888, Engels specifically exempts the "primitive communistic society" from this summation of all history. Evidently separate and antagonistic classes appear only after this initial form of society.

43.   Marx and Engels, *Communist Manifesto*, in Feuer, pp. 11–12.

44.   Marx and Engels, *Communist Manifesto*, in Feuer, pp. 23–24. "We therefore reject every attempt to impose on us any moral dogma whatsoever as an eternal, ultimate, and forever immutable moral law on the pretext that the moral world, too, has its permanent principles which transcend history and the difference between nations. We maintain . . . that all former moral theories are the product, in the last analysis, of the economic stage which society reached at a particular epoch . . . morality has always been a class morality. . . . That . . . there has been, on the whole, progress in morality, as in all other branches of human knowledge, cannot be doubted. But we have not yet passed beyond class morality. A really human morality, which transcends class antagonisms . . . becomes possible only at a stage of society which has not only overcome class contradictions but has even forgotten them in practical life," F. Engels, *Anti-Dühring*, ch. IX (1877–1878), in Feuer, p. 272.

45.   Marx and Engels, *Communist Manifesto*, in Feuer, pp. 14, 9–10.

46.   Marx and Engels, *The German Ideology*, p. 26; see pp. 24–27.

47.   Marx and Engels, *Communist Manifesto*, in Feuer, pp. 18, 20–21, 27–29.

48.   F. Engels, *Socialism: Utopian and Scientific*, English edition, 1892, in Feuer, pp. 105–106, 109, 111. "Freedom of the will . . . means nothing but the capacity to make decisions with real knowledge of the subject. . . . Freedom therefore consists in the control over ourselves and over external nature which is founded on knowledge of natural necessity; it is therefore necessarily a product of historical development. The first men who separated themselves from the animal kingdom were in all essentials as unfree as the animals themselves, but each step forward in civilization was a step towards freedom . . . ," Engels, *Anti-Dühring*, ch. XI, in Feuer, p. 279.

49.   The whole of the historical process up to the dissolution of the classes and disappearance of class antagonisms is really "pre-history," according to the estimate of Marx. "The bourgeois relations of production are the last antagonistic form of the social process of production . . . at the same time the productive forces developing in the womb of bourgeois society create the material conditions for the solution of that antagonism. This social formation constitutes, therefore, the closing chapter of the prehistorical stage of human society," Marx, Perface to *A Contribution to the Critique of Political Economy*, in Feuer, pp. 44. The young Marx (1844) did not view communism as the final stage in human history: "Communism is the phase of negation of the negation and is, consequently, for the next stage of historical development, a real and necessary factor in the emancipation and rehabilitation of man. Communism is the necessary form and the dynamic principle of the immediate

future, but communism is not itself the goal of human development—the form of human society," *Economic and Philosophical Manuscripts*, in Bottomore, p. 167.

50.　F. Engels, "On the History of Early Christianity," (1894–1895), in Feuer, pp. 168–169.

51.　See K. Marx, "The Communism of the Paper *Rheinischer Beobachter*," (1847), in Feuer, p. 267 f.

4

THE EVOLUTION OF HISTORY:

Comte and Spencer

The theory of human progress had been left by eighteenth-century thinkers in France resting on an induction with weak and shifting foundations. Their successors, however, Henri Saint-Simon and Auguste Comte, sought to elevate it into a scientific hypothesis by arriving at social laws as valid as the laws governing the physical universe. In the process the study called sociology was born. Saint-Simon, in 1814, left no doubt that he believed in human progress and perfection in the not too distant future. "The imagination of the poets had placed the golden age in the cradle of the human race. . . . The golden age is not behind us, but in front of us. It is the perfection of the social order. Our fathers have not seen it; our children will arrive there some day, and it is for us to clear the way for them."[1]

Already in 1812 Saint-Simon proclaimed himself a determinist in his conception of the processes of human history, and the plain substitution of a "law" of history for the plan of providence made an appearance.

In the development of the sciences and arts the human spirit follows a predetermined course which is superior to the greatest intellectual forces, which appear only as instruments destined to produce successive discoveries at given times. Although this force derives from us, it is no more in our power to escape its influence or to master its action than it is to change at our pleasure the primitive impulse which makes our planet circle around the sun. Secondary effects alone are subject to dependence on us. All we can do is to obey this law (our veritable providence) with understanding, taking into account the course which it prescribes for us instead of being blindly pushed by it. . . .[2]

The key to the securing of human progress depended on a true understanding of the nature and direction of history. "Philosophical history," or scientific history, could attain to essential history in which all trivia and accidentals were eliminated from consideration. Unacquainted with the works of German philosophers of history such as Herder or Kant, and unaware of the masterpiece of Vico, Saint-Simon recognized only Condorcet as a predecessor. As a result, he was convinced that he had discovered philosophical history. "In fact," he wrote,

> history in a scientific sense has not yet come out of its swaddling clothes. This important branch of our knowledge is nothing but a collection of more or less well-established facts. The facts are not tied together by any theory. . . . No historian has yet placed himself in a general vantage point.[3]

It was some time before Saint-Simon settled on one theory to tie together the historical facts. His theory postulated three successive organic systems, one more perfect than the other, all driving toward the perfection of man as their goal. Polytheistic ideology coupled with a social order based on slavery was characteristic of the first system, or organic civilization. Following on the first was a civilization featuring a theological ideology together with a feudal social organization. The third system had, or was to have, a scientific or positive ideology while its social order was industrial. The first historical system had already passed through its life cycle while the second was on its deathbed and the third was just beginning to attain youthful vigor. These three systems did not succeed one another as if they were completely cut off from one another in time, but there was considerable overlapping from one to the other in time. Periods of transition of a totally different character intervened between the three organic systems. This succession should be considered a "law," the law of alternating epochs. The intermediate periods were periods of criticism or revolution, while the systematic periods were periods of organization or construction. One period of criticism had been experienced by ancient man, the age of the disintegration of the ancient world, while another period of revolution or transition was taking place in Saint-Simon's day, which was especially clear in the events of the French Revolution. Universal history, for Saint-Simon, unfolded in a rhythm of organic and critical epochs, though the movement toward human perfection was assured by the succession of ever more perfect systems.[4]

The Evolution of Historical Humanity:
The Comtean Synthesis

Many of Saint-Simon's insights find their fullest and most coherent exposition in the positivistic system of Auguste Comte. While the question of originality may be disputed, there is little doubt that the elaborate synthesis of Comte eclipsed the unorganized "philosophical history" of Saint-Simon. Before striking out on his own, the young Comte had been secretary to the aging Saint-Simon for several years, but the role of disciple was not one that he relished. The final break between the two came in 1824, and Comte turned to tutoring in mathematics for a livelihood. From 1826 to 1829, with time out for a severe mental breakdown and attempts at suicide, he delivered a series of lectures on his new system. The complete Comtean system appeared in its first form in the six-volume *Cours de philosophie positive* (1830–1842), which incorporated the earlier conferences. Once again we come across a claim to the discovery of a new science, for which Comte finally fashioned the name sociology. Last of the sciences in the chronological order of discovery, sociology was the highest in the order of rank, or so Comte believed. This discovery not only rounded out the circle of the sciences but made possible a philosophy of science and the various sciences as a whole. A philosophy of the history of mind seen through the development of the sciences is the keystone in the Comtean system.[5]

"In order to understand the true view and character of the Positive Philosophy," Comte wrote, "we must take a brief general view of the progressive course of the human mind regarded as a whole; for no conception can be understood otherwise than through its history." The study of the history of mankind revealed a "great fundamental law" at work in the progress of human intelligence and knowledge which held for all times. Comte's "discovery" turned out to be remarkably similar to earlier insights of Saint-Simon, Turgot, and even Vico.

> The law is this: that each of our leading conceptions—each branch of our knowledge—passes successively through three different theoretical conditions: the *Theological*, or fictitious; the *Metaphysical*, or abstract; and the *Scientific*, or positive. In other words the human mind, by its nature, employs in its progress three methods of philosophizing, the character of which is essentially different, and even radically opposed: viz., the theological method, the metaphysical, and the positive. Hence arise three philosophies, or systems of general conceptions of the aggregate of phenomena, each of which excludes the others. The first is the necessary point of departure of the human understanding; and the third is its fixed and definitive state. The second is merely a state of transition.[6]

In the "theological" state, the first condition of the human race, the mind, dominated by imagination, believed all phenomena to be produced immediately by supernatural beings or gods, all the while engaged in the futile effort to know the nature of things and their "first and final" causes. This state reached its peak in Catholic theology, which synthesized all such explanations of reality by reference to the decrees of a unique God. The "metaphysical" state, a modification of the first stage, finds the mind still seeking absolutes, but divinities and divine decrees are replaced in their explanatory roles by immanent metaphysical entities such as proximate causes, substances, and powers, which are believed to inhere in all beings. Imagination still reigns over reason in this transitional state, and the summit is reached in the pantheistic synthesis, where nature combines in itself all the metaphysical entities. The final stage of the human mind is reached in the "positive" state, where reason has reached maturity, and observation, experiment, and historical comparison increasingly replace imagination. Having given up the vain search for causes and absolutes, the mind applies itself to the facts of experience and the study of their connecting laws, which are nothing but

> invariable relations of succession and resemblance. What is not understood when we speak of an explanation of facts is simply the establishment of a connection between single phenomena and some general facts, the number of which continually diminishes with the progress of science.[7]

Several general "facts" support this estimate of the development of human intelligence. "Our most advanced sciences still bear very evident marks of the two earlier periods through which they have passed." Not only have the most progressive sciences as astronomy and physics developed in this pattern, but the maturing process of the individual mind displays the same pattern. "Each of us is aware," Comte wrote, "if he looks back upon his history, that he was a theologian in his childhood, a metaphysician in his youth, and a natural philosopher in his manhood." In addition to the support of these general facts for the law of three stages, Comte thought that abstract reason pointed in the same direction. It may be true that there is no real knowledge which is not based on observed facts, at least for the positive generation, but it is also true that facts cannot be observed without the guidance of some theory. "Between the necessity of observing facts in order to form a theory, and having a theory in order to observe facts, the human mind would have been entangled in a vicious circle but for the natural opening afforded by Theological conceptions." The impasse could be hurdled only by theories that ranged far ahead of the facts; this is the fundamental reason for the theological character of primitive knowledge. On the other hand, the "spontaneous philosophy" of the theological stage could not be succeeded all at once in one great step by humanity to the positive philosophy; an intermediate system of metaphysical conceptions was necessary in which a gradual refining process took place. Only by passing through this gradual evolution could the human mind advance to the positive stage of knowledge where the illusory quest for causes yielded to the search for the invariable laws governing all phenomena.[8]

Intimately connected with the law of three stages, and, in fact, a verification of it, is the Comtean classification or hierarchy of the sciences. The different kinds of human knowledge have passed through the three stages at different rates because of the nature of the knowledge in question. In turn, knowledge depends on the nature of the phenomena with which it is concerned.

> All observable phenomena may be included within a very few natural categories, so arranged that the study of each category may be grounded on the principal laws of the preceding, and serve as the basis of the next ensuing. This order is determined by the degree of simplicity, or . . . of generality of their phenomena.

One can arrange phenomena and their respective sciences in a logical, or a priori, order which is successively more concrete and particular and at the same time increasingly dependent on the preceding class. Astronomy begins the classification, followed by physics, chemistry, physiology, and ending with the new science of Comte, social physics or sociology. Mathematics can be placed at the head of this listing, being at once the most simple and abstract and the general instrument for the investigation of the laws of phenomena. If a close look is taken at the historical development of the sciences, one finds that the three successive stages of human knowledge have appeared in actuality according to the postulated, a priori, order. Hence the Comtean law of the three stages and the Comtean classification of the sciences confirm one another.

> The general law which governs this history [the law of the three stages] . . . cannot be verified unless we combine it with the scientific gradation just laid down; for it is according to this gradation that the different human theories have attained in succession the theological state, the metaphysical, and finally the positive.[9]

Comte's six-volume masterpiece is arranged in an order that follows the gradation of the sciences according to the three stages of progress in knowledge. Beginning with mathematics, the analysis proceeds step by step until it reaches sociology, the most original part of the system. Fundamental to the whole system is the basic positivistic principle which "regards all phenomena as subjected to invariable natural Laws." This did not mean that Comte accepted Saint-Simon's project of reducing the explanation of all phenomena to a universal law like gravitation.

> While pursuing the philosophic aim of all science, the lessening of
> the number of general laws requisite for the explanation of natural
> phenomena, we shall regard as presumptuous every attempt, in all
> future time, to reduce them rigorously to one.

It did mean that there was one general method to be pursued if knowledge
of any kind were to become truly scientific.[10] It also entailed the view
that the positivistic knowledge of laws governing the various provinces
of reality was the only knowledge possible.

> Our positive method of connecting phenomena is by one or other of
> two relations,—that of similitude or that of succession—the mere fact
> of such resemblance or succession being all that we can pretend to
> know; and all that we need to know; for this perception comprehends
> all knowledge which consists in elucidating something by something
> else,—in now explaining and now foreseeing certain phenomena. Such
> prevision applies to past, present, and future alike. . . .[11]

Having made his laborious way through the other five fundamental
sciences, Comte takes up the question of "humanity in a state of association," the province of social physics. In physiology-biology it has been
shown that "there is no other essential difference between humanity and
animality than that of the degree of development admitted by a faculty
which is, by its nature, common to all animal life . . . ." Since all animals,
especially the higher, manifest a "reasonable" or "rational" approach to
the life they are capable of, Comte rejected as meaningless the scholastic
definition of man as a reasonable or rational animal. What distinguishes
humanity from the higher animals is history, "the consecutive states of
humanity," and "the necessary influence of human generations upon the
generations that follow, accumulating continuously." The historical evolution of humanity is the peculiar object of social physics, but an "abstract"
history, preferably "without the names of men, or even of nations," studied
according to the method of the positive scientist-philosopher. Through
his analyses of historically evolving humanity Comte hoped to raise the
last and highest of the sciences to the positive level, thus rounding out
the scientific project.[12]

Scientific history or sociology, like physics and biology, must have its
statics and dynamics. Social statics investigates the conditions of co-
existence, concentrating on the theory of order. Social dynamics studies
the laws of succession, focusing on the laws of progress.

> The philosophical principle of the science being that social phe-
> nomena are subject to natural laws, admitting of rational prevision,
> we have to ascertain the precise subject, and the peculiar character
> of these laws. The distinction between statical and dynamical condi-
> tions of the subject must be extended to social science. . . . It cor-
> responds with the double conception of order and progress; for order

> consists . . . in a perfect harmony among the conditions of a social existence; and progress consists in social development; and the conditions in one case and the laws of movement in the other, constitutes the statics and dynamics of social physics.[13]

The basic law of social statics appears to be the law of "cohesion," meaning that there is harmony and solidarity between the various phenomena of the social order which make their evolution inseparable.

> Not only must political institutions and social manners . . . and ideas . . . be always mutually connected; but, further, this consolidated whole must be always connected, by its nature, with the corresponding state of the integral development of humanity, considered in all of its aspects, of intellectual, moral, and physical activity.[14]

Conceiving human society as a collective organism, Comte is led to see in society, as in the individual organism, a harmony of structure and function working toward a common end through the action and reaction among the parts and upon the environment. The principle of organic cohesion, or interconnection, secures harmony and order in the development of social structures and is as important as the laws governing social dynamics. The laws of dynamics secure the general movement toward progress, which Comte considers to be an obvious fact of history. The fundamental law here is the law of the three stages of intellectual development. Comte does not view progress as a simple linear movement but rather as a general motion tending to prevail, around which cluster variations and oscillations. Factors like race, climate, and particularly deliberate human action cause these oscillations, but their efficacy as causal factors is limited. They cannot invert the general order of the movement, subject as it is to natural laws, but they may accelerate or retard it.[15]

Human progress rests first of all on man's increasing control over the environment, for without this basic improvement, progress in the more properly human areas would not have been possible. "All human progress, political, moral, or intellectual, is inseparable from material progression, in virtue of the close interconnection which, . . . characterizes the natural course of social phenomena."[16] Technological advance presupposed, one can discern three stages of improvement in the political and moral areas as well as the intellectual, which, by reason of the law of cohesion, are intimately connected with parallel stages in the other areas. Progress, or social evolution of humanity, is based on man's three basic functions of activity, feeling or emotion, and intellect. We already know well that the social evolution of intellect consists in the progress from the theological and metaphysical stages to the positivist plateau. Progress in the area of political action consists in the advance from wars of conquest through the phase of defensive wars to the peaceful and industrial stage. An evolution from egoism to universal altruism marks the presence of progress in the area of feeling or emotion; from egoism to a domestic altruism directed toward the family, thence to a collective altruism whose object is the state, and finally a truly universalistic altruism focusing on humanity as a whole. The love of humanity is inseparably connected with the peaceful stage of industry and the positive phase of intellect, since the note of universality is equally present in each.

It may be true that Comte did not base his entire philosophy of history on the single factor of intellectual evolution, but this factor remains basic to his reconstruction of the history of humanity. Universal history displayed a grand drama of three acts which paralleled the stages in the intellectual development of humanity: the first theological age, the middle metaphysical age, and the final positive age just beginning. The whole of the history of mankind from its animistic beginnings in prehistory to the fourteenth century A.D. constituted one theological age in the Comtean schema. Fetishism, or animism, opened the drama of the history of man, and it was succeeded by a polytheistic epoch with several phases: a period of theocratic polytheism (the Oriental empires); a period of intellectual polytheism (the Greek period); and, finally, a period of social polytheism, which was also a transition to social monotheism (the Roman period). A fully monotheistic period followed in Catholic feudal society which brought the theological age of humanity to a close. The metaphysical age of humanity lasted from 1300 to 1800, a transitional and revolutionary age beginning with the Renaissance, continuing with the Reformation, and culminating in the French Revolution. The whole of the metaphysical, critical age was but one of preparation for the final age of humanity, the age of positivism.[17]

Having reached the end of his historical analysis, Comte rejoiced once again in the explanatory value of his "theory of evolution," or the law of three stages.

> From the earliest beginnings of civilization to the present state of the most advanced nations, this theory has explained, consistently and dispassionately, the character of all the great phases of humanity; the participation of each in the perdurable common development, and their precise filiation; so as to introduce perfect unity and rigorous continuity into this vast spectacle . . .[18]

A law of such synthesizing qualities can be only the expression of historical reality, capable not only of capturing the whole of the past but also of connecting the past with the future. The European community, the most advanced part of the human race, has "exhausted" the theological and metaphysical life and is now at the "threshold" of the fully positive stage of humanity. Elements for a new social order, more stable and more homogeneous than mankind has ever experienced, are present in Western civilization, and all that is needed is their coordination and organization. "The mere knowledge of the law of progression becomes the general principle of solution," since the coordination must be first of all intellectual and only then expand into the moral and political areas.

In order to terminate the revolutionary, metaphysical age of the last centuries the stabilizing force of order must be re-established. "No real order can be established, and still less can it last, if it is not fully compatible with progress; and no great progress can be accomplished, if it does not tend to the consolidation of order."[19] Comte believed that the Catholic Church had been the main advocate of hierarchy and order on the European scene, while the critical and individualistic spirit of the Reformation had been the chief factor for progress. The new age of humanity was to be neither Catholic nor Protestant, but simply "positive," fulfilling the law of evolving humanity by combining order and progress in the final positivistic system.

> The regeneration of social doctrine must, by its very action, raise up from the midst of anarchy a new spiritual authority which, after having disciplined the human intellect and reconstructed morals, will peaceably become, throughout western Europe, the basis of the final system of human society.[20]

This new breed, imbued with the truth of positive social science, was to administer a system of universal education, patterned on the three stages of intellectual development, and draw up a final code of ethics.[21]

By 1848, in the *Discours sur l'ensemble du positivisme*, a new dimension had been added to the first rationalist form of the system. Undoubtedly, the affective side of humanity had not been overlooked in the earlier *Cours*, but it took the friendship with Clothilde de Vaux to direct the Comtean synthesis plainly on the path of love. Order and progress were to have a companion, if not a leader. "Love is our principle; Order our basis; and Progress our end."[22] Along with the exaltation of love, positivism became a religion, the new religion of humanity. Positivism, Comte now believed, required a "central point" toward which feeling, reason, and activity alike could converge.

> Such a center we find in the great conception of Humanity toward which every aspect of Positivism naturally converges. By it the conception of God will be entirely superseded, and a synthesis be formed, more complete and more permanent than that provisionally established by the old religions . . . . Thus Positivism becomes in the true sense of the word, a Religion, the only religion which is real and complete.[23]

The new spiritual authority required for the final positivistic age, the "philosophers of the future," was to constitute a wholly new class and become "priests of Humanity." When Comte went on to fabricate a calendar of saints and ritualistic observances, it became apparent that he was serious about wishing to replace Christianity with his new religion. He even predicted that before 1860 he would preach the good news of positivism in Notre-Dame. Comte's final program for the future of man cannot be better described than as "Catholicism without Christianity."[24]

The Comprehensive Evolution: The Spencerian Critique

"To have no God, and to talk of religion, is . . . at once an absurdity, and an impiety," or so it would seem to nine out of ten, was John Stuart Mill's opinion of the final religious form of Comtean positivism.[25] An early admirer and even promoter of Comtean views, Mill, like others, found it increasingly difficult to accept the pronouncements of the high priest of humanity. This did not lead Mill to repudiate the whole of the positivistic system, but his attachment to the system came to be defined within fairly narrow limits. In his *System of Logic* (first edition, 1842), Mill revealed a continuing respect for Comtean methodology. The idea of progress "in a trajectory" must be viewed as a "theorem" of social science, while any "cyclical" repetition of historical events—that proposed by Vico, for example—must be rejected. As practiced on the Continent, the method of social science consisted in an attempt to discover the law of progress from the general facts of history, Mill believed. Even if such an attempt were successful, it could never result in a "law of nature," or "scientific law," but would only be an "empirical law," or factual generalization.

> Until that law could be connected with the psychological and ethological laws on which it must depend, and by the consilience of deduction a priori with historical evidence, could be converted from an empirical law into a scientific law, it could not be relied on for the prediction of future events.[26]

Generalizations derived from the course of history, or "empirical laws," cannot stand on their own but must rely for their necessity on psychological and "ethological" laws which govern the activities of men and the relations between men and circumstances. Thus Mill accepted what he called the Comtean "inverse deductive method," but held against Comte that psychology must be included in the circle of sciences as the starting point for moral and social science.

This being understood, Mill believed that the Comtean law of three stages approached the stature of a scientific law. "This generalization appears to me to have that degree of scientific evidence which is derived from the concurrence of the indications of history with the possibilities derived from the constitution of the human mind." Whatever be the decision that the future may bring of the Comtean law of evolution, Comte's method is the pattern to be imitated in social studies. "We may not only succeed in looking into the future history of the human race, but in determining what artificial means may be used, and to what extent, to accelerate its natural progress." Superior minds, even in England, were turning to the project of finding "the derivative laws of social order and social progress." One major requisite of systematic social studies was the explanation of the main facts of universal history. Hence Mill found a prominent spot for a philosophy of history in his program for social studies. "A philosophy of history is generally admitted to be at once the verification and the initial form of the Philosophy of the Progress of Society." With the construction of a philosophy of history, controlled and directed by sociological evidence, the Comtean ideal would be fulfilled, and sociology itself would at last take its proper place among the sciences and "the circle of human knowledge would be complete."[27]

Mill may have had some important reservations about the Comtean system, especially when it was transformed into a religion, but Herbert Spencer emphatically rejected almost the whole of Comtean positivism. The law of three stages, Comte's classification of the sciences, the authoritarian conception of society, the ignorance of biological evolution, the religion of humanity, all of these were ridiculed by Spencer at one time or another.[28] Undoubtedly, there are important doctrinal differences between Spencer and Comte, but there are also points of similarity. Above all stands the philosophical project of the coordination and unification of all knowledge, especially scientific knowledge. Comte had been attracted by Saint-Simon's vision, in which all phenomena would be connected with one most general law, as the law of gravitation, but he thought the project impossible of attainment. Spencer not only thought it possible to subject all phenomena to one universal and axiomatic law, the "persistence of force," as he called it, but he also believed that a formula deduced from this law would also "yield a total and specific interpretation of each phenomenon in its entirety, as well as of phenomena in general."[29] This is at once the goal of all philosophy and the limit of knowledge.

Spencer had little first hand acquaintance with the Comtean system, at least in his formative years, though he did read a few pages of the Martineau translation of the *Cours*. Scarcely an avowed practitioner of the Comtean "cerebral hygiene," if for no other reason than its Comtean lineage, Spencer admitted that he could not read a book whose point of view differed from his own. Mill's *Logic* served as an introduction to Comte, but Spencer's mind had already been captured by other ideas. A mechanical engineer by profession, he soon became interested in social problems and began to publish articles in the field. By 1840 he had come into contact with a theory of biological evolution of the Lamarckian variety which greatly impressed him. In 1857, while rereading some of his earlier essays which embodied ideas on biological evolution, the notion of evolution struck him as having universal dimensions, a universal law applying to all orders of phenomena, inorganic, organic, and "super-organic," as he later labeled them.

> Whether it be in the development of the Earth, in the development of Life upon its surface, in the development of Society, of Government, of Manufacturers, of Commerce, of Language, Literature, Science, Art, this same evolution of the simple into the complex, through successive differentiations, holds throughout. From the earliest traceable cosmical changes, down to the latest results of civilization, we shall find that the transformation of the homogeneous into the heterogeneous is that in which progress essentially consists.[30]

In 1860 Spencer conceived of a vast synthesis in which all the scientific knowledge of his time would be assembled in one coherent philosophical system. This project was initiated by the *First Principles of a New System of Philosophy*, which appeared in 1862, and it was continued in other works where the principles of biology, psychology, sociology, and morality were elaborated.[31] Spencer's fundamental principles remained remarkably consistent with those stated in the earliest work of the synthesis, the *First Principles*. Here the central theme is his view of evolution as conceived in 1857, but now it is part of a grand scheme which takes in every facet of all knowable reality, past, present, and future.

A philosopher, if he is true to his calling, must not only take into account all knowledge and all phenomena but should also point to the mysterious and unknown. Hence, before an exposition of his synthesis of all scientific knowledge that deals with phenomena and appearances, Spencer devotes a section of the *First Principles* to the "Unknowable," which is epitomized in the perennial conflict between religion and science. Religion can be defined, at least in its credal aspect, "as a theory of original causation" which has evolved through the same phases as Comte had postulated. From the primitive fetishism (or ghost theory) through polytheism and monotheism to pantheism, the hypothetical causal agency has become increasingly less concrete and more generalized. Atheism should be added to this listing, according to Spencer, since it too asserts some causal agency as the adequate cause of appearances.[32] Religion has not developed in this fashion unaided, for evolving science has played the principal agitating role in the movement of religious hypotheses toward abstraction and unification. Using the term "science" in its "true" sense, "as comprehending all positive and definite knowledge of the order existing among surrounding phenomena," it is apparent that progress in science has consisted in the increasing discovery of established order among phenomena, or laws, which has continually reduced the area of disorder, the point of insertion for supernatural or religious agencies. The continuing grouping of special phenomena under limited laws and of these laws under more and more general laws necessarily involves a progression from more concrete to more abstract causes. The total progression or evolution of science and religion together is a movement toward abstraction and the inconceivable, that is, the unthinkable and unknowable.[33]

All religious creeds have one thing in common, "that the existence of the world, with all that it contains and all which surrounds it, is a mystery ever pressing for interpretation." Setting out with the assertion of an impenetrable mystery, every religion then proceeds to give some interpretation of this mystery, thus asserting it is not a mystery. An examination of their several hypotheses for the explanation of the universe, and indeed of every possible hypothesis, indicates that one and all are invalid.

> Thus the mystery which all religions recognize turns out to be a far more transcendant mystery than any of them suspect—not a relative mystery but an absolute mystery . . . that the Power which the universe manifests to us is utterly inscrutable.[34]

The same conclusion results from an examination of ultimate scientific ideas, whether objective as force, space, and time, or subjective, such as sensations.

> In all directions his investigations eventually bring him face to face with an insoluble enigma. . . . He learns at once the greatness and the littleness of the human intellect—its power in dealing with all that comes within the range of experience, its impotence in dealing with all that transcends experience. . . . He [the scientist], more than any other, truly *knows* that in its ultimate essence nothing can be known.[35]

Consequently, in face of the ultimate reality, religious and scientific conceptions are equally inept. "Ultimate religious ideas and ultimate scientific ideas alike turn out to be merely symbols of the actual, not cognitions of it."[36]

If this be so, the conflict between religion and science should gradually cease as the limits of possible knowledge are established. Religion and science are necessary correlatives and correctives for one another. Once science becomes aware that its explanations are "proximate and relative" and religion becomes more fully convinced that the mystery it contemplates is ultimate and universal, a permanent peace will be established.

> Thus the consciousness of an Inscrutable Power manifested to us through all phenomena has been growing ever clearer . . . . This certainty that on the one hand such a Power exists, while on the other its nature transcends intuition and is beyond imagination, is the certainty toward which intelligence has from the first been progressing. To this conclusion Science inevitably arrives as it reaches its confines; while to this conclusion Religion is irresistibly driven by criticism. And satisfying as it does the demands of the most rigorous logic at the same time it gives the religious sentiment the widest possible sphere of action, it is the conclusion we are bound to accept without reserve or qualification.[37]

One wonders whether Spencer overreached himself, since he seems to have left little room for philosophy in his assessment of the roles of religion and science. Philosophy is shut out from investigating the nature of the "Power," as this is impossible, and what is left over seems to be the province of science. Philosophy is "knowledge of the highest degree of generality." At this point Spencer acknowledged Comte as a precursor because of his attempt to organize scientific knowledge into a coherent system, but his indebtedness to Comte is surely greater than this. "Science concerns itself with the co-existences and sequences among phenomena, grouping these at first into generalizations of a simple or low order, and rising gradually to higher and more extended generalizations." Philosophy carries this process to completion by taking these independent generalizations and contemplating them together "as corollaries of some ultimate truth." As the widest generalizations of science comprehend the limited generalizations of its own department, so the generalization of philosophy comprehends and consolidates the widest generalizations of science. "Knowledge of the lowest kind is un-unified knowledge; Science is partially unified knowledge; Philosophy is completely unified knowledge."[38] The Spencerian philosophy is completely unified in the supreme and fundamental "given," "the persistence of force."

As a confirmed mechanist, Spencer attempted to reconstruct all phenomena with the twin elements of matter and motion. The existence of these elements is governed by universal laws that apply to the inorganic, the organic, and the superorganic domains at once. All the laws, however, are deducible from one postulate, the "persistence of force," or, in other words, the law of the conservation of energy. Other fundamental laws, such as the indestructibility of matter, that is, force in its static state, and the law of the continuity of motion, that is, force in its dynamic state, are only aspects of the supreme and indemonstrable axiom. Four secondary propositions are also ultimately deducible from the first law: the persistence of the relations or laws among forces; the equivalence of forces, meaning that force is never lost but only transformed; the law that everything moves along the line of least resistance or of greatest attraction; finally, the law of rhythm or alternation of motion. The system is not yet complete, as one must not only explain how one or another of the elements behaves but also come up with a formula that expresses the combination of these factors in each change and in the one total process of phenomena. This formula is the law of the continuous redistribution of matter and motion, which results in opposite transformations, those of evolution and dissolution.[39]

Everywhere we look, Spencer believed, we see two opposite processes taking place, that of concentration and that of diffusion. These opposed processes should be explained in terms of matter and motion. "The change from a diffused, imperceptible state to a concentrated, perceptible state is an integration of matter and concomitant dissipation of motion." The opposite change, one from a "concentrated, perceptible state to a diffused, imperceptible state" is "an absorption of motion and concomitant disintegration of matter." Taken together these two opposed processes constitute the "history" of every sensible phenomenon. Despite the complexities of these processes, it remains true that there is always progress either toward integration or disintegration.

> Everywhere and to the last, therefore, the change at any moment going on forms a part of one or other of the two processes. While the general history of every aggregate is definable as a change from a diffused, imperceptible state to a concentrated, imperceptible state, every detail of the history is definable as part of either the one change or the other. This, then, must be the universal law of redistribution of matter and motion, which serves at once to unify the seemingly diverse groups of changes, as well as the entire course of each change.[40]

Having unified the two opposed processes under the law of the redistribution of matter and motion, Spencer now names them evolution and dissolution. "Evolution under its simplest and most general aspect is the integration of matter and concomitant dissipation of motion; while dissolution is the absorption of motion and concomitant disintegration of matter." This complete formula covers the whole "history" of everything that has a history, and, indeed, the whole process of knowable reality.[41]

After this sample of his logic and terminology, we need not delay over Spencer's continuing analysis of the process of evolution, nor over the more complete definition given later. It is important, however, to realize that the law of evolution applies equally to all knowable phenomena, from those of the primitive nebulae to the social facts of the most civilized state of man, from natural history to human history.

> When we think of Evolution as divided into astronomic, geologic, biologic, psychologic, sociologic, etc., it may seem to a certain extent a coincidence that the same law of metamorphosis holds throughout all its divisions. But when we recognize these divisions as mere conventional groupings . . . when we regard the different existences with

which they . . . deal as component parts of the one Cosmos, we see at once that there are not several kinds of Evolution having certain traits in common, but one Evolution going on everywhere after the same manner.[42]

Social change and development, the province of human history, consequently, is easily absorbed into such a far-reaching formula and synthesis. Social and cultural evolution conform to the laws of cosmic evolution, being nothing other than a progressive integration of matter followed by increasingly perfect differentiation and coordination in the parts. Development and change in human history are naturalistic processes just like that of the cosmos as a whole, for they are simply one part of the one cosmic process.

Like Comte, Spencer pictured society as an organism. No doubt his view that the same evolutionary law governs social life as well as corporeal life led him to press the organismic concept of society beyond the point of mere metaphor. Social evolution parallels the evolution of the homogeneous ovum into the heterogeneous individual, where the process is one of multiplication of size, of complexity of structure and function, and growing interdependence of parts. The principal difference between an organism and society is that consciousness in the former is localized, whereas in the latter it is diffused throughout the individual units. There is little need to enter into Spencer's systematic development of the comparison between human society and the living organism, but considerable tension appears at this point in his thought. Spencer was much more of a philosophical and social individualist than Comte, and how this was to be reconciled with the organismic concept of society is not clear.

In general, Spencer viewed human society as evolving from militarism to industrialism, a classification anticipated in the writings of both Saint-Simon and Comte. The movement of societies is from the predominantly aggressive and military to the pacific and dominantly industrial type. Compulsory cooperation is the foundation of the militant society, while voluntary cooperation is the basis of industrial societies. In a military society the individuals are completely subject to the central government, somewhat after the fashion of the individual organism, which is governed by the central nervous system. Industrialized society, on the other hand, is decentralized, sustained as it is by the free transactions of individuals, and Spencer is hard put to find any organismic analogy worthy of mention. The grand movement in history from militarism consists in progress toward a state of perfect adaption of man and society to the environment, but it always remains dependent on the character of the peoples within the various societies.[43]

An integral part of the Spencerian synthesis was the vision of progress everywhere toward what is called "equilibration," or a balance between the antagonistic forces of evolution and dissolution.[44] Within this large cyclical framework Spencer offered an optimistic view of man's future with clearly marked individualistic features.

> The adaption of man's nature to the conditions of his existence cannot cease until the internal forces which we know as feelings are in equilibrium with the external forces they encounter. And the establishment of this equilibrium is the arrival at a state of human nature and social organization, such that the individual has no desires but those which may be satisfied without exceeding his proper sphere of action, while society maintains no restraints but those which the individual voluntarily respects. The progressive extension of the liberty of citizens and the reciprocal removal of political restrictions are the steps by which we advance to this state. And the ultimate abolition of all limits to the freedom of each, save those imposed by the like freedom of all, must result from the perfect equilibration between men's desires and the conduct necessitated by surrounding conditions.[45]

Evolution only can end in the establishment of the "greatest perfection and complete happiness," for the "penultimate stage of equilibration" implied "the highest conceivable state of humanity."[46]

The choice of words is not accidental. Spencer's optimism was confined to the penultimate stage of equilibration. True to his fundamental principles, he was driven to take account of the alternate and opposed process of dissolution. "The universally co-existent forces of attraction and repulsion, which . . . necessitate rhythm in all minor changes throughout the Universe, also necessitate rhythm in the totality of its changes . . . alternate epochs of Evolution and Dissolution."[47] The specter of an everlasting cycle of evolution and dissolution arose, willy-nilly, from the axioms of Spencer. He may find it more profitable and interesting to contemplate the process of evolution, but from the fundamental "given," the persistence of force, he deduced that universal evolution would be followed by universal dissolution. But the universal law of rhythm continues to hold, and from there it was a short step to the opinion that "we can no longer contemplate the visible creation as having a definite beginning or end."[48]

NOTES

1. H. Saint-Simon, "The Reorganization of the European Community," in F. Markham, *Henri de Saint-Simon, Social Organization, The Science of Man and Other Writings* (New York: Harper & Row, 1964), p. 68. One can consult F. E. Manuel's excellent work, *The New World of Henri Saint-Simon* (Notre Dame, Ind.: University of Notre Dame Press, 1963), for a complete exposition of Saint-Simon's thought.

2. Saint-Simon, cited by Manuel, p. 151, from Jean Dautry's *Saint-Simon, Textes choisis* (Paris: 1951), p. 69. Saint-Simon believed that one law, the law of gravitation, governs the whole of reality, the physical and the moral worlds, from which every other law and fact can be deduced. History, as one province of the moral world, could become a science after the fashion of physical science. Addressing the Institut de France in 1813, he said: "Your studies have no unity. They are only a series of disjointed ideas, because they are not related to any general concept . . . select an idea to which all other ideas can be related, and from which all principles can be deduced as consequences—then you will have a philosophy. This philosophy will necessarily be founded on the idea of universal gravitation . . . the object of this philosophy being to deduce from this principle, as directly as possible, the explanation of every kind of phenomenon," "Essay on the Science of Man," in Markham, p. 25. Later Saint-Simon admitted that his efforts in this direction were unsuccessful.

3. Saint-Simon, *Travail sur la gravitation universelle, in Oeuvres*, Vol. XL, p. 246, as cited by Manuel, p. 152. The whole of Chapter 12, "Man before History," pp. 148–157, is useful.

4. See Manuel, ch. 19, "Epochs Organic and Critical," pp. 219–236.

5. Several works that have proved useful for an understanding of Comte and positivism can be cited: the summary article of the Comtean specialist, H. Gouhier, "Auguste Comte's Philosophy of History," reprinted from the *Journal of World History*, Vol. II, No. 3, in G. Metraux and F. Crouzet, *The Nineteenth Century World* (New York: New American Library, 1963), pp. 464–484; F. E. Manuel, *The Prophets of Paris* (Cambridge, Mass.: Harvard University Press, 1962), pp. 251–296; H. De Lubac, *The Drama of Atheist Humanism* (Cleveland: World Publishing, 1963), pp. 77–159; W. H. Simon, *European Positivism in the Nineteenth Century* (Ithaca, N.Y.: Cornell University Press, 1963).

6. H. Martineau, *The Positive Philosophy of Auguste Comte*, 2 vols. (London: 1853), an adaption and abridgment of the six-volume *Cours*, I, ch. I, pp. 1–2.

7. Martineau, Vol. I, p. 2. See A. Comte, *A General View of Positivism*, trans. J. H. Bridges of *Discours sur l'ensemble du positivisme* (New York: R. Speller, 1957), ch. I, p. 50, "The true Positive spirit consists in substituting the study of the invariable Laws of phenomena for that of their so-called Causes, whether proximate or primary; in a word, in studying the *How* instead of the *Why*."

8. Martineau, Vol. I, ch. I, pp. 3–5.

9. Martineau, Vol. I, ch. II, pp. 25, 29.

10. Martineau, Vol. I, ch. I, pp. 5, 17. "The consideration of all phenomena as referable to a single origin is by no means necessary to the systematic formation of science. . . . The only necessary unity is that of Method . . . . As for the doctrine, it need not be one; it is enough that it should be homogeneous." The first five volumes of the *Cours* treat of mathematics, astronomy, physics, chemistry, and biology in that order. Comte admitted that the history of science did not conform exactly to his logical classification: "In the main, however, our classification agrees with the history of science; the more general and simple sciences actually occurring first and advancing best in human history, and being followed by the more complex and restricted, though all were, since the earliest times, enlarging simultaneously," p. 24.

11. Martineau, Vol. II, ch. XIII, p. 515. Comte constantly refers to the "relative" character of the positivist philosophy, yet he is obviously committed

to the absolute features of his law of three stages. "Mental immutability being thus discarded, the relative philosophy is directly established: for we have been thus led to conceive of successive theories as accelerated approximations towards a reality which can never be rigorously estimated,—the best theory being, at the time, that which best represents the aggregate of corresponding observations . . . to which sociological philosophy adds a complete generalization, and henceforth a dogmatic sanction," pp. 518–519.

12.   See Martineau, Vol. I, ch. VI, p. 465; Vol. II, ch. III, p. 105; ch. VII, p. 183 f. "Sociology is radically connected with biology, since the original state of humanity essentially coincides with that in which the superior animals are detained by their organic imperfection—their speculative ability never transcending the primitive fetishism which man would never have issued from but for the strong impulsion of the collective development," Vol. II, ch. XIV, p. 547. Comte spoke of the "vast organic system" linking the lowest form of life with that of man, but he rejected Lamarckian biological evolution in favor of Cuvier's critique. "We rest upon the great natural law that living species tend to perpetuate themselves indefinitely, with the same chief characteristics, through any exterior changes compatible with their existence. In non-essentials the species is modified within certain limits, beyond which it is not modified, but destroyed," Vol. II, ch. XI, p. 417. Despite the insistence on the historical evolution of humanity, the same principle applies to the nature of man. "Biological principles . . . show that the human organism, in all times and places, has manifested the same essential needs, differing only in their degree of development and corresponding mode of satisfaction," Vol. II, ch. VII, p. 187.

13.   Martineau, Vol. II, ch. III, pp. 74–75.

14.   Martineau, Vol. II, p. 78.

15.   See, e.g., Martineau, Vol. II, p. 90 f. "True liberty is nothing other than a rational submission to the preponderance of the laws of nature, in release from all arbitrary personal dictation," ch. I, p. 47.

16.   Martineau, Vol. II, ch. IV, p. 118. "We must conclude the social state, regarded as a whole, to have been as perfect, in each period, as the co-existing conditions of humanity and of its environment would allow. Without this view, history would be incomprehensible . . . ," ch. III, p. 89.

17.   See Martineau, Vol. II, chs. VI–XI, pp. 149–433.

18.   Martineau, Vol. II, ch. XII, p. 465.

19.   Martineau, Vol. II, ch. I, p. 3.

20.   Martineau, Vol. II, ch. XII, pp. 465–466.

21.   Not only did Comte insist on progress through the three stages as the program to be followed in the positivist system of general education but he claimed to have experienced personally the truth of the three stages during his siege of madness in 1826. Then he had felt himself regress backward through the various stages to fetishism under mental strain, and, while recuperating, he ascended through the same phases to positivism and health. See Manuel, *The Prophets of Paris*, p. 281.

22.   Comte, *A General View of Positivism*, ch. VI, p. 355; see ch. II, pp. 116–119.

23.   Comte, *A General View of Positivism*, pp. 364–365. "Thus, in the conception of Humanity, the three essential aspects of Positivism, its subjective principle, its objective dogma, and its practical object are united. Toward Humanity, who is for us the only true Great Being, we, the conscious elements of

whom she is composed, shall henceforth direct every aspect of our life, individual or collective. Our thought will be directed to the knowledge of humanity, our affections to her love, our actions to her service."

The individual appears to be lost to sight in the "great organism" of humanity, since "the life of the individual is in every respect subordinate to the evolution of the race," p. 378. Comte was convinced that this was the only view possible for scientific history. "It is our filiation with the Past, even more than our connexion with the Present, which teaches us that the only real life is the collective life of the race; that the individual life has no existence except as an abstraction. Continuity is the feature which distinguishes our race [species] from all others," p. 404.

24.   One should compare Comte's religion of humanity with that announced earlier by his former master, Saint-Simon, in *New Christianity* (1825).

25.   J. S. Mill, *Auguste Comte and Positivism*, 2d ed. (London: 1866), pp. 132–133; see also Simon, pp. 172–200.

26.   J. S. Mill, *A System of Logic*, 9th ed. (London: 1872), pp. 596–597 [London, 1961 reprint]; compare with *The Positive Philosophy of Auguste Comte*, p. 224 f. and Mill's *Autobiography*, 3d ed. (London: 1874).

27.   Mill, *A System of Logic*, pp. 605–607. H. T. Buckle, in *The History of Civilization in England* (1857), continued the search for laws of historical and social development, but the results were minimal. Buckle's working model was that of the natural sciences, and he thought that history could become a "science" if the laws by which the facts are governed could be discovered. Statistical studies proved that human actions are governed by laws, or so Buckle believed. From this point Buckle was driven to embrace a pure and frank determinism.

28.   See Simon, pp. 217–219.

29.   See H. Spencer, *First Principles*, American edition of the 1880 version (New York), e.g., pp. 453–470.

30.   H. Spencer, "Progress: Its Law and Cause," in *Essays Scientific, Political and Speculative* (New York: 1892), Vol. I, p. 10. "On passing from Humanity from its individual forms to Humanity as socially embodied, we find the general law more variously exemplified. The change from homogeneity to heterogeneity is displayed in the progress of civilization as a whole, as well as in the progress of every nation; and is still going on with increasing rapidity," p. 19.

31.   The program is outlined in the Preface to the first edition of *First Principles*, which was reprinted in the 1910 edition, New York and London, pp. xi–xvi. Spencer's first book, *Social Statics*, was published at his own expense in 1850, and many of his later notions appeared here, including the evolution of man from the animal level. Spencer claimed that his use of the expression "social statics" derived from Mill's *Logic* rather than directly from Comte.

Spencer's notion of biological evolution was developed prior to and independently of Darwin's. It is interesting to observe that Darwin accepted the doctrine of progressive change, long a postulate of the theorists of human society and history. "The inhabitants of the world at each successive period in its history have beaten their predecessors in the race for life, and are, in so far, higher in the scale." And, "As natural selection works solely by and for the good of each being, all corporeal and mental environments will tend to progress toward perfection," *The Origin of Species*, 6th ed. (London: 1911), pp. 492, 669. There is something to be said for the view that the theory of organic evolution is a derivative of concepts and theories long operative among socioeconomic theorists; see, for example, Malthus, *An Essay on the Principle of Population*.

See F. G. Teggart, *Theory and Processes of History* (Berkeley, Calif.: University of California Press, 1941) [1961 reprint], pp. 128–140, and P. G. Fothergill, *Historical Aspects of Organic Evolution* (London: Hollis and Carter, 1952), pp. 108–109.

32. Spencer, *First Principles*, Part I, ch. II, p. 36.

33. Spencer, *First Principles*, ch. V, pp. 86–87.

34. Spencer, *First Principles*, ch. II, pp. 38–39.

35. Spencer, *First Principles*, ch. III, p. 56.

36. Spencer, *First Principles*, ch. IV, p. 57. "If every act of knowing is the formation of a relation in consciousness parallel to a relation in the environment, then the relativity of knowledge is self-evident. . . . Thinking being relationing, no thought can ever express more than relations," ch. V, p. 72. "Debarred as we are from everything beyond the relative, truth, raised to its perfect form, can be for us nothing more than perfect agreement, throughout the whole range of our experience, between those representations of things which we distinguish as ideal and those presentations of things which we distinguish as real. If, by discovering a proposition to be untrue, we mean nothing more than discovering a difference between a thing expected and a thing perceived, then a body of conclusions in which no such difference anywhere occurs, must be what we mean by an entirely true body of conclusions," Part II, ch. II, pp. 115–116.

37. Spencer, *First Principles*, ch. V, pp. 90–91.

38. See Spencer, *First Principles*, Part II, ch. I, pp. 108–111.

39. See Spencer, *First Principles*, chs. III–X, pp. 131–230; the matter is summarized by Spencer in ch. XXIV, pp. 453–463.

40. Spencer, *First Principles*, ch. XII, pp. 238, 240.

41. See Spencer, *First Principles*, p. 240, and ch. XIII, p. 258.

42. Spencer, *First Principles*, ch. XXIV, p. 459. "Not only is the law thus clearly exemplified in the evolution of the social organism, but it is exemplified with equal clearness in the evolution of all products of human thought and action, whether concrete or abstract, real or ideal . . . ," ch. XV, p. 295.

43. This matter, only hinted at in the *First Principles*, is fully developed in *Principles of Sociology*, 3 volumes (1876, 1879, 1895). *The Study of Sociology* (1873) and the eight volumes of *Descriptive Sociology* (1873–1881) complete his treatment of "super-organic evolution."

44. Spencer, *First Principles*, Part II, ch. XXII, p. 407.

45. Spencer, *First Principles*, p. 432.

46. See Spencer, *First Principles*, pp. 436, 462. "This general principle of equilibration . . . was traced throughout all forms of Evolution—astronomic, geologic, biologic, mental and social. And our concluding inference was that the penultimate stage of equilibration, in which the extremest multiformity and most complex moving equilibrium are established, must be one implying the highest conceivable state of humanity."

47. Spencer, *First Principles*, ch. XXIII, p. 452.

48. Spencer, *First Principles*, ch. XXIV, p. 463.

SUMMARY

Though Herbert Spencer died in the twentieth century and Giambattista Vico was born in the seventeenth, only little more than a century stretched between the final edition of Vico's *New Science* and the first version of the Spencerian cosmic evolution. That century witnessed a gradual secularizing process in which a traditional Christian interpretation of history first formulated in Augustine's *City of God* was brought down to earth and transformed into the philosophy of history. Voltaire symbolizes the beginnings of this development. Combating a providential view of history proposed in too easy and confident a manner by Bossuet, Voltaire made a strong case for the "other causes" of human events, causes immanent to the historical order. The term "philosophy of history" did not mean much more to him than that. Vico, on the other hand, was more truly a prophetic figure. Bossuet had been almost completely preoccupied with the city of God, the ultimate goal of divine providence as he saw it. Vico directed attention to the city of man and the plan of divine providence manifested there. With Vico, too, an assessment of man's past hardens into a picture of his future. No doubt the rhythmic cycles of *corso* and *ricorso* do not match one another exactly in details, yet the vision of an "ideal history" through which all nations and civilizations must ordinarily pass was not just a methodological device. If, as it appears, this "ideal history" is equated with the plan of providence for the profane historical process, then providence and the historical process are not easily distinguished.

In arriving at the philosophers of progress one comes to the very borders of the philosophy of history. It is not altogether clear where Vico stood on the idea of human progress, but for the writers of the Enlightenment it was almost an axiom. Almost, but not quite. Voltaire, to say

85

nothing of Rousseau, was not so inclined. But they were not in sympathy with one of the strong passions of the eighteenth century. The golden age lay ahead of man in history and not in the past. Different goals were prophesied, some vague in the extreme, others with liberalistic, socialistic, or nationalistic features. Some viewed the earthly goal as a fond hope while others thought it inevitable, written in the very processes of human history so legibly as to constitute a law. The latter, consistently enough, were bound to see the developments of the past leading up to the prophesied future. This view did not sit comfortably next to the prejudice of the enlightened against the Christian past. Eventually the Romantic movement, with its fondness for every corner of the past, undermined the "catastrophic" or "cataclysmic" view of the historical process so common during the Enlightenment and substituted for it the "organic" view. Botanical and biological metaphors for the processes of history were more and more pressed into service. This transition is already well underway in the writings of Herder.

All of the classic philosophers of history built on the foundations of the philosophy of progress, though the superstructures they erected bear marked differences. One group, especially among the Germans, still paid lip service to the notion of divine providence, but human authorship is everywhere evident in their master plans for history. A very imposing summit was reached in Hegel's system, which covered every inch of reality and of history. Behind "phenomenal history," the external and perceptible events, Spirit was at work in its own dialectical way securing the consciousness and reality of its freedom through the activities and creations of the human spirit. Incarnated first in the ancient Orient, Spirit exchanged this form for more progressive ones successively in the Greek, Roman, and modern German worlds. Step by dialectical step Spirit and freedom marched through history in the form of the state until the final universalistic unfolding took place in the German world of Hegel's day. Hegel may have protested that philosophy has no knowledge of the future, but it is difficult to see how any other incarnation of Spirit could take place.

Marx and Engels were quick to accuse Hegel of bringing the grand movement of history to a premature halt. Undoubtedly, this was so because Hegel had misconstrued the nature of the dialectic; its foundations were ill conceived and must be transposed. Transposing the foundations meant giving a "materialist" or economic thrust to the dialectic. At the bottom of all historical movement lay the inevitable clash between the productive capacity and social structure of each age, epitomized in the class conflicts. Step by economic step history passed from the primitive communistic society through the various successive class societies, the ancient society resting on slavery, the medieval society relying on serfdom, and the modern capitalist society built on the proletariat, to the classless Communist society of the future. History might be aiming ineluctably at the truly human society of the future, but the movement could be helped along where obstructionist and reactionary forces did not co-operate. The Marxist philosophy of history was also a philosophy of revolutionary action. Doubtless, Marx and Engels were not altogether outside of the empirical tradition and claimed a "scientific" foundation for historical materialism. Yet, when the slogans of "scientific socialism" are brushed aside, a religious apocalyptic and a secularized version of the Judaeo-Christian messianic kingdom comes unmistakably into view.

At the same time that Hegel was identifying the "cunning of reason" with the plan of divine providence, French writers had already abandoned the notion of divine providence in favor of an open search for the "iron laws" of historical evolution. More plainly in the tradition of the empirical scientist than Hegel or even Marx, the positivist aimed at a science of history patterned after the model of the natural sciences. One influential synthesis that sought to take in the whole of reality appeared in the positive philosophy of Comte. Comte's philosophy of history was based ultimately on the famous law of the three stages of mankind's intellectual evolution in which the peculiarly rational element in man gained steadily at the expense of his animality. Theological fictions and metaphysical abstractions were being replaced by a positive science of facts and connecting laws governing the whole of phenomenal reality. No doubt social phenomena had their own set of laws and could not be rigorously subjected to laws from other domains, but there was only one scientific method. Essential history pertains to the new and final science of sociology, and the philosophy of history was on its way to becoming a preserve for sociologists, ethnologists, and anthropologists. Comtean positivism ended in a religious system dedicated to humanity, complete with ritual, priests, saints, and high priest. Once again the noted French logic was able to point clearly to the implications of leading elements in the philosophical tradition behind the classic philosophies of history.

Despite pointed differences in doctrine, it can be claimed fairly enough that the perfection of positivistic tendencies was reached only in the evolutionism of Spencer, perhaps the most representative sociologist of the nineteenth century. Comte's "law of evolution," applicable to historical humanity only, was subsumed under a truly universal law of evolution which was deducible, as other laws, from a single axiom of the Spencerian philosophy. Social and historical evolution of mankind is only one instance of a universal cosmic law. Not merely analogous to physical and biological evolution, "super-organic" evolution is identical with these, being governed by precisely the same law. Human history, in this view, along with the philosophy of history, had no privileged standing and could be easily subjected to some monistic principle deriving from physics or biology. Despite his pioneering status in the area of theoretical biological evolution, Spencer opted for a mechanistic reductionism rather than follow the path charted by Herder and the Romantics.

Historicism, Complete and Incomplete

PART TWO

5

THE CRITICAL HISTORIANS AND PHILOSOPHERS:

Ranke to Rickert

The ambiguity of the word "history" itself is well known. A variety of meanings have been associated with the word, yet a basic double-barrelled meaning seems to be the foundation of the others. History can designate the human past, that is, the human past as actuality and reality. Or it can mean the record, the account, the narrative of past human actions, the human past as recorded or reconstructed by the chronicler or historian. This ambiguity is significant, as it points out two possible areas of investigation and concentration for the philosopher of history. The "classical" philosophies of history just reviewed were concerned, in the main, with history as past actuality, the actual course of the human past as a whole. Insights of these philosophers of the past were often projected into the future, either as a fond hope or as a strict necessity, depending upon the firmness with which they clung to their views. This type of the philosophy of history is now generally designated as the "speculative" philosophy of history. As the nineteenth century wore on, professional historians and philosophers turned increasingly to the problems of history as record or narrative, to the processes of historical thinking and reconstruction of the past. Today this concentration is often referred to as the "critical" philosophy of history.[1] Resulting from the shifting of interest to historical accounts and historical thinking was the precising of the critical and historical method and the rise of scientific and critical history. History had become a science, or so it was believed, though not a science after the fashion of the natural sciences. By the end of the nineteenth century this conception of history was a commonplace among German philosophers as well as historians.

But philosophers were not content to let the matter rest there. Critical historians of the nineteenth century, especially among the Rankean school, laid claim to autonomy and the rank of science for their studies, principally because of the refinements of the historico-critical method. Critical philosopher-historians, on the other hand, initiated their own analyses of the critical bases of scientific history, thus generating what came to be known as the critical philosophy of history. Enthused, if not overwhelmed, by the results of their investigations, philosopher-historians such as Wilhelm Dilthey, Benedetto Croce, and Robin Collingwood were led to make a new and much more pretentious claim for historical knowledge. History had become philosophy and philosophy had become history. The hybrid of philosophy-history which resulted can be called historicism, "a philosophic system which perceives in all spiritual reality, in the knowledge of truth, in religion, morality and law, only change and evolution . . . rejecting all that is permanent, eternally valid and absolute."[2]

Reflecting on this development, historians have come to distinguish two major phases in the evolution of historicism: one is primarily methodological, associated with the critical school of Rankean historians; the other is predominantly philosophical and is intimately bound up with the thought of historical-minded philosophers such as Dilthey, Croce, and Collingwood.[3]

Critical Historians

Already in 1637 Descartes had pointed to a principal difficulty confronting anyone who might be so bold as to claim that history could be scientific.

> Even the most faithful record, although it may neither change the facts, nor enhance their value, in order to make them worthy of being related, at least always omits the least dignified and the least illustrious circumstances. Thus, the rest does not appear such as *it really was*. . . .[4]

Two centuries later the presentation of the past "as it really was" had become the goal of the professional historian, and the great historians of the nineteenth century believed that they were well on the way to achieving this objective. Leopold Ranke, perhaps the greatest, and certainly the most influential, of the German historians of the nineteenth century made this youthful boast, amid protestations of modesty.

To history has been assigned the offices of judging the past, of in-
structing the present for the benefit of future ages. To such high
offices this work does not aspire. It wants only to show what actually
happened (*wie es eigentlich gewesen*).

A modern British historian, not without exaggeration, refers to Ranke's
influence in these terms. "Three generations of German, British, and even
French historians marched into battle intoning the magic words 'wie es
eigentlich gewesen' like an incantation—designed, like most incantations,
to save them from the tiresome obligation to think for themselves."[5]
Certainly it would be an exaggeration to maintain that the critical
and historical method began with the German historians of the nineteenth
century, or even with the earlier scholars at Göttingen in the late eighteenth century. Similar ambitions can be traced easily as far back as the
ancient Greek historians. True as this may be, and despite a long and
impressive list of predecessors, the refinement of the historico-critical
method, and especially its elevation to the status of an ideal and model
for aspirants to the professional rank of historians, belongs to Ranke and
the Rankean school. Their aim was an accurate picture of the past, attained through scrupulous care in ascertaining and assessing the facts,
together with an objectivity in presentation. "Everything hangs together,"
wrote Ranke, "the critical study of the genuine sources, impartial perception, objective presentation: the aim is to present the whole truth." "The
strict presentation of the facts . . . is undoubtedly the supreme law."
Painstaking research and analysis, reliance on the best and primary sources
only, abstention from judgments not strictly warranted by the evidence,
all this and more became the normal method for the critical and scientific
historian at work. It is in this sense that most nineteenth-century historians
claimed autonomy and the rank of science for their discipline. One can
agree that Ranke "inaugurated modern critical historiography" and effectively made it a universal ambition for historians through the historical
seminar at Berlin.[6]
Early in his career Ranke rejected *a priori* philosophies of history,
particularly the version of Fichte.

From *a priori* ideas one used to infer what must be. Without realizing
that these ideas are exposed to many doubts, men set out to find
them reflected in the history of the world. From the infinitude of
facts, one selected those which seemed to confirm these ideas. And
this has been called the philosophy of history. One of these ideas
which the philosophy of history presses time and again, as an irrefut-
able claim, is that the human race moves along a course of uninterrupted progress in a steady development toward perfection. . . .
But this is by no means true . . . from the beginning to the present
day the nations of the world have developed in the most diverse
manner.

Ranke held to the view that the methods of philosophy and history are radically different. "There are only two ways of acquiring knowledge about human affairs: through the perception of the particular, or through abstraction: the latter is the method of philosophy, the former of history." Unlike the abstract philosopher, the true historian "must feel a participation and pleasure in the particular itself."[7]

Leader though he may have been in the development of modern critical historical scholarship, Ranke was deeply imbedded in the Romantic tradition, which was so lovingly attached to the event in its singularity and uniqueness. "The event in its human intelligibility," this was the principal goal of the Rankean historian. Hence the well-known statement of Ranke that each generation or period was "immediate" to God. "I am committed to the view that every epoch stands in an immediate relation to God and that its value does not depend on what it produces but simply on its existence." Each event, each series of events like a generation or historical period, was unique and must be understood in and for itself, impartially and without prejudgment. "Nothing exists entirely for the sake of something else." One generation is not a mere steppingstone on which another and later generation ascends, but each has its own irreplaceable value and worth, and its own intelligibility also.

Nevertheless, Ranke always maintained a more universal interest, an interest in the whole of human history, which, it is true, is a unique and particular event in its own way. He conceded that history could never produce the unity of a philosophical system, but there was no denying that it has "an inner connection of its own." No doubt generations and periods do not exist sheerly for the sake of others, but there is "a deep and pervasive connection" between the past and the present. "Critical method, objective research, and synthetic construction can and must go together." Longer and longer series of successive and contemporary events linked together by historical connection formed an epoch or a century. If it ever came to be possible to synthesize the sequence of centuries or epochs, "each with its unique essence, all linked together," then one would have attained to "universal history." This should be the final goal of the historian and of the discipline of history. "The discipline of history," Ranke believed, "is of itself called upon, and is able, to lift itself in its own fashion from the investigation and observation of particulars to a universal view of events, to a knowledge of the objectively existing relatedness."

Ranke held no very high opinion of the "abstract categories" of the aprioristic philosophers of his acquaintance. He believed that the study of history, unaided or unencumbered by such philosophy, could of itself result in "a solidly rooted understanding of the entire history of man." Hence the final goal of the historian was attainable through his own method, "to comprehend the whole while obeying the dictates of exact research."[8] Such an ambition for universal history may sound suspiciously akin to a philosophy of history in the classic sense, though of modest proportions. However, this view of the matter would not do full justice to Ranke's understanding of universal history. He repeatedly expressed the opinion that universal history or world history had no human recognizable goal. Freedom and necessity, he tells us, are rubbing shoulders at every minute in history, and at any moment something unexpected and original may emerge. The individual makes a difference in the course history may take in the future, and the free choices of men have a real part to play in the processes of history. If there are laws in the historical process, they are not only unknown to us but are more secret and profound than we can possibly understand. Undoubtedly, the historian viewing the course of events retrospectively finds developments there explicable and perhaps even apparent from his vantage point, but such a necessity attaches as much to the historian's understanding of the events as to the events themselves.[9]

Whatever the estimates of Ranke as a philosopher for historians, the legacy he left to the German historians was a rich one, if not an unmixed good.[10] His passion for objectivity and impartiality on the part of the historian at work amounted, at times, to a seeming "amoralism" and "passivity" in the face of historical realities. This attitude, if pressed to the limit, could easily lead to a more plainly philosophical historicism, "an interpretation of history which acknowledged no standards outside the object."[11] The ambition for the elevation of history to the stature of an autonomous discipline and science, freed from all aprioristic and positivistic philosophical interlopers, could reinforce the tendency toward a philosophy like historicism which claimed to derive from historical study alone. And Ranke's own peculiarly "vaporous" brand of Romantic idealism, with its efforts "to grasp intuitively the 'general,' the 'tendencies' or 'objective' ideas in history through contemplation . . . of the unique and individual,"[12] left the field of history prey for any philosophy with more muscular outlines. A full-blown philosophical historicism presented just such a posture.

By and large, historians of the nineteenth century were repelled by the *a priori* philosophies of history which abounded in the first generations of that century, but they were even more opposed to the positivistic branch with its search for the "iron laws" of the human past. For the latter history could become a science only if it modeled itself according to ideals and practices of contemporary natural science. A few historians were attracted by the charms of the positivistic tradition. H. T. Buckle, for example, in his *History of Civilization* (1857), urged historians to model their efforts on those of the natural scientist and thus create a "science of history." Buckle's "laws" of European history, which entailed a denial of human freedom, were not well received among professional historians.

Another exponent of much the same point of view was the French critic, philosopher, and historian Hippolyte Taine. "History is an art, but it is also a science." Taine believed that history could become a science, not in the fashion of geometry, perhaps, but like the sciences of physiology and geology.

> Here as elsewhere we must search out the causes after we have collected the facts. No matter if the facts be physical or moral, they all have their causes; there is a cause for ambition, for courage, for truth, as there is for digestion, for muscular movement, for animal heat. Vice and virtue are products, like vitriol and sugar; and every complex phenomenon arises from other simple phenomena on which it depends.

History was to become a sort of social psychology, but this correlation could be made only on the condition that history be treated as a science. Lying behind the "elementary moral state," a sort of permanent condition of man, are the three general causes of Taine: race, milieu (environment), and moment (time). Out of this complex interplay of forces a certain type or dominant psychology arises that characterizes entire epochs and periods of history. At this point the process of increasing generalization reaches the level of a law.

> Here as elsewhere we have but a mechanical problem; the total effect is a result, depending entirely on the magnitude and direction of the producing causes. The only difference which separates these moral problems from physical ones is that the magnitude and direction cannot be valued or computed in the first as in the second.

Taine then proceeded to enumerate a number of general laws of history which need not detain us.[13]

Nothing could be more calculated to upset historians, at least in the Romantic tradition, than to conceive the historical world as a "mechanical problem." Johan G. Droysen, in his *Grundriss der Historik* (1867), agreed with Taine that history was at once an art and a science, but rejected the view that the method of natural science was the only scientific one. "As if it were not a scientific task," he wrote, "to seek ways of investigation, of verification, of understanding for the movements and effects of human freedom and personal peculiarities." The "moral world," which the historian studies, is a reality of much different outlines than the physical world, which the natural scientist investigates, as it is shot through and through with human freedom and individual difference. Moreover, the world of the human past is not known to us directly and immediately as is the physical world but must be "framed out of the sources, a more or less subjective apprehension, view or copy." The insight that "history exists not outwardly and as a reality, but only as thus mediated" is the greatest service that the critical school of historians have contributed to the development of historical methodology, Droysen believed. He candidly admitted that historians had not as yet placed their science and their method on a firm footing, but he was hopeful for the future.

> We certainly possess immediately and in subjective certainty an understanding of human things, of every expression and impression of man's creation or behavior which is perceptible to us. . . . What we need to do is to find methods, in order to secure objective rules and control for this immediate and subjective grasp of events, especially as we now have before us, to represent the past, only the views of others or fragments of that which once existed . . . to establish, not the laws of objective history, but the laws of historical investigation and knowledge.[14]

Droysen touches here on a point that escaped the notice of historians in the positivistic tradition. The past is known to us partially at best, and then most often through the "sources," which, in turn, are personal and perhaps mainly subjective impressions of that actuality. The most pressing need for the historian was the establishment of the "laws of subjective history," that is, objective criteria for the critical investigation of the historical world. Within a generation manuals of historical methodology such as Bernheim's *Lehrbuch der Historischen Methode* (1889) and Langlois and Seignobos' *Introduction aux Études Historiques* (1897) answered this need from the side of the professional historian.[15] At the same time, a number of German philosophers began to challenge directly the positivistic understanding of history.

Critical Philosophers of History

Among the German philosophers who grappled with the problem of the nature of historical study were the neo-Kantians Wilhelm Windelband and Heinrich Rickert. Windelband, in his rectorial address at Strassburg in 1894, proposed a distinction between history and the natural sciences which was developed by Rickert. In the address, entitled *Geschichte und Naturwissenschaft*, Windelband held that the human mind can deal with any subject matter in one of two ways, either by generalizing and laying down laws or by describing individual facts. The first method, proper to the natural sciences, Windelband called the nomothetic, while the second, characteristic of his historical studies, he referred to as the idiographic method. Any subject matter can be approached from either standpoint. Hence the very same subject matter can be studied nomothetically by the natural sciences or idiographically by the historical sciences. This does not mean that the historian is confined to a mere description of individual events without connections; rather, connections are traced between events, causes assigned, and a unified series exposed. In doing this, however, the historian has no intention of discovering universal and necessary laws, but his whole emphasis is on the individual and unique, whether it be a singular event or a complex whole or series of events.

Two years later Rickert began to publish *Die Grenzen der naturwissenschaftlichen Begriffsbildung*, which takes up the problem of distinguishing historical or cultural studies from the natural sciences at the point that Windelband left off. Rickert develops his position in terms of the formation and limitation of scientific concepts. The natural scientist forms concepts with general contents, selecting the features that are common to all the members of a group. These concepts in turn are formed into a system or systems of laws, the system becoming ever more abstract and consequently less and less concrete in the process. The laws that the natural scientist seeks involve changes which repeat themselves, thus rendering generalization possible. Furthermore, the natural scientist in arriving at his laws always treats the causes as equal to or adequate for their effects. Finally, it is evident that the nearer the natural scientist is to his goal the farther he is from the perceptible reality. Hence, if we wish to become acquainted with the unique and perceptible reality, some method other than that of the natural sciences must be used. That method is the method of the historical sciences.

In forming his concepts the historian uses general terms, but combines them to form a concept with individual rather than general content. In turn, these concepts or unique objects are selected from reality because of their importance for the historical whole or series of events that the historian is considering. Only those features of this unique object are selected that make it important or significant for the particular historical series of complex wholes under consideration. The historian goes on from there to combine his unique and complex individuals into ever larger and more complex wholes, rendering them concrete by retaining perceptible characteristics, and showing their unity by tracing the causal connections between the individual events or parts. Historical synthesis is always concerned with a single subject whether it is a single life or a period in the life of a people, a subject forming a unit with beginning and end. Knowing the outcome, the historian seeks to comprehend the chain of events that led up to the final event. Hence the historian always deals with a unique teleological series with definite parts bound together by causal connection. From the viewpoint of historical synthesis, the causes need not always be equal to the effect, for one may find great effects proceeding from causes comparatively or seemingly minimal. At any rate, such a series or whole is always unique, unrepeatable, an individualized whole, regardless of how extensive the period covered. In sum, the synthesis of historical science treats the individual fact as a part of an individualized complex whole, while the synthesis of natural science treats the individual fact as an example under a universal law.

It may be true that history is concrete compared with the abstractness of natural science, yet the historian also abstracts from the fullness of empirical reality in determining the complexes of personages and events to be considered as historical wholes and in focusing his attention on some of the many determinable wholes to the exclusion of others. Thus the historian is always selecting from the richness of reality, and this selection must be based on some standard if the results are not to be completely subjective. Selection takes place, in the view of Rickert, by reason of the historical significance or meaningfulness of the event or whole. Only those facts that embody, or somehow causally affect, the embodiment of cultural values are important or significant historically. One source of values for the historical judgment is immanent to the historical reality itself, and the historian in judging according to the standards of value current with the events he is studying is making an objective judgment. Another source is to be found in the general cultural tradition of the historian himself, and judgments in accord with these standards are reasonable and can be objective. These are sufficient grounds for the selection and judgment of the historian, but the philosopher must take a different view of the matter.

In his *Die Probleme der Geschichtsphilosophie* Rickert takes up the problem of absolute values in connection with the construction of a universal and world history. The philosopher realizes that Europe is only one cultural unit among many and that its standards and values are valid perhaps only for it. How can one combine the various cultural traditions in a comprehensive view, putting all in their proper place with their true value according to an objective and universal standard, if all values are relative? This can be done, Rickert holds, if one is convinced that the values of one's cultural tradition, despite their historical and relative characteristics, are true approximations to a system of absolute values. Admittedly, one does not know the absolute values to the full, but in actual value standards their traces are manifested, while the historical changes of standards show a slow progress toward a fuller and clearer understanding. Hence, there is a place for the philosophy of history over and above the work of the historian, but it will not consist in attempting to find causal laws for the historical process, since these contradict the very nature of historical reality. The philosophy of history will first of all make an epistemological and logical analysis of historical studies. It will also set forth the most general values that determine the meaning of history and from which concepts for historical interpretation derive. Finally, a philosophy of history will grasp all the specialist's knowledge of the partial processes of history as a whole in the light of the highest values and single out the most important elements of progress or regress that appear, dividing the whole into broad periods whose limits are determined by objective philosophical principles. This will be true world history.[16]

NOTES

1. See W. H. Walsh, *Philosophy of History: An Introduction* (New York: Harper & Row, 1960) [reprint of revised edition of 1958], pp. 9–28. A. C. Danto, *Analytical Philosophy of History* (London: Cambridge University Press, 1968), pp. 1–16, prefers to speak of "substantive" and "analytical" philosophies of history.

2. Pope Pius XII, "Address to the Tenth International Congress of Historical Studies," 1955, trans. in *The American Ecclesiastical Review*, Nov. 1955, p. 341. Historicism, or Historismus in the German usage, is a term that some scholars avoid because of the varied meanings, often equivocal, associated with it. See A. Lalande (ed.), *Vocabulaire Technique et Critique de la Philosophie*, 9th ed. (Paris: 1962), pp. 416–417. E. H. Carr, *What Is History* (London: Macmillan, 1961), p. 86, n. 1, avoids using the term because "Professor Popper's widely read writings on the subject have emptied the term of precise meaning." The works that Carr refers to are Popper's *The Open Society* (Princeton, N.J.: Princeton University Press, 1950) and *The Poverty of Historicism* (London: Routledge, 1957). An echo of Popper's usage can be found in M. D'Arcy, *The Matter and Meaning of History* (New York: Meridian, 1961).

H. Meyerhoff, *The Philosophy of History in Our Time* (New York: Double-day, 1959), pp. 299–301, is devastating in his criticism of Popper's arbitrary and equivocal usage of the term and points to the more usual understanding of the term (pp. 9 f., 27). G. Barraclough, *History in a Changing World* (Norman, Okla.: University of Oklahoma Press, 1956), p. 1 f., uses the term in much the same way as Pius XII and Meyerhoff. D. Lee and R. Beck, "The Meaning of Historicism," *The American Historical Review*, Vol. LIX (1953–1954), pp. 568–577, also repudiate Popper's usage. Aware that the term has acquired various meanings, Lee and Beck suggest two final definitions: "the belief that the truth, meaning, and value of anything, i.e., the basis of any evaluation, is to be found in its history; and, more narrowly, . . . the anti-positivistic and anti-naturalistic view that historical knowledge is a basic, or the only requirement for understanding and evaluating man's present political, social, and intellectual position or problems," p. 577. These meanings are rather close to that given by Pius XII. Lee and Beck also consider historicism to be "the heir of the idealistic antirationalism of the late eighteenth and early nineteenth centuries," p. 575.

3. The German historian Frederich Meinecke, *Entstehung des Historismus*, 2 vols. (Munich: 1936), gave a somewhat different interpretation of historicism than the one accepted above. "The quintessence of historicism consists in the replacement of the generalizing view of historico-human forces by an individual-izing view." At that time Meinecke believed that the principles of historicism had been most completely formulated in Goethe's works, while their consum-mation had been achieved in the works of the great German historian Leopold Ranke. A detailed analysis by C. A. Beard and A. Vaghts of Meinecke's work on Historismus appears in *The American Historical Review*, Vol. XLII (1936–

1937), pp. 460–483. A short and characteristic statement of Meinecke on much the same topic can be found in "Values and Causalities," trans. F. Stern, *The Varieties of History* (New York: Meridian, 1956), pp. 268–288.

It is clear that Meinecke refers to what is now called the Rankean phase of historicism. P. Geyl, *Debates with Historians* (New York: Meridian, 1958), p. 21, sums up in this way: "*Historicism* was the term that came into use for the approach to history that was derived from his [Ranke's] example. Minus the mystical urge, no doubt, but the abstaining from judgment, the accepting, the acknowledging of no other standards than those supplied by the historical process itself—these came to constitute the spirit in which history was studied." For the distinction between historicism as a methodology and as a philosophy or *Weltanschauung*, see H. P. Rickman, *Pattern and Meaning in History* (New York: Harper & Row, 1962), pp. 50–59.

Dilthey, Croce, and Collingwood were by no means the only thinkers of the period concerned with the nature and problems of historicism. H. Stuart Hughes, *Consciousness and Society* (New York: A. Knopf, 1961), pp. 183–248, gives a thoughtful analysis of Dilthey, Croce, F. Meinecke, and E. Troeltsch in relation to historicism.

4. R. Descartes, *Discourse on Method*, I (London: 1960), p. 40, trans. A. Wollaston, emphasis added. See L. Levy-Bruhl, "The Cartesian Spirit and History," in R. Klibansky and H. J. Paton (eds.), *Philosophy and History* (New York: Harper & Row, 1963), pp. 191–196, and E. Cassirer, *The Philosophy of the Enlightenment* (Boston: Beacon Press, 1955), pp. 197–223.

5. Carr, p. 3. The American Historical Association, founded in 1884, elected Ranke, then almost ninety, as its first, and only, honorary member. The text from Ranke appears in his very first work, *Geschichte der romanischen und germanischen Völker*, dating from 1824.

6. J. W. Thompson, *A History of Historical Writing* (New York: Macmillan, 1942), Vol. 2, pp. 168–186. The texts of Ranke are from *Sammtliche Werke*, 3d ed. (Leipzig: 1874–1890), Vol. XXI, p. 114, cited in Thompson, p. 184, n. 59, and from *Geschichte der romanischen und germanischen Völker von 1494 bis 1514*, Preface, appearing in Stern, p. 57. A valuable estimate of the achievements of the Göttingen school of criticism appears in H. Butterfield, *Man on His Past* (Boston: Beacon, 1960), pp. 32–62.

In *The Varieties of History* Stern has collected representative statements of historians from the second half of the nineteenth century expressing the belief that history had become scientific. Included are the prospectuses of such historical journals as the *Historische Zeitschrift* (1859), the *Revue historique* (1876), and the *English Historical Review* (1886), as well as the inaugural lectures of Fustel de Coulanges (1862 at Strasbourg), Theodor Mommsen (1874 at Berlin), and John B. Bury (1902 at Cambridge). Also included are Lord Acton's letter to the contributors to the *Cambridge Modern History* (1896) and the programmatic statement of the *Revue de synthèse historique* (1900). Despite differences, all seem to agree that history is a science particularly because of its critical apparatus, though Henri Berr's vision of scientific history in the *Revue de synthèse historique* encompassed sociology and psychology and stressed historical synthesis.

7. *Weltgeschichte*, first to third editions (Leipzig: 1888), Part IX, section 2, pp. vii–xi, trans. in Stern, pp. 58–59.

8. See Ranke, pp. xiii–xvi, in Stern, pp. 60–62.

9. See H. Butterfield, *Man on His Past*, "Ranke and the Conception of

'General History,' " pp. 100–141, and T. Von Laue, *Leopold Ranke: The Formative Years* (Princeton, N.J.: Princeton University Press, 1950).

10.   One can compare Thompson's critical estimate of Ranke with that of Gooch, *History and Historians in the Nineteenth Century* (Boston: Beacon, 1959), pp. 72–97, which ends on this adulatory note: "he remains the master of us all." Also useful is F. Schevill, *Six Historians* (Chicago: University of Chicago Press, 1956), "Ranke: Rise, Decline and Persistence of a Reputation," pp. 125–155. C. G. Iggers, "The Image of Ranke in American and German Historical Thought," *History and Theory*, Vol. 2 (1962), pp. 17–40, observes that American historians detached Ranke's critical methodology from his idealistic philosophy, while in Germany he was considered a champion of the idealist tradition against the inroads of positivism.

11.   See P. Geyl, "Ranke in the Light of Catastrophe," in Geyl, p. 9.

12.   See Iggers, p. 18.

13.   See S. J. Kahn, *Science and Aesthetic Judgment: A Study in Taine's Critical Method* (London: Routledge, 1953), esp. pp. 60–72. Texts cited are from Taine's *History of English Literature* (Edinburgh: 1871), Vol. I, pp. 8, 17, trans. H. van Laun. The dictum of Taine, "*Après la collection des faits, la recherche des causes,*" is considered by some to be the epitome of positivistic history; however, see Kahn, pp. 228–229.

A generation later the German historian Karl Lamprecht was pursuing the same path as Taine. While admitting that Ranke was a master of the art of description, Lamprecht considered him a leading representative of the Romantic idealist tradition, which stressed at once the individual in the historical process and the "idea" lying behind great concourses and concatenations of events. A naturalist treatment of historical reality modeled after that of the sociologist or anthropologist was necessary if one wished to comprehend historical developments. Lamprecht repeated Taine's view that "history is applied psychology" and came up with a point of view that resembled that of Herder. "As the individual psyche has its specific development in the years of the child, of the adolescent, of the man, and of the aged, there must exist for the socio-psyche too, a canon of development which runs through, in unbroken succession, a series of cultural periods." See K. Lamprecht, *What Is History*, trans. E. Andrews (New York: 1905), pp. 15–16, 29, 171. Lamprecht thought that universal laws of historical development could be attained if only the method he initiated in his *German History* were followed.

One can compare Lamprecht's conception of history with that of eminent sociologists of the same period. Emile Durkheim, for example, formulated his views on the matter in these words (1903): "History can only be a science on the condition that it raises itself above the particular; it is true that then it ceases to be itself and becomes a branch of sociology. It merges with dynamic sociology. It can remain an original discipline if it limits itself to the study of each national individuality, taken in itself and considered in its diverse moments of becoming. But then it is only a narrative of which the object is above all particular. Its function is to place society in the state of remembering their past; this is the eminent form of the collective memory.

"After having distinguished these two conceptions of history, it is necessary to add further that more and more they are destined to become inseparable. There is no opposition between them, but only difference of degree. Scientific history or sociology cannot avoid direct observation of concrete facts, and on the other hand national history, or history as art, can only gain by being penetrated by the general principles at which sociology has arrived," *L'Année Sociologique*, Vol. 6 (1903), pp. 124–125.

14.   See J. G. Droysen, *Outline of the Principles of History*, trans. E. Andrews (Boston: 1893), pp. 105–118, as cited in Stern, pp. 137–144. Droysen can scarcely be considered a disciple of Ranke, being a leading member of the ardent nationalist Prussian school of historians. In the Preface to one of his earlier works he expresses this sentiment: "my object is to express and justify the love of and belief in the fatherland."

15.   Bernheim's manual distinguished three stages in the development of history: narrative or descriptive, pragmatic or didactic, and genetic or evolutionary. In the last stage history attains to the rank of a science. It is interesting to compare Bernheim's definitions of the science of history in the different editions of his manual. The first edition (1889) states that "History is the science of the development of mankind in their activity as social beings." Due to a controversy with Lamprecht, Bernheim was led to expand the original definition in the edition of 1903. "The Science of history is the science which investigates and narrates in causal connection the facts of the development of mankind in their activities (individual as well as typical and collective) as social beings." The definition of the science of history is still more expanded in the edition of 1908. See J. Huizinga, "A Definition of the Concept of History," *Philosophy and History*, R. Klibansky and H. J. Paton (eds.), pp. 1–2.

It must be recognized that both of these manuals have been since classified in the positivist tradition by some. R. G. Collingwood, *The Idea of History* (Oxford: Clarendon Press, 1946), p. 176, following Benedetto Croce, considers Bernheim a follower of the positivist historians, though his own idealist views must be taken into account. H. Marrou, *The Meaning of History* (Baltimore: Helicon Press, Inc., 1966), e.g., pp. 55–56, classifies Langlois and Seignobos among the positivists also, but Marrou's personalist views undoubtedly have had some influence on this opinion. In fact, there are some who rate Ranke himself as a positivist.

16.   We have been using the analyses of Rickert's views on the methodology and philosophy of history given by F. M. Fling, "Historical Synthesis," *The American Historical Review*, Vol. IX (1903), pp. 1–22, and by H. A. Hodges, *The Philosophy of Wilhelm Dilthey* (London: Routledge, 1952), pp. 225–228, 238–245.

According to Collingwood, pp. 168–169, Rickert distinguishes four types of science, combining two criteria intimated by Windelband, methodology and subject matter. Historical studies are not only idiographic but are also concerned with what has meaning and value, while the natural sciences are not only nomothetic but are related to facts without value or meaning. So one can have four types of sciences: the nonvaluing, which are either generalizing, as pure natural science, or individualizing, as the quasihistorical sciences of geology and evolutionary biology; and the valuing sciences, either generalizing, as the quasiscientific studies of history as sociology, economics, and politics, or individualizing, as history proper.

6

UNDERSTANDING THE MEANING OF HISTORY:

Wilhelm Dilthey

In 1882 Wilhelm Dilthey succeeded to Hegel's chair in philosophy at the University of Berlin, where he had been a lecturer in philosophy some years earlier. During his first years at Berlin Ranke was at the height of his career, and all through his life Dilthey maintained a profound respect for Ranke, who appeared to him to be "the personified capacity of the historical mind." Not simply a philosopher but more truly a philosopher-historian, Dilthey engaged in research and in the critical editing of texts from Schleiermacher, Kant, and Hegel. The history of thought and ideas remained one of his principal preoccupations. His specifically philosophical writings extended over the period of 1864 until his death in 1911 and all are bound together by one enduring theme. That theme is his determination to write a critique of historical reason. Dilthey was determined to do for "historical reason" what Kant had done for "pure reason" and "practical reason," for the master of German thought had not ventured into this area. In 1883 appeared Dilthey's *Einleitung in die Geisteswissenschaften* (Introduction to the Sciences of Mind), which was meant to be only the beginning of his major philosophical interest, the critique of historical reason. The project was never completed, though Dilthey issued major essays from time to time on the topic. These, assembled by his literary executors in one volume, constitute substantially the *Kritik der historischen Vernunft* that he so persistently attempted to compose. Of the three tasks assigned to the philosophy of history by Rickert, Dilthey shows an interest only in the first two, the epistemological analysis of historical studies and the determining of the general principles that lie behind historical interpretation and give meaning to history.[1]

Despite the defining of his objective in Kantian terms, Dilthey was not a neo-Kantian as Windelband and Rickert but differed significantly from Kantian orthodoxy. He agreed with Kant that the facts of consciousness are the only secure foundation for philosophizing; but what is given in consciousness is not merely rational consciousness but rather a sum total of feeling, volition, and thought.

> I was led, by my historical and psychological study of the whole man, to make this whole man . . . this willing, feeling, thinking being the foundation for explaining knowledge and its concepts, such as those of the external world, time, substance, cause, however much it may seem that knowledge weaves these concepts only from the material of perception, ideation, and thought.[2]

Agreeing with Kant in the point of departure for philosophy, Dilthey declined to follow him much further. In his theory of knowledge there is no *a priori*, for he views all thought structures as arising out of experience and deriving their meaning from their relation to experience. Experience is the foundation for all knowledge and is the only evidence we can have that anything exists. In experience there is given not only the self and its activities but also the external world as it is found in lived experience. The fundamental reality is the human being, a mind-body unit living his life in interaction with his physical and social environment, and from this interaction all experience and thought arise. For Dilthey life and knowledge, activity and contemplation are bound up in an inseparable whole. This complex structure of thought and action together must be the foundation of philosophy, since reality somehow is a process of interaction between them. This he called a life philosophy. "Life is the fundamental fact which must form the starting point for philosophy. It is that which is known from within, that behind which we cannot go."[3] Continued interaction of the thought and action of all members of a society form a life stream in which the varied human potentialities are realized. The life stream should be studied especially in the human and creative expressions of life, while at the same time each part of the life stream is closely connected with every other part of it. In the end, philosophizing and the study of history come very close to coincidence and identity. "Life is the fullness, variety and interaction—within something continuous—experienced by individuals. Its subject matter is identical with history. History is merely life viewed in terms of the continuity of mankind as a whole."[4] It is sufficiently clear that the term "life" for

Dilthey refers to human life, the life of mankind with its historical achievements, and bears little relation to the biological features of human life.

History and Understanding

Dilthey's preoccupation with history and the human sciences (*Geisteswissenschaften*), as he called them, antedates the remarks of Windelband and Rickert on this subject, but his own views gradually crystallized under the impact of their neo-Kantian expositions. Side by side with the development of the natural sciences, Dilthey held, a group of studies has "grown naturally from the problems of life." These studies are the human studies, having the same subject matter, which is mankind, or humanity, or simply the human-social historical reality. Because this group of studies refer to the same subject matter of humanity and moreover develop directly from the problems of life, it is necessary to distinguish them from the natural sciences. The range of the human sciences is very broad, including "history, economics, law, politics and psychology, and the study of religion, literature, poetry, architecture, music and philosophic world views and systems."[5] Dilthey labels this group of studies *Geisteswissenschaften*, and he means to exclude from the listing such apparently related disciplines as human biology, physical anthropology, or physiological psychology. This restriction is consistent with his use of the term "life," which refers to that which is distinctively human and not that which is had in common with animals.

One reason for the difference between the natural sciences and the human studies is their differing proximity to life and common experience.

> Scientific thinking [in the natural sciences], the productive achievements of which are esoteric, has become detached from our practical contact with the external world; but, in the human studies a connection between life and science is retained so that thought arising from life remains the foundation of scientific activity.[6]

Our knowledge of the world arises in the course of our active life and intercourse with it, as our relation to the object is not merely cognitive but active and vital. Individuals as well as social groups enter into this active relation with their environment, and from this they build up a body of experience and a set of ideas. The human sciences rest directly on this body of common experience, while the starting point of the natural sciences does not. Hence, the results of the natural sciences in the form of scientific theories and hypotheses are "esoteric," because their initial point of departure is "esoteric" as well. The human sciences stand nearer than the natural sciences to common experience and life.[7]

Another, and more fundamental, difference between the natural sciences and the human studies flows from the community of nature between object and subject in the latter. "It is not conceptual procedure which forms the foundation of the human studies but the becoming aware of a mental state in its totality and the rediscovering of it by empathy. Here life grasps life. . . ."[8] The same human nature that is experienced in oneself is studied in the human sciences and history. As the human sciences advance in their goal of understanding life, they leave behind more and more the merely physical side of events and mechanical causality, which are relegated to the role of conditions and means of comprehension only.

> This is the turning toward self-knowledge, the movement of the understanding from the external to the internal. This tendency makes use of every expression of life in order to understand the mental content from which it arises. . . . This tendency does not depend upon an external point of view from which life is surveyed; it is founded directly on it.[9]

The term "understanding" (*Verstehen*) for Dilthey is a technical term. To further complicate matters, Dilthey's explanation of the term seems to have passed through several stages. Common to all is the view that "understanding" rests on what has been called an "inside" view of human nature which we all possess.[10] In the earlier phase of his exposition of "understanding," the aspects that interest him most are those which contrast the experiential foundations of the human studies with those of the natural sciences. The natural sciences begin with sense data and cannot find any principle of unity in them; consequently, the unity of the physical world must be supplied by hypothesis. The human studies, on the other hand, rest upon a direct apprehension of their object in a living unity, for the investigator finds the object given in himself by inner perception and rediscovers it in his understanding of others and history. "To understand another person is not merely to know that he is having a certain experience, but to feel the reverberation of that experience in myself, to relive it (*nacherleben*) or reconstruct it imaginatively (*nachbilden*)." Hence Dilthey recommends that genuine knowledge in the human studies must always be derived from and interpreted in close dependence on the concrete experience of life in inner understanding. General concepts and perhaps even laws operative in history and society can be formulated by the human studies, but the object must be understood before it is known, and it always remains more understood than known.[11]

In the last years of his life Dilthey recognized more and more the dependence of all "understanding" upon the physical expressions of mental life. "Understanding is our name for the processes in which mental

life comes to be known through the expressions of it which are given to
the senses."[12] Understanding cannot be achieved by mere introspection
or self-observation, and if more than a purely subjective understanding
of man is desired, then an objective source is to be found in the "expressions of life." Dilthey distinguishes three major groups of the "expressions of life." Statements of logical relations, or treatises containing them,
fall into the first group, and understanding of these is directed at "pure
thought-content." Understanding here may be precise, but it is never
deep, since the logical relations can be considered without any reference
to any underlying living experience. The second group consists of human
actions, which are the execution of purposes, and consequently express
the purpose of the agent or agents, though not intentionally. Understanding of this class of the expressions of human life is possible but not
always especially fruitful. At best, the action or group of actions manifests
one response only to a particular set of circumstances and not the
underlying character or outlook of the man or group, which contains
endless possibilities of action. The third and final group is made up of
the expressions of living experience in the fullest sense, and Dilthey calls
them "expressions of lived experience." These stem from the urge "to
express the inner self, and somehow to place it before oneself and com-
municate it to others."[13] Here is the ideal field for understanding and
interpretation, and in its highest forms it consists in works of creative
genius, whether artistic, scientific, philosophical, religious, and so on.

> The copies which still give us a feeble intuition of Zeus of Pheidias,
> of Dürer's Apocalypse or the Ninth Symphony, a drama or a philo-
> sophic system, a poem by Goethe or Newton's *magnum opus* is
> mathematical physics, whether it be an individual creation, or a rela-
> tion between concepts which gives expression to some matter of fact—
> in all these cases there is an external fact which arose as the expres-
> sion of an inner reality and thus brings this reality to understanding.[14]

Such expressions of vital experience reveal more about their author than
he himself knows, emerging as they do from the very depths of the soul.
    Only the higher forms of understanding are free from uncertainty,
because they are free from inference, and this exalted form of understanding occurs in the understanding of the works of creative genius. The
experience expressed is a self-contained whole, while the expression itself
is one that has been elaborated precisely for this purpose. Consequently,
the direct perception of the inner in the outer without any added inference is enough to reveal to us a coherent living whole. In the highest
forms of understanding there is a process of reliving step by step in the
true temporal and causal order the experience of another mind. This is
most easily done when the experience has already passed through the
consciousness of the other and is expressed in a lasting work, and it is

the hermeneutic art that makes possible understanding of this experience.
The hermeneutic art cannot be taught but must be acquired by personal
contact with the great creative expressions of life. Furthermore, it demands
something of creative genius in its practitioner.

> Scientific exposition or interpretation, as an understanding which re-
> produces [its object] in accordance with an art, has always something
> of genius in it, i.e., only through inner affinity and sympathy does it
> attain a high degree of perfection. . . . This inner relation, which
> makes transposition possible, forms therefore the presupposition of
> all hermeneutical rules.[15]

The results reached in interpretation may never be demonstratively certain, but the process carries with it a conviction all its own. No chain
of inferences into which one may pretend to resolve the process will
ever substitute for this understanding. Interpretation is not the result of
logical reflection but arises out of the same creative imagination from
which the creative expression of life itself derived. In fact, it can even
relive factors that were not present to the explicit consciousness of the
originator but that are made accessible through the finished work.[16]

The expressions of life upon which understanding essentially depends
are themselves impregnated with an historical and dynamic character.
They proceed from life and are themselves an incident in its development. Structurally the expressions of life reach out beyond themselves
into the past and the future, and from this characteristic flows their historical and dynamic quality. Through these expressions we are introduced
immediately into the historical world.

> It is through the idea of the objectification of life that we first obtain
> a glimpse into the essence of the historical. Everything here has arisen
> by mental agency, and therefore bears the character of historicity.
> It is woven into the sensible world itself as a product of history. From
> the distribution of the trees in a park, the arrangement of the houses
> in a street, or the purposive tool of a handicraftsman to the sentence
> pronounced in the law courts, we are surrounded every hour by things
> which have come to be in the course of history. That which the mind
> today imparts of its own character to its manifestations, tomorrow,
> if it exists, is history. . . .[17]

To characterize this world of the expressions of life, or the objectifications of mind, Dilthey borrows Hegel's expression "objective mind"
(*objectiver Geist*), but he is careful to observe that he does not mean it
in the Hegelian sense.[18] The objective mind is not a metaphysical assumption but the term Dilthey uses for a range of empirical facts that
man can understand because the human mind has been responsible for
their production. The totality of the human world is called the "social-

historical world," or the "historical world," or simply "life." From the point of view of its basic structures and enduring manifestations it is called objective mind.

> By this [the objective mind] I mean the manifold forms in which what individuals hold in common have objectified themselves in the world of senses. In this objective mind the past is a permanently enduring present for us. Its realm extends from the style of life and the forms of social intercourse, to the systems of purposes which society has created for itself, to custom, law, state, religion, art, science and philosophy.

From the earliest moments of his childhood the individual is orientated in the world of objective mind, and it "is the medium in which the understanding of other people and their expressions takes place."[19]

From the point of view of its dynamism the historical world is referred to as a "dynamic system" or "system of interactions" (*Wirkungszusammenhang*).[20] This concept effectively expresses the nature of historical reality. From the smallest unit of historical life, the smallest that can be studied as a unity or whole in itself, through the larger wholes up to the comprehensive whole of world history everything we encounter is a dynamic system or a system of interactions. These systems of Dilthey are not simple causal systems but teleological and creative ones, generating values and fulfilling ends. "This system of interactions is distinguished from the causal order of nature by the fact that, in accordance with the structure of mental life, it creates values and realizes purposes. . . . Historical life is creative; it constantly produces goods and values and all concepts of these are reflections of its activity." In fact, this process begins with the individual, who can be considered as a dynamic system on a small scale.

The human individual is a mental unity whose unifying center lies in himself, but there are other channels through which the creative teleological process works. The individual is the point of intersection of various cultural systems and a member of various associations and societies, and in these too we find a structural unity comparable to that of the individual together with a continuance of the creative and teleological process. Still more complex and wider dynamic systems are the nation, the age, and the historical period. These higher systems are more self-contained than the others, and the historical periods or ages are the most self-centered of all.

> An epoch is centered on itself in a new sense. The common practices of an epoch become the norm for the activities of the individuals in it. The pattern of the systems of interaction of the society of an epoch has constant features. Within it the relations in the comprehension of objects show an inner affinity. The ways of feeling,

the inner life and the impulses which arise from it, are similar to each other. The will, too, chooses similar goals, strives for related goods and finds itself committed in a similar way.

The historical world is a whole composed of lesser unities and wholes, a dynamic system composed of particular and lesser dynamic systems, and this conception must dominate historical studies.[21]

The same notion of the historical world is necessary if the human studies are ever to become objective and true sciences. In his interpretation of events and understanding of historical personalities, the historian depends essentially on his conception. Because common factors like the state, religion, or the law of the land have shaped an historical personality to a considerable degree, it is not possible to understand such an individual thoroughly unless the historian has a general knowledge of these factors. Consequently, Dilthey is convinced of the interdependence of "interpretation, criticism, linking of sources, and synthesis into a historical whole." This is merely another instance of the general feature of interrelatedness present in all the human studies. "Criticism, interpretation, and intellectual synthesis differ in their tasks, but the accomplishment of these tasks always demands insights gained from the others." If one applies the rules of strict demonstration to the procedure followed by the historian in the reconstruction of the past, there seems to be a circular movement, but Dilthey is not overly concerned. Even in the case of knowledge of motives in political history, which he places at the bottom of the scale of historical knowledge from the viewpoint of certitude, probability of a high degree can be built up.[22]

Dilthey tried to resolve the problem of the interrelatedness of the human studies and of the consequent interdependence of various steps in the process of historical understanding. One answer, he felt, lies in the very nature of the historical world itself, consisting as it does in a "system of interactions." Another answer is to be seen in the very nature of the inquiring human.

> The comprehension of the system of interactions arises, primarily, in the experiencing subject for whom the sequence of inner events unfolds in structural relations. These connections are then rediscovered in other individuals through understanding. Thus the fundamental form of the connections arises in the individual who combines present, past, and possibilities of the future into the course of his life.[23]

In the end, we are driven back to the connectedness of life itself, behind which we cannot go. "Life contains as the first categorical definition, fundamental to all others, being in time."[24] The temporal structures of the individual human life are essentially the same as those of the life of mankind in time with which history proper has to deal. All human life has this historical character and the temporal dimension. Indeed, Dilthey tells us, all the meaning in life is based on its temporal and historical character.

> The connectedness of a life can only be understood through the mean-ing the individual parts have for understanding the whole . . . and every part of the life of mankind can only be understood in the same way. Meaning is the comprehensive category through which life be-comes comprehensible.[25]

Meaning and History

Equally important in Dilthey's thought with the concept of "under-standing" is that of "meaning" (Bedeutung), for understanding is the process of grasping meaning imbedded in the historical and human world. From the life of an individual, even from his particular experiences, to the life of mankind as a whole stretches a world of meaning.

> We come face to face with the category of meaning. The relation contained in it defines and clarifies the conception we have of our lives; it is also the point of view from which we grasp and describe the coexistence and sequence of lives in history. . . . It is quite generally the category which is peculiar to life and to the historical world. Indeed it is inherent in life because it is the particular relation-ship which exists between its parts; all life contains this relationship which is essential for describing it.[26]

Meaning penetrates and permeates the historical world and thereby sharply distinguishes it from the physical world, which is studied by the natural scientist. Something of the range and breadth of the concept of "meaning" for Dilthey is indicated by this passage: "Whenever connec-tions occur in history and wherever there is freedom within reality we must apply the concept of meaning. Wherever life is past and has entered understanding there is history. And where history is there is meaning in all its variety."[27]

As in the case of a number of concepts that Dilthey employs, there is difficulty in assessing the elusive concept of "meaning" in his thought. One sense of the word "meaning" is that of importance, but it does not seem that any text of Dilthey necessarily demands such an understanding of the term. Another sense of the word "meaning" is that of signification, the relation between a sign and the thing signified, whereby the sign indicates or expresses or "means" the thing signified. Undoubtedly this sense of the term is present in the thought of Dilthey, though it is not the sense that is emphasized. Working not only from texts but from all available forms of expression, the historian can find meaning in all of them in the sense that they are outward signs referring to an inner reality. Yet this is not the aspect of "meaning" that Dilthey considers most fruitful in the process of understanding history, nor is it completely adequate for the fullest understanding of life and history. The sense of "meaning" emphasized by Dilthey points to the nature of life as a process and a self-developing unity, the relation between the parts and whole of life. "The category of meaning designates the relation, rooted in life itself, of parts to the whole." And again, "Meaning is the special relation which the parts have to the whole within a life."[28] We have already encountered something of this crucial aspect of "meaning" in discussing Dilthey's concept of "understanding," and it is of special relevance when the objects of the hermeneutic art are those highest forms of the expressions of life that Dilthey calls "expressions of lived-experience."

The place to begin in trying to fathom some of the depths of the concept of "meaning" is with the individual and the course of his life, as does Dilthey. One can say that the individual life, in a way, "represents the historical universe," while from it "the specific historical categories arise." Autobiography is the highest and most instructive form in which the understanding of an individual life confronts us, for the man who understands it is at the same time the one who created the autobiography.

> The person who seeks the connecting threads in the history of his life has already from different points of view created a coherence in that life which he is now putting into words. He has created it by experiencing values and realizing purposes in his life, making plans for it, seeing his past in terms of development and the future as the shaping of his life and of whatever he values most. He has, in his memory, singled out and accentuated moments which he experienced as significant; others he has allowed to sink into forgetfulness. The future has corrected his illusions about the significance of certain moments . . . from an endless, countless multiplicity, a selection of what is worth recording has been prepared. Between these parts we see a connection which neither is, nor is intended to be, the simple likeness of the course of a life of so many years, but which, because understanding is involved, expressed what the individual knows about the continuity of his life.

Dilthey singles out three famous autobiographies for analysis, those of Augustine, Rousseau, and Goethe. How do these writers grasp the continuity between the different parts of their life? It is in terms of the categories of purpose, value, significance, and meaning. Augustine is an exemplar of the category of purpose above all, directing himself exclusively to the relation of his life with God. Rousseau, on the other hand, wanted above all to justify his individual existence; here the category of value stands out. Goethe, finally, exemplifies in his autobiography the category of meaning, looking at his life from the viewpoint of universal history. No one of these categories is understood in terms of a cause and effect relationship. But each of these categories is not equally fruitful for the understanding of a life. "The connectedness of life" cannot be established from the category of value only, applying as it does only to experiences in the present without connection, nor purely from the category of purpose, which refers to the future and involves subordination of the parts of life. "Only the category of meaning goes beyond mere co-existence or subordination of the parts of life. As history is memory, and as the category of meaning belongs to memory, this is the category which belongs most intimately to historical thinking."[29]

Being the comprehensive category of life, meaning is the principal category under which historical knowledge apprehends its object, which is life. This is possible only because the historian himself understands his own life as a meaningful structural unity, despite the fact that he neither recalls the experience of his birth nor has experienced death. "The present includes the presentation of the past in the memory, and that of the future in the imagination, which explores its possibilities, and in the activity which sets ends among these possibilities. Thus, the present is filled with pasts and pregnant with the future."[30] The individual in the continuity of these experiences becomes conscious of himself as a unitary being extending in time. Looking back on the course of his life, the individual experiences a structural unity, that is, "connections quite independent of the temporal sequence and the direct causal relations in it, which join the parts of a life into a whole." Decisions, or plans of life, once made can produce activities that extend over many years, persisting without being reexamined, despite long interruptions by occurrences of quite a different kind. Time in nature and time in history or human life are entirely different. If the individual goes on to try to understand this structural unity, to explore the character of the whole and the contributions made by its various parts, he is seeking the meaning of his life. "The contribution to the whole made by any part is the meaning (Bedeutung) or significance (Bedeutsamkeit) of that part, and the resultant character of the whole is its meaning (Bedeutung) or sense (Sinn)." The meaning of life lies entirely in the relations between parts and whole within it.[31]

The meaning of one's life, in Dilthey's sense, is not a matter of contemplation purely, nor rooted in a determined process, for the future is a realm of active freedom, of "possibility." One's decisions and one's plans for life can change the actuality of one's life, and hence the meaning of it.

Our conception of the meaning of a life is constantly changing. Every plan for a life expresses a conception of the meaning of life. The purposes we set for the future condition how we determine the meaning of the past. The actual pattern of life is judged in terms of the meaning we give to what we remember.

If this is so, then it would seem that every meaning given to life, the life of mankind as a whole as well as that of the individual, is provisional. This is Dilthey's view. "One would have to wait for the end of a life and, in the hour of death, survey the whole to ascertain the relation between the whole and its parts." The same can be said of the meaning of history as a whole. "One would have to wait for the end of history to have all the material necessary to determine its meaning."[32] And yet Dilthey does not intend to leave the impression that no meaning can be perceived in history. "What we see is always a limited relation between elements of history and the whole of the past. But what is decisive is that we see a real, though limited, meaning; in no succeeding context can it be cancelled. Hence the historian sees truly."[33]

The meaning of the individual life is not fully understood even after its completion except in the light of history. The biographer surveys the course of an individual life that has ended, but he sees the individual as the center of his world, a value in himself, and all meaning relations are viewed in reference to the individual. This approach is limited and one-sided.

> Universal movements intersect in the individual life; if we are to understand them we must seek for new foundations outside the individual. . . . *We must turn to new categories, shapes and forms of life which do not emerge from the individual life.* The individual is only the crossing point for the cultural systems and organizations into which his existence is woven; how can they be understood through him?[34]

The historian, on the other hand, takes the view that the individual, instead of being *the* center of meaning, derives his meaning from his place in the historical and social process in which he is caught up.

> The individual person in his own independent existence is a historical being. He is determined by his place in time and space and his position in the interaction of cultural systems and communities. The historian has, therefore, to understand the whole life of an individual as it expresses itself at a certain time and place. It is the whole web of connections which stretches from individuals concerned with their own existence to the cultural systems and communities and, finally, to the whole of mankind, which makes up the character of society and history.[35]

The historian, properly speaking, is not concerned with the meaning of individual lives except of those who rank as historical personages, but he is concerned with the meaning of the historical process, that is, with the "objectifications of life" and the "dynamic systems" or "systems of interactions." In Dilthey's view all the dynamic systems (*Wirkungszusammenhang*) are also meaning systems (*Bedeutungszusammenhang*), and the historian must regard them in this light. The events of history fall naturally into groups or relatively self-contained processes in which forces of many kinds combine, strengthen, modify each other, and produce some common effect or historical change of significance. Such are Dilthey's dynamic systems. The wholeness of such systems depends primarily upon the unity of the result effected in them, and this wholeness flows from the unity of social end or social value pursued or realized in them.

> Every individual is, also, a point where systems intersect; systems which go through individuals, exist within them, but reach beyond their life and possess an independent existence and development of their own through the content, the value, the purpose, which is realized in them. . . . Some kind of knowledge of reality is inherent in them; standpoints for valuation develop within them, purposes are realized in them; they have a meaning. . . . This is already the case in some of the systems of culture, for instance, art and philosophy, in which there is no organization to link the parts. Furthermore, organized associations arise. . . . In the family and in the different intermediate forms between it and the state, as well as in the latter itself, we find the highest development of common goals within a community. Every organized unit in a state . . . has a meaning of its own in the context of mankind.[36]

As in the individual life, the relations between ends and values, and the way in which particular decisions and events are subordinated to their realization, constitute the meaning of that life, so too in the cultural systems and societies of the historical process.

On a still higher level of the dynamic systems are states or nations and ages or periods of history. The state or the nation is the comprehensive framework for all the lesser dynamic systems, cultural and organizational, and may even take over some of their functions such as education. "A composite structure occurs. In it the organization of power and interrelated purposive systems are linked into a higher unity. Common features arise in it. . . ." The life of a nation is centered around common beliefs, ideals, values, purposes, and ways of doing things, and hence there is a visible concord or agreement among the different spheres of life in a nation. Yet this uniformity and harmony cannot be ascribed to one of the spheres, such as economics, as Marx believed.

> Whatever effects proceeded from the strength and character of certain achievements, the kinship which links the different spheres of

life within a nation originates, above all, from common depths which no description can exhaust. They exist for us only in the expressions of life which emerge from them and express them.[37]

On the highest level of the dynamic and meaningful systems is the historical period or age, which is supranational.

> In the course of historical events periods can be delimited in which a unity of mental culture embracing everything from the conditions of life up to the highest ideas, took shape, reached its zenith, and disintegrated again. In each such period there exists an inner structure, common to them all, which determines the connections of the parts to the whole, the course of events and the modifications in the tendencies. . . .

The age or epoch embraces all lesser systems and organizations, including nations, in its broad expanse, stamping common features on its activities, products, and ideas. "From highly varied and variable elements a complex whole forms. And this determines the meaning of all that is active in the age. . . . Everything in an age derives its meaning from the energy which gives it its fundamental tendency." All the expressions of life, in stone and on canvas, in deeds or words, in constitutions and legislations, are filled with the spirit of the age (*Zeitgeist*), which is its meaning.

> The whole system of interactions of the age is determined from within by the links between life, the world of feelings, valuations and goals. Every activity which becomes part of this context is historical; the context forms the horizon of the age and, through it, finally, the meaning of every part in the system of the age is determined.[38]

The consideration of different ages and periods in history leads to the question of the great changes involved in the transition from one age to another. Each age, Dilthey says, refers back to the preceding one, which contains not only its own peculiar active forces but also strivings and creative activities preparing for the new age. There are "inner connections" between one age and the next, as there are in all of life and history, but it is a mistake to see these connections as the development of some rational purpose. "It is a dream of Hegel's that the ages present stages in the development of reason." There is change from age to age in history, because of the insatiability of human needs, on the one hand, and the finiteness of every shape or configuration that historical life takes as answers to these needs, on the other.

> Every configuration of historical life is finite and, therefore, contains, balanced against each other, joyful power and pressure, expansion and narrowness of existence, satisfaction and deprivation, giving rise

to power tensions and redistribution; thus actions constantly arise . . .
only at a few points of historical life is there momentary calm. . . .
History is movement.

From this combination of momentary calm with ideals realized and
harmonized and the insatiable needs of man forever springing into creative yet disturbing activity "the essential nature of history is revealed.
It is based on irrational factuality. . . ."[39]
And thus we come to the final question, the meaning of history as
a whole. Dilthey unconditionally rejects any attempt, such as that of
Hegel or Comte, to find a general direction in the movement of universal
history from which a meaning of the historical world might be derived.
"The whole search for the goal of history is completely one-sided."

> The manifest meaning of history must, first of all, be sought in what
> is always present, in what always recurs in the structural relations, in
> the patterns of interaction, in the formation of values and purposes
> in them, in the inner order in which they are related to each other,
> that is, in everything from the structure of the individual life up to
> the last all-embracing unit; this is the meaning which history always
> has; it rests on the structure of the individual existence and reveals
> itself through the objectifications of life, in the composite patterns
> of interactions. This regularity determines the past development and
> the future is subject to it.[40]

But is this the last word on the matter of the meaning of history?
"Are the experienced connections, the experienced values, meaning and
purpose the last word of the historian?" At this point plain and unvar-
nished historicism appears. "The historian cannot renounce the attempt
to understand history from within. . . ."[41] Dilthey decisively rejects interventions by philosophers of transcendental leaning like Rickert into the
empirical sphere of the historian. History is indeed aware of the postulating
of something unconditional as value, norm, or good in various ages,
but it knows nothing of their universal validity. "If we eliminate the
foundation in transcendental philosophy there is no method for ascertaining unconditional norms, values or purposes. There are only those which
claim unconditional validity, but which, because of their origin, are
tainted with relativity."[42] The understanding of history "from within"
leads inevitably to "the total recognition of the immanence to historical
consciousness of even the unconditionally held values and norms."

> The historical consciousness of the finitude of every historical phe-
> nomenon, of every human or social condition and of the relativity of
> every kind of faith, is the last step towards the liberation of man.
> With it man achieves the sovereignty to enjoy every experience to
> the full and surrender himself to it unencumbered, as if there were
> no system of philosophy or faith to tie him down. Life is freed from

knowledge through concepts; the mind becomes sovereign over the cobwebs of dogmatic thought. Everything beautiful, everything holy, every sacrifice relived and interpreted, opens perspectives which disclose some part of reality. And equally, we accept the evil, horrible and ugly, as filling a place in the world, as containing some reality which cannot be conjured away. And, in contrast to relativity, the continuity of creative forces asserts itself as the central historical fact.[43]

NOTES

1. Biographical details on Dilthey appear in W. Kluback, *Wilhelm Dilthey's Philosophy of History* (New York: Columbia University Press, 1956), pp. 1–51. In addition to Kluback's work, there are valuable expositions of Dilthey's thought in H. A. Hodges, *Wilhelm Dilthey, An Introduction* (London: K. Paul, 1944), and *The Philosophy of Wilhelm Dilthey* (London: Routledge, 1952) and H. P. Rickman, *Pattern and Meaning in History* (New York: Harper & Row, 1962). The latter work contains a translation of approximately one third of Dilthey's final thought on history, which is assembled in Volume VII of Dilthey's works, published by the Teubner Verlag, Stuttgart. Rickman's work was originally published by George Allen and Unwin, London, 1961, under the title of *Meaning in History*.

2. W. Dilthey, *Gesammelte Schriften*, Vol. I, p. xviii, trans. H. Holborn, "Wilhelm Dilthey and the Critique of Historical Reason," *Journal of the History of Ideas*, Vol. XI (1950), p. 100.

3. Dilthey, *Gesammelte Schriften*, Vol. VII, p. 261, Rickman trans., p. 72. An excellent analysis of Dilthey's theory of history is given by Rickman (pp. 14–63).

4. Dilthey, *Gesammelte Schriften*, Vol. VII, p. 256, Rickman trans., p. 163. See Kluback, pp. 54–56. A detailed exposition of Dilthey's theory of knowledge is given by Hodges, *The Philosophy of Wilhelm Dilthey*, pp. 26–71.

5. Dilthey, *Gesammelte Schriften*, Vol. VII, p. 79, Rickman trans., p. 68.

6. See Dilthey, *Gesammelte Schriften*, Vol. VII, pp. 134–136, Rickman trans., pp. 78–80.

7. See Hodges, *The Philosophy of Wilhelm Dilthey*, pp. 259–260.

8. Dilthey, *Gesammelte Schriften*, Vol. VII, p. 135, Rickman trans., p. 79.

9. Dilthey, *Gesammelte Schriften*, Vol. VII, pp. 80–81, Rickman trans., p. 69.

10. See Dilthey, *Gesammelte Schriften*, Vol. VII, p. 191, and Rickman, pp. 37–43. The concept of *Verstehen* or "interpretative understanding" entered decisively into German sociology through Max Weber and remains a distinguishing feature. See R. Aron, *German Sociology* (New York: Free Press of Glencoe, 1964), pp. 75–78, 109–110. An outstanding proponent among American sociologists is Pitirim Sorokin, as we shall see in a later chapter.

11. Hodges, *The Philosophy of Wilhelm Dilthey*, p. 118; see also pp. 116–128. Hodges notes the similarity between Bergson's concept of intuition and that of understanding in Dilthey, but the differences between the two are even more noteworthy. Bergson holds that the passage from intuition to concept

is a distortion of the lived experience or reality, while Dilthey believes that the more abstract forms of thought can be, in their own way, a true reflection of mental reality. Knowledge, as distinct from understanding, can widen experience by inferences far beyond the range of understanding, but wherever knowledge advances it must take understanding with it, and it can never exhaust the combined data of lived experience and understanding. Hodges cites an illuminating text from Dilthey on this subject. "There is no scientific process which could leave this living reproduction behind it as a subordinate moment. Here is the mother earth to which even the most abstract operations in the human studies must constantly return to draw their strength. Understanding here can never be transmuted into rational conception. It is vain to try to make the hero or the man of genius intelligible by appeal to all kinds of circumstantialities. The most proper approach to him is the most subjective. For the highest possibility of grasping what was powerful in him lies in the lived experiences of his effects upon ourselves, in the permanent conditioning of our own life by him. Ranke's Luther . . . proceeded from such a relation to the living power of a hero," Dilthey, *Gesammelte Schriften*, Vol. V, p. 278, in Hodges, *The Philosophy of Wilhelm Dilthey*, p. 128.

12.　　Dilthey, *Gesammelte Schriften*, Vol. V, p. 332, in Hodges, *The Philosophy of Wilhelm Dilthey*, p. 129.

13.　　Dilthey, *Gesammelte Schriften*, Vol. VII, p. 320, in Rickman, pp. 116–121.

14.　　Dilthey, *Gesammelte Schriften*, Vol. VII, pp. 320–321, in Hodges, *The Philosophy of Wilhelm Dilthey*, p. 132.

15.　　Dilthey, *Gesammelte Schriften*, Vol. V, p. 278, in Hodges, *The Philosophy of Wilhelm Dilthey*, p. 141.

16.　　See Hodges, *The Philosophy of Wilhelm Dilthey*, pp. 129–142, and Kluback, pp. 15–19, 75–78, where the influence of Schleiermacher's practice and theory of hermeneutics on that of Dilthey is observed.

17.　　Dilthey, *Gesammelte Schriften*, Vol. VII, pp. 147–148, in Hodges, *The Philosophy of Wilhelm Dilthey*, pp. 263–264.

18.　　Dilthey, *Gesammelte Schriften*, Vol. VII, p. 150 f, in Rickman, pp. 126–127.

19.　　Dilthey, *Gesammelte Schriften*, Vol. VII, p. 209, Rickman trans., p. 120.

20.　　See Rickman, pp. 24, 115, and Hodges, *The Philosophy of Wilhelm Dilthey*, pp. 267–269.

21.　　Dilthey, *Gesammelte Schriften*, Vol. VII, pp. 155–156, Rickman trans., pp. 129–131.

22.　　See Dilthey, *Gesammelte Schriften*, Vol. VII, pp. 161–162, in Rickman, pp. 140–141; also pp. 137–138, 143, 151–152, 259–260, in Rickman, pp. 81–82, 94, 127–128, 164–165.

23.　　Dilthey, *Gesammelte Schriften*, Vol. VII, p. 155, in Rickman, p. 131.

24.　　Dilthey, *Gesammelte Schriften*, Vol. VII, p. 192.

25.　　Dilthey, *Gesammelte Schriften*, Vol. VII, p. 232, Rickman trans., p. 105.

26.　　Dilthey, *Gesammelte Schriften*, Vol. VII, p. 73, Rickman trans., pp. 99–100.

27.　　Dilthey, *Gesammelte Schriften*, Vol. VII, p. 255, Rickman trans., p. 162.

28.　　Dilthey, *Gesammelte Schriften*, Vol. VII, pp. 233–235, Rickman trans., pp. 106–107; see also pp. 261–262, 319–322. See also Hodges, *The Philosophy of Wilhelm Dilthey*, pp. 142–147. Dilthey further observes that "the significance which a fact receives as a fixed link in the meaning of the whole is a relation in life and not an intellectual one. . . . The significance emerges from life itself," *Gesammelte Schriften*, Vol. VII, p. 240, Rickman trans., p. 75. And again, "Life does not mean anything other than itself. There is nothing in it which points to a meaning beyond it," *Gesammelte Schriften*, Vol. VII, p. 234, Rickman trans., p. 107.

29. Dilthey, *Gesammelte Schriften*, Vol. VII, pp. 198–201, Rickman trans., pp. 85–89.

30. Dilthey, *Gesammelte Schriften*, Vol. VII, p. 232, Holborn trans., p. 108.

31. See Dilthey, *Gesammelte Schriften*, Vol. VII, pp. 71–72, in Rickman, pp. 97–98, and Hodges, *The Philosophy of Wilhelm Dilthey*, p. 272. Dilthey distinguished between time in nature, or linear time, and time in history, or concrete time. Time in nature is like "a line consisting of parts of equal value"; whereas concrete time "consists . . . of the uninterrupted progress of the present, what was present constantly becoming the past, and the future becoming the present. The present is the filling of a moment of time with reality . . . ," *Gesammelte Schriften*, Vol. VII, p. 72.

32. Dilthey, *Gesammelte Schriften*, Vol. VII, p. 233, Rickman trans., p. 106.

33. Dilthey, *Gesammelte Schriften*, Vol. VII, p. 341, Rickman trans., pp. 163–164.

34. Dilthey, *Gesammelte Schriften*, Vol. VII, p. 251, Rickman trans., pp. 92–93.

35. Dilthey, *Gesammelte Schriften*, Vol. VII, p. 135, Rickman trans., p. 79.

36. Dilthey, *Gesammelte Schriften*, Vol. VII, pp. 134–135, Rickman trans., pp. 78–79; see also Hodges, *The Philosophy of Wilhelm Dilthey*, pp. 286–287. One listing given by Dilthey of the cultural systems runs as follows: "the simplest and most homogeneous systems of interaction . . . are education, economic life, law, politics, religion, social life, art, philosophy, science." He also enumerates certain characteristics of such systems and is careful to observe that none of the systems, nor, it would seem, even the ensemble, includes the whole of the individual; see (*Gesammelte Schriften*, Vol. III, pp. 165 f, as in Rickman, pp. 145 f.)

37. See Dilthey, *Gesammelte Schriften*, Vol. VII, pp. 169–171, Rickman trans., pp. 149–151, 282–285, where Dilthey rejects any such notion as "a real super-individual unit, whether this unit is determined transcendentally or in terms of racial psychology."

38. Dilthey, *Gesammelte Schriften*, Vol. VII, pp. 185–187, Rickman trans., pp. 155–156.

39. Dilthey, *Gesammelte Schriften*, Vol. VII, pp. 287–288, Rickman trans., pp. 157–158; see also p. 187, in Rickman, pp. 156–157.

40. Dilthey, *Gesammelte Schriften*, Vol. VII, pp. 172–173, Rickman trans., p. 161; see also Hodges, *The Philosophy of Wilhelm Dilthey*, pp. 299–304.

41. Dilthey, *Gesammelte Schriften*, Vol. VII, p. 173.

42. Dilthey, *Gesammelte Schriften*, Vol. VII, p. 289, Rickman trans., p. 166. Dilthey himself says that "the individual is an intrinsic value in the mind-affected world; indeed it is the only intrinsic value we can ascertain beyond doubt," *Gesammelte Schriften*, Vol. VII, p. 212, as in Rickman, p. 111. Returning again to this problem, Dilthey states: "History itself produces principles which are valid because they make the relations contained in life explicit. Such

principles are the obligation which is based on a contract and the recognition of the dignity and value of every individual simply as a man. These truths are universally valid because they impart order to every aspect of the historical world," *Gesammelte Schriften*, Vol. VII, p. 262, Rickman trans., p. 74. Rickman, pp. 58–59, points to Dilthey's continuing concern with historical relativism and summarizes there the two lines of argumentation that Dilthey uses to justify his holding to the intrinsic value of the individual. Time and again Hodges, in *The Philosophy of Wilhelm Dilthey*, refers to this facet of Dilthey's thought; see, e.g., pp. 147, 244, 303–304, 324, 352 f, 356 f.

43.   Dilthey, *Gesammelte Schriften*, Vol. VII, pp. 290–291, Rickman trans., pp. 167–168. Dilthey, of course, is aware that philosophizing is compounded of two distinct activities, the critical analysis of the foundations of knowledge and the drive toward the formulation and speculative development of *Weltanschauungen*, or the metaphysical endeavor. His *Critique of Historical Knowledge* is devoted to the first of these philosophical problems, while its conclusion points to the relativity and historicity of the supposed universally valid principles to which the second of the problems might appeal for foundation. Yet in "The Dream," a lecture delivered on the occasion of his seventieth birthday, something of a different accent emerges. There three types of philosophy are presented: materialism or positivism, classical or objective idealism, and a middle view—that of Dilthey—the idealism of liberty and freedom. Then Dilthey expressed this opinion: "Every world-view is conditioned historically and therefore limited and relative. A frightful anarchy of thought appears. The very historical consciousness that has brought forth this absolute doubt, however, is able to set limits for it. The world views are divided by an inner law. . . . These types of world views exist along side each other through the centuries. The liberating element here is that the world views are grounded in the nature of the universe and in the relationship between the finite perceptive mind and the universe. Thus each world view expresses within its limitations one aspect of the universe. In this respect each is true. Each, however, is one-sided. To contemplate all the aspects in their totality is denied to us. We see the pure light of truth only in various broken rays. . . . Historical consciousness shatters the last chains that philosophy and the natural sciences could not break. Man has now achieved freedom. . . . Confidently we may recognize in each of these world views an element of truth. And if the course of our life brings us closer to a particular aspect of the incomprehensible harmony, if the truth of the world view which this particular aspect expresses fills us with creativity, then we may quietly surrender. For truth is present in them all." The entire text is to be found in *Gesammelte Schriften*, Vol. VIII, pp. 218–224, and has been translated by Kluback, pp. 103–109. Kluback's translation is also reproduced in its entirety in H. Meyerhoff, *The Philosophy of History in Our Time* (New York: Doubleday, 1959), pp. 37–43.

7

PHILOSOPHY-HISTORY:

Benedetto Croce

Benedetto Croce almost completely dominated Italian literary and philosophical life during the first half of the twentieth century. Immensely well read and in large measure self-educated, Croce spent the greater part of his long life in Naples as a private scholar with neither university degree nor academic status, independent financially as well as intellectually. The range of his thought was truly encyclopedic, and by the end of his life his writings numbered over sixty volumes. As a young scholar he enthusiastically studied the antiquities of Naples, thus coming to a knowledge of the historian's craft through painstaking and detailed historical investigation. By 1893 the young antiquarian was becoming more and more interested in a theoretical understanding of the historian's work, that is, in the critical philosophy of history. He read Vico's *New Science* for the first time as well as the works of outstanding German authorities in the field such as Dilthey. The result was the first of his theoretical writings on history, an essay entitled, "History Subsumed under the General Concept of Art." There Croce expressed his opinion on the nature of history in very simple terms. "Historical writing does not elaborate concepts, but reproduces particular events in their concreteness; and for that reason we have denied it the character of a science. It is therefore easy . . . to conclude that if history is not science it must be art."[1] In 1902 Croce was still repeating the same thesis in his *Aesthetic.*

History does not search for concepts, nor does it create concepts; it does not deduce, nor does it induce, but it directs itself *ad nar-*

123

randum, but not ad demonstrandum; it does not create universals and
abstractions, but pure intuitions. The hic et nunc and the individuum
omnimode determinatum is the realm of both art and history. Therefore history is reduced to the universal concept of art.[2]

In his first theory about history Croce had identified the individuality
of history and art, though he did hold that history was distinct from art as
the narration of the real from the narration of that which is possible only.
From 1895 to 1899 Croce was engaged in studies of Marxism; in 1899 he
published Historical Materialism, which was critical of Marxian theory, and
went on to deny the possibility of a deterministic philosophy of history.
Several years later appeared his first systematic work in philosophy, the
Aesthetic, which was followed shortly by the first version of his Logic.
After these publications, Croce decided it was time to become better
acquainted with the work of Hegel, Marx's philosophical master. In 1906
he published the results of these reflections under the title, "What Is
Living and What Is Dead in Hegel's Philosophy." Under the influence of
Hegelianism, Croce felt that he should write a multivolumed Philosophy
of the Spirit, the first two volumes consisting of revised versions of the
Aesthetic and Logic, with the series being rounded out by volumes on
economics and morals (practical philosophy) and on historiography. By
1913, with the publication of the volume on history, History: Theory and
Practice, the "systematic" phase of Croce's writing career was over. From
this time on he shied away from further syntheses, though volume after
volume of later thoughts continued to appear, consisting principally of
historical works, essays, observations, and so on. In the meantime Croce
had arrived at a new theory about the nature of history which appeared
first in the revised Logic of 1909 and was more fully developed in the
volume on historiography.[3] He no longer viewed history as a form of art
but identified it with philosophy, and this view remained Croce's principal
thesis concerning the nature of history.

> The conception of history that we have reached—namely, that which
> has not its documents outside itself, but in itself, which has not its
> final and causal explanation outside itself, but within itself, which
> has not philosophy outside itself, but coincides with philosophy,
> which has not the reason for its definite form and rhythm outside
> itself but within itself—identifies history with the act of thought it-
> self, which is always philosophy and history together. . . .[4]

Historicism reached its apogee in this conclusion, and one can understand why Croce claimed that his historicism was a complete and perfected
type as compared to that of Ranke. Furthermore, the tables had been
turned on Hegel himself, who "aimed at resolving history into philosophy,"
while Croce believed that he had succeeded in "resolving philosophy into
history, considering it as an abstract moment of historical thought itself.

. . ." Such a resolution was possible only within the confines of Croce's logic and idealistic philosophy.

> The modern theory of logic has withdrawn philosophy from heaven or from the peak on which it practised its sterile contemplation of the Ideas. It has invited and constrained it to descend toward the earth, while, in the same act, it has withdrawn history from its lowly function as a collector of anecdotes, a chronicler of what happens, and has raised it toward heaven or the peak of the Ideas, making it meet philosophy half-way, embrace it and mingle with it into a new spiritual personality.[5]

Hence a brief look at the logic and idealist frame within which the new personality of philosophy-history emerged will not be out of place.

The Idealistic Logic

Though Croce was by no means a thoroughly disciplined follower of Hegel, there is little question that the German philosopher was responsible for prominent features of Croce's thought. Croce himself described his philosophy as the "philosophy of spirit." In this view mind or spirit alone is real, and there is no reality that is not spirit. Spirit is creative and its creativity consists in the interpretation of its dynamic, concrete self, which is reality.

> When being is conceived as something external to the human spirit, and knowledge as separable from its object, so that the object could exist without being known, it is evident that the existence of the object becomes a datum, something, as it were placed before the spirit. . . . Philosophy as we go on unfolding it, shows that there is nothing outside the spirit, and there are therefore no data confronting it. The same conceptions of the external, mechanical and natural world are not external data but data of the same spirit. The spirit fashions that so-called "eternal" world.[6]

The activity of spirit can be distinguished into two fundamental types, Croce held, the theoretical and the practical, or the activities of knowing and doing. The theoretical or knowing activity of spirit is an active process with two forms, one intuitional the other conceptual, or, as Croce names them, aesthetic and logic. Aesthetical knowledge is knowledge of the individual arrived at by the use of the imagination and it produces images. Logical knowledge, on the other hand, is knowledge through the intellect and of the universal, and it produces concepts. The practical activity of the spirit has two forms also, economic, as Croce labels it, and ethical or moral. Economic activity is directed to the useful, while ethical or moral activity is directed to the good. Thus the four activities of spirit are directed toward the beautiful and the true, the useful and the good. These four are distinct, pure, universal concepts, each giving us the whole of reality under one aspect.

Conceptual thinking, as opposed to intuitional, is characteristic of the second and major type of the theoretical activity of spirit. It universalizes what is given in intuition, and concepts are not possible without intuition. Yet it is conceptual thinking alone that bears the fullness of the cognitive activity of the spirit.

> Expressivity, universality, and concreteness are . . . the three charac-
> teristics of the concept. . . . Expressivity affirms that the concept is
> a cognitive act, and denies that it is merely practical. . . . Universality
> affirms that it is a cognitive act *sui generis*, the logical act, and denies
> that it is an intuition . . . or a group of intuitions. . . . Concreteness
> affirms that the universal logical act is also a thinking of reality, and
> denies that it can be universal and void, universal and inexistent. . . .[7]

The pure concept is neither feeling nor intuition but thought, and thus it is distinguished from aesthetical activity or from any immediate knowledge or a logical experience. Furthermore, the pure concept is universal and concrete, or concretely universal and universally concrete, and thus distinguished from pseudoconcepts, which are either concrete without being universal or universal without being concrete. Concrete universality or immanent transcendence as a characteristic of the pure concept at once assures its reality and its rationality.

Croce calls the concepts of natural science and of mathematics pseudoconcepts. The pseudoconcepts of natural science are concrete but not universal, while those of mathematical science are universal but not concrete. A scientific concept, say of house, cat, or rose, represents a group of objects but is merely a class name. Certain common qualities are abstracted from all existing houses or cats or roses and taken as representative of the class, or some particular characteristic is employed for the same purpose. In either case the concept thus fashioned is concrete but not universal. In mathematical science, on the other hand, the concepts may be universal but are not concrete or real. Wherever reality is thinkable, and as far as thought can reach, the concept of triangle with its properties is valid. Yet such concepts lack reality and concreteness, for nowhere in reality is there an existent corresponding to them. Thus Croce concludes that the mathematico-natural sciences consist of thought about pseudoconcepts or fictions.[8]

If this is so, then one can say that neither truth nor error is to be found in these disciplines but only a practical value or usefulness. The natural and mathematical sciences are not knowledge but action, not cognitive activity but utilitarian, not part of theoretical or thinking activity of spirit but rather pertaining to the practical activity of spirit, namely, that called economic. The natural sciences measure and calculate, fashion classes and types, and formulate laws, but all of this is done to manipulate reality to our purposes and is not thought or knowledge at all.

> What are called cognitions about natural things are not properly cognitions, but abstractions executed upon the living reality of the world, being abstractions, they are the product of a practical operation, in which things are stamped and marked in order that they may be found again and used when necessary, not in order that they may be understood. Rather does that very act of abstraction make them unintelligible, external things, soulless objects, blind forces without the spirit that moves them. They become things which are ordered and classified, placed in relationship among each other, measured, calculated, and not known at all. Such is the operation of the so-called natural sciences.[9]

Thinking of the pure concepts pertains to philosophy and history, though in different ways. "The thinking of the pure concept, of the concept as itself, of the universal that is truly universal and not mere generality or abstraction is Philosophy, and Philosophy cannot be otherwise defined than as the thinking, or the conceiving of the pure concept." Croce goes on to observe that pure concepts can be expressed in two ways, one characteristic of philosophy, the other of history. "Since the pure concept can be expressed either in the form of definition or in that of universal judgment, there corresponds to this duplication the distinction of the two forms of knowing, Philosophy in the strict sense, and History."[10] But as his thought progresses, Croce no longer seems to hold for two forms of knowing but for one sole form of philosophy-history. There are inseparable elements of universal truth and contingent or individual truth in every judgment and thought. Even pure definitions, which pertain to philosophy, have an individual or historical element about them. On the other hand, the universal (individual) judgment or historical judgment has a predicate, which is a universal capable of definition, and a subject, in which the universal is realized or incarnated. Philosophy provides the pure concepts capable of serving as predicates to the historical judgment, which is at once both individual and universal.

> Philosophy and history are not two forms, they are one sole form: they are not mutually conditioned but identical. The *a priori* synthesis which is the reality of the individual judgment and of the definition, is also the reality of philosophy and history.[11]

The New Historiography

"Every history is contemporary history." Croce aimed this paradoxical statement directly at the "detached" historians of the Rankean school who would have one believe that the writing of history demanded such an impartiality and objectivity that no present affection or attachment should influence the assessment of the past. Croce's viewpoint in this matter is principally that of the historian reconstructing and narrating the past rather than seeing history as past actuality. "If we think rigorously, the term 'contemporaneous' can be applied only to that history which comes into being immediately after the act which is being accomplished, as consciousness of the act." Consequently, he repudiates the common distinction between contemporary history, or history of the immediate past, and noncontemporary history, history of the more remote past. All historical writing and narration, whether of the immediate or remote past, flows from some present interest or purpose. "Only an interest in the life of the present can move one to investigate past fact. Therefore this past fact does not answer to a past interest, but to a present interest, insofar as it is unified with an interest of the present life." But this is not all that Croce intends to convey by the proposition that all history has the intrinsic characteristic of contemporaneity. Bound up essentially with the present interest of the historian is what is called a "re-living" of the event in question, or "an internal vital evocation." Without this vital and imaginative activity on the part of the historian there is no true history, since "the condition of its existence is that the deed of which the history is told must vibrate in the soul of the historian, or (to employ the expression of professed historians) that the documents are before the historian and that they are intelligible."[12] It is not possible to write a history for which documents are lacking, for it would be an unverifiable history and thus not history at all, but documents alone are in no way sufficient. "Critical exposition of the document, intuition and reflection, consciousness and auto-consciousness," all of these are necessary if true history is desired. Without artistic experience of the great masterpieces of the past how can one write a history of painting? "Without the capacity for living again, or rather an actual living again of these particular states of the individual soul" how can anyone hope to write a history of some custom or practice of a previous age?[13] There is an indissoluble link between life and history, or document and historical writing, and if this link is broken, then whatever the result, it will not be history. This link is the capacity to relive and rethink the past experience and event as it happened.

The link between life and history, between document and historical narrative, is broken in many instances, one of which is the chronicle. Heretofore, Croce believes, the distinction between chronicle and history has not been made properly.

> The truth is that chronicle and history are not distinguishable as two forms of history . . . but as two different spiritual attitudes. History is living chronicle, chronicle is dead history; history is con-

temporary history, chronicle is past history; history is principally an act of thought, chronicle an act of will. Every history becomes chronicle when it is no longer thought, but only recorded in abstract words, which were once upon a time concrete and expressive.

In some cases all that chronicles bequeath to posterity is a series of names, and no reliving of the events or experiences in question is possible. Such is the case of the history of Hellenic painting, where all that survives is a list of artists' names without the works of art. Another example is chronicles composed by one who simply lists events chronologically without adverting to their content or his experience of them. One cannot relive what is not given in such a chronicle. Or it may even be a question of the chronicler recording events he had not experienced nor understood. Again no reliving of these events is possible to the historian. If all of this is true, then the chronicle does not have priority over history. "First comes history, then chronicle. First comes the living being, then the corpse; and to make history the child of chronicle is the same thing as to make the living be born from the corpse, which is the residue of life, as chronicle is the residue of history."[14] Here Croce has passed from the concept of history as record to that of history as actuality. Unquestionably, the past was first lived, and then recorded, if only ineptly, in chronicles.

It is an easy step from here to a similar view concerning the whole of the class of "sources" which the historian uses. If history separated from the living reality becomes dead chronicle, so too the document itself, when separated from life, becomes a dead thing. The sources of the historian are not extrinsic to historical criticism and synthesis but are truly constituted as such, that is, as living, by the historian.

> Document and criticism, life and thought, are the true sources of history—that is to say, the two elements of historical synthesis; and as such, they do not stand face to face with history, or face to face with the synthesis . . . but they form part of it and are constituted by it. Hence the idea of a history with its sources outside itself is another fancy to be dispelled, together with that of history being the opposite of chronicle. The two erroneous fancies converge to form one. Sources, in the extrinsic sense of the empiricists, are equally with chronicle, which is a class of those things, not anterior but posterior to history.[15]

Croce, of course, is aware that no history can be written or relived without the sources. He willingly concedes that the collection of documents and the preservation of the remains of the past are of inestimable service for the true historian. The moment will come when the documents will live again and be present to the spirit of the true craftsman. Great tracts of history which now exist only as dead chronicle and many documents which now are mute one day will live and speak again. None of this is fully understandable, Croce holds, unless his fundamental idealist principle is granted.

> It will be impossible ever to understand anything of the effective process of historical thought unless we start from the principle that the spirit itself is history, maker of history at every moment of its existence, and also the result of all anterior history. Thus the spirit bears with it all its history, which coincides with itself. To forget one aspect of history and remember another is nothing but the rhythm of the life of the spirit. . . . The spirit, so to speak, lives again its own history without those external things called narrative and documents; but those external things are instruments that it makes for itself, acts preparatory to that internal vital evocation in whose process they are resolved.[16]

Not only does the historian through an elaborate reliving and re-thinking process constitute his sources as such but he can be said to "create" the historical fact.

> A fact is historical insofar as it is thought, and since nothing exists outside thought, there can be no sense whatsoever in the question, What are historical facts and what are non-historical facts? A non-historical fact would be a fact that has not been thought and would therefore be non-existent. . . .[17]

The historian is never faced with the problem of choosing among several facts, because his interest is in a special problem of the past for which there is one solution, "a problem that generates other problems, but is never a problem of choice between two or more facts, but on each occasion a creation of the unique fact, the fact thought."[18] In this fashion Croce neatly sidesteps at once two great problems of the working historian: the problem of selectivity from an infinitude of facts and the question of certitude in the results. There is no infinity of facts from which the his-torian is forced to select in Croce's opinion, for the historian creates the historical fact by his reliving and rethinking it. This process bears within itself the highest form of certainty and assurance. "How could that which is a present producing of our spirit ever be uncertain?"[19]

If Croce's theory about the nature of historical thinking is correct, then a number of historical attitudes and the "histories" produced in accord with them must be censured. These "psuedo-histories" are of three kinds: philological history, poetical history, and practistical, or rhetorical, history. By philological history Croce means the brand of history practiced in Germany after the 1820s, history "without truth and without passion." Practitioners of this type of history need have no experience or affinity with their subject, and, in truth, are encouraged to lay aside any personal interest they might have as an obstacle to impartiality and objectivity. Furthermore, they view their sources as extrinsic and given, though they do test authorities quite severely and accept only those worthy of faith. It is quite clear that this procedure is at odds with Croce's notion of "contemporary history." The results of the philological historian are comparable to that of the dead chronicle. "It is always a question of faith, that is of the thought of others and of thought belonging to the past, and not of criticism, that is to say, of our own thought in the act. . . . Hence philological history can certainly be *correct*, but not *true*. . . ."[20]

The poetical historian goes to another extreme, substituting "sentiment" for the lack of interest of the philological historian, and "aesthetic coherence" for the truly logical one. Here Croce is confronting a view not altogether unlike the one he himself held earlier when he regarded history as a form of art. The indifference of the philological historian seems to be overcome by a criterion of values used by the poetical historian, but they are "values of sentiment" and not true values, which are "values of thought."

> Since history is history of the spirit, and since spirit is value, and indeed the only value that it is possible to conceive, history is clearly always history of values, and since the spirit becomes transparent to itself as thought in the consciousness of the historian, the value that rules the writing of history is the value of thought. . . .

The interest of the poetical historian is also misconceived, as it is not "that of life which becomes thought, but of life which becomes intuition and imagination."[21] It is eminently clear that Croce considers imagination an indispensable feature of historical thinking and synthesis; indeed, he believes that without it historical thought is sterile and empty. Yet necessary as imaginative reliving of the past is for the historian, it is not the whole of the process but must culminate in a rethinking or in thought. Hence it is radically distinct from the free poetic imagination.

> We have demanded the vivid experience of the events whose history we have undertaken to relate, which also means their re-elaboration as intuition and imagination. Without this imaginative reconstruction or integration it is not possible to write, read, or understand history. . . . The imagination that is inseparable from the historical synthesis [is] the imagination in and for thought, the concreteness of thought, which is never an abstract concept, but always a relation and judgment. . . .[22]

Croce swiftly disposes of practistical history, or rhetorical history with its various practical ends related to education and instruction. This kind of history is composed of two elements, history proper and a practical end, converging into one, which is the practical act. Moral education, the end of practistical history, pertains properly to the practical activity of spirit, which is ethical. History proper pertains to the theoretical and knowing activity of spirit, which is conceptual and culminates in thought.

On the same principles that Croce has rejected the history of some historians, philological, poetical, and practistical, and distinguished history proper from chronicle, he severely castigates the so-called histories of nature. "The history of historians has always the individually determinate as its object and proceeds by internal reconstruction, whereas that of the naturalists depends upon types and abstractions and proceeds by analogies."[23] We have already seen what Croce thinks of the concepts and constructions of the natural scientist. The naturalist deals with fictitious concepts and imaginary entities, which are useful but not to be ranked along side of, nor confused with, thought or knowledge. When these fictions are set forth as historical facts and their serial order as history, all that can result is a myth. Evolutionists, for example, "run on without meeting any obstacle, from the cell, indeed from the nebula, to the French Revolution and even to the socialist movements of the nineteenth century." "Cosmological romances" is the title Croce reserves for this form of pseudohistory. "The evolutionists of today are creators of myths."[24] A further difficulty with "histories" of nature is that "internal reconstruction," an essential feature of historical thinking for Croce, is impossible with regard to natural things. It is patently impossible to imagine oneself truly as a blade of grass or as a cow and without this reliving and rethinking of the past no true history is possible. The same can be said of trying to imagine oneself in the condition of Neolithic man, or even in some states of recent man. Hence Croce consistently levels the same objection not only at natural history but also at prehistory, and in truth at every history, even the history of yesterday, if it is impossible really to think it again.[25]

Croce is much less successful in dilineating positively the characteristics of his new historiography than he is in deflating other conceptions and pseudohistories. One compact expression of his view runs as follows.

> History is thought, and, as such, thought of the universal, of the universal in its concreteness, and therefore always determined in a particular manner. There is no fact, however small it be, than can be otherwise conceived (realized and qualified) than as universal. In its most simple form—that is to say, in its essential form—history expresses itself with judgments, inseparable synthesis of individual and universal.[26]

All of this is in conformity with Croce's opinion of what constitutes true knowledge, the theoretical activity of spirit. History is the concrete-universal, the individual-universal, thought.[27] There is only one kind of judgment; it is both individual and universal, and it is identical with historical judgment and knowledge. "Every judgment is an historical judgment or, quite simply, history . . . historical judgment is not simply a variety of knowledge, but it is knowledge itself; it is the form which completely fills and exhausts the field of knowing."[28]

The exaltation of history to such a rank in the edifice of knowledge necessarily brings about the humbling of philosophy. Limited to an epistemological and methodological function, philosophy becomes a constituent element of history.

> Philosophy, in consequence of the new relation in which it has been placed, cannot of necessity be anything but the methodological moment of historiography: a dilucidation of the categories constitutive of historical judgments, or of the concepts that direct historical interpretation. And since historiography has for content the concrete life of the spirit, and this life is life of imagination and of thought, of action and morality . . . and in this variety of forms remains always one, the dilucidation moves in distinguishing between aesthetic and logic, between economic and ethic, uniting and dissolving them all in the philosophy of the spirit.[29]

The Dialectic of Progress

At first sight Croce's view of the relation between philosophy and history precludes any speculative philosophy of history. "There is neither philosophy nor history, nor philosophy of history, but history which is philosophy and philosophy which is history and intrinsic to history."[30] It is easy to understand, then, Croce's remark that the philosophy of history is dead. This view is arrived at not so much by pointing to philosophy's inclusion in history but by demonstrating the inadequacy of the theories that have been paraded as philosophies of history. Croce distinguishes between the deterministic and positivistic conception of history and the philosophy of history in a narrower sense. "The 'philosophy of history' represents the transcendental conception of the real, determinism the immanent."[31] Croce believed that the deterministic conception of history was first on the scene, but was followed inevitably by the transcendental philosophies of history.

Hippolyte Taine is taken as the representative of the deterministic and positivistic conception of history. "First collect the facts, then connect them causally; this is the way that the work of the historian is represented in the deterministic conception. . . ."[32] Croce is convinced that the inquiry after causal connections for the facts of history is a fruitless venture at best, for it sets up an infinite regression with an endless postponement of explanations. The naturalistic method must be judged a failure. The failure of positivism leads necessarily to the transcendental philosophy of history, to the renunciation of the "category of cause for another, which cannot be anything but that of end, an extrinsic and transcendental end. . . ."[33] The transcendental philosopher of history no longer searches for causal connections between facts but attempts to confer a "meaning" on the brute facts, "representing them as aspects of a transcendental process, a theophany." In Croce's estimation there is a strong strain of pure poetry running through the transcendental philosophies of history, as "facts are no longer facts but words, not reality but images." Pure poetry has its place, Croce admits, but its appearance in the philosophies of history is incongruous, history being the true conceptual knowledge of spirit, poetry a form of intuitional knowledge performed by imagination. "Images and words are placed there as ideas and facts . . . as myths: progress, liberty, economy, technique, science are myths, insofar as they are looked upon as agents external to the facts."[34]

However, Croce's criticism of the deterministic conception of history and of the transcendental philosophy of history has not yet reached the heart of the matter. Both, in the end, proceed with a false notion of history. "At bottom the false persuasion still persists that history is constructed with the 'material' of brute facts, with the 'cement' of causes, and with the 'magic' of ends, as with three successive or concurrent methods."[35] Such a view of the methodology of the historian is not that of Croce, as is clear. One must return to the true starting point of the historian, not to the facts already naturalized and disorganized but "to the mind that thinks and constructs the fact." From this starting point it is easy to see that there is no need for any further search for causes or for extrinsic ends.

> If we really do make live again in imagination individuals and events, and if we think what is within them—that is to say, if we think the synthesis of intuition and concept, which is thought in its concreteness—history is already achieved: what more is wanted? There is nothing more to seek. . . . The fact historically thought has no cause and no end outside itself, only in itself. . . .[36]

Croce's radical historicism once again shows some of its features in the last statement, but its fuller outlines stand out in his discussion of the problem of progress in history. On this question we "are concerned with the whole of reality, and with history only when it is precisely the whole of reality." Hence Croce is confronting directly the problems of a speculative philosophy of history here, and his views on the matter constitute such a philosophy of history. He even conveniently labels his position as "the dialectic conception of progress." Fundamental to this view is the notion that "development is a perpetual surpassing, which is at the same time a perpetual conservation."[37] Furthermore, it is a mistake to speak of the end of history as being extrinsic to history itself or unattained. "Where the end has been correctly conceived as internal—that is to say, all one with development itself—we must conclude that it is attained at every instant,

and at the same time not attained, because every attainment is the formation of a new prospect. . . ." If this is so, then it is incorrect to conceive
history as a passage from evil to good or from good to evil. "The true solution is that of progress understood not as a passage from evil to good . . .
but as the passage from the good to better, in which the evil is the good
itself seen in the light of the better." There are no facts or epochs in
history that are not productive in their own way, and none is to be condemned by the historian. "There are no good and evil facts, but facts that
are always good."[38]

It is a short step from the "dialectical conception of progress" to a
complete relativism.

> Every particular form, individual action, institution, work, thought,
> is destined to perish: even art . . . perished. Finally, truth itself per-
> ishes, particular and determined truth, because it is not rethinkable,
> save when included in the system of a vaster truth, and therefore at
> the same time transformed. But those who do not rise to the concep-
> tion of pure historical consideration . . . are prone to attribute the
> immortality which belongs to the spirit in universal to the spirit in
> one of its particular and determined forms. . . .[39]

In his last major theoretical writing on the theme of history Croce
put forward a conception of history as an "ethical discipline," yet he did
not abandon his historicism.[40] "Historicism . . . is the affirmation that
life and reality are history and history alone." He maintained to the end
that "reality is history and is only historically known" and that there is
"no reality beyond history which is absolute immanence." Historicism is
now conceived as the heir to humanism, for it contains in itself "liberation
from transcendence of all kinds," from transcendental religion as well as
transcendental philosophy.[41]

NOTES

1. B. Croce, "La storia ridotta sotto il concetto generale dell'arte," *Primi Saggi*
(Bari, Italy: 1919), p. 24, as cited in H. S. Hughes, *Consciousness and Society*
(New York: Random House, 1961), pp. 207–208.

2. Croce, *Estetica* (Bari, Italy: 1909), p. 32, as cited in A. A. de Gennaro,
The Philosophy of Benedetto Croce (New York: Citadel, 1961), p. 43.

3. See the excellent study of Croce in Hughes, *Consciousness and Society*,
pp. 82–89, 200–229.

4. Croce, *History: Its Theory and Practice*, trans. of *Teoria e storia della
historiografia* by D. Ainslie (New York: Harcourt, 1960), p. 117. This work was
originally published by George G. Harrap, London, 1921, under the title of *The
Theory and History of Historiography*.

5.   Croce, *History as the Story of Liberty*, trans. of *La storia come pensiero e come azione* by S. Sprigge (New York: Meridian, 1955), pp. 264, 307–308. This work was originally published by George Allen and Unwin, London, 1941.

6.   Croce, *Logic as the Science of the Pure Concept*, trans. of *Logica come scienza del concetto puro* by D. Ainslie (London: 1917), p. 110.

7.   Croce, *Logic*, pp. 44–45. See de Gennaro, pp. 7–14, 33–42.

8.   See Croce, *Logic*, pp. 23–26, 45.

9.   Croce, *History as the Story of Liberty*, p. 288.

10.   Croce, *Logic*, pp. 255–256.

11.   Croce, *Logic*, p. 324. See R. G. Collingwood, *The Idea of History* (Oxford: The Clarendon Press, 1946), pp. 194–197.

12.   Croce, *History: Its Theory and Practice*, pp. 11–12.

13.   Croce, *History: Its Theory and Practice*, pp. 14–15.

14.   Croce, *History: Its Theory and Practice*, pp. 19–20.

15.   Croce, *History: Its Theory and Practice*, pp. 23–24. Croce expands on this point in *History as the Story of Liberty*, pp. 17–18, where he writes, "the present state of my mind constitutes the material, and consequently the documentation for an historical judgment, the living documentation which I carry within myself. . . . Man is a microcosm, not in the natural sense, but in the historical sense, a compendium of universal history. The documents specifically known as such by research workers will loom very small in the total mass of documents if we bear in mind all those other documents upon which we continually rely, such as the language we speak . . . customs . . . intuition and reasoning . . . experiences. . . . Without these other documents some of our historical recollections would be difficult, nay altogether impossible. . . ."

16.   Croce, *History: Its Theory and Practice*, p. 25.

17.   Croce, *History: Its Theory and Practice*, p. 108.

18.   Croce, *History: Its Theory and Practice*, pp. 110–111; see also pp. 72–74.

19.   Croce, *History: Its Theory and Practice*, p. 15.

20.   Croce, *History: Its Theory and Practice*, p. 29. Ranke is the principal target for Croce's remarks, and he receives lengthy criticism for his "pure" historiography in *History as the Story of Liberty*, pp. 80–92.

21.   Croce, *History: Its Theory and Practice*, pp. 36–37.

22.   Croce, *History: Its Theory and Practice*, p. 39. Compare "The Imagination, the Anecdote and Historiography," in *History as the Story of Liberty*, pp. 119–124.

23.   Croce, *History: Its Theory and Practice*, p. 129.

24.   Croce, *History: Its Theory and Practice*, pp. 129–130. Consistently with his idealist philosophy Croce views the concept of nature itself as a "myth" and "abstraction." "There is not a double object before thought, man and nature, the one capable of treatment in one way, the other in another way, the first cognizable, and the second uncognizable and capable only of being constructed abstractly; but thought always thinks history, the history of reality that is one, and beyond thought there is nothing, for the natural object becomes a myth when it is affirmed as object, and shows itself in its true reality as nothing else but the human spirit itself . . . ," p. 133. In *History as the Story of Liberty*, p. 263, the following statement is made: "our proposition . . . denies the reality of nature as an abstraction, and being an abstraction, is the work of the human

mind, which posits it and projects it into an outwardness which is just the mind itself or an aspect of it."

25. See Croce, *History: Its Theory and Practice*, pp. 130–135, and *History as the Story of Liberty*, p. 289.

26. Croce, *History: Its Theory and Practice*, p. 60. Compare "The Identity of the Judgment of Events with the Knowledge of Their Genesis," in *History as the Story of Liberty*, pp. 143–145.

27. Croce, *History: Its Theory and Practice*, p. 106.

28. Croce, *History as the Story of Liberty*, p. 30.

29. Croce, *History: Its Theory and Practice*, p. 151.

30. Croce, *History: Its Theory and Practice*, p. 83.

31. Croce, *History: Its Theory and Practice*, p. 64.

32. Croce, *History: Its Theory and Practice*, pp. 64–65.

33. Croce, *History: Its Theory and Practice*, p. 67.

34. Croce, *History: Its Theory and Practice*, pp. 68–70.

35. Croce, *History: Its Theory and Practice*, p. 80.

36. Croce, *History: Its Theory and Practice*, pp. 75–76. For Croce there are no such things as "brute facts," for it is the mind that affirms their existence. "Who, as a matter of fact, affirms their existence? Precisely the spirit, at the moment when it is about to undertake the search for causes. But when accomplishing that act the spirit does not already possess the brute facts . . . and then seek the causes . . . but it makes the facts brute by that very act—that is to say, it posits them itself in that way, because it is of use to it so to posit them." Furthermore, the very search for causes in history is a naturalistic approach, with all the defects Croce assigns to the method of natural science. "The search for causes, undertaken by history, is not in any way different from the procedure of naturalism . . . which abstractly analyses and classifies reality. And to illustrate abstractly and to classify implies at the same time to judge in classifying—that is to say, to treat facts, not as acts of the spirit, conscious in the spirit that thinks them, but as external brute facts," p. 73. Croce, consequently, was contemptuous in his attitude toward "social science" and especially sociology; see S. Hughes, "The Evaluation of Sociology in Croce's Theory of History," in W. J. Cahnman and A. Boskoff (eds.), *Sociology and History* (New York: Free Press of Glencoe, 1964), pp. 128–140. Yet all of the experts are agreed that Croce's works in the field of history, many of them written after his work on the theory of history, happily conform to the traditional pattern of history writing. By this time Croce is moving toward his theory of history as an "ethical-political" discipline.

37. Croce, *History: Its Theory and Practice*, pp. 83–84; see also pp. 85–86.

38. Croce, *History: Its Theory and Practice*, pp. 85, 89. Hence, Croce argues that if a fact or an epoch seems evil, then it is because the fact or epoch has not yet been thought historically. "A fact that seems to be only evil, an epoch that appears to be one of complete decadence, can be nothing but a non-historical fact . . . one which has not been historically treated . . . ," pp. 87–88.

39. Croce, *History: Its Theory and Practice*, pp. 91–92.

40. See Croce, *History as the Story of Liberty*, pp. 15–16, 110, 287, and Hughes, *Consciousness and Society*, pp. 213–222. Circumstances in Fascist Italy forced him to become an advocate of liberal institutions and ways of life. History had become the "story of liberty."

41. See Croce, *History as the Story of Liberty*, pp. 63–65, 312–316, 32–33.

8

CRITICAL PHILOSOPHY-HISTORY:
Robin Collingwood

Like Dilthey and Croce, Robin Collingwood was at once a philosopher and historian. Professor of philosophy at Oxford, he was also an accomplished archaeologist and historian of Roman Britain. Interesting parallels have been drawn between the philosophical development of Collingwood and that of Croce. Both became dissatisfied early with the "realist" philosophers of their acquaintance because of artistic and historical interests. Both went on to study Hegel for themselves and to do competent work in history. And both found their way to a form of idealism and eventually to an identification of philosophy and history. Collingwood learned much from Croce, yet his own historical views were independently argued and more carefully worked out. Nevertheless, there is little doubt that in his final years he came very close to the historicism of Croce, following him even in the rapprochement between history and action.

Collingwood felt himself out of place among the philosophers at Oxford, who, in his opinion, were "neglecting history." He went so far as to speak of a "conspiracy of silence" about the place of the historical element in the theory of knowledge proposed there. To his "realist" contemporaries he would have liked to address these words: "Your positive doctrines about knowledge are incompatible with what happens, according to my experience, in historical research; and your critical methods are misused on doctrines which in historical fact were never held by those to whom you ascribe them." Instead of these words, Collingwood addressed a number of essays and works on the same topic to his fellow-philosophers

138

at Oxford and to the world at large. From the vantage point of his fiftieth year, he came to see that his life's work, in the main, had been "an attempt to bring about a rapprochement between philosophy and history."

> From the first . . . I was also demanding a philosophy of history. This meant, in the first instance, a special branch of philosophical inquiry devoted to the special problems raised by historical thinking. . . . But this demand for a new branch of philosophy soon developed into the demand for a new kind of philosophy.[1]

The New Historicist Logic

In *An Essay on Philosophical Method* Collingwood still distinguished between philosophy and history, but it is evident that the logic and philosophical method therein proposed is one which relies heavily on a concept derived from history which he called the "scale of forms." The central teaching of this work is the view that philosophical concepts or universals are related to one another as lower to higher in a process of development. Different forms of goodness, such as pleasure, utility, and moral goodness, for example, are not just different specifications of goodness existing side by side but are related to one another in a "scale of forms."

> Each term, which is in itself simply one specific form of goodness, has also a double relation to its neighbours: in comparison with the one below, it is what that professes to be; in comparison with the one above, it professes to be what that is. This . . . purely logical relation . . . is a synthesis of . . . four relations . . . : difference of degree, difference of kind, a relation of distinction, and relation of opposition. The higher term is a species of the same genus as the lower, but it differs in degree as a more adequate embodiment of the generic essence, as well as in kind as a specifically different embodiment; it follows from this that it must not only be distinct from it, as one specification from another, but opposed to it as a higher specification to a lower, a relatively adequate to a relatively inadequate, a true embodiment of the generic essence to a false embodiment. . . . The higher thus negates the lower, and at the same time reaffirms it: negates it as a false embodiment of the generic essence, and reaffirms its content, that specific form of the essence, as part and parcel of itself.[2]

All philosophical concepts or universals are thus interrelated among themselves somewhat like stages in an historical process, each incorporating or reaffirming in itself the notes and characteristics of its predecessors, while bearing itself some of the possibilities of its successors. Collingwood seems to hold that a definitive term is never reached in our conceptions of goodness, truth, and so on, though a relative culmination and termination is always at hand in our present conceptions.

> Each term in the scale, therefore, sums up the whole scale to that
> point. Wherever we stand in the scale, we stand at a culmination.
> Infinity as well as zero can thus be struck out of the scale, not be-
> cause we never reach a real embodiment of the generic concept, but
> because the specific form at which we stand is the generic concept
> itself, so far as our thought yet conceives it. . . . All lower stages in
> the scale are telescoped into this situation.[3]

Precisely the same notion of a "scale of forms" permeates Collingwood's views on philosophical definitions, judgments, inferences, and
philosophical systems. Of special interest is the application to philosophical
systems. The philosophy of the successful and competent philosopher
arises by "objective necessity" out of his situation in the history of thought,
and since his situation and problem are unique, the philosophy deriving
from it can never be accepted by his successors without modification.

> The philosopher in constructing a system, has place in a scale whose
> structure is such that every term in it sums up the whole scale to that
> point; however far up the scale he goes, he never comes to an abso-
> lute end of the series, because by reaching this point he already comes
> in sight of new problems; but he is always at a relative end, in the
> sense that, wherever he stands, he must know where he stands and
> sum up his progress hitherto, on pain of making no progress hence-
> forth.[4]

The same features are exhibited in the history of philosophical thought as
a whole, at any rate in its successful instances and to the perceptive historian. "All of the philosophies of the past are telescoped into the present
and constitute a scale of forms, never beginning and never ending, which
are different in degree and in kind, distinct from each other and opposed
to each other." If this is so, then there can be no such thing as a permanent system of philosophy or a perennial philosophy, at least so far as
its contents are concerned. "What is permanent and essential is not this or
that system, for every particular system is nothing but an interim report on
the progress of thought down to the time of making it. . . ."[5]

At the time of the writing of this *Essay* Collingwood still believed in
a philosophy distinct from history, but he did not work out such a philosophy himself from the principles therein laid down.[6] By 1939 he had come
to hold, like Croce, that "philosophy as a separate discipline is liquidated
by being converted into history."[7] In his *Autobiography* Collingwood
explicitly holds to the view that in studying the history of philosophy one
is not confronted with the task of answering two questions about the
thought of any philosopher, the historical question as to what in fact this
philosopher thought and the philosophical question as to whether in truth
he was right in his thought. He argues that the historical question is the
only question to be asked and only the historian can answer it. There is no

further question. Philosophy seems to have disappeared completely and only history remains. This later position developed rather easily and naturally out of the concept of a "scale of forms," but it is more immediately related to a new logic briefly expounded in the *Autobiography*, the "logic of question and answer."

By reason of his experience as an historian-philosopher, Collingwood came to believe that truth in its proper sense means that truth which can be spoken of in relation to a philosophical theory or an historical narrative as a whole. If this is granted, then no logic of bare propositions suffices but only the logic of question and answer. Truth is "something that belonged not to any single proposition, nor even . . . to a complex of propositions taken together, but to a complex consisting of questions and answers." At the center of this logic of question and answer lies the opinion that truth is the historical answer given to a certain question arising out of a particular historical situation. The concept of a "scale of forms" is already pregnant with this opinion. Hence, if one wishes to know this truth, he must place himself in the situation that gave rise to the problem it professes to answer. "Anyone who wishes to know whether a given proposition is true or false, significant or meaningless, must find out what question it was meant to answer." It is plain that only an historical inquiry can bring this off. "This question 'To what question did So-and-So intend this proposition for an answer?' is an historical question, and therefore cannot be settled except by historical methods."[8]

At this point the "realist" philosophers hurry forward with the distinction between the historical question and the philosophical question, but Collingwood is not moved by their arguments. Is there not a question other than the question of fact, the question of whether such and such a philosopher was right in his theories? This "realist" distinction is erroneous "because it presupposes the permanence of philosophical problems." Anyone who studies the history of political theory, Collingwood believed, will be convinced that the "history of political thought is not the history of different answers given to one and the same question, but the history of a problem more or less constantly changing, whose solution was changing with it." Much the same should be said of the history of personal ethics. "Ideals of personal conduct are just as impermanent as ideals of social organization. Not only that, but what is meant by calling them ideals is subject to the same change."[9] Nor must one stop at the spheres of politics and ethics, for every recognized branch of philosophy, even metaphysics, displays the same fluidity.

> Metaphysics . . . is no futile attempt at knowing what lies beyond the limits of experience, but is primarily at any given time an attempt to discover what the people of that time believe about the world's general nature; such beliefs being the presuppositions of all their "physics," that is, their inquiries into detail. Secondarily, it is the

attempt to discover the corresponding presuppositions of other peoples and other times, and to follow the historical process by which one set of presuppositions has turned into another.

Metaphysics must renounce the claim to be anything more than an historical inquiry into the "absolute presuppositions" of various times and peoples. Now truth or falsity does not apply to these presuppositions. They are matters of belief, and not answers to any questions at all. The truth or falsity of metaphysics in this historicist logic pertains only to answers about questions concerning the history of the absolute presuppositions.[10]

Hence there are no eternal problems, much less any eternal answers. There is no ground on which a distinction between the historical question and the philosophical question can be erected. Furthermore, in the interpretation of a philosopher, we come to understand the problem confronting him and his solution to it in the very act of historical inquiry. "One and the same passage states his solution and serves as evidence of what the problem was. The fact that we can identify his problem is proof that he has solved it; for we can only know what the problem was by arguing back from the solution." If truth consists in finding out what question a philosopher is trying to answer, together with the answer given, then it is achieved simultaneously with the knowledge of the fact by the historian. "For me, then, there were not two separate sets of questions to be asked, one historical and one philosophical, about a given passage in a given philosophical author. There was one set only, historical."[11] Thus it is easy to understand how Collingwood could come to the following conclusion.

> Logic is an attempt to expound the principles of what in the logician's own day passed for valid thought; ethical theories differ but none of them is erroneous, because any ethical theory is an attempt to state the kind of life regarded as worth aiming at, and the question always arises, by whom? Natural science is indeed distinct from history and, unlike philosophy, cannot be absorbed into it, but this is because it starts from certain presuppositions and thinks out their consequences, and since these presuppositions are neither true nor false, thinking these together with their consequences is neither knowledge nor error.[12]

History, it would seem, had become the only kind of knowledge possible to man. Collingwood in this way narrowly escaped from absolute scepticism, a problem he had to face at every turn in his thought.

A Critical Philosophy of History

Collingwood's critical philosophy of history appears in its clearest form in *The Idea of History*, which was put together posthumously from a number of lectures and essays by a close associate. Despite the fact that much of the layout of the work is due to the editor, the thought is everywhere Collingwood's, even the very plan of the work. Much of the matter gathered in *The Idea of History* dates from 1936 when Collingwood had not yet fully made up his mind to accept the view that philosophy had become history, no more and no less. In truth, at this time, he still distinguished between philosophy and history, as he had in *An Essay on Philosophical Method.* Firmly convinced that the theories of knowledge taught in his time at Oxford accounted only for mathematical, theological, and scientific knowledge, Collingwood was concerned about the new historical techniques springing up everywhere but unaccounted for in English philosophical thinking.

> A special inquiry was therefore needed whose task should be the study of this new problem or group of problems, the philosophical problems created by the existence of organized and systematized historical research. This new inquiry might justly claim the title philosophy of history, and it is to this inquiry that this book is a contribution.[13]

The first task in such an inquiry into the nature of historical thinking and knowledge is to delineate the proper subject matter of the historian. Now the ordinary historian conceives his subject matter as the history of human affairs only. But what is the reason for this confinement? Has not the evolutionary conception of nature, whose implications were worked out by philosophers like Bergson, Alexander, and Whitehead, abolished the distinction between human history and natural history, between historical process and natural process, and resolved nature into history? Is not the historicity of all things, natural as well as human, a thesis defended by such philosophers as Alexander?[14] If it is granted that natural processes are historical processes, then the historian needlessly and arbitrarily restricts himself to the study of human affairs; rather, he should go on to study all processes in time. Collingwood is very alive to the force of this argument, yet he decisively rejects the idea that historical processes and natural processes are one. One need but advert to the method used by the historian to see that it is not designed to solve problems of natural change and natural process, but those of human change and historical process.

A distinction must be made between the "outside" of an event and its "inside," and with this distinction in hand it will be easy to explain the historian's confinement to human affairs only. By the "outside" of an event is meant everything belonging to it that can be described in terms of bodies and their movements. By the "inside" of an event is meant that which can be described only in terms of thought. The passage of Caesar with a certain number of men on a certain date across the river called the Rubicon is the "outside" of this historical event. But the event also has an "inside." The "inside" of this crossing the Rubicon refers to Caesar's defiance of the Roman senate, which became an overt act of treason by crossing the Rubicon, the boundary between Gaul and Italy.

> The historian is never concerned with either of these to the exclusion of the other. He is investigating not mere events (where by a mere event I mean one which has only an outside and no inside) but actions, and an action is the unity of the outside and inside of an event. . . . His work may begin by discovering the outside of an event but it can never end there; he must always remember that the event was an action, and that his main task is to think himself into this action, to discern the thought of its agent.[15]

In the case of nature, the distinction between the outside and inside of an event does not arise, for natural events are mere events, not the acts of agents and having no inside. The natural scientist, like the historian, does go beyond the discovery of mere events but in a different direction. Instead of the movement from the outside of the event to the inside, the naturalist goes beyond the event by observing its relation to other events and thus attempts to bring it under a general formula or laws of nature. For the natural scientist nature is always mere phenomena and a spectacle for contemplation. The events of history, on the other hand, are never mere phenomena nor sheerly spectacles for contemplation but things to be looked through to discern the thought within them. The thought within an historical event, the action of man, is the purpose or intention of the act and expressed in it. "Reflective acts may be roughly described as the acts which we do on purpose, and these are the only acts which can become the subject-matter of history." Once the thought inside the historical event is discovered, that is, its intention or purpose, then the event is already understood and there is no need for the historian to inquire further into its causes. "When he knows what happened, he already knows why it happened."[16]

It is evident that not all human activity falls within the field of inquiry of the historian, but only those acts which have an inside, that is, thought and purpose. Collingwood excludes activity that flows from man's animal nature, from his natural appetites and impulses, from the subject matter of the historian. Such human actions are nonhistorical, being implicated in a process that is natural and not historical.

> The historian is not interested in the fact that men eat and sleep and make love and thus satisfy their natural appetites; but he is interested in the social customs which they create by their thought as a framework within which these appetites find satisfaction in ways sanctioned by convention and morality.

Collingwood suggests that psychology, if it would be true to its name, study these irrational and nonhistorical elements in man.

Mind also realizes the presence in itself of elements that are not rational. They are not body; they are mind, but not rational mind or thought. To use an old distinction, they are psyche or soul as distinct from spirit. These irrational elements are the subject-matter of psychology. They are the blind forces and activities in us . . . not parts of the historical process: sensation as distinct from thought, feelings as distinct from conceptions, appetite as distinct from will.[17]

The reflective and purposive human actions that are the subject matter of historians are not to be identified with what is called practical action. It is plain that there can be a history of politics, warfare, morals, and even of economic activity. These forms of human activity are shot through and through with plan and purpose, though one may be less than certain about the whole of economic activity. But history is not to be confined to this world of practice, as if no other human activity were pursued with plan and purpose. Art, science, philosophy, and religion are also subjects for historical treatment, because in these, no less than in the more practical activities, man proceeds according to plan and thinks with purposes in mind. In each of these spheres of what is commonly called theoretical activity of the human mind, whether it is scientific or philosophical, artistic, or religious, a certain problem or question confronts man, and his reflective, purposeful thought is the response or answer to the situation. Indeed, this is already practical activity or action in its beginnings. "To conceive a purpose or to form an intention is already a practical activity. It is not thought forming an anteroom to action; it is action itself in its initial stage."[18] One can understand why Collingwood eventually called for a new logic of question and answer from this view of thought as action. Not only for the world of practice but in every type of theoretical activity pursued by man the particular problem or question that man faces is the key to the understanding of human thought and action.

Collingwood admits that it is possible to make generalizations from the data of history to detect types and patterns of activity repeated over and over again in history, but he questions the value of such generalizations and then denies to them any universal validity. Here, of course, he is rejecting the possibility of history in the pure positivistic tradition, whether that of Comte and Spencer or that of Taine and Lamprecht, among others. If the historical event is understood from within, its purpose known in and from the historical context, then there is nothing of value left for generalization to do. "Nothing is added to our understanding of that process by the statement (however true) that similar things have happened elsewhere." As for the validity of such historical generalizations, Collingwood seems to admit that types of behavior patterns recur, so long as minds of the same kind are placed in the same kind of situation. Positivistic history, perhaps, can establish uniformities and recurrences, but it cannot guarantee that such "laws" will hold good beyond the historical period or situation to which they pertain. And if one should attempt to rise above historical periods and ages and come up with universal and unchanging conditions of human nature, delusion is the only result.

> To regard such a positive mental science as rising above the sphere of history, and establishing the permanent and unchanging laws of human nature, is therefore possible only to a person who mistakes the transient conditions of a certain historical age for the permanent conditions of human life.

The only way of investigating mind or human nature is in its historical manifestations through the methods of history. "History is what the science of human nature professed to be."[19]

Collingwood attempts to justify this view through a rather complicated and not completely consistent or finished analysis of what historical knowledge is. Fundamental to his theory of history is this proposition: "historical knowledge is the re-enactment in the historian's mind of the thought whose history he is studying."[20] Lining up alongside of Croce in this opinion, he takes a position plainly opposed to those historians who placed passivity, impartiality, and objectivity in the front ranks of the perfections possessed by the true historian. "Historical knowledge is the knowledge of what mind has done in the past, and at the same time is the redoing of this, the perpetuation of past acts in the present." The historian can truly know the past only by rethinking the same thought that created the situation under investigation, and thus come to an understanding of the situation. Hence the object of history is not something outside the mind that knows it; it is an activity on the part of the historian himself and is known only on the condition of this reenactment. "To the historian, the activities whose history he is studying are not spectacles to be watched, but experiences to be lived through in his own mind; they are objective, or known to him, only because they are subjective, or activities of his own."[21] Thought can never be mere object, for to know what someone has thought or is thinking involves thinking it for oneself. Now historical knowledge is not just concerned with the thought or purposive activity of an individual, for it is by historical thinking in the sense explained that one knows what is called the "corporate mind" of a community or an age. Furthermore, it is not restricted to knowledge of the remote past but is the type of thinking involved in knowing the thoughts of a friend and even the past thought of oneself. "Historical knowledge is the only knowledge that the human mind can have of itself. The so-called science of human nature or of the human mind resolves itself into history."[22]

Historical knowledge is self-knowledge as well, for it reveals to the historian the powers of his own mind. Since all the historian can know as a historian is thought that he can rethink for himself, the fact that he has succeeded in doing so shows him that his mind is able to think in these ways. Historical thought of this nature is to be identified with the historical process, which is a process of thoughts. In proper historical thinking the mind not only discovers within itself the possibilities of which historical thought reveals the actuality but develops these possibilities effectively by bringing them from a latent to an actual state. In such an historical process man fashions a definite human nature for himself.

> The body of human thought or mental activity is a corporate possession, and almost all the operations which our minds perform are operations which we learned to perform from others who have performed them already. Since mind is what it does, and human nature, if it is a name for anything real, is only a name for human activities, this acquisition of ability to perform determinate operations is the acquisition of a determinate human nature. Thus, the historical process is a process in which man creates for himself this or that kind of human nature by re-creating in his own thought the past to which he is heir.[23]

Clearly the historical process, as Collingwood conceives it, differs immensely from any natural process, even the evolutionary conception of natural process. Historical events differ from natural events not only in having an inside as well as an outside but because they are also part of a vastly distinct process. Here again Collingwood comes very close to the conception of historical development that he earlier labeled the scale of forms. Evolution as a natural process abolishes one specific form in producing another. "The past, in a natural process, is a past superseded and dead." Evolutionistic historians and philosophers confuse the natural process "in which the past dies in being replaced by the present, and an historical process, in which the past, so far as it is historically known, survives in the present."[24] The historical past, unlike the natural past, is a living past, kept alive by the act of historical thinking itself. In the historical process the past is "incapsulated" in the present, at least insofar as it is known. "Since the historical present includes in itself its own past, the real ground on which the whole rests, namely the past out of which it has grown, is not outside it but is included within it."[25]

Thus far Collingwood has only intimated that historical thinking is a type of scientific knowledge, but he has something further to say on this matter. In elaborating on this characteristic of historical knowledge Collingwood delivers a scathing critique of what he calls "scissors-and-paste" history, which was practiced, he holds, even by the great German critical historians of the nineteenth century. History is scientific, because "it is wholly a reasoned knowledge of what is transient and concrete."[26] If this is so, then the scientific historian cannot ape the scissors-and-paste historian, who depends completely for his knowledge on the testimony of authorities or sources. "History constructed by excerpting and combining the testimonies of different authorities I call scissors-and-paste history."[27] For such a pseudohistorian history means repeating statements that other people have made before him, and he is able to write history only if he is supplied with ready-made statements on the subjects that interest him. Even the Rankean critical historian succumbed to a form of scissors-and-paste history by reason of his ultimate dependence upon sources and authorities, however purified by the critical method. Now it is precisely this dependence on authorities that leads Collingwood to deny the title of scientific historian to any scissors-and-paste historian. He admits that the acceptance of the testimony of others is necessary for practical and everyday life, and in some instances he concedes this belief may even rate the name of knowledge. Yet belief in the testimony of others, even if honored with the title of knowledge, can never claim to be scientific knowledge. Scientific knowledge is reasoned knowledge, demands autonomous activity by its practitioner, and in the process the scientist becomes his own authority. Now this claim can be justified for the historian, if his statements are made on his own authority, and are the result of reasoning. It follows that "scientific history contains no ready-made statements at all."[28]

> By explicitly recognizing this fact it is possible to effect . . . a Copernican revolution in the theory of history: the discovery that, so far from relying on an authority other than himself, to whose statements his thoughts must conform, the historian is his own authority and his thought autonomous, self-authorizing, possessed of a criterion to which his so-called authorities must conform and by reference to which they are criticized.[29]

The autonomy of the historian can be seen at its simplest in the work of selecting from the variety of facts available to the historian. Not even the worst of historians merely copies out his authorities, for he is always leaving things out of the narrative on his own authority. Autonomous activity is even more plain in that which is called historical construction, where phases in a process not described by the authorities are interpolated by the historian. The clearest demonstration of the historian's autonomy is given by historical criticism. The historian puts his authorities on trial, questions and cross-examines them, extorting information withheld, consciously or unconsciously, in the original statements, even rejecting something explicitly told him by the authorities or sources. If this is so, then the criterion of historical truth cannot be the fact that a statement is made by an authority, for the authority itself is on trial. The criterion of historical truth is to be found in the historian himself.

In addition to selecting from his material, the historian goes beyond what his authorities tell him in two ways—in criticizing the authorities and in reconstructing phases of the past not reported by the authorities. In the latter operation the historian interpolates between statements, expressed or implied, of his authorities through the use of his imagination. Now this construction of the past which is authored by the imagination is neither fanciful nor arbitrary, since it is necessitated by evidence. To designate this activity of interpolation, with its twofold character of necessity and of being imagined, Collingwood uses the term "a *priori* imagination." This form of imagination must not be confused with the "ornamental" imagination or plain fancy. Admittedly, the latter is useful for making the historical narrative attractive, but without the "structural" or a *priori* imagination there would be no narrative to adorn. The a *priori* imagination bridges the gaps between what the authorities say, thus giving continuity to the past, but always as demanded by evidence. This structural and a *priori* imagination has other functions also. Besides the historical function, it operates in the field of art as well as in the common perceptual activity of man. Both of these forms also have the character of necessity about them just as the historical function, but the historical function differs in having as its special object the past, which is not an object of possible perception. At this point the historian's reconstruction of the past appears to be "a web of imaginative construction stretched between certain fixed points provided by the statements of his authorities." If these points are frequent enough and the threads of the web spun with due care by the historical imagination, then the whole picture appears to be verified by the data from the authorities and very close to the reality it represents.[30]

This conception, however, overlooks the crucial part played by the historical imagination in the work of historical criticism. The supposedly fixed points between which the historical imagination spins its web are not given ready-made but must be achieved by critical thinking. The web of imaginative construction cannot derive its validity from historical facts, for the historian is as responsible for the one as for the other. Through criticism of the authorities the historian accepts, rejects, modifies, or reinterprets what his authorities tell him. Thus it is the historian who is responsible for the statements he makes after criticism, that is, for the historical facts themselves. "The web of imaginative construction is something far more solid and powerful than we have hitherto realized. So far from relying for its validity upon the support of given facts, it actually serves as the touchstone by which we decide whether the alleged facts are genuine." The same a *priori* imagination which does the work of historical criticism also supplies the means of historical criticism. Statements are accepted from the sources if the picture of the past to which they lead the historian is a coherent and continuous picture, one that makes sense. It is the historian's picture of the past that justifies the very sources used in its construction.[31] Yet it is not an arbitrary picture, for it must be in accord with the evidence, but the notion of evidence must not be too narrowly construed, as if it were to be found only in the historian's sources. "The whole perceptible world . . . is potentially and in principle evidence to

the historian. It becomes actual evidence in so far as he can use it." Now
evidence of itself is historically dumb, and it becomes historical evidence
only when someone contemplates it historically and interprets it. The
principles by which the evidence is interpreted are everything the historian
knows: "historical knowledge, knowledge of nature and man, mathematical
knowledge, philosophical knowledge; and not only knowledge, but mental
habits and possessions of every kind."[32]

Nevertheless, we still have not yet arrived at the ultimate criterion of
historical truth. The historian himself is part of the historical process, and
the very principles by which evidence is interpreted are subject to change,
as well as the evidence itself.

> The historian himself, together with the here-and-now which forms
> the total body of evidence available to him, is a part of the process
> he is studying, has his own place in that process, and can see it only
> from the point of view which at this present moment he occupies
> within it.

There is no need for historical skepticism because of this, Collingwood
believes, as it is simply the discovery of another dimension of historical
knowledge, the history of history itself. However, for one who is well on his
way to equating knowledge with historical knowledge, as Collingwood is,
the question is not merely one of historical skepticism but of absolute
skepticism. Collingwood fights his way clear of this alternative by an appeal
to an innate or a priori idea of the past in man's mind. This is the ultimate
criterion of historical truth.

> That criterion is the idea of history itself: the idea of an imaginary
> picture of the past. That idea is, in Cartesian language, innate; in
> Kantian language, a priori. It is not a chance product of psycho-
> logical causes; it is an idea which every man possesses as part of the
> furniture of his mind, and discovers himself to possess in so far as
> he becomes conscious of what it is to have a mind. Like other ideas
> of the same sort, it is one to which no fact of experience exactly cor-
> responds. . . . It is the idea of the historical imagination as a self-
> dependent, self-determining, and self-justifying form of thought.[33]

Progress and History

It might be thought that Collingwood's concept of the historical
process demands progress in history and actuality as a necessity, but this
is not his opinion. We have already seen his notion that the historical
process is a process of thoughts in which the past lives on, or can live on,
in the present, while the natural process, even in evolutionary guise, is a
mere succession of events and forms in which the past is superseded by the

present. Hence he flatly denies that the historical process is a mere extension of the natural evolutionary process. As a consequence, he rejects any notion derived from the evolutionary concept of natural process such as a natural and necessary law of progress in history where the latest forms of social organization, art and science, and so forth, would necessarily be an improvement on the earlier forms. The assumption behind this conception is the view that progress is a law of nature, for evolution in nature is thought to have been progressive insofar as it had been an orderly process leading to the existence of man. Hence it is easy to pass from the laws of evolution to the laws of history, and, in fact, identify one with the other. But Collingwood finds an inconsistency in this extrapolation and is quick to point to it.

> The conception of a "law of progress," by which the course of history is so governed that successive forms of human activity exhibit each an improvement on the last, is . . . a mere confusion of thought, bred by an unnatural union between man's belief in his own superiority to nature and his belief that he is nothing more than a part of nature. If either belief is true, the other is false: they cannot be combined to produce logical offspring.[34]

Collingwood is no less critical of other conceptions of progress in history, which, while admittedly distinguishing historical progress from natural or evolutionary progress, nevertheless are products of historical ignorance rather than of historical knowledge.

> The old dogma of a single historical progress leading to the present and the modern dogma of historical cycles, that is, of a multiple progress leading to the "great ages" and then to decadence, are . . . mere projections of the historian's ignorance upon the screen of the past.[35]

Collingwood's notion of historical knowledge as a reenactment of the thought and experience of the past has a vital role to play in this conclusion. By reenacting the experiences of other ages in his mind, the historian has already accepted them as things to be judged on their own standards. Forms of life with their own problems, they are to be judged by their success in solving these problems and no others. Comparison of two historical periods or ways of life is not possible, for the two do not represent attempts to do one and the same thing. Furthermore, it must be recognized that no historian can know any period or age of history as a whole, since there are large tracts of life in each period for which no data are available and other data from the period that cannot be reenacted by the historian because of his vastly different mode of life. To describe one age as dark and another as bright or full of light is to express one's ignorance of that age designated as dark and decadent. To designate each

succeeding age as superior to its predecessor is not possible, for ages as a
whole cannot be known by the historian.[36] Even if ages as a whole could
be known, there are no eternal problems that face each age, much less
eternal answers for them. Hence, no judgment about historical progress
can be made, or so it seems. Yet Collingwood admits that there is a
"genuine meaning" to the question of historical progress.

> If thought in its first phase, after solving the initial problems of that
> phase, is then, through solving these, brought up against others which
> defeat it; and if the second solves these further problems without los-
> ing its hold on the solution of the first, so that there is gain without
> corresponding loss, then there is progress. And there can be progress
> on no other terms.[37]

With this definition of progress as a criterion, certain aspects of experience can be singled out from the past and the question of progress put
to them. Now in certain spheres of human life, such as the economic, the
moral, and the political, there are two processes to be considered, Collingwood believes. One aspect of these spheres of human life arises out of man's
animal nature and constitutes a natural process. There may be change and
even development in these natural processes, but the question of historical
process and progress is meaningless for them. For example, in the economic sphere there is no comparing the comforts and material satisfactions
of one way of life with another. "The happiness of a peasant is not contained in the happiness of a millionaire." In the moral sphere a succession
of animal desires conditions the course of the moral life which changes in
the individual and which differs from age to age and from climate to
climate. These changes and differences are part of the process of nature,
not of history. In each of these areas of human activity, however, there is
another aspect, one that pertains to the level of thought and is part of the
historical process. The question of historical progress means something
when viewed in this aspect of economic, moral, and political life. In the
economic life not all demands of man are for the satisfaction of animal
desires. The demand for savings to support one in old age arises out of an
individualistic economic system which may have solved other problems
but seems powerless in the face of this one. "A better economic system,
one whose substitution for this would be a progress, would continue to
solve the same problems which are solved by individualist capitalism, and
solve these others as well." So too in the moral problems. As products of
thought in time, these problems are part of the historical process, and
the notion of historical progress can be applied to them. Progress would
be the devising of new institutions that would at once solve the new
problems arising from the old institutions as well as those problems for
which the old had been devised. Much the same can be said of the

political area, where the historical process is quite as plain as in the economic and moral spheres.[38]

In the field of art there can be development in the mastery of techniques, but there is no progress from one form or work of art to another. Every fresh work of art is the solution of a fresh problem arising out of the artist's unreflective experience and not out of a previous work of art. Artists may do better or worse work in solving these problems, but the relation between good and bad art is not an historical one. The problems of art arise out of the flow of unreflective experience, and that flow is not an historical flow.[39] For the areas of science, philosophy, and religion, the question of historical progress can be easily answered in principle. There is no question of coping here with animal needs or desires, as in the economic, moral, and political spheres, but it is a question of pure historical process. To each of these areas in turn Collingwood applies his criterion for progress: the new solution must solve the problems solved by the old solution in addition to solving those generated by the old solution.[40] The result will be progress in science, philosophy, and religion.

In this sense, then, progress is possible in the different areas of life and human activity, excepting always the natural processes in the economic, moral, and political spheres, as well as the whole field of art. Whether progress has actually occurred is a question for historical investigation to answer. The plainest area of progress has been in science, and those who believe most strongly in the idea of progress appeal to the examples here as the strongest proof. Some go further and wish to make science the absolute mistress of human life, thus securing, they hope, progress in every other sphere of life. But, as has been observed, in some areas of human life progress is not possible, while in the others progress is possible, but it is achieved not by submitting to the rule of science but by improving these specific activities according to their own standards. In fact, progress comes about only as the result of historical thinking. "Progress is not a mere fact to be discovered by historical thinking; it is only through historical thinking that it comes about at all."[41] Progress, when it happens, comes about by the retention in the mind, at one phase, of what was achieved in the preceding phase. These two phases are related not merely by way of succession but by way of continuity. Essential to this process is the reenactment in the mind of the previous phase as the point of departure, but together with a development of it that is partly constructive or positive and partly critical or negative. This is the only way in which progress occurs, and historical thinking plays the fundamental role in the process.

NOTES

1. R. G. Collingwood, *Autobiography* (Oxford: Clarendon Press, 1939), pp. 28, 85, 77. T. M. Knox's Introduction to Collingwood's *The Idea of History* (New York: Oxford University Press, 1956), pp. v–xxiv, is helpful for understanding the development of Collingwood's thought. *The Idea of History* was published originally by The Clarendon Press, Oxford, in 1946.

2. Collingwood, *An Essay on Philosophical Method* (Oxford: Clarendon Press, 1933), pp. 87–88.

3. Collingwood, *Essay*, pp. 89–90.

4. Collingwood, *Essay*, p. 191. If one's philosophy is competently worked out from its place in the scale of forms, then it has a universal aspect about it. "As one form in a scale, an individual philosophy is one among many, a single moment in the history of thought, which future philosophers will have to treat as such; but as reinterpreting previous philosophies and reaffirming them as elements within itself it summarizes the whole previous course of that history, and is thus universal as well as individual," pp. 191–192.

5. Collingwood, *Essay*, pp. 194, 198.

6. See Collingwood, *Essay*, pp. 1, 26. In *The Idea of Nature*, which belongs to the period between the *Essay* and the *Autobiography*, Collingwood has this to say about the dependence of natural science on history and historical thinking: "I conclude that natural science as a form of thought exists and has always existed in a context of history, and depends on historical thought for its existence. From this I venture to infer that no one can understand natural science unless he understands history: and that no one can understand the question what nature is unless he knows what history is. This is a question which Alexander and Whitehead have not asked. And that is why I answer the question 'Where do we go from here?' by saying, 'We go from the idea of nature to the idea of history.'" (Oxford: Clarendon Press, 1945), p. 177. Collingwood's next work was entitled *The Idea of History*.

7. Cited by Knox, p. x, from Collingwood's notes for a work to be called *The Principles of History*.

8. Collingwood, *Autobiography*, pp. 36–39. This logic already appears in the earlier work, *The Idea of History*, e.g., pp. 269–281.

9. Collingwood, *Autobiography*, pp. 68, 62, 65.

10. Collingwood, *Autobiography*, pp. 65–67. Collingwood takes the same position in *An Essay on Metaphysics*.

11. Collingwood, *Autobiography*, pp. 70, 72.

12. Cited by Knox, pp. xii–xiii, from Collingwood's notes. Knox has this to say about Collingwood's final position. "He has still left us not clearly enlightened on the true conception of history. If he solved the problem of combining what is generally known as philosophy with what is generally known as history to form a new discipline to be called History . . . he never clearly expounded his solution in his writings," p. xix.

13. Collingwood, *The Idea of History*, p. 6; see also pp. 1–10. Later, in his *Autobiography*, Collingwood summarized his philosophy of history in three propositions which he arrived at only gradually. "By about 1920 this was my first principle of a philosophy of history: that the past which an historian studies is

not a dead past, but a past which in some sense is still living in the present," p. 97. "This gave me (1928) a second proposition: 'Historical knowledge is the re-enactment in the historian's mind of the thought whose history he is studying,' " p. 112. "So I reached (1930) my third proposition: 'Historical knowledge is the re-enactment of a past thought incapsulated in a context of present thoughts which, by contradicting it, confine it to a plane different from theirs,' " p. 114.

All of Collingwood's earlier work in the philisophy of history is now available in *Essays in the Philosophy of History*, W. Debbins (ed.) (New York: McGraw-Hill, 1966) [reprint]. This worthwhile volume also contains an excellent introduction to Collingwood's conception of the philosophy of history by the editor as well as an extensive bibliography of Collingwood's writings and of literature about Collingwood.

14.   See S. Alexander, "The Historicity of Things," in R. Klibansky and H. J. Paton (eds.), *Philosophy and History* (New York: Harper & Row, 1963), pp. 11–25.

15.   Collingwood, *The Idea of History*, p. 213; see also pp. 210–213. In a footnote on page 127 of his *Autobiography*, Collingwood observes that the term "action" is not to be understood too narrowly. "Some 'events' of interest to the historian are not actions but the opposite, for which we have no English word: not *actiones* but *passiones*, instances of being acted on. . . . It (*passio*) becomes an 'historical event' in so far as people were not merely affected by it, but reacted to this affection by actions of various kinds."

In *The Idea of History*, p. 217, Collingwood will admit natural processes as historical in character on one hypothesis only. "There is only one hypothesis on which natural processes could be regarded as ultimately historical in character: namely, that these processes are in reality processes of action determined by a thought which is their own inner side." Obviously, he does not think this hypothesis to be true.

16.   Collingwood, *The Idea of History*, pp. 309, 214; see also pp. 302–309. "The cause of the event, for him [the historian], means the thought in the mind of the person by whose agency the event came about: and this is not something other than the event, it is the inside of the event itself," pp. 214–215.

17.   Collingwood, *The Idea of History*, pp. 216, 231.

18.   See Collingwood, *The Idea of History*, pp. 309–315. The text cited is on page 312.

19.   Collingwood, *The Idea of History*, pp. 223, 224, 209. Collingwood denies any underlying spiritual substantiality to the mind. "Hume was therefore right to maintain that there is no such thing as 'spiritual substance,' nothing that mind is, distinct from and underlying what it does," p. 222.

20.   Collingwood, *Autobiography*, p. 112. See the section entitled, "History as Re-enactment of Past Experience," in *The Idea of History*, pp. 282–302. See W. H. Walsh, *Philosophy of History: An Introduction* (New York: Harper & Row, 1960) pp. 48–59.

21.   Collingwood, *The Idea of History*, p. 218.

22.   Collingwood, *The Idea of History*, pp. 219–220.

23.   Collingwood, *The Idea of History*, p. 226. Here Collingwood comes close to what is considered to be a leading thesis of the existentialist philosophers. Another statement from the *Autobiography*, p. 115, runs like this: "If he [the historian] is able to understand, by re-thinking them, the thoughts of a great

many different kinds of people, it follows that he must be a great many kinds of man. He must be, in fact, a microcosm of all the history he can know. Thus his own self-knowledge is at the same time his knowledge of the world of human affairs."

24.   Collingwood, *The Idea of History*, p. 225.

25.   Collingwood, *The Idea of History*, pp. 229–230. For a brief explanation of what Collingwood means by "incapsulation," see his *Autobiography*, pp. 141–143.

26.   Collingwood, *The Idea of History*, p. 234. Another statement of the scientific nature of history is expressed in this way. "It [history] is a science whose business is to study events not accessible to our observation, and to study these events inferentially, arguing to them from something else which is accessible to our observation, and which the historian calls 'evidence' for the events in which he is interested," pp. 251–252.

27.   Collingwood, *The Idea of History*, p. 257.

28.   Collingwood, *The Idea of History*, p. 275.

29.   Collingwood, *The Idea of History*, p. 236.

30.   Collingwood, *The Idea of History*, pp. 240–242; see also pp. 234–240.

31.   Collingwood, *The Idea of History*, pp. 242–245. In the lengthy section entitled "Historical Evidence," pp. 249–282, Collingwood holds that historical criticism as exercised by the scissors-and-paste historian can only lead to an historical inference or conclusion which is at the best permissive or probable. However, he is convinced that his method of question and answer leads to the certitude which is required of any scientific knowledge, "an historical argument which left nothing to caprice, and admitted of no alternative conclusion, but proved its point as conclusively as a demonstration in mathematics," p. 262. This idea, of course, fits nicely with his view that history is an inferential science leading to certitude in its conclusions. Crucial for this position is his view that the starting points of the scientific historian are his own autonomous statements and not statements accepted on authority. Collingwood has certainly successfully demonstrated that the procedure of the scientific historian, from top to bottom, is of a high rational order.

32.   Collingwood, *The Idea of History*, pp. 247, 248.

33.   Collingwood, *The Idea of History*, pp. 248–249.

34.   Collingwood, *The Idea of History*, p. 323; see also pp. 321–323.

35.   Collingwood, *The Idea of History*, p. 328; see also pp. 263–266.

36.   See Collingwood, *The Idea of History*, pp. 326–329.

37.   Collingwood, *The Idea of History*, p. 329.

38.   Collingwood, *The Idea of History*, pp. 330–331.

39.   See Collingwood, *The Idea of History*, p. 330.

40.   See Collingwood, *The Idea of History*, pp. 332–333.

41.   See Collingwood, *The Idea of History*, p. 333.

SUMMARY

Historicism opened a new chapter in the philosophy of history. A by-product of the romantic revolt against the rationalism of the Enlightenment, it pointed to the manifold richness of historical reality, the bewildering variety of historical forms, their uniqueness as well as their continuous growth and transformation in the course of history. The working historians were not quite prepared to yield their domain to the philosophers of history, whether of metaphysical leanings or of scientific stripe. With the Rankean school of historians historicism began to take on sharper features. A scientific and critical form was fashioned for it, since the autonomy of historical studies was at stake. In its first phase historicism was imbedded in the methodology of the critical historians of the nineteenth century. The aim was simple, to tell the truth, the whole truth in so far as this was possible, about sectors of the human past, personal opinion and prejudice being firmly set aside. Detachment, impartiality, objectivity, even passivity in the face of historical individuality, became prime virtues of the critical historian. Generalizations or regularities thought to be found in the historical process by those of positivistic bent were greeted with unconcealed suspicion and derision. In conflict with the individuality motif of the historian, they seemed to rule out unexpected changes in the course of history, and even to deny the freedom of man. As a methodology, historicism resented and resisted as well the intrusions of a priori or transcendental philosophers in the field of historical interpretation. Philosophy, it was held, focused on universals and abstractions, while historical inquiry centered on the individual and the concrete. History must be understood through the patient application of the historical method, without presuppositions forcing their way into the view

157

of the past. This did not mean that practitioners of the critical method denied the validity of transhistorical principles or values, at any rate as a necessary consequence of their methodology. It did mean that every human reality was open to historical investigation, including the transcendental values and unconditional principles held by man in the past. A philosophical starting point outside of history which pretended to say how history must have been, or how it must necessarily develop, was the principal target of the critical historians, whether metaphysically or positivistically inspired.

And yet there were implications and tensions in this methodological phase of historicism. One of these centered in the question of values. Was the historian to abstain from all value judgments excepting those in accord with the standards of the period he was investigating? Did this entail only a methodological setting aside of the historian's own values, as if irrelevant, in the process? How far should objectivity and impartiality extend, or, more truthfully, how far could it extend in reality? If one went on to observe the historical changes in the supposed unconditional and timeless values held by man, then the problem could become acute for the unwary historian. The purely passive and objective historian was expected to change his methodological value judgments from period to period, if a true assessment of the past were wished. The relativity and historicity of his own values and principles could hardly escape the notice of the historian given to thinking at all. Were not his own values, supposing he still clung to some at this point, part of the historical moment, imbedded in the historical process, passing as he was himself to pass from the scene of history? Join to this the implication that the historical method unaided could lead from the particular to the historical universal, perhaps the only true universal because it is concrete, and history with its method was well on its way to claiming the rank of philosophy as the queen of the sciences, if other sciences there were.

Thus the stage was set for the second phase of historicism. It became a philosophy, a *Weltanschauung*, a philosophy of history in the fullest sense of the word. It claimed to spring, pure and inviolate, from historical reality alone through the application of a truly scientific methodology. Hence the concentration on what came to be called the critical philosophy of history. If historical reality was the only reality, then its investigation must be rooted in the most critical of historical methodologies, the only true methodology leading to the only true knowledge. A leading principle from Vico's *New Science* became central to the historicist position.

> The world of civil society has certainly been made by men, and its principles are therefore to be found within the modifications of our own mind. Whoever reflects on this cannot but marvel that the

philosophers have spent all their energies on the study of nature, which, since God made it, He alone knows; and that they should have neglected the study of the world of nations, or civil world, which, since men had made it, men could come to know.[1]

This statement of principle was pushed to its limits by the historicists, Dilthey, Croce, and Collingwood. It meant, on the one hand, a whole-hearted concentration on the civil world, the human and historical world, which was sharply distinguished from the world of nature. The historico-human world, since it was fashioned by man himself, could be understood by man, while the natural world somehow evaded his best intellectual efforts. An unscalable wall came to be erected between the historico-human world and its knowledge and the world of nature with its natural science. For Dilthey both the starting points as well as the results attained by the natural scientist were "esoteric" abstractions that could never be permitted to contradict that more fundamental understanding of living experience which was historical knowledge. Croce went so far as to deny the reality of "nature" as understood by the natural scientist. The pseudoconcepts and fictitious laws of natural science might have their uses, but they could not claim to be knowledge. In the end only historical knowledge could validly make such a claim. Collingwood is not as sure of himself on this point as on others, but it is clear that he too denied the rank of knowledge to the intellectual efforts of the natural scientist, and historical knowledge eventually turned out to be the only type of scientific knowledge possible. History and nature were two worlds apart in the historicist position, if nature as such was thought to exist at all. Causality pertained primarily to the world of nature, and when it was admitted into historical explanations by the historicists, it was never thought to be a profound or final explanation.

Vico had also claimed that the civil world could be understood by man because the principles of its creation were to be found within the mind of man. If the cultural world was a product of man's mind, then it could not be viewed as an object independent of the mind of man. Its whole intelligibility proceeded from the mind of man its creator. Hence the historian must relive, or reexperience, or rethink the human past in his own mind on pain of not understanding it all. This thesis was common to Dilthey, Croce, and Collingwood. Without an intense act of imaginative reconstruction of the past event by the historian there could be no historical knowledge. This meant, first of all, that imagination found a prominent spot in the methodology of the true historian. It meant also that an affinity for the object, a capacity to relive and rethink it, was a

---

1.   *The New Science of Giambattista Vico*, trans. T. G. Bergin and M. H. Fisch (New York: Cornell University Press, 1961), sec. 331, pp. 52–53.

prime qualification for historical thinking. An extrinsic causal explanation could not substitute for this reliving and rethinking of the event, which at once offered an inside understanding of the event as well as a superior form of certitude. In place of the detachment, the objectivity, the passivity recommended for the historian by German historians of the critical school, attachment, subjectivity, and activity were paramount among the virtues of the historicist historian. Croce and Collingwood go on to assert that historical facts are the products of the thinking of the historian and do not exist apart from that thinking. Common to all is the insight into the mutual interdependence of historical criticism and historical synthesis or construction, a position in open opposition to distinctions appearing in standard manuals of historical methodology. The analyses of Collingwood on this point were the clearest, and his arguments cannot be avoided by any truly critical philosophy of history to this day.

A truly seminal thinker of the stature of Dilthey cannot be fully summed up by the appellation of historicist. His influence on the development of phenomenology and existentialism, to which Heidegger and Ortega y Gasset bear witness, can be matched in the development of sociology, at least among German and American sociologists like Max Weber and Pitirim Sorokin. And yet Dilthey is an historicist. If he did not go so far as to identify philosophy with history, there is no doubt that he was convinced of the fruitlessness of metaphysical inquiry. The historian cannot renounce the ambition to study history from within through his own methodology. The study of history reveals the relativity of all claims to unconditional values and transcendental principles. Hence history has freed man from the chains of all metaphysical dogmas and of every kind of faith. There is no method for ascertaining the validity of the so-called transcendental values. Man himself is the only intrinsic value that history reveals beyond a doubt. He should surrender himself to his place in the life stream, submit to the present experience and to his historical moment, and resign himself to historical immanence.

Dilthey may display idealist tendencies in his thinking, but he is very much more of an empiricist and realist than Croce, who claimed that the only reality was spirit or mind. Croce combined his brand of idealism with an interest in history to form what he called a pure or complete historicism, which offered liberation from transcendence of all kinds. There is no reality beyond history which is absolute immanence, and there is no way of knowing it except through historical thinking.

"The conception of history that we have reached," wrote Croce,

> namely, that which has not its documents outside itself, but in itself, which has not its final and causal explanation outside itself, but within itself, which has not philosophy outside itself, but within

itself—identifies history with the act of thought itself, which is always philosophy and history together.[2]. . .

Thus was Hegel surpassed. History could not be reduced to philosophy, but philosophy could and must be reduced to history.

Collingwood also ended up with a type of idealist-historicism. Through his penetrating analysis of the mutual dependence of historical criticism and historical synthesis or reconstruction he was driven to postulate an innate or a priori idea of history in the mind of every man. This imaginary picture of the past, part of the native endowment of the human, was the ultimate criterion of historical truth. Despite certain inconsistencies and waverings, he felt that philosophy must be absorbed by history. Even metaphysics was to become nothing more than an historical inquiry into the "absolute presuppositions" of various periods. The historical method, properly understood according to Collingwood's critique, was the only scientific method that produced true knowledge. The sciences of nature did not achieve truth nor knowledge, for their presuppositions or starting points were neither true nor false. Truth was identified with historical truth, and this was attainable only through an historical inquiry. Historical knowledge turned out to be the only kind of knowledge.

The historicist-philosophers concentrated on the critical philosophy of history and demonstrated no great interest, except a critical one, in the classical speculative philosophies of history. All agreed that the latter were projections of the historian upon the screen of the past, products of historical ignorance rather than of historical knowledge. At the same time, they did have something to say about the course of history. Dilthey denied that the meaning of history from beginning to end could be assessed by anyone for the simple and convincing reason that such a meaning depends on the knowledge of its outcome and end. Obviously this was beyond the intellectual powers of man. Yet a provisional meaning of history can be gathered from what is always present in history, the patterns, structures, and interactions of the dynamic systems and the objectifications of life. Created by man and expressing human values and purposes, they display an intelligibility that can be understood by the perceptive historian and student of the human sciences. This is the only meaning of history. Croce, who held no high opinion of sociology in any form, would not have been attracted to Dilthey's opinion, which seemed to hand over to the sociologist much of the investigation of meaning in history. For Croce the end of history is neither extrinsic to the historical process nor is it attained only at some final termination of the process. Identical with historical develop-

2.   B. Croce, *History: Its Theory and Practice*, trans. D. Ainslie (New York: Harcourt, 1960), p. 117. This work was originally published in 1921 by George G. Harrap, London, under the title of *The Theory and History of Historiography*.

ment itself, the end of history is internal to the process, attained at every instant, and consists at once in a perpetual conservation and a perpetual surpassing. This is Croce's dialectic of progress. Collingwood's scale of forms and notion of progress come close to matching the Crocean dialectic, though he does not seem to believe in its necessary fulfillment in actuality. Here too Collingwood arrives at a position that Croce himself eventually adopted. Both came to hold that theory and practice, history and action, were inseparable. If progress in historical reality was to take place, it would follow the pattern of dialectic or the scale of forms, but only historical thinking revealed the path, while historical, practical action was necessary to secure the goal. It was not sufficient to sit by and contemplate historical development. History had to be made by man. Unwittingly, perhaps, both Croce and Collingwood had taken a position not too many steps removed from the Marxist conception of history, though neither was attracted by its socialist ideology or its economic interpretation of history.

The Rhythms
of History

PART THREE

9

THE ORGANIC LOGIC
OF HISTORY

Oswald Spengler

Inspired by the Romantic movement, historians of the early nineteenth century rejected any simple and uniform explanation of past generations and peoples such as were to be found among the classical philosophers of history. Following in the track of Goethe and Herder, they preferred to look for what was proper and unique to each period and people. Intimately bound up with the Romantic tradition, however, was the notion of continuity in the historical process, the concept of organic growth often expressed in botanical metaphors. This view led historians to accentuate more and more the notion of an idea or institution developing, and it was even urged that the great Ranke had missed this insight.[1] By the 1860s and 1870s, the notion of historical development had found an ally in evolutionary and Darwinian theories coming from the life sciences, taking on new features in the alliance. The idea of linear progress, criticized by outstanding Romantic historians, became prominent once again, revitalized by an evolutionary viewpoint often modeled after the supposed logic behind the origin and survival of species. Evolutionistic-minded historians, ethnologists, anthropologists, and sociologists restored to favor the notion of history as progressing in a straight line, a view underlying many of the classical philosophies of history. Cultural and social evolution progressing inevitably in a direction in which the present was superior to the past, with the future holding certain if unknown further perfections, was a common assumption for the evolutionistic-minded.

Comte and Spencer, with the aid of Herder and Darwin, had won the day, it would seem.

Nevertheless, there were exceptions. The great Swiss historian Jacob Burckhardt, for example, was no proponent of progressive evolution in human history. "Neither man's spirit nor his intellect," he wrote, "has demonstrably improved in the period known to history." And for the optimists he had this caution: "Evil is assuredly a part of the great economy of world history."[2] Burckhardt did not hide his pessimism, and his prediction of a new race of military tyrants, "saviours" and "terrible simplifiers" at once, was not far off the mark. Others more eccentric than Burckhardt fused a pessimistic outlook with the revival of a cyclical view of history. Nietzsche, with his theory of the "eternal recurrence" of all things, is the outstanding exponent of this view of history, though there were other glaring exceptions to the evolutionistic-progressive view of the processes of history. No one of these voices gained much of a hearing in the late nineteenth and early twentieth century world of the West. The "century of hope" ran on without incident into the twentieth, filled with promise, or so it seemed.

By the end of the first decade of the twentieth century sensitive ears thought they heard an unfamiliar sound, the noises of approaching conflict. Among the listeners were Oswald Spengler and Arnold Toynbee, both exceptionally perceptive. What they heard seemed to be part of the last movement of a great symphony which had been played a number of times before in the history of man. History appeared to move with a rhythm to Spengler and Toynbee, and later to Pitirim Sorokin. No doubt this unlikely trio did not pick up quite the same beat; yet each found rhythmic patterns in the human past and thought they heard once again a finale. World War I, and later conflicts also for Toynbee and Sorokin, were not isolated episodes in the history of the West but symptoms of its approaching disintegration. Militarism for Spengler was symptomatic, representing one of the terminating features in the "physiognomic rhythm" of the life cycles of great cultures. Toynbee found a military beat of rout-rally-rout more expressive of the disintegration of civilizations, while, on the grand scale, he thought "the alternating rhythm of Yin and Yang" described exactly the history of civilizations. Sorokin, sociologist by profession, is not so lyric in his choice of terms: the Western world was not disintegrating in the sense of Spengler or Toynbee, but it was passing from one phase of the "super-rhythm" of the cultural supersystems to another.

Only Spengler, without further ado, can be called a "cyclical" philosopher of history, or a "prophet of doom." Both Toynbee and Sorokin are hopeful for the future, the one finding progress realized in the "higher religions," the other relying more, it would seem, on "creative altruism." Yet each of the trio thought he heard some rhythm in the grand movements of history. Much the same point of view was held by Alfred Kroeber, dean of American anthropologists.

Physiognomic and World-as-History

The publication in 1918 of the first volume of Spengler's *Der Untergang des Abendlandes* almost immediately thrust the author into the front ranks of the philosophers of history, and there he remains to this day. *The Decline of the West*, as it is known in its English version, was an instantaneous success, despite Spengler's lack of reputation and academic status. In Germany it soon became the center of a violent controversy, with the historians almost to a man condemning the work. Yet sales of the work mounted, reaching ninety thousand in a few years. Spengler, it seems, had become the philosopher of the hour for Germany, and "nineteen-nineteen was the Spengler year."[3] Doubtless the defeat of Germany in World War I had deepened a melancholic mood among the reading public at large, and a measure of consolation was offered by the pessimistic vision of Spengler. Nevertheless, the pessimism of the *Decline* did not issue from the disaster of the war, since before the outbreak of the conflict Spengler had worked out a first draft of his masterpiece which embodied the same vision.

Already in 1911, Spengler tells us, he had come to the view that war was imminent. Intending to "put together" some considerations about the political phenomena of the day and their possible developments, he happened upon the fundamental idea behind the pessimistic outlook of the *Decline*. "It became perfectly clear," he writes, "that no single fragment of history could be thoroughly illuminated unless and until the secret of world history itself, to wit the story of higher mankind as an organism of regular structure, had been cleared up." He began to see and sense relations and connections everywhere among the varieties of phenomena in the sociocultural order, and one insight above all others stood out: a view of "great morphological relations, each one of which symbolically represents a particular sort of mankind in the whole process of world-history, strictly symmetrical in structure." In this new light a different picture of the present situation revealed itself, a picture in which the approaching war was no longer seen as "a momentary constellation of casual facts," nor even as a unity or necessity of "cause and effect." Spengler saw the coming conflict and the present as "the type of a *historical change of phase* occurring within a great historical organism of definable compass at the point pre-ordained for it hundreds of years ago." The end of this phase would be a final conclusion, and the "history of West-European mankind will be definitely *closed*."[4]

This startling and pessimistic prediction about the fate of the Western world and civilization ran directly counter to the naive optimism and general assumption of inevitable progress so characteristic of the nineteenth century. Behind the pessimism, indeed the determinism, of the Spenglerian view of history lay a philosophy of life and becoming, a world view that derived largely from one of the earliest and most unsystematic exponents of German Romanticism, Goethe. Spengler never tires of acknowledging his debt to Goethe.[5] "We have before us two possible ways in which man may inwardly possess and experience the world around us," Spengler notes.

> With all possible rigour I distinguish . . . the organic from the mechanical world-impression, the content of images from that of laws, the picture and the symbol from formula and system, the instantly actual from the constantly possible, the intents and purposes of imagination ordering according to plan from the intents and purposes of experience dissecting according to scheme.[6]

Thus appears a fundamental presupposition of Spengler, the sharp contrast between two world views, the view of the "world-as-nature" and that of the "world-as-history," as he calls them.

Philosophers and thinkers who view the world-as-nature consider it in a mechanical, static, even dead way; for these the world is a world of "rigid being," a "thing-become," a realized actuality, existing in space and extension and governed by unchanging, timeless relations. Such is the world of mechanical causality, a world of cause and effect, a world of laws following the "logic of space." The world-as-history, on the other hand, is radically different from the world as nature. Here one confronts the world of "pure becoming, pure life . . . incapable of being bounded. It lies beyond the domain of cause and effect, law and measure."[7] World as history is governed by the "logic of time" rather than the "logic of space"; in this world destiny as the "organic necessity in life" fulfills itself rather than Causality with its "necessity of cause and effect."[8] There is no doubt at all that Spengler is enthused with the philosophy of "living experience" which sees the world-as-history.

Paralleling the two world views, according to Spengler, are two methods or ways of knowing the world, the "systematic" and the "physiognomic," the first characteristic particularly of natural science and the second proper to history.

> The Morphology of the mechanical and extended, a science which discovers and orders nature-laws and causal relations, is called Systematic. The Morphology of the organic, of history and life, all that bears the sign of direction and destiny is called Physiognomic.[9]

The "systematic" approach to reality views the world as nature; basing itself on empirical observation of the senses, it turns into a dissecting of the dead and lifeless where "that which is cognized becomes a rigid object."[10] Such is the scientific method of cognition where concepts and definitions, causal formulas and laws, abstract conceptual schemes and systems are fabricated. "Physiognomic," on the other hand, approaches the world as history. "Sympathy, observation, comparison, immediate and inward certainty, intellectual flair . . . are the means of historical research."[11] Characteristic of the "physiognomic" and historical approach to reality is the "method of living into (*erfuhlen*) the object, as opposed to dissecting it."[12] Now it is true that the scientific and historical methods are not completely divorced from one another.

> True science reaches just as far as the notions of truth and falsity have validity: this applies to mathematics and it applies also to the science of historical spade-work, viz. the collection, ordering and sifting of material. But real historical vision . . . only begins at this point.[13]

Real historical insight approaches the world-as-history through "intuitive vision," and particularly through the wise use of analogy, which is the way to understand "living forms."[14] In truth history is much like art, for it belongs to the domain of "significances" and the world of "universal symbolism." "Nature is to be handled scientifically, History poetically. . . ." The would-be world historian must be "guided by feeling" where "intuitive vision . . . vivifies and incorporates the details in a living inwardly-felt unity. Poetry and historical study are kin."[15]

Most historians, Spengler believes, have been deceived by the methods of natural science, pursuing the "logic of space," when all the while it was the "logic of time" with its "organic necessity" that they above all should have appreciated. The common approach to world history has led to a "simple rectilinear progression" of "meaningless proportions," the division of history into ancient, medieval and modern. Such a dividing and partitioning of the historical world Spengler calls the "Ptolemaic conception of history." Impatient with this popular Western prejudice, he speaks of it as "an empty figment of one linear history which can only be kept up by shutting one's eyes to the overwhelming multitude of facts." It "circumscribes the area of history," and, what is worse, "rigs the stage." "We select a single bit of ground [West Europe] as the natural center of the historical system, and make it the central sun." In place of the "Ptolemaic" vision of world history Spengler offers his own version, the "Copernican" conception. The latter admits "no sort of privileged position to the Classical or the Western Culture as against the Cultures of India, Babylon, China, Egypt, the Arabs, Mexico. . . ."[16] World history must not be seen as "a sort of tapeworm industriously adding on to itself one epoch after another." Rather, it reveals itself as a "picture of endless formations and transformations, of marvelous waxing and waning of organic forms."[17] This view of history, the "Copernican," calls for just that approach to reality and the world which Spengler had labeled the physiognomic. There is, then, a consistency of sorts among the Spenglerian concepts of the world-as-history, the physiognomic method, and the Copernican view of world history.

Cultures: Life Cycles and Prime Symbols

Moreover, there is a "logic of history," "a metaphysical structure of historic humanity," which Spengler had already hinted at in the reference to the "logic of time" and "organic necessity" which govern the world as history.[18]

> What gives this fleeting form-world [world-history] meaning and substance and has hitherto lain buried deep under a mass of tangible "facts" and "dates" that has hardly yet been bored through, is *the phenomenon of the Great Cultures*. Only after these prime forms shall have been seen and felt and worked out in respect of their physiognomic meaning will it be possible to say that the essence and inner form of human History as opposed to the essence Nature are understood. . . . Only after this inlook and this outlook will a serious philosophy of history become feasible.

The philosophy of history is well on its way to becoming a philosophy of culture, in the Spenglerian view, for "Culture is the *prime phenomenon* of all past and future world-history," and "world-history is their collective biography." Once the physiognomic method has been brought to bear on the great cultures of history, then it will be possible to "see each fact in the historical picture . . . according to its symbolic content, and to regard history . . . as an organism of rigorous structure and significant articulation." History has an organic structure because the great cultures, the prime phenomena of history, are "organisms" too; there can be symbolic content to each historical fact because it is the expression of a "primitive cultureform" which "underlies as ideal all the individual Cultures."[19] If cultures are organisms, then a method like the comparative morphology of plants and animals may be useful in helping to recognize their inward forms. But this must not be understood as some sort of capitulation to the demands of the systematic approach to the world as nature. Spengler has a very low opinion of the "dissecting morphology of the Darwinian . . . with its hunt for causal connexions" and recommends, consistently enough, the "morphology of Goethe" with its respect for "living nature" and the "organic logic."[20] In a rather striking passage Spengler gives us an idea of what he means by "morphology." Rather than a "trite history of human progress," he sees a drama of a number of mighty Cultures, each springing with primitive strength from the soil of a mother-region to which it remains firmly bound throughout its whole life-cycle; each stamping its own material, its mankind, in its own image; each having its own idea, its own life, will and feeling, its own death. . . . Each Culture has its own new possibilities of self-expression which arise, ripen, decay and never return . . . just as each species of plant has its peculiar blossom or fruit, its special type of growth and decline. These cultures, sublimated life-essences, grow with the same superb aimlessness as the flowers of the field. They belong, like the plants and animals, to the living Nature of Goethe, and not the dead Nature of Newton.[21]

Spengler's logic of history, or the logic of time, finds its foundation in the great cultures that have a "life-cycle" as all organisms do. Thus he speaks of a culture being "born," "blooming," and "dying." Or he can say that "every culture passes through the age-phases of the individual man. Each has its childhood, youth, manhood, and old age." Or again, Spengler refers to the "spring," "summer," "autumn," and "winter" of the great cultures.[22] Such expressions, or some very similar, can be found in the writings of a number of historians and were part of the common patrimony of the German Romantics, but now they are taken for much more than simple metaphors. In the Spenglerian view they point to clearly marked phases in the cycle of a culture, and assume a rigid, deterministic mold to which the prime objects of history must conform. "Every culture, every adolescence, and maturing, and decay of a culture, every one of its intrinsically necessary stages and periods, has a definite duration, always the same. . . ."[23] He speaks of the "*ideal* life of one millennium for each Culture," though it seems true that he would not wish to be held too closely to it in practice. As the ideal lifespan of man, at least in one reckoning, is three score and ten, so too a thousand years is the ideal lifespan of a culture.[24]

There is another well-known Spenglerian distinction that appears at this point, the distinction between culture and civilization.

Every Culture has *its own* Civilization. In this work, for the first time, the two words . . . are used in a *periodic* sense, to express a strict and necessary *organic succession*. The Civilization is the inevitable destiny of the Culture. . . . Civilizations are the most external and artificial states of which a species of developed humanity is capable. They are a conclusion, the thing-become succeeding the thing-becoming, death following life, rigidity following expansion, intellectual age and stone-built, petrifying world-city following mother earth and the spiritual childhood of Doric and Gothic. They are an end, irrevocable, yet by inward necessity reached again and again.[25]

The culture period comprises the spring, summer, and autumn of a society, the period of creative activity, when the soul of the countryside dominates.

Civilization is the winter of a culture, the period of material comforts and intellectual schematizations, when the intellect of the city predominates. With the appearance of the world city, the "megalopolis," the phase of civilization has begun, and it will be accompanied by a new "Caesarism," when democracy is succeeded by a "universal imperium" and dictatorship. The end and term of the culture as a whole is reached when a "second religiousness" or theosophy appears with its "messiahs" and "saviours" becoming the forlorn hope of the "masses." Then the culture-civilization dies, though some continue in a "petrified form" for hundreds and even thousands of years, as can be seen, according to Spengler, in China, India, and the Islamic world, distorting if not aborting the birth of a young culture. But the normal course is the final death of the culture, the end of the civilization phase, and one can see it realized in the Classical (Graeco-Roman) culture, for instance, and already underway in the Western culture.[26]

Spengler presses the organismic view of culture to the limit when he speaks of the "contemporaneity" of the phases of each of the great cultures. "Without exception," he states, "all great creations and forms in religion, art, politics, social life, economy, and science appear, fulfill themselves and die down *contemporaneously* in all the Cultures." Not only do the creative periods of the cultures parallel like periods in other cultures, but the whole of the life-cycle is matched in order and detail by all.

> The inner structure of one [culture] corresponds strictly with that of all the others . . . there is not a single phenomenon of deep physiognomic importance in the record of one for which we could not find a counterpart in the record of every other, and . . . this counterpart is to be found under a characteristic form and in a perfectly chronological position. . . .[27]

In the charts appended to the first volume of the *Decline*, one can see how far Spengler is willing to go with the belief that the life cycle and important events of the great cultures match those of others.

In fact, Spengler believes that the organismic view of cultures and history offers the possibility of predicting the future of the history of Western civilization and of reconstructing the past of the great cultures for which evidence is limited or lacking.

> History offers possibilities . . . of overpassing the present as a research limit, and of predetermining the spiritual form, duration, rhythm, meaning and product of the *still unaccomplished* stages of our western history; and reconstructing long-vanished and unknown epochs, even whole cultures of the past, by means of morphological connexions. . . . It is possible, given the physiognomic rhythm, to recover from scattered details . . . the organic characters of whole

centuries of history, and from known elements on the scale of art-expression, to find corresponding elements on the scale of political forms, or from that of mathematical forms to that of economics.[28]

The "truly Goethean method" makes such prophecy and reconstruction possible, and this method is rooted in "Goethe's conception of the prime phenomenon."

In the Spenglerian view of history cultures are the "prime phenomena," and "every culture is nothing but the actualizing and form of a single, singularly-constituted soul." Every great culture is a "superlative human individuality" with its own personality and soul. "I distinguish the *idea* of a Culture, which is the sum total of its inner possibilities, from its sensible *phenomena* or appearance upon the canvas of history, as a fulfilled actuality. It is the relation of the soul to the living body, to its expression. . . ."[29] The individuality, the personality, and what Spengler calls the style of each of the great cultures is intimately related to the "prime symbol" of that culture. "The *choice of prime symbol* in the moment of the Culture-soul's awakening into self-consciousness on its own soil . . . decided all."[30] Each of the departments and spheres of a great culture articulate and express the "prime symbol" of that culture, and this symbol can be called the "master-pattern" which determines the essential characteristics of a culture. The "prime symbol" imparts to the culture "its specific style and . . . historical form"; it is "inherent in the form of the state, the religious myths and cults, the ethical ideals, the forms of painting and music and poetry, the fundamental notions of each science. . . ."[31] Once again Spengler observes that the prime symbol reveals itself only to the physiognomic approach, as it speaks "only to the inner feelings, not to the understanding."

Spengler reproaches the historian of his time with ignorance of the "morphological relation" that exists among all the elements of a great culture. Political historians, for example, bring in pieces of religious, social, and art history to illustrate the political sense of an epoch, but they do so sparingly and even grudgingly. Historians of this stripe have forgotten, if they ever knew, that "visible history is the expression, sign, and embodiment of soul." They are unaware of the "interconnectedness" of events, nor do they advert to the "morphological relationship that inwardly binds together the expression-forms of all branches of a Culture."[32] Traditional historians have not been able to "bring up, out of the web of world-happening, a millennium of organic culture-history as an entity and person, and to grasp the conditions of its inmost spirituality. . . ." In short, they have been ignorant of the "prime symbol" or master-pattern which binds together all major elements of the great cultures. Had they approached world history with the "eye of an artist," with "physiognomic flair," they

would "feel the whole sensible and apprehensible environment dissolve
into a deep infinity of mysterious relationships."[33] And in this process they
would have stumbled on the metaphysics of the future, one "which
regards everything whatsoever as having significance as a symbol," and
through which the "Morphology of world-history becomes inevitably a
universal symbolism."[34]

Coupled with the Spenglerian view of the great cultures as distinct
personalities with characteristic styles and unique prime symbols is a frank
and unqualified historical and cultural relativism.

> Each culture has its own new possibilities of self-expression which
> arise, ripen, decay and never return. There is not one sculpture, one
> painting, one mathematics, one physics, but many, each in its
> deepest essence different from the others, each limited in duration
> and self-contained. . . .[35]

There is no human activity that is not the expression of the cultural soul,
bound up with a particular people and geographical area, and having
validity only for that culture. "There are no eternal truths. Every philosophy is the expression of its own and only its own time. . . . Truths are
truths only in relation to a particular mankind."[36] Spengler even gives the
impression that there is not one mankind but different species of man
developed in the different cultures. "Mankind is a zoological expression,
or an empty word." And, more explicitly, he observes that "every culture
possesses a wholly individual way of looking at and comprehending the
world-as-Nature . . . it has its own peculiar 'Nature' which no other sort
of man can possess in exactly the same form."[37] Each of the great cultures
has stamped its own mankind with its image, that of the prime symbol.
All the great sociocultural products, whether mathematics, science, philosophy, or the arts, express the style and meaning of the soul of a culture,
and that soul or idea only. Culture speaks its own language through all the
great compartments of cultural phenomena, a language that is incomprehensible to other cultures. "Each of the great Cultures, then, has arrived at
a secret language of world-feeling that is only fully comprehensible by him
whose soul belongs to that culture."[38]

Doubtless, Spengler is not fully consistent on this point. He declares
one culture to be "incomprehensible" to a member of another culture,
and yet much of the Decline is filled with detailed comparisons of cultures
and their products. Indeed, he does not hesitate to go so far as to assign
various "prime symbols" or master patterns to each of the great cultures.
Perhaps the very skilled and accomplished practitioner of the physiognomic method could be relied on somehow to rise above the limited
views and values of his own cultural milieu. Yet, consistently enough, in
the Preface to the revised edition of the first volume of the Decline,
Spengler refers to the relativistic character of his own findings. "I can

then call the essence of what I have discovered 'true'—that is, true for me—not true in itself, as dissociated from the conditions imposed by blood and history, for that is impossible."[39]

The Fate of the West

In the course of his comparison of the great cultures, Spengler confines himself to a period corresponding to that with which the conventional historian often works, though here and there he hints at a philosophical view that could be expanded into an explanation of all becoming. "Of the whole picture of world becoming . . . the becoming of the heavens, of the earth's crust, of life, of man," he writes, "we shall deal here only with that very small morphological unit that we are accustomed to call world-history . . . the history of higher mankind during 6000 years or so, without going into the deep problem of the inward homogeneity of all these aspects."[40] Within the 6000-year period mentioned, Spengler adverts principally to those cultures with which he might be expected to be somewhat familiar. His completed roster includes eight fully developed cultures, in addition to the Russian, whose true history had yet to begin. Of the eight great cultures, the Babylonian and Mexican receive only passing reference, while the Egyptian, Chinese, and Indian cultures merit fuller yet still limited analysis. The *Decline* is primarily a series of comparisons between the attitudes and values of what Spengler calls the Classical or Apollinian (Graeco-Roman) and the Western or Faustian (West European) cultures. Between these two is a culture Spengler calls the Arabian or Magian culture, one that is a rather strange amalgam of Iranian, Semitic, early Christian, and Islamic elements.

It is not necessary to follow in detail Spengler's complicated and often brilliant analyses and comparisons of the great cultures and their prime symbols.[41] His aim was to forecast the future of the Western or Faustian culture, and most of the controversy over the *Decline* centered around his interpretation of Western history. The history of the Western or Faustian culture begins, for Spengler, around the year 900 with the birth of the Faustian soul in Europe. Preceding the appearance of the Faustian spirit in the tenth century was a period of twilight, the "pre-cultural period" of four centuries, during which the memories of the Apollinian civilization and the still-enduring vestiges of the Magian struggled for possession of West European soil with the first stirrings of a new and indigenous spirit, the Faustian. Spring, summer, and autumn of the Faustian spirit, the culture period, resembles conventional delineations of the same era, the high Middle Ages, the era of absolutism and the Baroque being the summits. The winter or civilization phase of Faustian culture is ushered in with the French Revolution and Napoleon, and with the nineteenth century the winter of the West has begun. Even Spengler's assessment of the nineteenth century as one of materialistic and skeptical philosophies and of intellectual and artistic eclecticism matched by the emergence of the "fourth estate" does not differ radically from that of historical manuals. It is only when one comes to the twentieth century that the deterministic and pessimistic implications of Spengler's morphological method become quite clear.

An age of great wars is dawning, with the conflicts grouping more around new leaders, the new "Caesars," than around nations. Eventually one of the Caesars will triumph over the others and establish a universal imperium. Life at the same time will have descended to a low level of general uniformity where local and national differences fade, and a few "world-cities"—the "megalopolis"—will be the only centers of importance. In these "barrack-cities" will dwell great numbers of the "masses," a mob willing to follow any leader, and the educated and the intellectuals will have degenerated into the merely clever. Eventually every trace and form and style will have disappeared and a new primitivism will assert itself. From out of the desolation of the cities will appear a "second religiosity" or gnosticism through which the masses can hope to escape their misery. Then, having lost its "desire to be," the Faustian soul will wish itself back to the darkness, to the womb of the mother, the grave.[42] On this fatalistic and pessimistic note Spengler brings his work to a close.

> For us, however, whom a Destiny has placed in this Culture and at this moment of its development—the moment when money is celebrating its last victories, and the Caesarism that is to succeed approaches with quiet, firm step—our direction, willed and obligatory at once, is set for us within narrow limits, and on any other terms life is not worth the living. We have not the freedom to reach to this or that, but the freedom to do the necessary or to do nothing. And a task that historic necessity has set *will* be accomplished with the individual or against him.[43]

NOTES

1.   C. G. P. Gooch, *History and Historians in the Nineteenth Century* (Boston: Beacon, 1959), p. 537.

2.   See J. Burckhardt, *Force and Freedom: Reflections on History* (Boston: Beacon, 1964), pp. 56, 361.

3.   See H. Stuart Hughes, *Oswald Spengler*, rev. ed. (New York: Scribner, 1962), pp. 89–97.

4.   O. Spengler, *The Decline of the West*, authorized translation by C. F. Atkinson (London: G. Allen, 1926), Vol. I, ch. I, pp. 46–47, 38. *The Decline*

of the West was simultaneously published in the United States by Alfred A. Knopf, New York.

5.   See for example, Spengler, Preface, p. xiv. Hughes, in a series of chapters (2, 3, 4), gives an excellent synopsis of the intellectual milieu in which the *Decline* was written. Many of the ideas in the European air find an outlet in Spengler's work, but the question of the direct influence of thinkers and historians like Burckhardt, Dilthey, Bergson, Pareto, and so on, seems to be ruled out. Goethe and Nietzsche are the two acknowledged masters of Spengler (*Decline*, pp. 59–64). Hughes also observes that Spengler's doctoral thesis on Heraclitus (1903) already contained many of the leading ideas that were to appear in the *Decline*. P. Sorokin, *Modern Historical and Social Philosophies* (New York: Dover, 1963), ch. III, pp. 49–71, discusses a work of the Russian Nikolai Danilevsky, *Russia and Europe* (1871), which anticipates a number of insights fundamental to the organismic and cyclical interpretation of the cultural process. Yet neither Sorokin (p. 329) nor Hughes (p. 53) can detect any direct influence of Danilevsky's theories on Spengler's views.

6.   Spengler, Vol. I, p. 4.

7.   Spengler, Vol. I, ch. III, p. 95. In another place (ch. I, p. 48) Spengler says, "Man as an element and representative of the world is a member, not only of nature, but also of history—which is a second Cosmos different in structure and complexion, entirely neglected by Metaphysics in favor of the first."

8.   Spengler, Vol. I, ch. I, pp. 6–8.

9.   Spengler, Vol. I, ch. III, p. 100.

10.   Spengler, Vol. I, p. 102.

11.   Spengler, Vol. I, ch. I, p. 25.

12.   Spengler, Vol. I, ch. III, p. 105.

13.   Spengler, Vol. I, p. 96.

14.   Spengler, Vol. I, ch. I, pp. 4–5.

15.   Spengler, Vol. I, ch. III, p. 102.

16.   Spengler, Vol. I, ch. I, pp. 16–18.

17.   Spengler, Vol. I, pp. 21–22.

18.   Spengler, Vol. I, p. 3.

19.   Spengler, Vol. I, ch. III, p. 104.

20.   See Spengler, Vol. I, p. 104, n. 2.

21.   Spengler, Vol. I, ch. I, p. 21.

22.   Spengler, Vol. I, ch. III, pp. 106–107.

23.   Spengler, Vol. I, pp. 109–110.

24.   Spengler, Vol. I, p. 110.

25.   Spengler, Vol. I, ch. I, p. 31.

26.   The simplest reference is to the three tables appended by Spengler to Volume One. Table One is called "Contemporary Spiritual Epochs"; Table Two, "Contemporary Cultural Epochs"; and Table Three, "Contemporary Political Epochs."

27.   Spengler, Vol. I, ch. III, p. 112. This view had been announced at the very beginning (ch. I, p. 4) in these words: "It is, and always has been, a matter of knowledge that the expression-forms of world-history are limited in number, and that eras, epochs, situations, persons are ever repeating themselves true to type."

28.   Spengler, Vol. I, pp. 112–113.

29.   Spengler, Vol. I, pp. 129, 104–105.

30.   Spengler, Vol. I, ch. V, p. 180.

31.   Spengler, Vol. I, pp. 174, 175.

32.   Spengler, Vol. I, ch. I, pp. 6–7.

33.   Spengler, Vol. I, ch. IV, p. 159; ch. V, p. 163; ch. IV, p. 145.

34.   Spengler, Vol. I, ch. V, p. 163; ch. I, p. 46.

35.   Spengler, Vol. I, ch. I, p. 21.

36.   Spengler, Vol. I, pp. 41, 46.

37.   Spengler, Vol. I, ch. IV, p. 131. Another statement of the same position appears in ch. V, p. 169: "Every artist has rendered 'Nature' by line and tone, every physicist . . . has dissected 'Nature' into ultimate elements, and how is it that they have not all discovered the same? Because everyone of them has had his own Nature, though . . . every one believed that he had it in common with all the rest. . . . Nature is a function of the particular Culture."

38.   Spengler, Vol. I, ch. V, p. 178.

39.   Spengler, Preface to rev. ed. of Vol. One, p. xiii.

40.   Spengler, Vol. I, ch. III, p. 104.

41.   One can consult Hughes, pp. 77–79, or Sorokin, pp. 80–83, for a brief synopsis.

42.   Hughes, pp. 80–86.

43.   Spengler, Vol. II, p. 507.

10

THE WHEEL OF CIVILIZATION:

Arnold Toynbee

In 1914, as he expounded Thucydides to some undergraduates, a young Oxford don suddenly found himself illuminated with a profound inspiration, and the vision behind Arnold Toynbee's A *Study of History* began to take shape. Later, the incident seemed to Toynbee to have had this message: "The experience that we were having in our world now had been experienced by Thucydides in his world already. . . . His present had been my future." In the flash of this sudden insight Toynbee had perceived the "philosophical contemporaneity" of the Hellenic world of Thucydides with his own Western world, notwithstanding the nonsense such a vision made of the usual chronological notation. Nor was this the whole of the illumination, for it unfolded into the vision of the "philosophical contemporaneity of all civilizations." Comforting support for this view was to be found, Toynbee believed, in the recent scientific discoveries that reduced the five or six thousand years that had elapsed since the emergence of "civilizations" to an infinitesimally brief period in comparison to the age of the human species as a whole. "History revealed itself as a sheaf of parallel, contemporary, and recent essays in a new enterprise, the enterprise of civilization."[1]

A number of events, including war duties in the British Foreign Office, intervened before Toynbee had the time to give serious and prolonged meditation to the inspiration of 1914. Mulling over the problem of the genesis of civilization one day in 1920, he was introduced to Oswald Spengler's *Untergang des Abendlandes*, which, it can easily be imagined, struck him with dismay. Leisurely perusal of Spengler's work, however,

179

revealed certain defects, especially on the very question of the geneses of civilizations. On this point Spengler seemed most "unilluminatedly dogmatic and deterministic." "Where the German a *priori* method drew blank," it was possible that another approach, one employing "English empiricism," might uncover the answer.[2] So Toynbee set out to work on a project that would take the better part of a half century to complete. In the meanwhile critics were taking note, and all perceived a marked change in the later volumes. As one put it, the *Study* ceased to be a "study of the life cycles of comparable civilizations" and became a "history of salvation."[3]

Several principles, or assumptions, underlie Toynbee's monumental work. One of these concerns the "intelligible units" of historical study. For Toynbee there are two distinct units or societies in the general field of historical studies. The first of these, primitive societies, are the object of the investigations of the anthropologist or prehistoric archaeologist. Civilizations, the other species within the genus of historical societies, are the subject matter of the historian properly speaking, that is, those distinctive groupings and achievements of mankind that appeared some five or six thousand years ago in human history.[4]

Allied with the opinion that history is the study of civilizations is Toynbee's view of the "continuity of history." Several mistaken notions about the unity of history and the unity of civilization must be discarded first. Above all, Western historians must come to accept the fact that Western civilization is just one member of the species. The canonized formula of "ancient + medieval + modern history" has seduced Westerners into treating the transition from one of twenty-one civilizations to another as the turning point of all human history. Any unity of history built on this Western pride must be rejected. To be rejected as well is any unity of history based on theories of the "diffusionist" school of anthropology, which holds that civilization developed in one area of the world only, from which it spread. This group needs to be reminded that the "spark" or "germ of original creation" may flower anywhere in virtue of the uniformity of human nature.[5]

In place of the discredited theories about the unity of history and civilization Toynbee substitutes his view of the continuity of history. The parent-child relationship of civilizations is the continuity one finds in history. "The continuity of history is not a continuity such as is exemplified in the life of a single individual, but a continuity made up of the lives of successive generations." Three such generations of civilizations, upon reflection, can be seen as adequate to more than cover the historian's span of five to six thousand years, since "the last term in each series is a civilization that is still alive."[6]

Another assumption underlies Toynbee's *Study*: it is the use of the history of the Graeco-Roman world, or the Hellenic society, and its derived

Western civilization as the exemplar and archetype according to which the histories of other civilizations can be plotted. The wide knowledge Toynbee had of the Graeco-Roman world disposed him to make. it the model for the plotting of the essential course of all civilizations: If the leading phenomena accompanying the decay of the classical world and the birth of Western civilization could be isolated, then it would be possible to search for analogues in other societies. With the recognition of these analogues, the identification of the death of an older civilization and the birth of a new civilization could then be made. This was the methodology used by Toynbee, particularly in the first volumes of the *Study*.[7]

Toynbee identifies three phenomena in the transition from the Hellenic civilization to its filial descendant, Western civilization: "a universal state as the final stage of the old society; a church developed in the old society and in turn developing the new; and the chaotic intrusion of a barbarian heroic age."[8] Applying these criteria to other existing civilizations, the Orthodox Christian, the Islamic, the Hindu, and the Far Eastern, Toynbee comes up with a listing of twenty-one civilizations, fifteen of which are related as parent or offspring to one or more of the others, and the whole covering three generations. Despite the admission that "the comparable units of history remain inconveniently few for the application of the scientific technique, the elucidation and formulation of laws," Toynbee "intends to hazard the attempt."[9]

The Cycle of Civilizations

Much after the fashion of Spengler, though without recourse to the former's organismic analogy for a civilization, Toynbee proposes a cyclical pattern for civilizations. Genesis, growth, breakdown, and disintegration is the cycle that all identifiable civilizations have passed through, excepting, of course, those still with us. Yet even among the existing civilizations the cycle is in its last phase or approaching it. "Of the living civilizations every one has already broken down and is in process of disintegration except our own," and Toynbee displays no great confidence in the future of Western civilization. Hence we should review briefly Toynbee's explanation of the patterned cycle of civilizations.

Geneses of Civilizations

Of the twenty-one civilizations that had been identified at this point, fifteen are of the affiliated variety, that is, they have sprung from other civilizations. Only six, the Egyptiac, the Sumeric, the Minoan, the Sinic, the Mayan, and the Andean are primary civilizations, civilizations of the first generation, that is, ones that have sprung immediately from the condition of primitive societies. The problem is to explain how six societies had achieved that level of human accomplishment designated as civilization, beginning some six thousand years ago. Undoubtedly, the change from a primitive society can be described as a "transition from Yin to Yang." However, even the Chinese formula has not carried the problem much closer to a solution, as Toynbee seems to recognize. "We have now to seek for the positive factor . . . which has set human life in motion again by its impetus." Two positive factors that immediately suggest themselves for consideration, race and environment, are eliminated, at least as deciding factors in the geneses of civilizations.

> Neither race nor environment, taken by itself, can be the positive factor which, within the last six thousand years, has shaken humanity out of its static repose on the level of primitive society and started it on the hazardous quest of civilization.[10]

The factor on which Toynbee finally settles is one that he refers to as "challenge-and-response."

Coming to the opinion that the problem could not be solved through the use of the "scientific method," which, after all, was devised for the study of inanimate nature and not for the study of living things, Toynbee turns to the area of religious symbolism for clues. In the sphere of what he calls mythology, and particularly in Goethe's *Faust*, something of an answer can be perceived. The suggestion arises from this quarter that man achieves civilization as a response to a challenge in a situation of special difficulty. Applying this clue to the geneses of the six "unrelated" or original civilizations, one can find it verified, Toynbee believes, since all were born in response to a challenge of the physical environment. Passing on to the "affiliated" civilizations, those of the second and third generations, the same formula of challenge-and-response is seen to be applicable, though the challenge comes from a different area than the physical environment. "The essential challenge was a human challenge arising out of their relationship to the society to which they were affiliated." The "human environment" was the challenge presenting itself to "affiliated" civilizations. In both cases a successful response to a peculiarly challenging situation led to the foundations of civilizations in the "unrelated" and original class, and to the geneses of the "affiliated" class also.[11]

But this is not to say that success in the face of challenge was the only response on the part of the societies concerned. Obviously a great number—some 650 according to one reckoning—never advanced beyond the stage of the "primitive society." But to confine the investigation to civilizations proper, failure in the face of a challenge is characteristic of the "abortive civilizations," a new classification. Such civilizations "got as far as begetting a civilization," but in each case the "embryo succumbed to a challenge which proved too strong for it." Eventually Toynbee will find three representatives of the class of "abortive civilizations": the Far Eastern Christian, the Far Western Christian (Celtic), and the Scandinavian.[12]

Growths of Civilizations

A question arises almost immediately as to whether once a civilization is born growth is necessary, provided, of course, that it has not proven to be an instance of the "abortive civilization." Some civilizations, Toynbee believes, have not grown to maturity, though they managed to stay in existence for some time. In these instances the challenges offered were of such a nature as to evoke a *tour de force* which so engaged the energies of the society that little was left over for continuing growth. Thus we come upon another classification and grouping of civilizations, the "arrested civilizations," and one can point to five specimens. Three of them, the Polynesian, Eskimo, and Nomad, found their decisive challenge in conditions arising from the physical environment, while the other two, the 'Osmanli (Ottoman) and Spartan, were challenged to a standstill by elements of the human environment. One and all of the "arrested civilizations," after achieving their *tour de force*, settle down into a static and stationary type of society which resembles the societies of the bees and ants.[13]

Toynbee offers this explanation for the civilizations that manage to continue to grow.

> Civilizations, it would seem, grow through an *elan* which carries them from challenge through response to further challenge, and this growth has both outward and inward aspects. In the Macrocosm growth reveals itself as a progressive mastery over the external environment; in the Microcosm as a progressive self-determination or self-articulation.[14]

Either of these manifestations of growth, progressive conquest of the external environment or developing self-determination, can be possible criteria for the progress of the *elan* itself. Progressive self-determination is the standard Toynbee chooses as the norm according to which one can measure growth in a civilization.

Increasing control over the external environment can be achieved in two distinct areas, in the human environment and in the physical environment. Progressive mastery over the human environment usually takes the form of military conquest and expansion, while increasing control over the physical environment consists in improving material techniques. Military conquest and geographical expansion can be rejected immediately as a criterion of growth, for it ordinarily coincides with symptoms of the breakdown and disintegration of a civilization such as the universal state created by militarism.[15] To eliminate improving techniques in the control of the physical environment as a criterion of true growth of a civilization is not so simple a task. Modern archaeologists seem to take it for granted that "a supposed series of stages in the improvement of material technique is . . . indicative of a corresponding succession of chapters in the progress of civilization." Toynbee will not accept any archaeological scheme and its series of "ages," distinguished perforce by labels indicating certain technological improvements, if they are taken as representing corresponding stages in the progress of civilizations. Such a conception is suspect at the very outset because of its undoubted appeal to the preconceptions of our modern society, which is "fascinated by its own recent technical triumphs." Furthermore, it is a classic example of where the scholar tends to become the slave of materials which the accidents of time alone have deposited for examination. By the very nature of his work the archaeologist is bound to the material vestiges and products of early man, the techniques, while everything else has perished. Finally, the evidence from historical civilizations is decidedly against viewing improvement in technology as the criterion of true growth.

> When we turn to the evidence we . . . find cases of technique improving while civilizations remain static or go into decline, as well as examples of the converse situation in which techniques remain static while civilizations are in movement—either forward or backward as the case may be.[16]

True growth and progress in civilizations consists in progressive self-determination, though, it seems, the progress in technology paves the way for true growth.

> The process liberates forces that have been imprisoned in a more material medium and thereby sets them free to work in a more ethereal medium with a greater potency . . . [and] a consequent transfer of energy, or shift of emphasis, from some lower sphere of being or action to a higher.

Again Toynbee comes up with a label for this movement or shift of energies from the lower to the higher, and it is called "etherialization." Through increasing control of material techniques it becomes possible for the society to concentrate its energies on inner and more spiritual challenges. Challenge-and-response have been elevated from the material and external to the spiritual and internal.

Growth means that the growing personality or civilization tends to become its own environment and its own challenge and its own field of action. In other words, the criterion of growth is progress toward self-determination.[17]

Toynbee now turns to the question of how this process actually works in a society, and the answer can be simply stated: "growth of civilizations is the work of creative individuals or creative minorities." The action of the creative individual, or of the creative minority, can be described as a movement of "withdrawal-and-return." In the case of individuals there is a withdrawal from social life, voluntary or involuntary, for the purpose ultimately of personal enlightenment followed by a return to society with the mission of enlightening the rest of that society. This process can be seen exemplified in St. Paul, Buddha, Muhammed, and Machiavelli. Withdrawal followed by a return is characteristic of the creative minorities also. For a time these minorities—really subsocieties—are markedly withdrawn from the general life of the society, but then return to make distinctive contributions to the larger society. In the past, Italy and England have been examples of this movement in relation to the earlier chapters of Western civilization as a whole, and, for the future, Russia offers a distinct possibility.[18]

It is not sufficient to advert simply to the movement of withdrawal-and-return, for unless the "creations" of the individuals or minorities concerned are accepted in some way by the majority of the society, growth will not follow. The "cake of custom" has to be broken, and social acceptance of the contribution must follow in some way or there is no true growth of a civilization. In practice, social acceptance is secured by *mimesis*, or imitation by the majority, of the externals of the "act of creation" by the pioneers. No doubt this is a "short cut" taken by the uncreative majority, exposing the civilization to the perils of a breakdown, yet it seems to be the inevitable path of growth.[19]

As a result of the growth in a civilization, there arises differentiation within the society itself, but more markedly a differentiation of the civilization as a whole from its neighbors. Evidence for the latter can be seen most easily in the domain of art, for "every civilization creates an artistic style of its own." Yet this characteristic artistic style is not the only phenomenon that differentiates civilizations, but "civilizations lay differing degrees of emphasis on particular lines of activity." Characteristic of the Hellenic civilization was a predominantly aesthetic outlook on life, while a predominantly religious outlook distinguishes the Indic and, its affiliate, the Hindu, civilizations from others. Our own Western civilization displays "a penchant toward machinery," which, on the whole, seems quite unattractive to Toynbee. At this point Toynbee refuses to go any further with the analysis, not being prepared to follow Spengler's journey into the "fantastic" nor to accept the latter's "prime symbols." "The variety manifested in human life and institutions is a superficial phenomenon which masks an underlying unity without impairing it." Civilization can be compared to seeds, no doubt, each with its own destiny, but "the seeds are all of one kind."[20] Spengler's absolute cultural relativism is not the variety Toynbee accepts, for he is convinced of the fundamental sameness of human nature everywhere.

Breakdowns of Civilizations

The breakdown of civilizations is a more obvious problem for Toynbee than the growth of civilizations. All of the identified civilizations, living and dead, have broken down except possibly the Western. A breakdown, in Toynbee's terminology, means "the termination of a period of growth," and is to be distinguished from the disintegration of a civilization. Can one describe the nature of such recurring termination to the period of growth in a civilization? Toynbee has few doubts in the matter and gives the following summary. "The nature of the breakdowns of civilizations can be summed up in three points: a failure of creative power in the minority, an answering withdrawal of mimesis on the part of the majority, and a consequent loss of social unity in the society as a whole."[21] The next step will be to ascertain the causes of breakdowns, but it is already clear that it is a question of causes arising from within the society itself.

In vigorous fashion Toynbee disposes of various deterministic theories that would place the cause of breakdowns in the operation of some cosmic force outside the control of man. Lucretius' theory of "cosmic senescence," Spengler's "organismic" theory of civilizations, and a theory called the "dysgenic," concentrating on biological elements, are all disposed of rapidly by Toynbee. The last of the "deterministic" theories, that of the "theory of cycles" in human history, found in Plato and Virgil, merits closer attention from Toynbee, and not without reason. Has he not continually pointed to Western civilization as the only one of the species that has not yet broken down? One might be led to believe from his own reading of history that Western civilization is somehow compelled to "join the majority of its species." Even more clearly, Toynbee has been attempting to delineate recurrent elements in civilizations, the geneses, the growths, the breakdowns, and, to come, the disintegrations. He readily admits the presence of recurrent elements in history and offers an explanation through the medium of a metaphor. Recurrence joined with progress can be seen in the movement of a wheel of a vehicle in relation to the movement of the vehicle itself. The wheel's circular movement does not compel the vehicle itself to travel in circles.

Thus the detection of periodic repetitive movements in our analysis of civilization does not imply that the process itself is of the same cyclic order as they are. On the contrary, if any inference can legitimately be drawn from the periodicity of these minor movements, we may infer that the major movement which they bear along is not recurrent but progressive.[22]

Toynbee, at this point, has chosen to concentrate on lesser recurrences such as challenge-and-response or withdrawal-and-return, and movements of that nature, while ignoring the larger cycles of genesis, growth, breakdown, and disintegration. Later he returns to the larger aspects of the problem and rejects any Spenglerian notion that would have Western civilization bound to the fate of disintegration. Man is free, though within limits, is Toynbee's belief, and we need have no despair in the face of the ominous symptoms discernible in the state of Western civilization. As long as "the divine spark of creative power is still alive in us," prospects for our civilization can be hopeful.

Consistently enough, Toynbee also rejects any decline in control over the physical environment through decline in techniques, and the loss of mastery over the human environment through geographical contraction caused by military aggressors, as causes of the breakdowns of civilizations. Increase in mastery over the physical environment by improvement in techniques, together with developing control over the human environment by geographical expansion and military conquest, were eliminated before as criteria for the measurement of growth. Now the same processes in reverse are rejected as causes of the breakdowns of civilizations. The cause of the breakdown of a civilization is the "loss of self-determination," as the criterion for growth of a civilization was determined to be "progress in self-determination."[23]

A civilization loses its capacity for self-determination because of the attractions of mimesis. The "uncreative majority" of a civilization is bound, it seems, to take the short-cut to progress by mimesis, but this path is only a mechanical and superficial imitation of the "creative minority." The latter in turn may become infected with the spirit of mimesis themselves, and then the civilization becomes an "arrested civilization." Or the leaders, having lost the creative spark, may have recourse to the device of compulsion in order to retain their leadership, but then the rank and file of the society mutiny. In this situation the leaders have degenerated from a "creative minority" to a "dominant minority," while the "uncreative majority," the followers, have become a "proletariat," a group in but not of the society. This loss of harmony between the leaders and followers brings on a corresponding loss of self-determination on the part of the civilization as a whole, and breakdown has occurred.[24]

Now it may be true that "loss of self-determination" is the ultimate cause of breakdowns, but it has different sources and manifests itself in different forms. Basically, the sources of breakdowns appear to be two: "new wine in old bottles" and the "nemesis of creativity." The first source consists in a situation where new dynamic forces are introduced into an existing set of institutions, the "new wine in old bottles." Ideally, there should be a harmonious adjustment of existing structures and institutions to the new forces, and where these occur the society will continue to grow. If, on the other hand, there have been complete frustrations in the adjustment of structures to the new creative forces, then a breakdown of the civilization can be diagnosed. It is possible that a delayed and violent adjustment of structures to the new elements may occur with revolutions. The symptom, revolutions, does not permit a diagnosis of breakdown, but revolutions do indicate that the future growth of the society is questionable.[25] At the root of the breakdown, in this case, appears to be a complete failure of mimesis on the part of the uncreative majority.

Another general source of the breakdowns of civilizations is the "nemesis of creativity," and the expression "pride goes before a fall" sums up the meaning quite nicely. There is a passive way of succumbing to the nemesis of creativity where the "ex-creators," those responsible for earlier contributions, are found "resting on their oars." Their complacency and passivity toward the present situation is rooted in an idolization of the past, their past. It may take several forms, such as the worship of the creator's own personality or that of the society in some phase of the past, or, in a more specific way, the idolization of some particular institution or technique of the past. There are also more active forms of succumbing to the nemesis of creativity, and militarism or the intoxication with success manifest it. Fundamentally, it appears to be a question of pride, pride in one's past achievements, whether they be institutions, techniques, victories or successes, even the past of the society as a whole. Pride, leading to sloth or to ambition, tends to stifle the creativity necessary for continuing growth of the civilization, bringing it to a standstill, and thus we have a breakdown.[26]

Disintegrations of Civilizations

The first problem that arises is whether disintegration is a natural and inevitable sequel to breakdown. Toynbee's answer to the problem is that some civilizations have not disintegrated after breakdown but rather have entered upon a long period of petrifaction. Hence there is an alternative to disintegration following upon a breakdown, and it is a "petrified civilization." The classic example of petrifaction is the Egyptiac civilization, which lingered on during "two supernumerary millennia," inert and petrified, something like the "petrified forms" diagnosed by Spengler. Another example of petrifaction is adduced in the case of the Far Eastern civilization in China, while various fossilized fragments of otherwise extinct civilizations are also added to the listing.[27]

Toynbee's further researches into the problem of disintegration do not reveal anything startlingly new. In the very first pages of the Study he had settled on three leading phenomena, which he derived from his fundamental model of the Hellenic world, as indicative of the death of an old civilization and the birth of a new one. These three key phenomena, which had accompanied the decline of the Graeco-Roman world, turn out to be the leading results accompanying the disintegration of any civilization. Where one finds such elements as a universal state, a universal church, and a Völkerwanderung, one has found the products and symptoms of a civilization that is disintegrating.

The outstanding criterion for the recognition of a disintegration is a schism of the body social into three fractions: a "dominant minority," an "internal proletariat," and an "external proletariat." The formerly creative minority has become uncreative, yet strives to retain its leadership of the society now by force, thus transforming itself into a dominant minority. Because of this compulsion, "secessions" from the body social take place among the formerly uncreative majority, thus creating the schism of the body social. The uncreative majority originally included not only residents within the borders of the society but also primitive neighbors who had been following the leaders of that society, and from these two elements in the followers spring the two proletariats after secession and schism, the internal and the external.[28] Yet the movement of social schism has another aspect to it, and it is better described as "schism-and-palingenesia." No doubt there is some ambiguity in the choice of terms, Toynbee admits, for he is not exactly referring to a rebirth but to the three leading phenomena discovered in the Hellenic model disintegration. Each of the three fractions of the disintegrating society is able to achieve a characteristic creation, and these constitute, at least for the time being, the palingenesia.[29]

The now-dominant minority has created the universal state, the internal proletariat has brought about the emergence of a universal church, and the external proletariat has been responsible for the eruption of barbarian war bands. Toynbee is able to find abundant certification among various civilizations of the past for the threefold pattern accompanying the schism in the body social. He then embarks on a long journey of analysis of the corresponding "schism in the soul" of individual members of the disintegrating societies. These constitute the more fundamental "schisms" and underlie the more superficial schism in the body social.[30] There is little need for us to accompany Toynbee on that journey. More to our purpose is the "rhythm in which new challenges constantly meet successful and successive responses." This "rhythm" need not end, unless a challenge arise with which the society is unable to cope. In this tragic case the civilization has suffered a breakdown, and at this point, too, a "correlative rhythm" begins, the rhythm of disintegration, excepting, of course, the case of a "petrified civilization." Throughout the whole process of disintegration the very same challenge presents itself continually to the society. Partial and temporary successes in the face of this continuing challenge are followed alternately by failures until there is a final failure and dissolution of the civilization. There is a definite rhythm here, Toynbee believes, and the military language of "rout-rally-rout-rally . . ." expresses it as well as any. "Three-and-a-half beats seems to be the pattern which fits the histories of a number of disintegrating societies."[31]

Reluctant to leave the fascinating problem of the disintegrations of civilizations, Toynbee finds a "master-tendency" at work in disintegrations, a tendency toward "standardization and uniformity," and one unlike another master tendency found during the growth stage of civilizations. During growth the tendency was toward "differentiation and diversity," but during disintegration all phenomena manifest a certain standardizing uniformity. On a superficial plane one can notice the uniformity of three and a half beats in the rhythm of disintegration. A more significant uniformity is evident in the uniform schism of a disintegrating society into three sharply divided classes and the uniform works of creation achieved by each. Even more remarkable, Toynbee thinks, is the uniformity of ways of behavior, feeling, and life revealed in the deeper schisms of the individual souls.[32] Nevertheless, one need not be overly disturbed by the appalling lockstep manifest in disintegrating civilizations, nor even by the more disheartening treadmill cycle of civilizations. Inspired by Goethe's *Faust* once again, Toynbee ends his treatment of the cycle of civilizations on an optimistic and poetic note.

> The work of the Spirit of the Earth, as he weaves and draws his threads on the Loom of Time, is the temporal history of man as this manifests itself in the geneses and growths and breakdowns and disintegrations of human societies; and in all this welter of life and tempest of action we can hear the beat of an elemental rhythm whose variations we have learnt to know as challenge-and-response, withdrawal-and-return, rout-and-rally, apparentation-and-affiliation, schism-and-palingenesia. This elemental rhythm is the alternating beat of Yin and Yang; and in listening to it we have recognized that, although strophe may be answered by antistrophe, victory by death, creation by destruction, birth by death, the movement that this rhythm beats out is neither the fluctuation of an indecisive battle nor the cycle of a treadmill. The perpetual turning of a wheel is not a vain repetition if, at each revolution, it is carrying the vehicle nearer its goal; and, if palingenesia signifies the birth of something new and not just something that has lived and died before, then the Wheel of Existence is not just a devilish machine for inflicting everlasting torment on a damned Ixion. On this showing the music that the rhythm of Yin and Yang beats out is the song of creation. . . .[33]

The reader may be forgiven if he finds less music in the air than Toynbee after this rapid review of his cyclical view of civilizations. It has not yet appeared where Toynbee's vehicle is headed, if anywhere. A remarkable *tour de force* by Toynbee himself in the later volumes will point the vehicle of progress in a definite direction and mark out the path.

Progress and Religion

The third and final series of volumes of A *Study of History* begins with a doubt about the validity of the procedure followed in the earlier volumes. So far Toynbee has been working on the assumption that a comparative study of the geneses, growths, breakdowns, and disintegrations of the twenty-one civilizations would succeed in identifying everything of significance in the history of mankind since the time when the first civilization emerged from the primitive societies. Research has indicated that the typical products of a disintegrating civilization, the universal state, universal church, and barbarian war bands, are linked with still other civilizations, both contemporary and noncontemporary. It would seem that as a consequence the typical results of disintegration cannot be considered purely as by-products of one civilization but that they demand study on their own. Until one examines the claims of institutions of each of these three kinds to be intelligible fields of study in themselves, and also considers the alternative possibility that they might be parts of some larger whole embracing them and the civilizations alike, Toynbee believes that one "cannot be sure that we have brought within our purview the whole of human history above the primitive level."[34]

We can reverse the order of Toynbee's examination of universal states, universal churches, and barbarian war bands and regroup his conclusions according to this final scale of values by beginning with the latter. The barbarian war bands, and the "heroic age" arising from their "secession" from the disintegrating civilization, on the whole are not considered to have much long-range value in the history of civilizations. No doubt one can find some worth in their heroic legends, which were developed during their own peculiar sort of challenge after initial triumphs, but posterity is not overly indebted to the *Völkerwanderung*. In some instances there has been a service performed for mankind by the barbarian war bands; the interloping barbarian did in some cases provide a link between the defunct civilization and its newborn successor.[35] Toynbee is prepared to admit a certain usefulness of some barbarian groups for the "continuity of history," but this function is limited to the linkage between first- and second-generation civilizations.

Barbarian war bands are the characteristic creation of the external

proletariats of dying civilizations, while the universal state is the characteristic solution to the ever-present challenge confronting a disintegrating
civilization of the dominant minorities. Hence universal states have more
than one feature about them; not only accompaniments of social breakdown and products of dominant minorities, they are the expressions of a
particularly notable rally in the rhythm of rout-rally. They set a term to
the "time of troubles" which had come upon the society. As checks to the
process of disintegration, universal states "cling to life," but one should not
mistake this tenacity for true vitality. It is the obstinacy of the aged who
refuse to die. Yet some members of the crumbling society mistake the
universal state for final terms and goals of the process rather than recognizing them for what they are, means to a further end.

> Universal states show a strong tendency to behave as if they were
> ends in themselves, whereas in truth they represent a phase in the
> process of social disintegration and, if they have any significance be-
> yond that, can have it in virtue of being a means to some end that is
> outside and beyond them.[36]

This is not to say that the dominant minorities responsible for the establishment of universal states have in mind any other purpose than the
conservation of the disintegrating society. In the long run their purpose is
not fulfilled, for another purpose aside from their intention is ultimately
realized.

There can be only three possible beneficiaries of the "services" unconsciously rendered by a universal state: the internal and external proletariats
(and their characteristic creations) or some alien and contemporary civilization. If the service is rendered to the internal proletariat, as we shall see
that it always has been, then in reality the universal state will be ministering to one of the higher religions, which derive from the creative act of
the internal proletariat. An "empirical survey" of the service "involuntarily"
offered by universal states and of the "uses made of these facilities by
internal proletariats, external proletariats, and alien civilizations" offers
convincing support for the position that "the sole sure beneficiary from
the services afforded by a universal state is the internal proletariat." Among
these services are included the peace and order authored by the universal
state, and what is called by Toynbee the general "conductivity" of
empires.[37] The same conclusion appears if a study is made of the "institutions" of the universal state, their net of communications and transport,
their languages, legal systems, calendars, armies, citizenships, colonies,
provinces, and even imperial cities. "Passing in review" all of these institutions leads to the inescapable conclusion that "the principal beneficiaries
of the institutions maintained by universal states have been universal
churches." The higher religions and their universal churches are the ends
to which the benefits of universal states are unconsciously and ultimately
ordered.

Toynbee defends his view of the ultimate purposes of universal states against several contrary views of the nature of religion. One such view holds that the "higher religions are essentially and incurably antisocial," and consequently were responsible for the demise of the empires. Toynbee rejects this view as a basic misunderstanding of the nature of the higher religions, for "the spiritual progress of individual souls in this life" will in fact bring with it more social progress than could be attained in any other way.[38] The universal churches cannot reasonably be viewed "as cancers eating away at the living tissues of civilizations." Still another, less unsympathetic, view is possible of the relation between the universal churches and civilizations: perhaps the churches could be considered as "chrysalises" or as "part of the reproductive system of civilizations, serving as egg, grub, and chrysalis between butterfly and butterfly." There is a partial truth here, Toynbee believes, for all of the existing civilizations do have a universal church in their background through which they are affiliated to the civilizations of the second generation. Nevertheless, if one climbs to the "bird's-eye viewpoint" from which all civilizations can be seen simultaneously, then it is apparent at once that "the church-chrysalis is not the only medium through which one civilization can be affiliated to another." We have already seen that Toynbee is of the belief that the external proletariats (barbarian war bands) were responsible for the birth of some of the second-generation civilizations, and the other civilizations of this generation are seen to be the result of the activity of the dominant minorities. What is true about the view that holds the universal churches to be "chrysalises-mediums" is that

> all the known universal churches were developed within the disin-
> tegrating bodies social of civilizations of the second generation; that
> none of the civilizations of the third generation, though several of
> them are (and all of them may be) broken-down and disintegrating,
> shows any convincing evidence of producing a second crop of uni-
> versal churches.[39]

If this is so, then it is at least possible that the original assumption of the *Study* was partially in error by assuming that civilizations were the "protagonists in history." The histories of civilizations might have to be envisaged and interpreted in terms not of their own destinies, but of their effect on the "history of Religion."[40] A third species within the genus of societies that are "intelligible fields of study" has now appeared on the scene, and its members are the higher religions. The churches that embody the higher religions "are a distinct, and higher, species of the genus" that now includes the primitive societies, civilizations, and higher religions. And what is it that serves to distinguish this last and highest species from the others?

The distinguishing mark of the churches was that they all had as a

member the One True God. This human fellowship with the One
True God, which had been approached in the primitive religions and
had been attained in the higher religions, gave to these societies
certain virtues not to be found in primitive societies or civilizations.[41]

Perhaps one might be forced to conclude that the higher religions of
Christianity, Islam, Hinduism, and Mahayana (Buddhism), are the "protagonists in history" rather than the civilizations.

Convinced that the higher religions are instances of a new and
spiritually higher species than civilizations, Toynbee reverses his field
to consider "civilizations in terms of churches" rather than "churches in
terms of civilizations," as he had previously attempted. As representatives
of a lower species, and thus subordinate to the higher religions, civilizations can be classes as either "overtures" (chrysalises) to higher religions
or "regressions" (cancers?) from higher religions. Civilizations as a whole
are to be judged in relation to their "spiritual sequel." On this rating,
civilizations of the first generation appear to pertain, though only indirectly, to the classification of "overtures" to higher religions. On the
one hand, they gave birth to the secondary civilizations from which
emerged the higher religions and developed the "rudimentary higher religions" whose inspiration contributed to the growth and development of
the higher religions. Clearly the secondary civilizations are perfect representatives of civilization overtures, having been the sources of the higher
religions. Third-generation civilizations must be classed as "regressions"
from the higher religions, having no "spiritual sequel," having, rather, set
out to live a new "secular life" of their own.[42]

The Modern Western civilization, as the only member of the
third-generation type that has not yet broken down (although it is in the
state of disintegration) finds itself, on the principles of Toynbee, in an
unenviable position. However, though at the moment it appears as a
"civilization-regression," there may be some opportunity for it to move
closer to the "overture" variety of civilization.

> Perhaps the one conceivable justification for the existence of the
> Modern Western Civilization, on the view of history that we are now
> presenting, was that it might perform for Christianity and her three
> living sister religions the service of providing them with a mundane
> meeting-ground on a world-wide scale, by bringing home to them the
> unity of their own ultimate values and beliefs, and by confronting
> them alike with the challenge of a recrudescence of idolatry in the
> peculiarly vicious form of Man's corporate worship of himself.[43]

As lower and subordinate species, civilizations find their ultimate
purpose and significance in ministering to the progress of religions. Here
is the second, and last, of the "master-keys" that Toynbee has to offer
for the unlocking of the secrets of history. Once again the metaphor of

the chariot and its wheel is called in to do the duty of expressing this
final truth.

> If the movement of the chariot of Religion was constant in its direc-
> tion, the cyclic and recurrent movement of the rise and falls of civ-
> ilizations might be not only antithetical but subordinate. It might
> serve its purpose, and find its significance, in promoting the chariot's
> ascent toward Heaven by periodic revolutions on Earth of the "sor-
> rowful wheel" of birth-death-birth.

If one should ask why such a "sorrowful" means is necessary for the
progress of religion, then the answer lies "in the truth that Religion
is a spiritual activity and that spiritual progress is subject to a 'law' proclaimed by Aeschylus . . . 'we learn by suffering.' "[44]
    Christianity, whose essence "is the essence of the higher religions as
a class," can serve as the exemplar of spiritual and religious progress.
Christianity in its direct lines, according to Toynbee, goes back through
Christ to the Hebrew prophets, from there to Moses, and from Moses
to Abraham. Accompanying, or rather ministering, to these steps in the
progress of Christianity were the disintegrations, in order, of the Hellenic, Babylonic, Egyptiac, and Sumeric civilizations. From the debris
of four civilizations arose eventually the higher religion of Christianity.[45]
No doubt something of the same type of progress can be seen in the
cases of the other three higher religions, Islam, Hinduism, and Mahayana
Buddhism. Surely this is a "sorrowful wheel" to behold.
    But what of the future? Does not the growing unification of the
world, brought about by the universal features of Modern Western civilization, afford a precious opportunity for that unity of mankind which
Toynbee appears to see as the ultimate goal? "There can be no unity
of Mankind without the participation of God." Only the higher religions,
which "offer fellowship with the One True God" and, further, have "as
a member the One True God," could conceivably be the societies capable
of bringing this off. But why not one "commonwealth of God," one
civitas Dei, one highest religion, at whose birth modern Western civilization could assist—if need be, through its disintegration? Toynbee is
attracted by such a concluding finale to his vision of the progress of religion through the cycles of civilizations, but he does not go all the way
with it. Attached in his own way to Christianity, and yet fully aware of
the virtues of her three "sister religions," he cannot bring himself to
visualize some synthetic highest religion that would be capable of "ministering to the whole gamut of the Psyche's elemental needs for expression." A truly "universal Religion" is "doomed to disappointment."
    Any claim to catholicity on the part of the four living higher religions
singly and exclusively must be judged an invalid claim, though it is
possible to regard the claim of catholicity as valid if the four are con-

sidered collectively. Calling upon Jung's psychology for support, Toynbee believes that "each of the living higher religions, and their principal sects, have been attuned to some particular psychological type or subtype." Consequently, any one of them that "claimed already to be *the* Universal Religion must be unaware of its own intrinsic limitations." Yet some estimate can be given of the "relative value" of the higher religions. Of the four "faculties" that Toynbee accepts as characteristic of the psychological makeup of man—feeling, thinking, intuition, sensation—the religion making the most use of the highest faculty would be, relatively speaking, the best of the lot. "Feeling" is highest in order of rank among the "faculties" of man, and hence Christianity, the only one of the four higher religions using "feeling" as its dominant approach to reality, must be rated the highest. "The most valuable instruments in the orchestra of Religion would be those that played the music of Love, and . . . Christianity would head the list because, in Christianity, feeling was the predominant faculty." On another count, however, Hinduism must be judged in the lead at the present, because of its "spontaneous charity toward all revelations—past, present, and to come—which was the first spiritual requirement in an age in which the whole of Mankind had been united in a single Great Society through the 'annihilation of distance' by a Western technology."[46]

It may be possible that the future will bring a political unification of the world by Western civilization, a universal state embracing the entire surface of the planet in one commonwealth. A "virtual universality" on the planes of economics and technology has been attained already by Western civilization, and so political unification is not impossible. In such a situation "the historic living churches might eventually give to their unity in diversity by growing together into a single terrestrial Church Militant." Yet this would not be a "universal religion" of a new and highest type, and such a "unity in diversity" would preserve the specific nature of the higher religions. For this reason the Hindu acceptance of all revelations is the model for all the religions within a "literally ecumenical mundane framework."

> The divers higher religions must resign themselves to playing limited parts, and school themselves to playing these parts in harmony, in order, between them, to fulfill their common purpose of enabling every human being of every psychological type to enter into communion with God.[47]

Even if such a single church militant were effected on the earth, one must not think that paradise would be achieved, or that purely human society would be completely erased from the history of man.

The replacement of a multiplicity of civilizations and a diversity of higher religions by a single Church Militant on Earth would not have purged Human Nature of Original Sin; and this moral limitation on the possibility of perfection in This World has a political implication which limited the possibility still further. So long as Original. Sin continued to be an element in terrestrial Human Nature, there would always be work in This World for Caesar to do. . . . Human Society on Earth would not be able wholly to dispense with institutions . . . the perfect reflections of the moral imperfections of Human Nature; and these social products of Original Sin would always have to be administered by a secular arm.[48]

This world is "a province of the Kingdom of God," but it is a "rebellious province," and would always remain so because of original sin.

True progress for mankind is not to be conceived of as social progress but as "increasing spiritual opportunity for souls in their passages through this earthly life," and such opportunity is offered by each of the higher religions. "The progress of individual souls through this World towards God, and not the progress of Society in This World, is the end in which the supreme value is found."[49]

NOTES

1. A. Toynbee, *Civilization on Trial*, in *Civilization on Trial and The World and the West* (New York: Meridian, 1958), pp. 18–19.

2. Toynbee, *Civilization*, pp. 20–21.

3. See H. Stuart Hughes, *Oswald Spengler* (New York: Scribner, 1962), p. 186. The literature on Toynbee, much of it critical, is extensive. Several worthwhile cooperative efforts are A. Montagu (ed.), *Toynbee and History* (Boston: Beacon Press, 1956), and the more compact E. Gargan (ed.), *The Intent of Toynbee's History* (Chicago: Loyola University Press, 1961). Not to be omitted from any listing of Toynbee's critics is Pieter Geyl's *Debates with Historians* (New York: Meridian, 1958), pp. 109–202. An exhaustive bibliography appears in Toynbee's twelfth volume of *A Study of History*, entitled *Reconsiderations* (New York: Oxford, 1964), pp. 680–690.

4. A. Toynbee, *A Study of History*, Vol. I of D. C. Somervell's authorized abridgment (London and New York: Oxford, 1946), pp. 11, 35.

5. See Toynbee, *Study*, Vol. I, pp. 36–41.

6. See Toynbee, *Study*, Vol. I, pp. 11, 42. Toynbee's critics take note that he has nowhere very clearly defined what civilization is, though he makes repeated efforts to distinguish it from a primitive society. The problem is taken up again in *Reconsiderations* (pp. 273–280) in answer to the critics. There a definition is given: "an endeavor to create a state of society in which the whole of mankind will be able to live together in harmony, as members of a single, all-inclusive family," p. 279.

7. In *Reconsiderations* Toynbee devotes a great deal of space to answering this criticism (pp. 144–216). He still is not altogether convinced that the

"Hellenic model" was misused, though now he finds room for "Chinese" and "Jewish" models also.

8.   Toynbee, Study, Vol. I, p. 14.

9.   Toynbee, Study, Vol. I, p. 47.

10.   Toynbee, Study, Vol. I, pp. 245, 51–52, 67, 59.

11.   See Toynbee, Study, Vol. I, pp. 60–77. Evidently for Toynbee, "English empiricism," the method he was going to substitute for Spengler's a priori approach to the genesis of civilizations, is not to be identified with the "scientific method."

12.   Toynbee, Study, Vol. I, p. 153; see also pp. 153–160. Table V, appended to this volume, attempts to portray in one chart Toynbee's reconstructions of civilizations.

13.   See Toynbee, Study, Vol. I, pp. 164–185. The "arrested" civilizations are distinguished from the "abortive" as "infantile paralysis" differs from "infantile mortality."

14.   Toynbee, Study, Vol. I, p. 189.

15.   See Toynbee, Study, Vol. I, pp. 189–192.

16.   Toynbee, Study, Vol. I, pp. 192–193.

17.   Toynbee, Study, Vol. I, pp. 198, 208.

18.   Toynbee, Study, Vol. I, p. 214; see also pp. 217–240.

19.   See Toynbee, Study, Vol. I, p. 216.

20.   See Toynbee, Study, Vol. I, pp. 241–243.

21.   Toynbee, Study, Vol. I, p. 246. The difference between a "breakdown" and "disintegration" is clarified in a note by Somervell, pp. 273–274.

22.   Toynbee, Study, Vol. I, p. 254; see also pp. 246–254. Toynbee returns to the larger aspects of the problem in Volume Two of the abridgment, pp. 261–301, and especially pp. 271–279.

23.   Toynbee, Study, Vol. I, pp. 255–273.

24.   See Toynbee, Study, Vol. I, pp. 275–279.

25.   See Toynbee, Study, Vol. I, pp. 279–307.

26.   See Toynbee, Study, Vol. I, pp. 307–360.

27.   See Toynbee, Study, Vol. I, pp. 360–363.

28.   See Toynbee, Study, Vol. I, pp. 364–368, 371–428.

29.   See Toynbee, Study, Vol. I, p. 369. Later, it seems that "palingenesia" is restricted to the "universal church," though one is not altogether certain; see pp. 531–532.

30.   See Toynbee, Study, Vol. I, p. 429; see also pp. 430–532.

31.   Toynbee, Study, Vol. I, pp. 548–549.

32.   Toynbee, Study, Vol. I, p. 555.

33.   Toynbee, Study, Vol. I, pp. 556–557.

34.   Toynbee, Study, Vol. II (New York and London: 1957), pp. 1–2.

35.   Toynbee, Study, Vol. II, p. 140; see also pp. 120–143, especially the chart on page 142.

36.   Toynbee, Study, Vol. II, pp. 2–3.

37.   Toynbee, Study, Vol. II, p. 21; see also pp. 11–21.

38.   Toynbee, Study, Vol. II, pp. 79–80. The opinion rejected is that of

J. G. Frazer's *The Golden Bough,* though Gibbon's *Decline and Fall* comes in for criticism also.

39.   Toynbee, *Study,* Vol. II, pp. 82, 86, 87. Toynbee admits that this "rather patronizing view of the role of the churches in history" had been his own view for a number of years.

40.   Toynbee, *Study,* Vol. II, p. 87.

41.   Toynbee, *Study,* Vol. II, p. 104.

42.   Toynbee, *Study,* Vol. II, pp. 88, 92, 111; the whole section, pp. 109–115, should be read. On page 111, Toynbee says, "when the life of a civilization has served as an overture to the birth of a living church, the death of the precursor civilization may be regarded not as a disaster, but as the proper conclusion of the story." On page 113, he notes, "we must conclude that the renaissance of a dead civilization [certain aspects are involved in a third-generation civilization] spells a regression from a living higher religion and that, the farther the revival is pushed, the greater the backsliding will be."

43.   Toynbee, *Study,* Vol. II, pp. 92–93. Later, Toynbee returns to the "prospects of the Western Civilization," pp. 302–349, but I can find no noteworthy modification of the earlier position. Nor is there much difference to be seen in the volume of *Reconsiderations,* though caution in assessing the symptoms and prospects of the West is a new characteristic.

44.   Toynbee, *Study,* Vol. II, pp. 92, 88.

45.   Toynbee, *Study,* Vol. II, pp. 88–89.

46.   Toynbee, *Study,* Vol. VII of the original, pp. 734–735.

47.   Toynbee, *Study,* Vol. VII of the original, p. 734.

48.   Toynbee, *Study,* Vol. VII of the original, p. 556.

49.   Toynbee, *Study,* Vol. VII of the original, p. 564. In *Reconsiderations* Toynbee comes up with a new listing of higher religions as well as of civilizations.

11

THE RHYTHM OF THE SUPERSYSTEMS:

Pitirim Sorokin

Pitirim Sorokin, for many years chairman of the department of sociology at Harvard, seems to have been denied the thrill of Spengler's and Toynbee's one "moment of illumination" from which their theories sprang. He began life in 1889, the son of a poor Russian itinerant artisan and a peasant mother among the Komi people in the north of Russia. After an eventful and rather grim youth, Sorokin somewhat surprisingly became a student and then teacher at the University of St. Petersburg. Combining the career of an active revolutionary with that of budding scholar, he was no ordinary professor. By 1916, Sorokin had arrived at a sociological view that represented a sort of "synthesis of Comtean-Spencerian sociology of evolution-progress," updated and corrected by the latest Russian and European theories. "All in all," Sorokin confesses, "it was an optimistic *Weltanschauung*, fairly similar to the prevalent 'World View' of the Russian and Western thinkers of the pre-catastrophic decade of the twentieth century." But events of 1917 in Russia demanded Sorokin's reexamination of his "sweet and cheerful" view of things.

The Russian Revolution of 1917 and Sorokin's personal experiences for the next five years in Russia lent little support to his uncritically accepted views of progress and social evolution. The revolution, with its "explosion of the forces of ignorance, unhumanity, and death," led him to question the "progressive, rational-positivistic sociology." Questioning soon developed into rejection of the old views during the five years that Sorokin lived in Communist Russia. "There was too much hate, hypocrisy, blindness, sadistic destruction, and mass-murder to leave my 'cheerfully progressive' views intact."[1] Banished from Russia by the Communists in 1922, after having been at one point sentenced to death, Sorokin continued to search for a more realistic theory, first in Europe and, after 1923, in America, where he remained. During his years of teaching sociology at the University of Minnesota, the new views were taking shape and finally matured while at Harvard.

The seeds of Sorokin's more mature view of the historical process are already apparent in *Contemporary Sociological Theories*, published in 1928. There he urges his fellow-sociologists to pay greater attention than was customary in the nineteenth century to the "cyclical, rhythmical and repeated phenomena in social life and history." It was entirely possible that such a concentration might make Vico's ambition of a new science of history a reality. The reference to Vico, rather than to Comte, is prophetical, for Sorokin's matured view is much closer to the *corsi* and *ricorsi* of Vico than to the unilinear three-stage law of Comte.

> Studying more and more different repeated social phenomena, we approach more and more to solution of the great sociological problem: what in the incessantly changing process of history is relatively permanent, and what is quite temporary; what is relatively universal, and what is purely local; what relations between two or more phenomena are incidental, and what are really causal. In this way sociology may more and more transform itself into this real "Scienza Nuova" of which the great Vico dreamed, and which he tried to establish.[2]

Sorokin's mature views appear in the four-volume *Cultural and Social Dynamics*, published between 1937 and 1941 while at Harvard. In the Preface to the first volume of this massive work Sorokin states his purposes in characteristic clear fashion:

> These volumes are an investigation of the nature and change, the dynamics of integrated culture: its types, its processes, its trends, fluctuations, rhythms, tempos. The main material with which this investigation deals is that provided by the Graeco-Roman and Western civilizations during the more than twenty-five hundred years of their history. In briefer fashion it touches also on the Egyptian, the Babylonian, the Hindu, the Chinese, and the Arabic cultures. It is not, however, a *history* of these cultures, but a *sociology of their change*. . . . Of the semi-historical disciplines which it resembles, it is nearest to what often is styled Philosophy of History.[3]

The *Dynamics* is a work of about 3000 pages, studded with tables of comparative statistics ranging over twenty-five centuries and more of human history. Immense labor lies behind the publication of these volumes, and scores of scholars and specialists all over America and Europe assisted in the compilation of the statistics. We have no need nor any intention of treading into this area; rather, we wish to present as simply as possible the major outlines of Sorokin's philosophy of history. Fortunately, some of the fundamental positions are summarily restated in Sorokin's later works.

The Sociocultural World

The foundation of the whole superstructure of Sorokin's philosophy of history and sociology is the constantly reiterated principle that the subject matter of social science differs vastly from that of other scientists. The chosen area of the social scientist is the totality of the sociocultural world, which is easily distinguishable from the physical and biological worlds, at least in its higher reaches.

> In contradistinction to the inorganic phenomena that have only one physico-chemical component, and to organic phenomena that have two components—physical and vital (life)—the cultural or super-organic phenomena have the "immaterial" component of meaning (or meaningful value or norm) that is superimposed upon the physical and/or vital components.

Once the element of meaning or value has been added to some physical object or to a biological organism it immediately enters into another world, the sociocultural world. "Any phenomenon that is an 'incarnation' or 'objectification' of mind and meanings superimposed upon its physical and/or biological properties is by definition a sociocultural phenomenon."[4]

Hence there are two dimensions to any cultural phenomenon. "Cultural phenomena have two aspects: the inner one, or the aspect of 'immaterial' (spaceless and timeless) meaning and value, and the external or 'material shell,' externalizing in the space-time continuum this meaning. . . ."[5] These aspects, the inner meaning and outer expression, are clearly distinct. A Shakespeare play, for example, can be "externalized" in various media: in books, on records, in dramatic action, in simple reading aloud, and so on. The "meaning," or inner aspect, of the play remains the same despite the use of widely differing "material vehicles." Furthermore, the identical physical "incarnation" can be used for the expression of extremely varied meanings; the ones just described obviously are not confined to being vehicles for Shakespeare's plays. Finally, the very same physical object or biological organism can bear a number of different meanings or values. The physical act of handing over money may be the repaying of a loan, a donation to charity, a bribe, or the initiation of some contract, moral or immoral. Cultural phenomena, consequently, differ markedly from phenomena of the physical and biological worlds.

The element of meaning is imposed upon physical and biological objects by persons who, in turn, are functioning not purely as physical objects or biological organisms but mainly as "mindful human personalities." Physically and biologically speaking there are no "kings" or "presidents" or "generals"; these "meanings" have been superimposed on the biological organisms by human beings and the sociocultural world they live in. Biologically considered, the organism of a "dictator" may be weaker than that of any of his subjects, but socioculturally his power is greater than that of his strongest subject. In and through their meaningful interactions with others, human beings objectify their meanings in and through a vast number of physical vehicles; they "materialize" the "immaterial" meanings, values, and norms of the human mind.[6]

Hence one can speak of a sociocultural world whose totality differs from the physical and biological worlds, and which is composed of individuals, meanings, and the material bearers or expressions of these meanings.

> The totality of the "immaterial" meanings-values-norms, not objectified as yet through the material vehicles but known to humanity; the totality of the already objectified meanings-values-norms with all their vehicles; finally the totality of mindful individuals and groups—past and present; these inseparable totalities make up the total sociocultural world, superimposed on mankind's physical and biological worlds.[7]

This totality, the sociocultural world as a whole, is field for investigation by the social scientist and sociologist. The natural scientist works with the physical and biological worlds, while the philosopher investigates "pure meanings" only.[8]

Sorokin's analysis of the sociocultural world reveals a variety of relations and interconnections among the sociocultural phenomena. Beginning with the most external and accidental types of connections between cultural phenomena, Sorokin ascends through more intimate and essential connections until he reaches the highest and ultimate level, the "meaningful-causal" type. At the bottom of this scale are interconnections, which he refers to as "cultural congeries." Such a grouping of cultural phenomena is not bound together by any causal or logical tie but purely by spatial (or temporal) proximity. The refuse area of any city or town would be an example of a "cultural congeries." Higher on the scale of interconnected cultural phenomena are what Sorokin calls the "semi-congeries united by an indirect causal bond." The contents of a man's pocket, for example, are not logically nor causally connected with each other, but they are directly related to the man's needs. Yet this relation between the objects in a man's pocket vanishes once the individual is removed from the situation. Both of the lower interconnections of cultural phenomena are reckoned as "congeries" rather than "systems" because of the sheerly accidental or loose relation between the elements.

At a higher level of interconnections lies the "system" or "unity" of cultural objects, that is, groupings which are bound together by much deeper ties than the congeries. A first and lower type of the systems are the "causal unities or systems," where the totality of cultural objects, phenomena, and processes are bound together into a "real unity or system by a direct causal tie." Sorokin gives the example of the outbreak of war or famine leading to the expansion of government regimentation in all societies of a certain type as an example of a causal unity or system. The two sociocultural phenomena are bound together in a causal unity by a direct causal tie, and hence one can speak of a causal unity or system.

On the highest level of the interconnections of cultural phenomena stands the "meaningful-causal systems or unities." Meaningful as well as causal ties bind together the cultural phenomena in such a system or unity. Before speaking of such systems, all of which are empirically grounded realities in the sociocultural world, Sorokin explains what he means by a "system of meanings." The interdependence in meaningful systems or unities is either logical or aesthetical, both of which differ from the purely causal bonds in a causal system. Logical unity exists where a number of propositions are "united into one meaningfully consistent and comprehensible whole," so that a radical change in one of the main propositions affects the others and necessitates changes in them in order to re-effect consistency. Sorokin believes that mathematics especially, followed by the natural and social sciences, the great philosophical systems, the creeds of the great religions, the great ethical systems, and even most of the law codes manifest such a consistency in their main propositions. The aesthetical type of meaningful system appears in all the great creations in the field of the fine and liberal arts, as all "display a seamless unity of style and content." Doubtless, individual creators have often failed to bring off such logical or aesthetical consistency in their creations, but such would not be considered by Sorokin to rank as meaningful systems. Failures would belong, it seems, to the general class of "cultural congeries," though ranking within this class as "meaningful congeries."

Thus far Sorokin has been concentrating on "systems of meanings" which pertain to the ideological level of culture only, but the real interest of the sociologist is with such systems when they enter fully and completely into the sociocultural world through actions and material vehicles. When such systems of meanings are "objectified" in the external order, they then have a behavioral as well as a material aspect and become "fully grounded in the empirical sociocultural world." When this is effected, then the system of meanings has become a "meaningful-causal system or unity." Empirically grounded systems of meanings are bound together not only by meaningful ties but also by newly developed causal relationships.

> When diverse persons, material objects, or energies become agents and vehicles of the same system of meanings, the component of the meanings throws a causal net over all such persons and vehicles and introduces a causal dependence where it would otherwise not have existed.

Harvard University, for example, presents just such a meaningfully related unity with consequent causal relations among the elements. Sorokin believes that almost all organized groups, from the family to the state, and all grounded cultural systems, from mathematics to the fine arts, are "causal-meaningful unities" of this type.[9]

Such unities or systems are the most integrated of all the systems in the sociocultural world. "The causal-meaningful unities are thus the most integrated kind of sociocultural grounded systems, and the causal-meaningful interconnections between cultural phenomena are the closest possible ties."[10] Not content to assert the empirical nature of the grounded and socialized cultural systems, Sorokin is most explicit about the full reality of such systems as a whole. "Both the elements of a sociocultural system, as well as the system as a whole are real, but the elements have the *reality of the parts, while the system has a reality of the whole.*"[11] Cultural systems truly grounded in reality are real precisely in their totality and unity and consequently can be expected to display properties like individuality and functions like change-in-togetherness which do not pertain to the elements in the system as such.[12]

Granted the validity of Sorokin's estimates of a sociocultural world, a specific method for the investigation of such a complexity seems to be called for. If the internal aspect, or the "meaning," of cultural phenomena marks the point of difference from other phenomena, the internal aspect, or "mentality," above all must be able to be understood by the investigator. "Any 'reading' of culture involves the understanding of its internal aspect and is impossible without such comprehension."[13] According to Sorokin, there are several possible ways of "reading" the book of culture. The first way, a "purely descriptive" reading, adverts only to pure spatial and temporal interconnections of cultural phenomena, treating everything as if it were a "cultural congeries." This approach to the sociocultural world completely misses the "real meaning" of sociocultural phenomena. Attainment to the "real meaning" of the cultural world is possible through the use of what Sorokin calls the "psychological" interpretation or through the "sociologico-phenomenological" method. If one approaches the internal aspect of cultural phenomena in an attempt to regard it "exactly in the same way as it was regarded by its creators or modifiers," then the psychological reading of the meaning of culture is being used.[14] In a number of instances the meaning or purpose of the cultural phenomena have been explicitly announced by their creators, and hence a psychological interpretation is possible and useful within limits. But there exists still another "real meaning" in cultural phenomena, and it is attainable only by means of the method that Sorokin labels the "sociologico-phenomenological."

Over and above, and indeed distinct from, the meaning or intention of the creator or modifiers of cultural phenomena there exists a "social meaning" that does not coincide with the psychological meaning. This is evident, Sorokin believes, if one takes into account "that the objective results of an activity deviate greatly from the subjective aims of those who undertake it." In a great number of cases of cultural complexes the "meaning of the creator and the social meaning do not at all coincide." Such a "discrepancy" between intention and effect "does not necessarily make a cultural complex meaningless." Furthermore, there are many cultural phenomena whose psychological meaning is unknown, since the motive or purpose behind them is not manifest through any direct evidence from the creators. "Yet they continue to be meaningful."[15] Hence Sorokin is convinced that a "social meaning" of cultural phenomena exists, and the "sociologico-phenomenological" method is able often to disclose it.[16]

One form, and the lowest form, of the "sociologico-phenomenological" method lies in the "causal-functional" approach to the internal aspect of cultural phenomena, adverting to the "causal-functional relationships between the component parts of a cultural value or complex."[17] This method uncovers causal relations between many of the variables in the sociocultural world which can be independent of the knowledge and intention of the persons responsible. A causal-functional formula establishes a uniformity of relation, or "patterns of uniformity," between the variables in question, as, for example, between urbanization and the crime rate, or between business cycles and the mortality rate. "Uniformity of relationship is the common denominator of causally united phenomena."[18] The "causal-functional" approach to cultural phenomena has as its area of investigation the "causal unities" or "causal systems" already referred to. This method is useful for the sociologist also, but it remains, to some extent, on the surface of the sociocultural world, rarely giving "an intimate or internal comprehension of the connection."[19] Often all that is known through this method is the pattern of uniformity, but there is little understanding of why such a regularity occurs. No doubt this is the common method of social scientists, but—and this appears to be

Sorokin's principal difficulty with the causal-functional method—it can never produce "a synthesis of all the variables."[20] The highest form of the sociologico-phenomenological method, the "logical" or logico-meaning-ful," is able to achieve such a synthesis often and to make intelligible the regularities in the sociocultural process.

"Hidden behind the empirically different, seemingly unrelated fragments of the cultural complex lies an identity of meaning, which brings them together into consistent *styles*, typical *forms*, and significant *patterns*."[21] If we have at hand an integrated cultural unity or system of the "meaningful-causal" variety, Sorokin is convinced that deep logical, or aesthetical, unity binds all of the relevant phenomena into a comprehensive, consistent whole. No longer is "uniformity of relationship" the common denominator of the system, as in the causal unity, but "identity (or similarity) of central meaning, idea, or mental bias that permeates all the logically related fragments."[22] No doubt, as already observed, there are "meaningful congeries" that, because of internal or aesthetic inconsistencies, do not present an integrated unity and thus a "meaningful system." How is one able to decide whether the cultural complex involved is either a congeries only or a system? The answer is simple: by the applications of logic to the culture complex in question. Question the elements as to their logical consistency, as to whether there are unifying principles that permeate all the components of a given configuration. If a given complex or culture is integrated, then the "major premise" should emerge through the logical method; the "identity of meaning" behind all the elements should become clear. No doubt, several "readings" of theories may be offered in explanation of the cultural complex, both suggesting different "major premises." The final test will be similar to that used in the natural sciences. That theory is best which describes the field of phenomena in question most accurately and embraces the largest number of phenomena.[23]

And yet one gets the impression that Sorokin, despite the array of statistics in the *Dynamics*, rests his "reading" of cultural systems and supersystems on something rather like "intuition."

> The properly trained mind apprehends, feels, perceives, senses and understands the supreme unity of Euclid's or Lobachevski's geometry of perfect mathematical deduction; of Platonic metaphysics; of Phidias's Athena; of a suite or concert by Bach; of a Shakespeare drama; of the architecture of the Parthenon or the Cathedral of Chartres. Such a mind comprehends their sublime unity internally, intimately; often feels it immediately and directly, senses it without any experimental or statistical manipulations and without indirect reasoning.[24]

The Rhythm of the Supersystems

In answer to the eternal question voiced by Pilate, "What is truth," Sorokin believes that there are only three possible positive answers. Agnosticism and skepticism are purely negative answers to the question and cannot form an adequate basis for any integrated system of truth. All the positive answers to the problem of truth fall into three classes, each "giving its own conception of truth, its source and its criteria." To these three classes of answers Sorokin attaches a label: "the ideational, the sensate and the idealistic systems of truth and knowledge."

> Ideational truth is *the truth revealed by the grace of God*, through his mouthpieces (the prophets, mystics, and founders of religion), disclosed in a supersensory way through mystic experience, direct revelation, divine intuition, and inspiration. Such a truth may be called *the truth of faith*. It is regarded as infallible, yielding adequate knowledge about the true-reality values.[25]

On another occasion Sorokin sums up the ideational answer to the problem of truth, value, and reality in these words:

> The ultimate, true reality-value is a supersensory and superrational God (Brahma, Tao, "Divine Nothing," and other equivalents of God). Sensory and any other reality or value are either a mirage or represent an infinitely more inferior and shadowy pseudo-reality and pseudo-value.[26]

A second answer to the problem of truth and the ultimate reality is radically opposed to the ideational and it is called the sensate system or answer. "Sensate truth is *the truth of the senses*, obtained through our organs of sense perception."[27] "The ultimate, true reality-value is *sensory*. Beyond it there is no other reality nor any other non-sensory value."[28] Consequently, there is a profound difference between the first two answers to the question about the ultimate reality and value in life, between the "ideational truth of faith" and the "sensate truth of the senses." But there is still one other positive answer possible, according to Sorokin, and it is the idealistic solution, which is not to be confused with the ordinary designation of idealism in philosophical circles.

Sorokin describes the idealistic answer in these terms:

> Idealistic truth is *a synthesis of both, made by our reason*. In regard to sensory phenomena, it recognizes the role of the sense organs as the source and criterion of the validity or invalidity of a proposition. In regard to supersensory phenomena, it claims that any knowledge of these is impossible through sensory experience, and is obtained

only through the direct revelation of God. Finally, our reason, through logic and dialectic, can derive many valid propositions—for instance, in all syllogistic and mathematical reasoning. . . . Human reason also "processes" the sensations and perceptions of our sense organs and transforms these into valid experience and knowledge. Human reason likewise combines into one organic whole the truth of the senses, the truth of faith, and the truth of reason.[29]

The idealistic, the ideational, and the sensate solutions to the fundamental problem of the nature of ultimate reality and value are the three main positive solutions given by the great thinkers of history. No other positive solution for the problem seems possible. The sensate position views the ultimate reality as sensory, finds its source in the truth of the senses, and judges all reality by this standard. The ideational solution considers the ultimate reality as supersensory, finds its source in the truth of faith (or intuition), and judges all things less than the superrational as shadowy beings at the best. A synthesis of the sensate and ideational is effected in some measure by the idealistic solution, which considers the ultimate reality as radically "ineffable and unutterable," combining in itself "the rational or logical, the sensory, and the superrational-suprasensory." Ultimately, this synthesis is effected by reason, and so one can speak of the truth of reason as the source and criterion of this middle position.

Sorokin believes that each of the views just outlined has something to be said for it. "Each source of knowledge—the senses, reason, and intuition—affords a genuine cognition of the manifold reality." Most of Sorokin's fellow-sociologists, presumably, would not deny the validity of sense knowledge or of logical reasoning, but ranking intuition along with such honored sources of knowledge was certain to arouse objection. Sorokin, consequently, time and again rises to the defense of intuitional knowledge; one summary he gives runs as follows:

Intuition in its ordinary form as a momentary and direct grasp of a certain reality—the grasp distinct from sensory perception or logical reasoning, yields a knowledge of this aspect of reality like, for instance, the certain validity of anyone of us that "I exist." In its extraordinary form, as a charismatic and mystic experience accessible, through the grace of God, to only a few prophets, great thinkers, great artists, and great religious leaders, it opens to us certain aspects of the true reality inaccessible to our logic and senses . . . even contemporary natural science and technology embody not merely the truth of the senses, but, in the field of mathematics and logic, for instance, a large portion of the truth of reason as well; and both of these truths are ultimately rooted in intuition or faith as the basic postulates of science.[30]

Sorokin is convinced that the three sources of knowledge, the senses, reason, and intuition, can achieve true knowledge of reality, but it is a partial knowledge, a partial truth, for ultimate truth and reality are "three-dimensional." "Each of these systems, when isolated from the rest, becomes less valid and more fallacious, even within the specific field of its own competence."[31] An undue stress or exclusive concentration on any of the three sources of knowledge can lead to error and falsehood in the end. Consequently, any cultural system built on a single foundation of sensory knowledge, or rational knowledge, or intuitional knowledge tends by its very nature to error and ultimate collapse.

Basic to Sorokin's understanding of the processes of history and cultural systems is the distinction he makes between "social systems" and "cultural systems." The two systems must not be confused, or one is apt to draw some hasty and erroneous conclusions after the manner of Spengler and Toynbee.

> By social system is meant an *organized group* that possesses a set of enforced, obligatory law norms defining in detail the rights, duties, social position and functions, roles and proper behavior of each and all its members toward one another, outsiders and the world at large; a set of prohibited actions-relations sanctioned by punishment; and a set of recommended non-obligatory norms of conduct. As a result of these norms, this organized group is a clearly differentiated and stratified body. . . .

Millions of organized groups of this type exist in the world, beginning with any association, the family, and ending with the caste, nation, state, and so on. Understood in this sense, a social system "does not coincide with a cultural system."[32] Many cultural systems, especially the fundamental ones, enter into the total culture of practically all social systems. Language, science, and religion are obvious examples of vast cultural systems that enter into the culture of most if not all social systems. Hence the boundaries of a social system and that of a cultural system do not coincide.

Even more significant, Sorokin holds, is the fact that there are many cultural systems that enter into the total culture of any social system. "The total culture of any organized group, even of a single person, consists not of one cultural system but of a multitude of vast and small cultural systems that are partly in harmony, partly out of harmony, with one another, and in addition many congeries of various kinds." What Sorokin is saying is that the total culture of any organized group, even of any individual, "is not wholly integrated into one meaningful-causal system."[33] Side by side with the meaningful-causal systems, large and small, there exists in the total culture of any organized group and of any individual a number of congeries, and the totality of this culture does not make one integrated cultural system.

Hence Sorokin criticizes both Spengler and Toynbee on their notions of cultures and civilizations. On the one hand, they understand their cultures and civilizations as a "real unity, in the sense of either a causal or causal-meaningful system." Spengler and Toynbee have assumed that their cultures or civilizations are completely integrated, thus representing a consistent and unified whole. The total culture of Egypt, India, the West, or China "cannot be completely integrated into one causal or meaningful-causal system," but represents the co-existence of many cultural systems and congeries. Furthermore, they "mix up" the cultural and social systems or groups and display an "additional inconsistency," even in this operation. In the main Toynbee's and Spengler's classifications of civilizations and cultures are "inconsistent classifications of organized groups and of a few semi-organized social bodies." These are the basic errors of their views about the philosophy of history.[34]

At this point one might be led to believe that Sorokin has over-reached himself by destroying the basic "unities" of both Spengler and Toynbee, hitherto so acceptable in historical circles, at least in principle. But Sorokin still has his own version of "meaningful-causal systems" to call upon as substitutes for the rejected variety. "Within any inhabited interaction area (no matter how small or large it is) and especially within any organized group (no matter how small or large it is), we find in its total culture the following *cultural* systems (as empirical systems of meanings, vehicles, and agents)."[35] After this statement of principle, Sorokin goes on to enumerate what he considers to be the five main cultural systems: systems of language, science, religion, fine arts, and ethics.

> These five main systems (essentially different from one another) exhaust the main fundamental cultural systems of any culture area. They embrace all the main categories of meaning and value: Truth, Beauty, Goodness or Justice, meaning by it all the practical values whatsoever, from the supreme *summum bonum* to the economic and utilitarian values.[36]

There can be no doubt that there exists a large number of other cultural systems, but they are either "composites or derivatives" from the above five, being combinations of their subsystems. Among the derivative systems that Sorokin finds worthy of mention are the philosophical, economic, and political systems, which are the main derivative cultural systems. At this time he believed that "philosophy has been a derivative cultural system, *sui-generis*."[37] Later he comes up with a slightly different estimation of the cultural systems. "Among the basic vast cultural systems are language, science, philosophy, religion, the fine arts, ethics, law, and the vast derivative systems of applied technology, economics and politics."[38]

To be recalled here is Sorokin's view of empirically grounded cultural systems, or the "meaningful-causal systems." Behind the cultural systems, properly speaking, unlike the congeries, there lies an "identity of meaning," a "major premise," which is articulated in and through each of the elements of the system and makes of the system one meaningful and causal whole or unity. Sorokin is of the opinion that such is the case in fact of the basic cultural and derivative systems just enumerated. "The bulk of the meanings-values-norms of science or of great philosophical, religious, ethical or artistic systems are united into one consistent ideological whole." And much the same can be said, with due modification, of derivative systems like economics and politics. Since the greater part of the total culture "of almost any population" is encompassed by the enumerated systems, human culture and the sociocultural world present a mainly rational character. Only the congeries, which are a "minor part" of humanity's total culture, are witnesses to nonrationality and irrationality in human culture.[39]

Sorokin pushes on to find even more rationality observable in the total cultures of many populations. "Besides these vast cultural systems there are still vaster unities that can be called cultural supersystems." Like the other cultural systems, "the ideology of each supersystem is based upon certain major premises or certain ultimate principles whose development, differentiation, and articulation makes the total ideology of a supersystem." Since the supersystems are the largest of all the cultural systems, their ultimate principles or major premises must be about the nature of the ultimate true reality or the ultimate true value.[40] Thus we are led back to the three systems of truth and value postulated by Sorokin, the ideational, the idealistic, and the sensate. As the only possible positive answers to the question of the nature of the ultimate reality value, they are the only possible integrating principles for the cultural supersystem. In this way the ideational, idealistic, and sensate supersystems of Sorokin are established.

> In each of these supersystems the ideological, behavioral, and material elements articulate, in all its parts—in its science and philosophy, fine arts and religion, ethics and law, way of life and social institutions—its major or ultimate premise concerning the nature of the ultimate, true reality-value.

A sensate supersystem is composed of sensate science, sensate philosophy, sensate religion, sensate fine arts, sensate ethics, law, economics, politics, and so on. Correspondingly, the ideational and idealistic supersystems embrace ideational and idealistic types of all the main cultural systems and derivatives.[41] Logically coherent as a meaningful whole or unity, the supersystem expresses in all of its compartments the solution arrived at in answer to the nature of the ultimate reality and value. Yet Sorokin must not be understood as believing that the total culture of any person or group is encompassed in one or other of the three supersystems. There are many cultural systems and congeries in a given culture that are not embraced by the supersystem. Furthermore, no one of the three supersystems has ever existed "monopolistically" without the co-existence of the other supersystems in some measure. In short, the total culture is never completely integrated, as was held against the views of Spengler and Toynbee.

Sorokin is convinced that his statistics and charts, appearing in the *Dynamics*, have demonstrated the empirical existence of the three supersystems. More than that, he believes his studies have also disclosed a "superrhythm" of the three supersystems.

> In the process of this study, the Graeco-Roman and Western cultures have disclosed one of the most tidal, embracing, long-time, three-phase rhythms, the Ideational-Idealistic-Sensate rhythm in its historical unfolding and flow. That the rhythm is one of the most all-embracing is unquestionable. That its recurrence has happened at least twice, during some twenty-five centuries studied, is also unquestionable. . . . Likewise, a somewhat similar, though not so pronounced, rhythm has been pointed out as happening several times in other—the Egyptian, the Hindu, the Chinese—cultures.[42]

According to Sorokin's estimate of all the main cultural systems of the Graeco-Roman and Western total cultures, a typical change from one supersystem to another has twice occurred. Beginning with the ideational supersystem, these cultures passed through an idealistic phase and then settled into the sensate supersystem. Such recurring and typical changes pose a problem for Sorokin, and several principles are called in to suggest an answer. One principle that Sorokin appeals to as a partial answer to such changes is the "principle of immanent change."

> From the moment of its emergence, any empirical sociocultural system is a self-changing and self-directing unity that bears in itself the reason for its change, the nature of its functions, the phases of its unfolding, and the essentials of its destiny.[43]

The cultural systems and supersystems are largely autonomous, independent, in the main, of external factors like the environment, and hence are the "reason" of their change.[44] This principle explains, Sorokin believes, why one of the forms of supersystems cannot remain forever dominant and eventually is replaced by another.

The answer just given is not completely satisfactory however, since it is not altogether clear how it differs from Spengler's "organismic" theory of cultures. Another principle is called in to help with the problem, and it is the "principle of limit" or of limited possibilities. The principle of immanent change may have accounted for continuing change among the supersystems from one form to another, but it has not accounted for the

triple sequence. "The recurrence is sufficiently accounted for by the principle of the limited possibilities of the main *integrated* forms of culture."[45]
As we well know by now, there are only three positive solutions to the
problem of the ultimate reality, the ideational, the idealistic, and the
sensate. These are the only possibilities around which a supersystem could
be integrated, and hence the only phases that an integrated form of
culture could have.

But there is still a "deeper reason," Sorokin believes, which makes
the change from one form to another in the supersystems an "absolute
necessity." "The super-rhythm studied seems to be possible only under
the condition that each of the three main systems of truth and reality—
and the corresponding form of culture—is partly true and partly false,
partly adequate and partly inadequate." A point is reached in the history
of supersystems when the existing form tends to become "monopolistic,"
wishing to expel all other systems of truth, and, in the process, displays
more and more its own inadequacy as a foundation for the social and
cultural life of the members of the society. The time arrives when the
false side of the supersystem outweighs the valid part, and then "the
society of its bearers is doomed either to perish, or it has to change its
major premise—to 'redefine the situation'—and with it, its system of
culture."[46]

The same situation occurs eventually under the new supersystem, and
"so these *corsi* and *ricorsi* must go on, and have been going on." In such
a light, all becomes intelligible to Sorokin.

> The recurrence of our supersystems of Ideational-Idealistic-Sensate
> systems of truth and reality, and of corresponding systems of culture,
> becomes not only comprehensible but logically and factually inev-
> itable. The only alternative to this inevitability is the perdition of
> the society and culture. Such is the deeper reason for the "why" of
> the super-rhythm studied.[47]

Thus the statement can be made elsewhere that "the creative 'eternal cycle'
will persist, as long as human history endures."[48]

Sorokin is confident that his theory of the superrhythms of the supersystems lies between the shallow unilinear optimism of the progressive-
evolutionists and the pessimistic and cyclical view of Spengler and, to a
lesser degree, Toynbee.

> Some of the cultural systems follow a cycle. Most do not. Some of
> the systems for a limited time develop along the linear trend. None
> does it perennially. In both cases the partisans of the neo-cyclical
> and the neo-linear interpretations elevate a partial and temporary
> case to a perennial and universal rule. For logical and factual reasons
> neither conception can be accepted.

In place of these misconceptions of the historic process Sorokin offers the rhythms of the supersystems, or what he calls the "creatively recurring and integralist" conception.

> In this integralist, creatively recurring conception of the life-courses of systems, we find "links" of the process that are linear within a limited duration and system. We also find "links" that are practically cyclical, recurring now and again; and there are also irregular fluctuations and oscillations. But taken as a whole, the historical processes display an ever-new variation on the old themes. . . .[49]

The "old themes" are the ideational, idealistic, and sensate forms of the supersystem.

Some reservation with regard to the theory of the rhythm of the supersystems appears when Sorokin says that nowhere does he claim "that such an order of succession is a universal uniformity."[50] The passage from the ideational to the idealistic to the sensate forms of the supersystem, or from the sensate through the ideational to the idealistic, is not a necessary and uniform sequence everywhere and for all time. "Nevertheless, it seems to be the prevalent temporal order."[51]

The Future of the West

In the final pages of the *Dynamics*, and elsewhere, Sorokin assumes the role of prophet, and the present state and fate of Western culture receive his concentrated attention. Speaking of modern Western society and to its members, he remarks, "It is high time to realize that this is not one of the ordinary crises which happen almost every decade, but one of the greatest transitions in human history from one of its main forms of culture to another."[52] Sorokin is warning the West that it is at present in one of the transitional periods between the phases of his superrhythm of the supersystems. If so, then the West is experiencing a situation met with only twice before in the history of Western culture. Consequently, short-term remedies and the popular issues alike miss the whole point: "the sensate form of culture, and way of life, versus another, different form."[53]

According to Sorokin's reading of the history of the West, an ideational form of the supersystem associated with Christianity replaced the former sensate system of the Graeco-Roman world some time during the fifth century. This ideational form in turn was supplanted by an idealistic supersystem during the thirteenth century. Finally, during the sixteenth century a sensate form of the supersystem became dominant in the West and remains so up to our time. In line with Sorokin's principles one can expect this sensate supersystem to exhaust its potentialities and call forth, in virtue of the superrhythm of supersystems, an ideational, or perhaps idealistic form, in turn. This is precisely how Sorokin diagnoses the present and future of Western culture.

> The major premise of the sensory nature of the true reality and value is the root from which developed the tree of our sensate culture with its splendid as well as its poisonous fruit. Its first positive fruit is an unprecedented development of the natural sciences and technological inventions. The first poisonous fruit is a fatal narrowing of the realm of true reality and true value.[54]

Once the West began to narrow the ultimate reality and value to the point of sensory values alone, then a number of logical consequences followed in all the main cultural systems of the West. Sorokin pursues the disastrous effects in detail among the fine arts, in the systems of philosophy and religion, in the systems of ethics and law, and among the economic and political systems. Then he points to the growth in crime, suicide, mental disease, revolution, and war as consequences and symptoms of the present crisis. All are held to be the inevitable consequences of an exclusive emphasis on the sensory major premise of the modern sensate Western culture.[55] Materialism, with its allies of mechanism, positivism, empiricism, hedonism, and utilitarianism, sums up this crisis in one word, and Sorokin's diagnosis. The degradation of man himself followed, and Communism and Nazism are only the clearest manifestations of the sensate evaluation of man as nothing but a biological organism. These views and practices, all in all, are logical consequences of the major premise of an exclusivistic sensate supersystem. These evils are its "poisonous growths" quite as much as science and technology are its "marvelous fruits." "Both spring from the same root of the limitation of true reality and value to the reality of the senses."[56]

Recognizing the present crisis for what it really is, Sorokin proposes a remedy. "Our remedy demands a complete change of the contemporary mentality, a fundamental transformation of our system of values, and the profoundest modification of our conduct toward other men, cultural values, and the world at large." Such a remedy, Sorokin admits, can be achieved only by the active, incessant, and strenuous cooperation of every individual. Yet it is not a product of wishful thinking, but based "upon a sound sociological induction." It was the way out of the crises of the past and is the solution for the present crisis. "The process always consisted in a replacement of the withered root of sensate culture by an ideational or idealistic root, and eventually in a substitution of a full-grown and more spiritual culture for the decadent sensate form." More explicitly, Sorokin says, "the problem of overripe sensateness was solved by the emergence of a new religion or the revitalization of an older religion."[57]

Sorokin points to the history of Egypt and Babylonia, to India and China, to the history of the Jews and that of the Graeco-Roman culture in relation to Christianity. History, he believes, supports the view that almost all the great religions arose or experienced a vital renaissance during periods of profound crisis.

> The respective societies were preserved from dissolution . . . not so much through the "practical and expert" manipulation of economic, political, genetic, or other factors, but mainly through the transmutation of values, the spiritualization of mentality, and the socialization of conduct and enoblement of social relations effected through the medium of *religion*.[58]

This is Sorokin's "sociological induction," and hence it is his remedy for the present crisis in the West. In short, the remedy is for each individual to embrace willingly, energetically, and consciously the next form of the supersystem which already looms on the horizon, the ideational form (or, though less likely, the idealistic). Disintegration of Western culture, that is, of the sensate form and supersystem, is well underway and cannot be checked.

Such in brief is Sorokin's philosophy of history. He is confident that his own theories of the processes of history, together with those of Spengler, Toynbee, and others, have "recreated" the old philosophy of history and reestablished its claims as a "school of thought" in the social sciences and in the humanities.[59] He appears to have become less confident that organized religious bodies, present or future, will have a place of honor in the new ideational (or idealistic) phase, because of the "chasm between preaching and practice."[60] "Creative altruism" has become the only cure for the maladies of the historic transitional period in which we live. Humanity must be "transfigured" into a new level of altruistic consciousness, which Sorokin designates by the name "supraconscious," a state of "egoless" ineffable organic integration with society, the cosmos of nature, and the infinite.[61]

NOTES

1. P. A. Sorokin, "Sociology of My Mental Life," in P. J. Allen (ed.), *Pitirim A. Sorokin in Review* (Durham, N.C.: Duke University Press, 1963), pp. 3–36. The citations appear on pages 27, 28, and 29. In this worthwhile volume Sorokin is confronted by some of his critics, and the last half of the work is devoted to Sorokin's replies. Included is A. Toynbee's "Sorokin's Philosophy of History," pp. 67–94. Another article of interest for our purposes is that of O. F. Anderle, "Sorokin and Cultural Morphology," pp. 95–121.

2.   P. A. Sorokin, *Contemporary Sociological Theories* (New York: Harper and Row, 1964), reprint of 1928 ed., p. 741.

3.   P. A. Sorokin, *Social and Cultural Dynamics* (New York: Bedminster Press, 1962), reprint of 1937–1941 ed., Vol. I, p. x.

4.   P. A. Sorokin, *Modern Historical and Social Philosophies* (New York: Dover, 1963) [reprint of the work formerly entitled, *Social Philosophies in an Age of Crisis* (Boston, 1950)], pp. 187, 189. The influence of Wilhelm Dilthey on Sorokin's conception of the sociocultural world with its distinguishing feature of meaning is pronounced, and Sorokin concedes it, with some reservation, in *Dynamics*, Vol. I, p. 26, n. 33.

5.   Sorokin, *Dynamics*, Vol. IV, p. 12; see also Vol. I, p. 66.

6.   See Sorokin, *Philosophies*, pp. 188–189.

7.   Sorokin, *Philosophies*, p. 189.

8.   See, e.g., Sorokin, *Dynamics*, Vol. IV, pp. 39–40, 67–68.

9.   See Sorokin, *Philosophies*, pp. 192–197. The citation is from page 196.

10.   Sorokin, *Philosophies*, p. 196.

11.   Sorokin, *Dynamics*, Vol. IV, p. 61.

12.   See Sorokin, *Dynamics*, Vol. IV, pp. 45–95, where the essential "structural and dynamic" properties of empirical sociocultural systems are discussed.

13.   Sorokin, *Dynamics*, Vol. I, p. 66.

14.   Sorokin, *Dynamics*, Vol. I, p. 57.

15.   Sorokin, *Dynamics*, Vol. I, p. 59.

16.   See Sorokin, *Dynamics*, Vol. I, p. 58, n. 1, where it is said, "I use the term phenomenological in a sense congenial with E. Husserl's term, indicating by it the socially 'objective' existence of a meaning, regardless of whether it coincides with the psychological meaning."

17.   Sorokin, *Dynamics*, Vol. I, p. 60.

18.   Sorokin, *Dynamics*, Vol. I, p. 23.

19.   Sorokin, *Dynamics*, Vol. I, p. 24.

20.   Sorokin, *Dynamics*, Vol. I, p. 47.

21.   Sorokin, *Dynamics*, Vol. I, p. 23.

22.   Sorokin, *Dynamics*, Vol. I, p. 24.

23.   Sorokin, *Dynamics*, Vol. I, p. 37; see also pp. 60–65.

24.   Sorokin, *Dynamics*, Vol. I, p. 25. See, e.g., Vol. IV, p. 432, n. 86, where Sorokin says, "My sequence of the phases is based not upon a mere counting of the number of such sequences that occurred, but on logico-meaningful, plus causal, analysis of the static and dynamic relationship between the main three supersystems and between the phases of their rhythm. Actual verification in the history of Greece, Rome, and Europe is only an additional test, much less important than the logico-causal connections between the supersystems and the order of their phases."

25.   P. A. Sorokin, *The Crisis of Our Age* (New York: E. P. Dutton and Co., 1957) [reprint of 1941 ed.], pp. 80–81; see also Sorokin, *Dynamics*, Vol. I, pp. 66–96, and the charts, pp. 97–99.

26.   Sorokin, *Philosophies*, p. 199.

27.   Sorokin, *Crisis*, p. 81.

28.   Sorokin, *Philosophies*, p. 199.

29.   Sorokin, *Crisis*, pp. 81–82.

30.   Sorokin, *Crisis*, p. 105. See also, e.g., *Dynamics*, Vol. IV, pp. 746–761. Again a marked resemblance between Dilthey's views and those of Sorokin can be noted. Sorokin's ideational, idealistic, and sensate systems of truth and reality are matched by the three major philosophical groupings that Dilthey postulates: materialism or positivism, the idealism of freedom and personality, and classical idealism. See W. Dilthey, "The Dream," appearing in translation in W. Klubach, *Wilhelm Dilthey's Philosophy of History* (New York: Columbia University Press, 1956), pp. 103–109.

31.   Sorokin, *Crisis*, pp. 112–113.

32.   Sorokin, *Philosophies*, p. 202.

33.   Sorokin, *Philosophies*, p. 203.

34.   Sorokin, *Philosophies*, pp. 209–217.

35.   Sorokin, *Dynamics*, Vol. IV, p. 110.

36.   Sorokin, *Dynamics*, Vol. IV, p. 120; see also pp. 110–120.

37.   Sorokin, *Dynamics*, Vol. IV, pp. 120–121.

38.   Sorokin, *Philosophies*, p. 197.

39.   Sorokin, *Philosophies*, pp. 197–198.

40.   Sorokin, *Philosophies*, p. 199.

41.   Sorokin, *Philosophies*, p. 200.

42.   Sorokin, *Dynamics*, Vol. IV, p. 424.

43.   Sorokin, *Dynamics*, Vol. IV, p. 73.

44.   See, e.g., Sorokin, *Dynamics*, Vol. IV, pp. 587–620.

45.   Sorokin, *Dynamics*, Vol. IV, pp. 737–738.

46.   Sorokin, *Dynamics*, Vol. IV, pp. 742–743.

47.   Sorokin, *Dynamics*, Vol. IV, p. 743.

48.   Sorokin, *Crisis*, p. 132.

49.   Sorokin, *Philosophies*, pp. 291–292. This matter comes up for prolonged investigation in *Theories* and again in *Dynamics, passim.*

50.   Sorokin, *Dynamics*, Vol. IV, p. 770.

51.   Sorokin, *Philosophies*, p. 296.

52.   Sorokin, *Crisis*, p. 315.

53.   Sorokin, *Crisis*, p. 22.

54.   Sorokin, *Crisis*, p. 311.

55.   See Sorokin, *Crisis*, pp. 30–271. The evidence given here is but a summary of the investigations of the *Dynamics.*

56.   Sorokin, *Crisis*, p. 314.

57.   Sorokin, *Crisis*, pp. 321–322.

58.   Sorokin, *Crisis*, pp. 322–323.

59.   Sorokin, *Philosophies*, pp. 321–322.

60.   P. A. Sorokin, *The Reconstruction of Humanity* (Boston: Beacon, 1948), p. 44.

61.   In 1955 Sorokin retired as head of the department of sociology at Harvard to establish the Harvard Research Center in Creative Altruism.

12

STYLES AND SUPERSTYLES:

Alfred Kroeber

Any study devoted to the philosophies of history of Spengler, Toynbee, and Sorokin, however brief, cannot overlook a congenial point of view held by Alfred L. Kroeber, the recognized dean of American anthropologists at his death in 1960 at the age of eighty-four. His distinguished scientific career began before that of any of the authors reviewed in this section, spanning some sixty years as a whole. Active in many ethnographical areas, well informed on a wide and amazing variety of anthropological topics, Kroeber was the acknowledged authority on native cultures in California. His many energies were heavily slanted toward concrete phenomena and the use of the "inductive method," where he followed the lead of such great anthropologists as E. B. Tylor and Franz Boas. His talents were not exhausted by ethnological field work; he gradually formulated theories on culture, progress, and history that invaded what is commonly considered a province of the philosophy of history. Cautious as well as modest, Kroeber made no claim to the title of philosopher of history and, in fact, repudiated the classical varieties in favor of the inductive method. Undoubtedly, this attachment to fact and observation restrained him in his more speculative and imaginative moments, and no clear-cut philosophy of history issued from his sixty years of anthropological study.

This is not to say that his views are irrelevant for our purposes or unworthy of attention. Of all American anthropologists, Kroeber perhaps was the most interested in fruitful association with historians and the historical approach to man. Time and again in various articles he points

220

to the necessity of the historical approach for anthropologists as well as the utility of the concept of culture. The concept of culture, he believed, could become a bridge between history and the natural sciences provided that the "microscopic" and static view of cultures be supplemented by the "telescopic" and dynamic approach. As Kroeber grew older, his interests turned more and more to projects like those of Spengler, Toynbee, and Sorokin. Many of his articles and studies manifest an abiding interest in what he called the "macroscopic" view of history and its "macrodynamics." One typical formulation of this concern runs as follows:

> Applied Anthropology, of a long-range variety . . . leans little on Economics or Sociology, but a great deal on History. Only it asks that History be viewed now and then with a maximum of elbow room and freedom of perspective; with emphasis, for the time being, not on the mere events of History, which are as unending as the waves of the sea, but on its secular trends; and that these trends be construed so far as possible in terms of the style-like patterns which so largely constitute civilizations, and of the developmental flow, interactions, and integration of these patterns.[1]

With such an attitude Kroeber could not help but be sympathetic to the philosophies of history proposed by Sorokin and Toynbee, though this kinship was not so strong as to forestall criticism of their views. Toynbee, on the one hand, was too "historical" in a sense, Kroeber believed, while Sorokin was too systematic and "philosophical" or unhistorical. Kroeber had much respect and admiration for Toynbee, but as he saw it Toynbee's *Study* was too much tied to the orthodox historical approach. Mainly political in its accents, this work was more interested in societies and events or actions than in civilizations or cultures and their specific qualities. As for Sorokin, Kroeber could not but agree with the inductive approach on which the *Dynamics* rested as well as with its macroscopic view of cultures and civilizations as a whole. Yet he believed that Sorokin's taste for systematization and conceptualization led him to an erroneous denial of the reality and unity of civilizations and to a nonhistorical, universalistic formulation or category such as a "supersystem." Of the philosophies of history reviewed in this section, Spengler's view was the most attractive to Kroeber, but he could not embrace this view without reservation, describing the *Decline* as full of "needless exaggerations, dogmatism, vehemence of expression, blind spots, inability to balance evidence."[2] His disagreement with Spengler is specified in detail in *Configurations of Culture Growth* (1944), where Spengler's prime symbols and life cycles are rejected as unproved.

Nevertheless, Kroeber did not reject the existence of a fundamental pattern characterizing each of the major cultures, and his views on cultures and civilizations with their configurations, patterns, styles, and superstyles can be compared with those of Spengler.

The Autonomy of the Cultural Order

At the outset of his long and distinguished career in anthropology Kroeber accepted the three-leveled tier of reality proposed by Spencer, that is the inorganic, the organic, and the superorganic or cultural, but with considerable reservation. Spencer, it will be recalled, had conceived the three levels as being welded together by one mechanistic and evolutionistic principle. Kroeber rejected this view and with it a more vitalistic, biological evolutionism which was being proposed as a monistic principle underlying and connecting the organic and superorganic orders of reality. Kroeber's early view of the superorganic or cultural level of phenomenal reality was directly opposed to any "reductionism," whether mechanistic or vitalistic. But there is more to his opposition to "reductionism" than this. He seemed to conceive the cultural or superorganic order as completely independent and autonomous, even "above the accidents of personality." "The social or cultural . . . is in its essence non-individual. Civilization . . . begins only where the individual ends; and whoever does not in some measure perceive this fact . . . can find no meaning in civilization."[3]

Supporting this belief in the existence of a cultural order independent of individuals was Kroeber's notion that history reveals such a coincidence and clustering of inventions and discoveries in various periods that it must be independent of the individuals concerned and would take place without them.

> The march of history, or as it is current to name it, the progress of civilization, is independent of the birth of particular personalities; since these apparently averaging substantially alike, both as regards genius and normality, at all times and places, furnish the same substrate for the social [cultural].

Consequently, Kroeber held, attention must be shifted from the biological, or individual and psychological, to the civilizational or cultural, if one wishes to understand the march and meaning of history. In such a light, "the presence of majestic forces or sequences pervading civilizations will be irresistibly evident."[4]

Later Kroeber backed off from this exaggerated position. "The risk . . . of consciousness of a separate order," he wrote in 1951, "is that of going on to reify its organization and phenomena into an autonomous sort of substance with its own inner forces—life, mind, society or culture. I have probably at times in the past skirted such lapsing. . . ." In his later years Kroeber retracted any "reification" of the superorganic or cultural, yet he continued to believe that such an approach has methodological value. An approach to the cultural order in terms of culture itself is not the only one, Kroeber admitted, but it is the one he liked and one he continued to justify. It seems that Kroeber largely equated this "immanent" attitude toward culture with what he viewed as the "historical approach." He did not see any absolute dichotomy between the "scientific" and the "historical" methods, but was convinced that the different levels of reality lend themselves more readily to one or the other method. Essential to the historical approach is the "integration of phenomena into an ever-widening context, with as much preservation as possible—instead of analytic resolution—of the qualitative organization of the phenomena dealt with." Narrative is only incidental to such "history," while "recognition of quality and of organizing pattern" is of much more importance. "Patterns or configurations or Gestalts are what it seems most profitable to distinguish and formulate in culture." This must not be conceived in too static a fashion, but one must go on to considerations of both "stylistic and whole-culture flow, as in the historic 'configurations' or profiles of movements."[5]

Even historians, Kroeber believed, were coming to realize the inadequacy of specific causal explanations and were more and more presenting "sequences of significant forms." He admitted that "the efficient causes of cultural phenomena unquestionably are men," but knowledge of persons and even societies of persons "have conspicuously failed to explain the cultural *forms.*" Not only have social psychology and related disciplines failed to derive specific effects in the cultural order from specific psychic or social causes but they have not even been able to describe cultural forms. Every historian knows, or so Kroeber believed, that cultural situations make more sense and have more meaning in proportion as the total cultural context and antecedents are known. "Cultural forms or patterns gain in intelligibility as they are set in relation to other cultural patterns. This interrelating of forms is evidently like the consideration of Aristotelian 'formal causes.'" Kroeber had high hopes for the future of anthropology, if this approach were continued. "Culture may well yet reveal 'laws' similar to the 'laws' which the linguist calls sound shifts; only they will presumably be, like these, primarily relations of forms (synchronic or sequential), not laws of efficient causality."[6]

On this score Kroeber criticized the "old-fashioned" historical approach of Toynbee, who did "not really come to grips with culture." Toynbee

> deals far more with directly efficient causes that reside in men than with the meaningful patterns that culture assumes. The ultimately significant causality which he finds is that of the moral attitudes of men toward their societies, especially in the privileged minorities. These are factors pretty far removed from considerations of how far a stylistic unity pervades a culture.[7]

In the end Kroeber admits that his approach to history and culture bears some resemblance to that of Spengler.

On the cultural level, and in any "historic approach" as defined above, recognition of patterns is the suitable and fruitful aim of nearer understanding. Causation [efficient] should not be denied because it is hard to determine; but to put its isolation into the forefront of the endeavor, as if we were operating in old-fashioned mechanics is naive. Spengler, with all his dogmatism and maniac exaggeration, was not wholly wide of the mark when he rejected nineteenth-century causality for culture and its history. And his "destiny," if deflated of its absolutism and quality of tragic doom—it is already externally non-teleological—shrivels to something not too different from the larger patterning of culture-wholes.[8]

The Comparative Study of Civilizations

One cannot easily speak of the events of history having a structure, Kroeber believed, but civilizations possess both a structure and content. In fact, civilizations "might be roughly defined as the residue of history when one abstracts the events in history." Thus far there has been little systematic approach to the problem of civilization units in history, Kroeber held. The historian ordinarily takes such units for granted but seldom approaches them from a comparative and systematic point of view. Anthropologists, on the other hand, are accustomed to dealing with "culture wholes," but most often confine their attention to small tribal societies, usually unlettered and possessing no written history as a consequence. Individuals like Spengler and Toynbee have attempted a comparative approach to civilizations, but a principal difficulty has been the delineation of the civilization units. Neither Spengler nor Toynbee agrees in their estimation of the number of such units or wholes, though Toynbee did attempt to establish certain criteria for delineating civilizations. Systematic comparison must be extended to civilizations if one wishes to find uniformities or regularities in history.[9]

The problem of finding and delineating civilizations is a genuinely historical one, Kroeber was convinced, because "human culture is . . . no longer something that we believe that we can derive directly from psychology." This approach to civilizations, or the structures of history, must not be conceived as some "philosophy of history aiming to string civilizations like beads on the thread of some pervasive principle." Rather, it is "a pragmatic or empirical approach such as sociologists or anthropologists are accustomed to make." Using this approach, one can trace culture contacts back as far as cultures themselves can be traced, even into Paleolithic times. Similarity of customs and institutions must not be referred to some spontaneous emanation from the common stock of human nature but are an historical product. Diffusion of inventions or institutions has been operative since the beginning of the story of mankind. A number of culture traits, for example, the use of fire, techniques of stoneworking, and domestication of the dog, have spread over the world, beginning some tens of thousands of years ago and more. Later discoveries like the alphabet eventually found their way into every culture. "Most anthropologists and culture historians," Kroeber writes, "would agree that in probably every human society, the major part of the content of its culture or civilization has been derived from the outside." Consequently, if all civilizations have derived a good measure of their contents from sources other than the associated society, it is at once apparent that no simple identification of society and culture can be made, and another criterion for delineating civilizations must be sought.[10]

There is no simple and easy approach to this problem, since the criteria for defining civilization units are many and complex.

> To the student of culture, civilizations are segregated or delimited from one another by no single criterion: partly by geography, partly by period; partly by speech, religion, government, less by technology; most of all, by those activities of civilization that are especially concerned with values and the manifest qualities of style.

In the end it will be "style" that determines the outlines of a civilization and segregates it from all others, since "styles" are probably the "best indicators" of civilizational delimitations.[11] With this choice Kroeber takes a stance closer to that of Spengler than to that of Toynbee, though he does not agree completely with either in their enumeration of civilizations.

The Concept of Style

Basic to Kroeber's understanding of cultures and civilizations is the concept of style. Rather an elusive concept, it does not lend itself to any easy analysis or definition. However, it is already clear that the word style is another term that Kroeber uses for the cultural forms or patterns one can find in the area of cultural phenomena. One definition is: "A historical style can be defined as the co-ordinated pattern of interrelations of individual expressions or executions in the same medium or art."[12] A later definition is more cautiously proposed: "A style may be provisionally defined as a system of coherent ways or patterns of doing certain things." Whether or not style can be defined, Kroeber is convinced of the reality to which the term is meant to point.

Aware of the origin and different usages of the term, Kroeber notes its derivation from the ancient writing tool, whence it came to be applied metaphorically to express the individual ways of expressing words or literary compositions, and from there it came to be used of the other arts. This meaning is the original one and has never died out. But another meaning has become more common, since the term was extended "to denote a social or historical phenomenon, the manner or set of related patterns common to the writers or musicians or painters of a period and country."[13] This social or historical meaning, Kroeber believed, is even more common than the original meaning. Then the term was taken over by the archaeologists for use in investigation of cultures whose remains were not usually accompanied by inscriptions or records. Here the term was expanded to cover objects which offered the possibility of a certain plasticity of form and ornament, thus permitting archaeologists to identify different periods within the same culture or to recognize the eruption of other cultures into an existing one. From this exposition it is already clear how Kroeber understands the term style when he speaks of it as the leading criterion in the identification of civilizations or higher cultures.

The extension of the concept of style is considerable, as Kroeber uses the term. There is really very little in a culture or civilization to which the term cannot be applied in some way. "From the fine arts the concept of style can be carried over into the 'public' arts of ritual and religion, and into the domestic arts of decoration, dress fashion, gastronomy, etc."[14] In the extension of the concept of style from the fine (and liberal) arts to what are referred to as the "public" arts and the domestic, decorative arts something of the properties of pure style are partially lost or blunted. Creativity, and its accompanying growth, is a principal property of style in its pure state, since it serves to distinguish "ways," those normally repetitive practical manners of doing things which endure for centuries, from "styles." Because the "public" arts and the domestic, decorative arts are related to needs and practical concerns of life that entail cumulative and traditional "ways," in them style subsists in a mixed and imperfect form. Creativity and growth are considerably modified, if not largely curtailed, by the traditional and cumulative elements involved. Much the same should be said of applied science and technology, and, in truth, of all the useful arts and even the social structures and relations to some degree. Style is present in all of these cultural elements but in an imperfect and mixed fashion. Yet pure creativity and hence pure style must not be restricted to the aesthetic area only, for it is also found in pure science and philosophy.

Creativity expressed in growth and change is so closely linked to pure style that "styles are the very incarnation of the dynamic process of history." Another property of pure style is a consistency of direction that involves a stylehistory following a definite pattern. Consistent with his view of the cultural order as autonomous and, in some measure, independent of agents, Kroeber refuses to speculate about the causes (efficient) of style. One can observe the circumstances in which styles form, but once this formation has taken place, the history of a style follows a definite pattern and direction.

From there on, however, the story of the career of a style has unity. Its history usually possesses an internal self-consistency proportional to the definiteness of the style itself. A style definite in its themes, its manners, its affects, can be expected to run a definite course in successive stages.[15]

This property of style, as creativity, pertains principally to those pursuits in which pure style is found, that is, to aesthetic and purely intellectual activities of cultures. In other words, philosophy and science tend to grow and behave in a patterned career much like that of the liberal and fine arts.

A final property of style, already implicated in the preceding, is that of irreversibility. Every style possesses a significant internal coherence, and because of it the style contains a considerable degree of irreversibility of direction in its history. Well-defined styles follow a course that not only has a beginning and end but is one way. True style neither retraces its steps after some growth nor does it suddenly go off in a new direction. It perseveres up to a culminating point at which the potentialities of the style are being utilized to the utmost. "It is because of this one-wayness of growth that we can speak of a style as if it were a life history."[16] Once having reached its culmination, the potentialities of the style tend to become exhausted, and there is really no place for the style to go. "The style forms, develops, matures, decays, and either dissolves or atrophies into a dead petrifaction."[17]

Internal consistency or coherence, creativity and growth, and irreversibility of direction are the properties of styles, especially in their pure state. This means that a life history can be recognized for styles in both the aesthetical and purely intellectual areas of human activity and to some degree even for other cultural areas. Art historians are usually able to agree about the sequential placing of anonymous art objects within a style and a period. Something of the same can be said for philosophies and pure science as well. Especially significant is the clustering of great men of genius in a limited time period, whether artistic, philosophical, or scientific, within each civilization. Several hundred pages of Kroeber's *Configurations of Culture Growth* are devoted to instances of this sort in history. What is also revealed here is the recurrence of stylistic patterns of growth within the same civilization. Creative activities tend to appear in history in pulsations or bursts of productivity which come to a rapid climax and then taper off. This is why Kroeber can speak of styles as "the very incarnation of the dynamic process of history."

He is aware that a problem arises with respect to the objective perception of "styles" by the historian or scientist. Admittedly, the mental process is different from that ordinarily used in scientific circles, but it is a common procedure in the area of the humanities, among art historians and others.

Style has indeed a subjective aspect, especially in connection with the emotion released as style is apperceived. Nevertheless the phenomena of all style also have an objective aspect. That they are most often readily identified by simple recognition does not mean that recognition rests permanently on a mysterious or rare subjective faculty; it rests also on experience with an exposure to the phenomena; and verification can always be expressed objectively.[18]

Superstyles and Civilizations

The same concern for objectivity appears when Kroeber takes up the problem of whether there might be some over-all design for living peculiar to each of the great civilizations.

The method of procedure must be from the particulars to the larger whole, else we lose ourselves in unprovable intuitions or even mysticism. The larger the whole, the more of a construct it necessarily is. But a construct built up from particulars, or supported step by step with particulars, has a chance of being prevailingly true. . . .[19]

Kroeber believed in the existence of an over-all pattern of life in the great civilizations, but reliance on the inductive method made him cautious and reserved in his remarks about such a phenomenon. A number of terms were used to designate this over-all design: total-culture pattern, master-plan, total-culture style, master-style, and superstyle. In his later writings there is a marked preference for terms that include "style" in some way. Civilizations can be considered "as being constituted—at least to large extent—of a collection of styles."[20]

In speaking of styles in relation to the different sectors of culture, Kroeber distinguished what he called value culture from reality culture and social culture. Style is operative most immediately and in a pure way in the area of value culture, things felt to be intrinsically valuable, that is, good, right, beautiful, pleasing, desirable. Style is less immediately operative in the area of reality culture, or concern with the mastering and directing of nature through technology and the useful arts. Style is least operative in the sectors of social culture, that is, in social structures and relations. Nevertheless, because social culture is always interwoven with value culture and reality culture, it partakes of some of the characteristics of style also.[21] The concept of style, appearing in its purest form in aesthetic and purely intellectual pursuits, extended from there to the more useful, practical arts and technology and even to social structures and relations, is now cautiously applied to the whole of a civilization, to its over-all design for living. But with reservation.[22]

A civilization can be considered a collection of various styles, whether of government, law, and social relations, of characteristic manners of production and economy as well as of religious belief and organization, and of styles of art and literature. In the most successful instances of civilization, Kroeber believed, the several styles not only co-exist within the civilization but tend toward a certain consistency among themselves. In proportion as this association of styles is integrated, one can usefully regard "a civilization as a sort of super style, or master style, possessing some degree of over-all design and being set, faced, or sloped in a specific and more or less unique direction."[23] This is especially apparent in the more dynamic and creative side of integrated civilizations.

Being composed of styles a civilization could conceivably share to some degree in the qualities or properties of style through the superstyle or master pattern of its living. As we have seen, Kroeber assigns three principal characteristics to styles and cultural patterns: consistency, growth and creativity, and irreversibility. If the civilization is an integrated association of styles with a superstyle or master pattern, then it is fairly obvious that there must be some sort of consistency or consonance among the various elements. On this point Kroeber tends to agree with Sorokin: "no civilization can be completely integrated."[24] To have admitted this is not to deny the historical reality or unity but to admit that "any whole-culture style that may be discoverable must be regarded as composite in origin, secondary and derivative." Any style of a whole culture is necessarily incomplete and partial, variable because of outside influences, and achieved only gradually by creative effort.[25]

Kroeber is convinced that the great civilizations displayed the quality of creativity and growth.

> Every cultural growth involves first of all the acceptance, by traditional inheritance, or by diffusion from elsewhere, of a body of cultural content; second, an adequate adjustment to problems of environment as well as social structure; and third, a release of so-called creative energies more or less subject to shaping by the factor of style.

These are the three components that enter into the growth of a civilization, but the process is a gradual one, especially if it is a question of a massive and notable civilization. Unless the society has solved its basic subsistential problems, satisfied the basic human needs as well as fundamental social relations, then none of this will take place. But this is not sufficient, because there must be the production of new culture content, the assimilation of content from without, and the forging of characteristic styles before the project of civilization is well underway. Finally, there takes place the growth of congruence between the contents and patterns or styles, and ultimately, "a defined and unique whole-culture of civilization, which is also a nexus of system of style patterns."[26] This is a gradual achievement in which culture growth, creativity, and total style development are but three aspects of one complex process. The superstyle or master pattern of the civilization emerges during the process of continued growth and creativity.[27]

As for the final quality of styles which is called irreversibility, it is simply a necessary consequence of the consistency of a pure style where the style pattern follows a definite one-way course or history. Kroeber is not so certain that this property can be carried over to civilizations and their superstyles. There have been well-defined civilizations, such as the ancient Egyptian, which have dissolved away and have been replaced by others. As integrated entities they no longer exist, and one can speak of them as dead, if it is so desired. Such a death is more aptly described "as the exhaustion of the potentialities in the super-style which is the most significant part of a civilization." This situation can be considered analogous to the "ultimate exhaustion" of the potentialities within any particular creative style. Closer to home is the example of the Dark Ages, when an exhaustion and breakdown of the styles and patterns of the Graeco-Roman civilization occurred in the West, accompanied by "contraction of population, wealth, curiosity, knowledge, enterprise, and invention."

But there is an alternative to the disintegration of a whole civilization which Kroeber labels "reconstitution." The history of our own Western civilization demonstrates the existence of such a phenomenon. During the Dark Ages there was not only the breakdown of the "North East Mediterranean Civilization" in the West but the way was also being prepared for the rise of a new civilization, the Western civilization. The first phase of the new civilization lasted from say 900 to 1300, the medieval period. During the period from 1300 to 1550 more or less, when the exhaustion of the style patterns of the high Middle Ages took place, Western civilization "emerged with reorientation and a broadened set of patterns." No doubt this "period of reconstitution" was a time of strain, crisis, and loosening of patterns, "but as they [the patterns] broke down they were also *reconstituting* themselves on ampler scope."[28] This "reconstitution" of patterns went on for some time, and with "the filling in of these newly enlarged patterns, the actualizations of their now greater potential," the second or modern phase of Western civilization began. Phases of reconstitution can also be found in the histories of China and Egypt, in the history of the northeastern Mediterranean (Graeco-Roman), and can be granted for India and Mesopotamia as well.

With this view of the matter it seems that Kroeber is backing off from a previous position which was similar to that of Spengler. If we replace the quality of styles which is called irreversibility with the term inevitability, the problem assumes clearer outlines. Kroeber held to the view that irreversibility is characteristic of styles, which meant that styles have a characteristic "life history" which terminates with the exhaustion of the potentialities of the particular patterned activity. Now he is facing the same question with respect to civilizations or superstyles, and his earlier answer inclines to affirming irreversibility and an inevitable life history for civilizations and their superstyles.

> The processes of cultural growth, from shadowy, groping beginnings, through selective commitment, to particular forms or patterns and growing control of these until they are achieved and their potentialities are realized—this process seems to be basic in the history of civilization. Its operations constitute what we call the rise of civilizations; its cessation or reversal, their decline or disintegration.[29]

It is true that Kroeber warned against any mechanical application of this principle, leaving room for "reconstitutions" of patterns. There can be little question that he tended to believe that a life history was the usual thing to be expected of the course of a civilization.

On other occasions, especially when the theme happens to be "reconstitutions" and the future of the Western civilization, another impression is given: two equally possible alternatives confront a civilization in crisis, reconstitution or dissolution and collapse.

> The course of a large multinational civilization may be more complex than a smooth rise-culmination-and-decline . . . . It may come in successive surges or pulses—what we have called phases. It is further plain . . . that the intervals between the pulses may be, at least over most of the area of the civilization, periods of pattern dissolution, preparatory to pattern reconstruction.[30]

When speaking of the future of Western civilization, Kroeber often refused to speculate, but pointed to the alternatives of collapse or reconstitution. Later he inclined toward the latter as the more likely possibility.[31]

NOTES

1. A. L. Kroeber, "Flow and Reconstruction within Civilizations," in *An Anthropologist Looks at History* (Berkeley, Calif.: University of California Press, 1963), p. 39. This work is a posthumous collection of essays from the last decade of Kroeber's life. The same statement terminates an earlier article, "Is Western Civilization Disintegrating or Reconstituting?" in *The Nature of Culture* (Chicago: University of Chicago Press, 1952), p. 408. This work is a collection of essays by Kroeber which were written over the course of a half century. They are viewed as embodying his "theory of culture." He admitted that he was no "formal theoretician," since his first interest had always been the phenomena themselves.

2. See A. L. Kroeber, *Style and Civilizations* (Berkeley, Calif.: University of California Press, 1963) [reprint of 1957 ed.], pp. 83–107, 118–127, 132–135, 163–182.

3.   A. L. Kroeber, "The Superorganic," originally published in 1917, and reproduced in its 1927 wording in *Culture*, pp. 44, 40. A general worthwhile assessment of Kroeber's views appears in A. Kardiner and E. Preble, *They Studied Man*
(New York: New American Library, 1963), pp. 163–177. Milton Singer's Foreword to Kroeber's *History*, pp. v–xiv, is also valuable.

4.   "The Superorganic," in Kroeber, *Culture*, pp. 46, 45. Kroeber's *Configurations of Culture Growth* (Berkeley, Calif.: University of California Press, 1944)
can be considered an effort to document this view of culture. Sorokin analyzed
this work in *Modern Historical and Social Philosophies* (New York: Dover,
1963), pp. 159–175, and believed his own position and that of Kroeber to be
quite similar (pp. 311–317).

5.   "Introduction to Part I," in Kroeber, *Culture*, pp. 4, 5; here the most
compact presentation of Kroeber's views on culture appears. With Clyde Kluckhohn, Kroeber conducted an exhaustive search into the concept of culture, and
the results were published in *Culture: A Critical Review of Concepts and Definitions* (New York: Random House, 1952). There one finds a certain understandable reluctance on the part of the authors to give a definition of their own, after
criticism of several hundreds of others. On page 283 (1963 reprint), we read:
"In science as of 1952, the word culture has acquired also a new and specific
sense (sometimes shared with civilization), which can fairly be described as the
one scientific denotation that it possesses. This meaning is that of a set of
attributes and products of human societies, and therewith of mankind, which are
extrasomatic and transmissible by mechanisms other than biological heredity, and
are as essentially lacking in sub-human species as they are characteristic of the
human species as it is aggregated in its societies." On page 308 they come up
with another description, though they make no pretense of defining culture: "We
think culture is a product; is historical; includes ideas, patterns, and values; is
selective; is learned; is based upon symbols; and is an abstraction from behavior
and the products of behavior." Finally, while still avoiding a new formal definition, the following appears on page 357: "Culture consists of patterns, explicit
and implicit, of and for behavior acquired and transmitted by symbols, constituting the distinctive achievement of human groups, including their embodiments
in artifacts; the essential core of culture consists of traditional (i.e., historically
derived and selected) ideas and especially their attached values; culture systems
may, on the one hand, be considered as products of action, on the other as
conditioning elements of further action."

6.   "White's View of Culture," in Kroeber, *Culture*, pp. 114, 115; see also
"The Concept of Culture in Science," p. 132 f., and so on. Some comparable
statements appear in Kroeber and Kluckhohn, pp. 325–338, 371–376. On page
328 we read, "It is, of course, equally legitimate to be interested in the interrelations of culture and personality. . . . What the joint cultural-psychological
approach can hope to do better than the pure-cultural one, is to penetrate
farther into causality. This follows from the fact of the immediate causation of
cultural phenomena necessarily residing in persons. . . . It cannot be said that
as yet the causal explanation of cultural phenomena in terms of either psycho-
analysis or personality psychology has yielded very clear results." Kardiner and
Preble, pp. 171–177, advert to the difficulties in Kroeber's approach to culture
in terms of "formal causality," which prescinds from, if it does not deny, "efficient
causality" of individuals. Kroeber and Kluckhohn, p. 371, n. 38, explain their
notion of causality: "We use this terminology here and elsewhere not because we
subscribe wholeheartedly to the Aristotelian theory of causation but because those
who attack culture as a 'cause' or 'explanation' are—whether they realize it or not

—thinking in these or highly similar terms. We are aware that contemporary thought rejects the notion that a cause is connected with its effect as if by a sort of hidden string. We ourselves think of causality as interdependence or co-variance—if a, then b (under defined circumstances). Even this relationship, alike in most aspects of physical and social science, is not more than a statement of high probability: certain events or abstracted parts of events tend strongly to recur together. This is essentially Hume's interpretation of causality in terms of generality. . . ."

7. See Kroeber, *Style and Civilizations*, pp. 125–127, and "The Role of Style in Comparative Civilizations," in Kroeber, *History*, pp. 82–83.

8. "Introduction to Part I," in Kroeber, *Culture*, pp. 9–10. In *Style and Civilizations*, pp. 152–153, Kroeber summarizes how his "historical approach" to culture and civilization differs from that of the ordinary historian: "Culture is a set of patterns, abstractions from behavior. The historian ordinarily deals directly with behavior—human actions or events—and only incidentally with its patterning. . . . The second main distinction . . . is that the student of culture can and does abstract from individuals, except as exemplifications, whereas the historian takes both individuals and masses as they come mixed in the record, and even does not exclude patterns."

9. "Delimitation of Civilizations," in Kroeber, *History*, pp. 5, 10. Kroeber does not insist very much on the distinction between culture and civilization, *Style and Civilizations*, p. 150. Different understandings of the relation between the terms culture and civilization are examined in detail in Kroeber and Kluckhohn, pp. 19–30, 70–73, 288–289, where the authors point out that the two terms have continued to be almost synonymous for many writing in English.

10. Kroeber, *History*, pp. 7, 3, 8. In an article from 1955, "On Human Nature," in *History*, pp. 200–213, Kroeber admitted that the period of cultural relativism was drawing to a close, during which the concept of human nature was in eclipse. "Now this period in turn is drawing to a close, and basic human nature is once more felt as an existent . . . it is clear that we cannot permanently ignore the basic genetic part of our psychology."

11. Kroeber, *History*, pp. 17, 14. See also Kroeber, *Style and Civilizations*, pp. 155–156.

12. Kroeber, *Style and Civilizations*, p. 32.

13. "The Role of Style in Comparative Civilizations," in Kroeber, *History*, p. 66.

14. Kroeber, *History*, p. 68.

15. "Reconstitution within Civilization," in Kroeber, *History*, pp. 41–42.

16. See Kroeber, *History*, p. 43 f.

17. Kroeber, *History*, p. 41.

18. "The Role of Style in Comparative Civilizations," in Kroeber, *History*, p. 85; see also pp. 70–71.

19. Kroeber, *Style and Civilizations*, p. 71.

20. "Reconstitution within Civilizations," in Kroeber, *History*, p. 40. The whole question of cultures, patterns, and processes is treated at great length in Kroeber's *Anthropology*, rev. ed. (1948). A number of chapters have been extracted from this work and published as *Anthropology: Culture Patterns and Processes* (New York: Harcourt, 1963). We use this work sparingly, since Kroeber's views continued to develop to the end of his life. One can consult the

above extract, p. 93 f., for detailed exposition of his views, though always to be
measured against later statements which we have depended on.

21.   See "Is Western Civilization Disintegrating or Reconstituting?" in Kroeber,
Culture, p. 402 f. Kroeber makes the same point in *Style and Civilizations*, pp.
61–70, and *passim*, but now pure science and philosophy are plainly included in
value culture, and a style history similar to that for the fine and liberal arts is
recognized (pp. 151–152).

22.   See Kroeber, *Style and Civilizations*, p. 152.

23.   "Reconstitution within Civilizations," in Kroeber, *History*, p. 57. It is
possible to consider a whole culture or civilization synchronically or statically
rather than diachronically and historically, Kroeber admits, but it is not the
more "normal" approach, since civilizations occur in time and take time to
build up. If the synchronic approach is used, then the generalized master pattern
of the culture or civilization most often ends up with a psychologically slanted
formulation. Perhaps this is so because a final subsuming term or label characterizing a culture or civilization can only be a psychological one. See "The Role
of Style in Comparative Civilizations," in Kroeber, *History*, pp. 72–74.

24.   Kroeber, *Style and Civilizations*, p. 182; see also pp. 173–182 for Kroeber's
estimate of Sorokin's views.

25.   Kroeber, *Style and Civilizations*, p. 71.

26.   "The Role of Style in Comparative Civilizations," in Kroeber, *History*,
p. 85.

27.   See Kroeber, *Style and Civilizations*, pp. 103–106.

28.   See "Reconstitution within Civilizations," in Kroeber, *History*, pp. 53–58,
and "The Time Profile of Western Civilization," pp. 28–38.

29.   "Have Civilizations a Life History?" in Kroeber, *History*, pp. 23–24.

30.   "The Time Profile of Western Civilization," in Kroeber, *History*, p. 35.

31.   "Reconstitution within Civilization," in Kroeber, *History*, p. 59.

SUMMARY

One would have thought that under the impact of the two phases of historicism the speculative philosophy of history should have truly expired, as Croce maintained. Certainly during the late nineteenth century no speculative philosophy of history appeared that could challenge the earlier versions of the classical period. But the 1900s witnessed a revival of the discredited speculative philosophy of history. Two differences marked this revival: (1) it was not the doing of professional philosophers but of historians, sociologists, and anthropologists; and (2) the unilinear and dialectical views of progress were replaced by a cyclical and rhythmical view of history with pessimistic overtones.

Historicism had opened a new chapter in the philosophy of history, but Spengler, Toynbee, Sorokin, and Kroeber reopened an earlier chapter, that of the classic philosophies of history. This is not to say that the latter escaped the critical eye of the historicists. Though their main efforts were directed along the lines of the problems of the foundations of historical knowledge and the value of historical synthesis, Dilthey, Croce, and Collingwood were convinced that any comprehensive theory that pretended to encompass the over-all course of human history was nothing but a subjective projection of the theorist. The writers reviewed in this section, on the whole, were not overly concerned about the problems of historical knowledge and not at all hesitant when it came to making use of or devising historical syntheses. They focused on the actual course of history, beginning with the emergence of the first great literate civilizations some five to six thousand years ago. No doubt Spengler, Toynbee, Sorokin, and Kroeber welcomed the assistance of the historicists in criticizing the classical speculative philosophies of history, but it is much less clear that

235

they had any taste for the more radical historicist critique of any philosophy of history with definite outlines.

Underlying many of the main varieties of the classical speculative philosophies of history was the idea of progress, or the growing perfection of mankind, which was secured through an inevitable unilinear or dialectical process. Our authors, each in his own way, ridiculed the optimistic foundation of the earlier philosophies of history, which was rooted in a Western and ethnocentric reading of the history of man. Hegel had stated this presupposition baldly: "The history of the world travels from East to West, for Europe is the absolute end of history, Asia the beginning." The authors reviewed in Part Three burst out of the confines of Western prejudice to survey on equal terms every civilization known to them. Avoiding what they believed to be an ethnocentric bias in favor of the Western civilization, they did not emerge unscathed from the dangers of the other extreme of absolute cultural relativism. They ended up with a cyclical and rhythmical version of the course of the great cultures and civilizations, which in some instances was much closer to the view of Vico than to that of the other earlier philosophies of history. In this way the speculative philosophy of history, at least for the writers considered here, became largely a matter of the philosophy of history of the higher cultures and civilizations of man. Eventually, as with Kroeber, a less ambitious name came to designate the project—the comparative study of civilizations. After Spengler, a scientific and empirical foundation is claimed for the varied historical rhythms proposed in this section.

Oswald Spengler set the pace and established the general framework for the views outlined in Part Three. A new Copernican philosophy of history must be substituted for the older varieties, which will not judge events and phenomena of another age or from another area by Western standards. The world of history is a cosmos of much different outlines and contours from that of the world of nature. Only the physiognomic method, which is sympathetic, intuitive, and akin to poetic and artistic vision or insight, is able to penetrate the realities of the world of history. Thus far the Spenglerian view differs only slightly from the common German Romantic tradition, but, as we know, this is not the whole of the story. Mechanical causality governs the world of nature, while the world of history is ruled by inexorable destiny. The prime phenomena and the prime forms of the historical world are the great cultures, which act so much like great organisms that they have a typical life history. By means of the physiognomic method one can approach these massive historical realities and find their radical unity and soul, which is expressible in a single master pattern. Each compartment of the great cultures expresses this prime symbol, which was chosen by the culture soul at the moment of its birth. Once this choice is made, a rigid life cycle takes place over the course of a millennium or so which ends in death and petrifaction.

Every culture is born, grows, matures, dies, and decays. The life cycle is found in every culture; not only the general order and outlines but also the important events and personages are matched in detail. Because of these physiognomic rhythms in every culture, one can reconstruct periods from the unknown past of cultures and predict their inevitable future of death and decay.

The life cycle of cultures is independent of all agencies other than destiny, which dictates a typical course for each. A culture follows its determined course irrationally and independently of the humans who share in its life. Rather than viewing cultures as depending on human agencies, Spengler held that the human participants in a culture are so deeply and profoundly stamped by the soul of that culture that "nature [human] is a function of the particular Culture." There is no common humanity nor one mankind but many culturally defined and limited humanities, one in name only. As there is no sphere of culture that does not articulate the prime symbol of the culture, so there is no human activity that is not the expression of the soul of the culture. There are no eternal truths, as there is no perennial philosophy, no one mathematics, no one physics, painting, sculpture, and so on. Truths are true only in relation to a particular culture soul and for that cultural humanity. Not only pessimistic and deterministic, the Spenglerian philosophy of cultures and history ends up with an absolute cultural relativism that is self-contradictory and self-defeating on its own terms. Only Western culture should have been intelligible to Spengler.

It would be unfair to Toynbee, Sorokin, or Kroeber to rate them as Spenglerians, for each occupies a much larger and more independent intellectual rank than that of a disciple or follower of Spengler. In the case of Sorokin, it is clear that his views were more influenced by Vico and Dilthey, for example, than by Spengler. Nevertheless, each of these authors concerned himself with much the same set of problems that Spengler faced, those pertaining to the "morphology" of the great cultures and civilizations. Because these problems had been circumscribed and defined by Spengler for a large audience, these writers could not easily avoid the Spenglerian frame of reference even if they had so wished. But in many key areas this frame was so modified by their views that it now bears many features that Spengler either denied or did not advert to, and where the old remain they are considerably toned down.

First is the question of methodology. The pure physiognomic method of Spengler could not be acceptable to Toynbee, Sorokin, and Kroeber. Each in his turn contended that his theory of history rested on empirical data and was the result of the application of an empirical, scientific, and inductive method. Whatever the estimate of the results obtained or of the way this method was used, their wishes on the matter are clear enough. At the same time, they did not deny a place of importance to something akin to the physiognomic of Spengler, whether it is called intuition, artistic insight, or *verstehen*. As an historian Toynbee could be relied on to take such a methodological element for granted. Kroeber and Sorokin traveled in more reputedly scientific circles, however, and were forced to defend the presence of this "subjective" element in their data and theories. Of the two, Sorokin especially pursued the point on a more philosophical and universal plane, noting that something like intuition is operative in all creative and basic intellectual insights, even in the mathematical and scientific areas.

Bound to the empirical order as Toynbee, Sorokin, and Kroeber were, they could not admit the "culture-monads" of Spengler, which appeared to be born, mature, and die in isolation and independence of all external influences. Toynbee replaced the Spenglerian conception with his version of the continuity of history, which turns out to be a continuity of civilizations. His notion of the three generations of civilizations, in which the second and third generations are direct descendants of the first, with the first, in turn, developing immediately from the condition of primitive society, places special emphasis on a continuity in history. Sorokin and Kroeber may not agree with the particulars in Toynbee's theory, but against Spengler they admit a wide diffusion of culture traits and items from one society to another as a plain fact of history. Kroeber goes further, claiming a difference in degree only and not in kind between primitive cultures and literate civilizations. Hence his continuity of history is more tightly knit than that of Toynbee, who postulated a difference of species between primitive societies and civilizations.

Once this has been said, there still remains a considerable degree of independence from external agencies in the civilization units of Toynbee and Kroeber and the comparable units of Sorokin. These authors consider growth in independence from external factors and the environment to be a norm for the growth and maturity of civilizations. Challenge-and-response is a principal theme of Toynbee's philosophy of history, and the growth of a civilization can be measured as the challenge, with its response become progressively spiritualized and internal to the society itself. Progressive self-determination is the criterion of growth for a civilization. Much the same is Sorokin's estimate: the greater and the better the integration of the social and cultural systems, the greater and better the self-determination and autonomy of these systems from external agencies. For Kroeber it would seem that the formation of a superstyle or master pattern by a civilization is indicative of its unity and maturity. No doubt, a complex process is involved, yet the unity and maturity of a civilization, as well as the concomitant coherence of its lesser styles in a superstyle, result principally from the creative activities of a civilization that has mastered problems of subsistence and social structure.

The cultures of Spengler are not only independent of external factors but follow a predetermined life cycle independent of the human participants. Here the question is one of absolute cultural determinism and destiny. The authors we have reviewed flatly reject the Spenglerian destiny, but each proposes a large rhythm or cycle for civilizations, which raises the question of determinism in the mind of their critics. Toynbee's cycle of civilizations, Sorokin's superrhythm of the supersystems, and Kroeber's life history of civilizations are not the rigid structures found in Spengler's life cycle of cultures, but there is little question of the presence of a large element of immanent and ostensibly predetermined change in their social and cultural units. On the basis of his necessary cultural cycle, Spengler confidently predicted the doom of the West. Toynbee, Sorokin, and Kroeber inclined toward this conclusion but ultimately fought their way clear of it. Toynbee claimed that his regular cycle of genesis, growth, breakdown, and disintegration applied to civilizations of the past but did not determine the future of the West. Had he not pointed to the ever-present spark of creativity in man which could freely upset any prediction of the future?[1] Similarly, Sorokin yielded a little in his estimation of the future of the West: the sequence of his superrhythm from the sensate to the ideational to the idealistic supersystem was of low probability, certifiable only in some civilizations of the past. However, it is only the sequence of the phases of his supersystems that Sorokin is prepared to abandon.[2] Kroeber, likewise, found transitional phases in the life histories of civilizations which were periods of reconstitutions of patterns rather than terminating phases of complete disintegration and dissolution. Each shied from the pessimistic finale predicted for the West by Spengler, Toynbee with an explicit reference to the freedom of man, Sorokin and Kroeber pointing to other historical possibilities. Patently the question of cultural determinism remained for Kroeber and Sorokin. In both cases the problem is linked with elements in their theories that were similar to the prime symbols of Spengler, the systems and supersystems, and Kroeber's styles, if not his superstyles. Toynbee had refused to travel very far along this Spenglerian path.

In his earlier days Kroeber had posited a cultural order that appeared to be autonomous and independent of human agents. Later he denied any reification of the cultural order while still subscribing to a methodological approach to culture that systematically suppressed individuals and events in favor of cultural patterns and styles together with their dynamic interrelationships. As we have seen, styles, once formed, follow a one-way–patterned career or history ending with decay or petrifaction, largely

---

[1] See A. Toynbee, Reconsiderations, Vol. 12 of A Study of History (London and New York: Oxford, 1946), pp. 235–242.
[2] See P. Sorokin, Society, Culture and Personality (New York: Harper & Row, 1947), p. 688.

independent of the individual human agents involved as well as of external factors. To this notion Kroeber joined the phenomenon of the clustering of geniuses and highly creative productions of a civilization within a limited time period. Pattern or style development was interrelated with these highly concentrated bursts of creative activity. Hence the patterns or styles must have a certain potentiality and have reached a certain stage of development before great men or great creations could be reasonably expected. Once this stage had been achieved, then geniuses and creative inventions appear in clusters or bursts of concentration. These bursts of productivity come to a rapid climax and then taper off, because the potentialities of that style or pattern become exhausted. In this context Kroeber offered his notion of cultural determinism:

> If . . . our purpose is to understand the history of human civilization, the cultural factors are decisive, just because they are the larger determinant. They determine what, where, and largely when and how. The individual determines the precise date, the particular manner or coloring of the event, and mnemonic label of his personality and name.[3]

Kroeber admitted to being something of a determinist, but his determinism is never fully spelled out. Sorokin also faced the problem of determinism, perhaps more directly than Kroeber. His cultural systems and the supersystems follow a "normal" life career which is not only the realization of the potentialities of the system itself but is determined mainly by the immanent properties of the system. External circumstances as a whole may be relevant to the course of a sociocultural system, but principally in the manner of retarding or accelerating the unfolding of its potentialities. But what of free will? Sorokin believed that he had the answer to the problem of determinism and indeterminism and offered a "synthesis" of the doctrines of free will and determinism in connection with the operations of his systems. The sociocultural system is at once determined and undetermined or free. It is undetermined because there is a fringe or border area within the system itself that is not completely covered by the potentialities of the system. Further, the system is largely undetermined by external agencies because of its autonomy and immanent activity. The sociocultural system is determined from within, as it is mainly self-determining within the limits of its potentialities and independence of external influence. This is what is meant by freedom. "Considering . . . that the determining potentialities of the system are the system itself and are its immanent properties, the determinism of the system turns into self-determinism. Self-determinism is the equivalent of freedom."[4]

---

[3] See A. Kroeber, *Anthropology: Culture Patterns and Processes* (New York: Harcourt, 1963), p. 175.

[4] See P. Sorokin, *Social and Cultural Dynamics* (New York: Bedminster Press, 1963), Vol. IV, p. 602 f.

The absolute cultural relativism of the Spenglerian frame of reference was another key element considerably modified among the writers we have just considered. Each practiced a methodological cultural relativism, which can be nothing more than a comparative study of civilizations without bias. None believed, as did Spengler, that his theories were true for themselves alone; they were considered to rest on objective fact and phenomena. Both Toynbee and Sorokin plainly believed in a human nature that was common to all mankind, and both held for universal and absolute values. A hint of philosophical relativism after the fashion of Dilthey may appear in Sorokin's three systems of truth, but as he explains his view it is difficult to see that any relativism not due to the human condition is left standing.[5] Some instance of a religious relativism appears in Toynbee's denial that any higher religion can be truly universal. All in all, Sorokin's and Toynbee's cultural relativism need not be considered much more than a methodological or comparative approach to civilizations. The situation was not exactly the same for Kroeber. Only during the last decade of his life do clear, if guarded, statements appear admitting the existence of a constant, generic human nature underlying cultures as well as some universal and perhaps absolute values. Cultural relativism is now seen to be of limited scope, and rooted in universality and permanence.[6]

One by one the Spenglerian methodology, culture-monads, and deterministic life cycles—and finally relativism—were shrunken to more manageable proportions by Toynbee, Sorokin, and Kroeber. The historical rhythms of these thinkers do not match those of Spengler. Cross-cultural diffusion is admitted by all, but Sorokin remained unconvinced of any simplistic cyclical or unilinear view of the processes of history, continuing to speak of the ever-new variations on old themes, the "variable recurrent pattern" of most of the sociocultural processes. Toynbee, of course, found a line of progress running through history, but it centered in the higher religions and the spiritual values secured by them and not in the civilizations themselves. By 1948, Kroeber admitted a limited but cumulative "progress of civilization," and by 1959, it was apparent that he was ready to come to terms with the evolutionistic view treated in Part Four.[7]

---

[5] See Sorokin, *Dynamics*, Vol. IV, p. 741 f.
[6] See A. Kroeber and C. Kluckhohn, *Culture, A Critical Review of Concepts and Definitions* (New York: Random House, 1952), pp. 352–353.
[7] See Kroeber, *Anthropology*, pp. 104–112; *The Nature of Culture* (Chicago: University of Chicago Press, 1952), pp. 317–319; *An Anthropologist Looks at History* (Berkeley, Calif.: University of California Press, 1963), pp. 84 f. and 199.

The Ascent
of History

PART FOUR

13

HUMANISTIC EVOLUTIONISM:

Julian Huxley

The difference between the views sketched in Part Three and those reviewed in this part are considerable. One notable difference involves the dimensions and temporal expanse of history. Spengler, Toynbee, Sorokin, and even Kroeber confined themselves to considering the conventional period of human history, beginning some five or six thousand years ago. In this section the dimensions and expanse of history are extended until its limits merge with those of the cosmos. Such an expansion of the borders of history to the point where human history and natural history form one continuous period is due to the acceptance of bioevolution as a fact coupled with the desire to promote it to the status of an all-inclusive philosophy of evolutionism. From this long and wide view of human history results the conviction that there has been a groping progress throughout the human past, an ascending movement that, despite some setbacks and detours, holds much promise for man.

Progress and Evolution Revisited

Customarily, the historian of sociocultural thought dates the period from 1860 to 1890 as the generation during which unilineary evolutionistic views dominated the reconstruction of man's past among ethnologists, anthropologists, and sociologists. Comte and Spencer were followed, in one fashion or another, by a host of individuals who came to be known as the classical school of ethnology or anthropology. Postulating unilinear cultural evolution the world over, they assumed that different groups of mankind started at a very early time from a general condition of lack of culture, and, owing to the unity of human nature and consequent similar responses to stimuli, developed everywhere approximately along the same lines. L. H. Morgan's *Ancient Society* (1877) reflects this point of view.

> As it is undeniable that portions of the human race have existed in a state of savagery, other portions in a state of barbarism, and still others in a state of civilization, it seems equally so that these three distinct conditions are connected with one another in a natural as well as a necessary sequence of progress.

By the beginning of the twentieth century anthropologists and archaeologists were abandoning the unilinear evolutionary postulate and its associated doctrine of unilinear progress as not in keeping with the facts of the past. One series of archaeological discoveries that hastened the disappearance of the simplistic evolutionary pattern was the discovery of upper paleolithic cave art in the last decades of the nineteenth century. This remarkable flowering of art occurred during a period dated variously (from 35,000 B.C. to 10,000 B.C.) and took place in a quite restricted area of the world. Most significant was the realization that the artistic accomplishments of the Franco-Cantabrian school had come to an end. "Art did not again reach a comparable level of aesthetic performance in western and west Mediterranean Europe for thousands of years," observes the archaeologist G. Daniel, and "indeed did not exist at all for thousands of years."[1] By the first decade of the twentieth century American anthropologists were taking up arms against the unilinear evolutionary theory. "Serious objections may be made against the assumption of a general sequence of cultural stages among all the races of man," wrote Franz Boas. "We recognize," he continued, "both a tendency of diverse customs and beliefs to converge toward similar forms, and a development of customs in divergent directions."[2] Boas, along with others, was convinced that the "evidence of archaeology" did not support any neat progressive-evolutionary view of the cultural development of man.

Beginning in 1936, the distinguished British archaeologist V. Gordon Childe, in a series of popularized accounts of the archaeological record, attempted to vindicate both the discredited idea of progress and the applicability of the notion of evolution to the sociocultural area. With suitable changes, fortified by an open appeal to the Marxist theory of history, Childe found both notions substantiated by archaeology. "Progress is real if discontinuous," he wrote. "The upward curve resolves itself into a series of troughs and crests. But in those domains that archaeology as well as written history can survey, no trough ever declines to the low level of the preceding one; each crest outtops its last precursor."[3] Progress is real but not continuous, since it follows the pattern of the Marxist economic dialectic.

In *Social Evolution* (1950) Childe examined Spencer's and Morgan's theories of social evolution, concluding that the "concept of cultural evolution as a rational and intelligible process has been vindicated." Furthermore, the evidence of archaeology permits this generalization about the large stages in the process of cultural evolution, if no others.

> Archaeology has demonstrated in the New World as well as in the Old that the earliest societies lived exclusively by hunting, fishing, or collecting, while farming invariably begins later. So, too, illiterate farmers always precede literate citizens. Thus . . . Savagery is older than Barbarism, Barbarism is older than Civilization.[4]

To go beyond this generalization about the empirical sequence of the three main stages in the cultural evolution of humanity was not possible if one adhered strictly to the evidence of archaeology, or so Childe believed.

At the centennial celebration held in honor of Darwin at the University of Chicago in 1959, social and cultural evolution was the discussion theme for one of the panels. Included in the points for discussion by this panel was a summary of the major "revolutions" in the history of humanity.

> Within human cultural evolution several major critical breakthroughs (sometimes called "revolutions" in prehistory and history) have been discerned in the accumulating empirical evidence. These are (1) food production, beginning gradually about 7000 B.C.; (2) a syndrome centering around 3000 B.C., in which writing, metallurgy, urbanization, and political structures were first evolved; (3) from about 600 B.C., religions organized both doctrinally and institutionally; (4) beginning about 1600 A.D., a level or grade of civilization characterized by the rapid and progressive development of science, technology, invention, industry and wealth.[5]

Among the distinguished panelists was Leslie White, long-time chairman of the department of anthropology at the University of Michigan. White objected to this summary on the grounds that there were too many "revolutions" enumerated. If culture is a "thermodynamic system" whose primary purpose is to harness energy and put it to work in the service of man, as White believed, then there have been only two major cultural revolutions in human history. The first cultural revolution, the "agricultural," consisted in harnessing solar energy in the form of domesticated animals and cultivated plants. The second great cultural revolution in human history, the "fuel" or "power" revolution, began in the eighteenth century with the harnessing of solar energy in the form of coal and petroleum. This revolution has not yet run its course despite the break-through in the use of atomic energy.[6]

Quite a different objection to the "official" summary of human history was made by Julian Huxley, a principal speaker at the centennial. Huxley was not convinced that the role of religion in the history of man was accurately portrayed by the prepared summary. An "evolutionary biologist," as he prefers to style himself, Huxley takes up the problems of human history, as is to be expected, from the viewpoint of evolutionary biology. "Human history is a continuation of biological evolution in a different form." This statement, made in 1959, does not represent a recent insight of Huxley, since he had been propounding the same point of view for a generation or so in his many writings. A few years before the centennial, Huxley had synthesized his views in something of a comprehensive system that he called evolutionary humanism. By no means unique in this vision, nevertheless Huxley has been its loudest and most easily identifiable pro-ponent. In fact, Huxley seems to be willing to go one step further than most by designating evolutionary humanism as a religion, "the new religion of the future."[7]

It is at once apparent that in his association of the concepts of evolu-tionism and that of humanism Huxley is at odds with a more professedly "scientific" and "objective" evolutionism such as that of White. Evolu-tionary humanism is plainly "anthropocentric," to use White's label, and differs radically on this score from the mechanistic and deterministic position of the latter. Huxley is convinced that his evolutionism and his humanism are both warranted by science and biological fact. "The human species, as the latest successionally deployment, represents the furtherest step yet taken in evolutionary progress. This is not just anthropomorphic wish-fulfillment, but a direct and necessary deduction from biological fact."[8] Nor is Huxley's humanism confined to the human species, but he takes special cognizance of the evolutionary value and worth of the individual person.

> The primacy of personality . . . has been . . . a *postulate* both of Christianity, and of liberal democracy; but it is a *fact* of evolution. By whatever objective standard we choose to take, properly developed human personalities are the highest products of evolution. . . .[9]

We can take a brief look at the rather unexpected alliance between evolutionary science and humanism offered by Huxley. First, it is necessary to give a rapid survey of what Huxley called the monistic evolutionary hypothesis, for it represents his most comprehensive and fundamental vision.

The Monistic Evolutionary Hypothesis

In 1956 Huxley's basic view was expressed in these words: "Our basic hypothesis is . . . not merely naturalistic, as opposed to supernaturalistic, but monistic as opposed to dualistic, and evolutionary as opposed to static. . . ." At that time Huxley was convinced that the "monistic evolutionary hypothesis best meets the known facts."[10] Three features stand out plainly in Huxley's formulation of his fundamental position—those of naturalism, monism, and evolutionism. Naturalism is consistently opposed to any supernaturalistic intervention in the natural order of events, and, radically, consists in a complete denial of any other order of reality than the natural. The processes of nature are orderly and flow according to natural forces and energies; there is no need to call upon another mysterious order of reality for explanation either of its orderliness or for the appearance of novelty. Huxley is quite willing to admit the existence of "spiritual forces," but they are simply one form of mental activity that is purely natural. Consequently, Huxley's naturalism leads to the denial of creation by some force external to the order of observable reality, and the postulation of immanent "self-creation."

> The process of the universe provided by modern science is of a single process of self-transformation, during which new possibilities can be realized. There has been a creation of new actualities during cosmic time; it has been progressive, and it has been a self-creation.[11]

Or, more plainly, "In the evolutionary pattern of thought there is no longer need or room for the supernatural. The earth was not created: it evolved. So did all the animals and plants that inhabit it, including our human selves, mind and soul as well as brain and body."[12]

Huxley's basic hypothesis is not only "naturalistic" but also "monistic." Statements made about the monistic features of his position are not as clear as others, but it appears that he was led by his notion of the continuity of nature and its processes to the view of a single "world stuff," or, as he earlier expressed it, the "ultimate world-substance," which has both mental or material aspects or capacities.

> The entire cosmos, in all of its appalling vastness, consists of the same world-stuff . . . [which] is not restricted to material properties. When organized in certain ways—as for instance in the form of human bodies and brains—it is capable of mental as well as material activities.[13]

This view should not be confused with that of White, who reduced everything to the single components of matter and energy. Huxley conceives the material aspect of the "world-stuff" as including both matter and energy, and he is concerned, perhaps inconsistently, to maintain the distinctiveness of human mental activity as compared with that of lesser organisms. There are some tensions at this point in Huxley's thought, and he willingly admits the existence of a mystery here.

> The clear light of science, we are told, has abolished any mystery, leaving only logic and reason. This is quite untrue. Science has removed the obscuring veil of mystery from many phenomena . . . but it confronts us with a basic and universal mystery. The mystery of existence in general, and of the existence of mind in particular. Why does the world exist? Why is the world-stuff what it is? Why does it have mental or subjective aspects as well as material or objective ones? We do not know. All we can do is admit the facts. This means that . . . we accept the universe . . . we must learn to accept it, and to accept its and our existence as the one basic mystery.[14]

The last and principal feature of Huxley's basic hypothesis is that of evolutionism, and this view seems to be responsible for both the monistic and naturalistic characteristics of his fundamental position. Due to the discoveries of "evolutionary science," man has a new comprehensive vision of the universe and all reality, including himself.

> The present is the first period in which we have been able to grasp that the universe is a process in time and to get a first glimpse of our true relation with it. We can see ourselves as history, and can see that history in its proper relation with the history of the universe as a whole.

Biology has provided the central component to the scientific vision of modern man, but the other natural and social sciences have also contributed to the insight that "all phenomena have a historical aspect."[15] As an evolutionary biologist, however, Huxley could not be expected to rest content with the use of the term historical as a description of the temporal dimension of the whole of nature. Natural phenomena not only have a temporal feature but "they are all processes in time, and they are all interrelated as partial processes within the single universal process of reality." Huxley believes that an expanded notion of biological evolution covers this situation nicely. "All reality, in fact, is evolution, in the perfectly proper sense that it is a one-way process in time; unitary; continuous; irreversible; self-transforming; and generating variety and novelty during its transformations."[16]

This is the comprehensive view of the evolutionary scientist, for a single evolutionary process takes in the whole of reality. "The over-all process of evolution in this comprehensive sense comprises three main phases . . . the inorganic, or, if you like, cosmological; the organic or biological; and the human or psychosocial." Doubtless, there are considerable differences to be noted in this one process as it operates in the three spheres of reality, and one should say that the "general process of evolution operates in three quite different ways." The three sectors of the universal process differ "radically" in their spatial and temporal extent, in the methods and mechanisms by which their self-transformations operate, in their rates of change, and in the results they produce. Furthermore, though now contemporary in a sense, they have succeeded one another in time, the biological succeeding the organic and the psychosocial succeeding the biological.[17] Yet, however distinct may be their specific features, the three sectors of reality are continuous or successional in time, and continuous in nature, if for no other reason than the view that all form part of "a single universal process of reality."

Biological Evolution in Action

A rapid review of Huxley's understanding of biological evolution is necessary for any comprehension of his view of human history or psychosocial evolution, since the latter is considered to be the extension of the former process, though in a different key. As a general biologist, Huxley is convinced of the unity of the evolutionary process in the biological sector of reality. The unity of biological evolution is demonstrated by a combination of common factors: the common mechanisms of life such as the apparatus of heredity; common principles such as the universal principle of natural selection; common trends such as adaptation, formation of species, specialization of type over long periods, and deployment of groups over a greater expanse of space. Furthermore, Huxley holds, there is the broad tendency toward biological advance, involving the appearance of new capacities, and, ultimately, resulting in the emergence of mental capacities on a new and unique level in man.[18]

Huxley employs two key concepts or principles to explain the unity of biological evolution: natural selection—the guiding force—and biological improvement—the resultant positive trends of the process. These principles can be expressed in the form of "two general evolutionary equations." The first equation is stated thus: "reproduction plus mutation produces natural selection"; the second in this fashion: "natural selection plus time produces the various degrees of biological improvement." Both evolutionary equations, Huxley believes, "result from a single property of all living matter—its property of copying itself, but with occasional inaccuracies."[19] One could hardly hope for a more succinct expression of biological evolution than that given here by Huxley. Nevertheless, he is convinced that the concepts, principles, and equations are derived from biological and scientific fact, not from *a priori* wishes or philosophical premises.

Huxley explains easily the concept of natural selection and its relevant evolutionary equation. The self-copying property of all living matter allied with reproduction provides the basis for both the continuity and specificity in life and its expansion. Mutation, on the other hand, the result of occasional inaccuracy on the part of the self-copying property, is the ultimate source of variation, which is transferable through heredity. Now mutation is a rather haphazard business, taking place in all directions without reference to biological consequences. The variations provided by mutation differ in the "biological advantage" they confer, or in their "survival value." Yet, the advantageous variations will be gradually bred into the stock, whereas the disadvantageous ones will be gradually bred out. This is the process of natural selection in its simplest outlines. "The discovery of the principle of natural selection," Huxley says, "made evolution comprehensible. . . . So far as we now know, not only is natural selection inevitable, not only is it an effective agency of evolution, but it is the only effective agency of evolution." Natural selection converts the accidents of mutation into "apparent design," or into "organized pattern." Huxley conveniently puts the explanation into a "nutshell." "The capacity of living substance for reproduction is the expansive driving force of evolution; mutation provides its raw material; but natural selection determines its direction."[20]

On closer analysis of natural selection it becomes clear that the process itself is composed of rather distinct processes that vary enormously in their effects. Yet, Huxley cautions, "we must not lose sight of their underlying unity. They all have this in common—they are all automatic and all selective." Then appears the fullest summary of the concept of natural selection, where its limitations are also noted.

> Natural selection converts randomness into direction and blind chance into apparent purpose. It operates with the aid of time to produce improvements in the machinery of living, and in the process generates results of a more than astronomical improbability. But it has its limitations. It is opportunist and it is relative: at any one time it can only produce results which are of immediate biological advantage to their possessors, in relation to the particular situation of the moment. So it can never plan ahead or work to a complete design. Furthermore, it often leads life into blind alleys, from which there is no evolutionary escape.[21]

Huxley next turns to an explanation of the second of his key concepts, that of biological improvement, and the second of his evolutionary equations, "natural selection plus time produces biological improvement." He is aware that biological improvement is not a generally recognized technical term among biologists, yet he believes that it can be "scientifically defined." "It is improvement of the various pieces of biological machinery by means of which living substance carries on the business of existence and survival." Since time is of the essence in considering improvement, Huxley adds the factor of time to his second evolutionary equation. On a short-range view of biological evolution all that one can see is competition and struggle among living things, and improvement "eludes us." But as soon as the time element is introduced into the vision, trends of biological improvement appear. "When we . . . take in the whole range of evolutionary time we see general advance—improvement in all the main properties of life, including its general organization."[22] In the enormous expanse of biological time, beginning some 2000 or 2500 million years ago, on Huxley's reckoning, it is easy to see

> all kinds of biological improvement. There are adaptions which benefit certain individuals at the expense of the species; minor adjustments of the species; specializations of a type for a particular way of life; and advances in the general efficiency of biological machinery.

Moreover, there has not only been biological improvement during the broad expanse of biological time but progress. Most biological improvements turn out to be finite; sooner or later they come to a stop. Yet, on occasion, one line of advance continues, passing from group to group, and for such continuity of improvement between groups Huxley thinks the term biological progress is well suited.[23]

> Progress is constantly leading life into regions of new evolutionary opportunity. Like other kinds of biological improvement, it goes in a series of well-marked steps. Its path follows a general direction, but sometimes makes surprising twists and turns. Each new deployment, after steadily advancing over its new terrain, comes to an impasse. There is sometimes a path out of the impasse, but it is generally a devious one. . . . It is not too hard to chart the general direction of progress, but it is extremely difficult to prophesy the detailed course . . . once we look back on the facts we realize that it could have happened in no other way. Progress is inevitable as a general fact; but it is unpredictable in its particulars.[24]

We need not follow Huxley's persuasive and rather fascinating account of the steps in the story of biological progress, but simply point to its outcome. "The last step in biological progress," Huxley believes, is "the attainment of true speech and conceptual thinking." Looking back through the millions and millions of years of biological progress, one can see how the last step in biological progress could come about only in an organism like man.

> Looking back into the past we see clearly enough that conceptual thought could only have arisen in an animal as against a plant; in a multicellular symmetry and a head; in one with a highly differentiated

bodily organization, which was therefore doomed to die; in a verte-
brate as against a fish; and among land vertebrates, only in a placental
mammal with a constant temperature. And finally, it could have arisen
only in a mammal which had become gregarious, which had a long
period of learning and experience, which produced only one young at
a birth, and which had recently become terrestrial after a long spell
of life in the trees. Clearly, the path of progress is both devious and
unique![25]

Psychosocial Evolution

Though admitting that "purely biological progress . . . has come to
an end," Huxley does not believe that the evolutionary biologist is necessarily prohibited from making suggestions as to how "human progress"
should be considered. We have already seen Huxley's opinion that the
human species represents the furthest step taken in biological progress, and
that human personality, properly developed, is the highest product of the
evolutionary process as a whole. Huxley recommends that human life and
human history be viewed *sub specie evolutionis*, somewhat as medieval
theologians urged men to think of life *sub specie aeternitatis*. In this light
one sees "human history as a recent and very special outgrowth of biological evolution." Without the evolutionary point of view human history
looks very different, especially to the historian who confines his attention
to the five or six thousand years of civilization, and even finds this period
intolerably long.

> But this is a minute interval to the biologist. Man is very young: the
> human deployment is in an explosive and very early phase. Man is
> the result of two thousand [later 2500] million years of biological
> evolution: he has every prospect of an equal or even greater span of
> psycho-social evolution before him.

Huxley suggests that those engaged in the study of man follow the pattern
established by the evolutionary biologist. A number of illuminating facts
and ideas, Huxley believes, have emerged from the analysis of biological
evolution as a single process. Similar results "will emerge from the study of
human history as an over-all unitary process . . . which will escape detection as long as history is treated merely as a record of separate sequences
of events."[26] In the main, this is the procedure followed by Huxley, and
the results are principally an unintegrated series of suggestions and ideas
relevant to the psychosocial order.

There are some significant analogies between psychosocial and biological evolutions, Huxley thinks, and this view squares with his fundamental position that the organic and human sectors of reality are only

different phases of the one evolutionary process and reality. In the human phase of the universal evolutionary process there is also a method or mechanism of transformation, as there is in biological evolution, and it has largely supplanted the latter, that is, natural selection. The new main method of transformation in psychosocial evolution is "the method of cumulative experience combined with conscious purpose."[27] Psychosocial evolution is "teleological," while "the process of natural selection is teleonomic . . . [directing] change toward better chances of survival . . . but without conscious purpose of planning."[28] The possibility of cumulative experience rests, of course, on the last step in biological progress, the attainment of true speech and conceptual thought. Genetic advance, and the apparatus of heredity, has ceded place of honor to cultural accumulation and transmission, while "unconscious" purpose has given way to conscious planning.

Not only is there a method of transformation operative in psychosocial evolution as in biological evolution but there is also a comparable unit of evolution involved, though it is "a new unit of evolution." In biological evolution the unit concerned is the biological species, but in psychosocial evolution the bearers of the evolutionary process are "communities based on different cultures," though not to the exclusion of the individual. The teleological character of the new method of transformation in the psychosocial evolutionary phase has resulted in a new tempo or rate of change: acceleration has replaced the more or less steady rate of change over long periods discernable in biological evolution. The time unit of major change in the history of man has decreased at an accelerating rate through the period of human evolution: from a unit of one hundred thousand years during the long period of prehuman evolution it has successively changed to a unit of a thousand years immediately after the end of the ice age to a unit of a century for most of recorded history to the present unit of a decade. Huxley's assessment is based principally on change in the area of cultural phenomena, but he finds it confirmed, in a more alarming way, in the growth of the human population. Not only has the total population been steadily increasing, but "the rate of increase has itself been steadily increasing." Huxley considers this acceleration as the greatest single threat to the future of man and his evolution. "Human fertility is now the greatest long-term threat to human standards, spiritual as well as material."[29]

There is one phenomenon occurring during the physical and psychosocial evolution of man for which Huxley can find no analogue in the history of evolution as a whole. There is a unique character about human "deployment" as compared with the expansions of other biological stocks, for it has not broken up into separate species as have other biological deployments. In the physical evolution of man, Huxley distinguished three stages, that of pre-men, proto-men, and men in the proper sense, or *Homo sapiens*. At the stage of or level of pre-men, or pre-human apes, many biological species resulted from a single stock, though all showed a trend toward the acquisition of more human characteristics. Proto-men, appearing perhaps a million years or so ago, while responsible for cultural advances like the discovery of fire, tools, clothing, and perhaps some sort of speech and ritual, are classed in species and genera different from ourselves by the biologist. Furthermore, all seemed to have been "biologically discontinuous" and thus constituted "a typical divergent radiation." Perhaps a quarter of a million years ago began the evolution of man in the proper sense of the word, the evolution of our own species, Huxley believes, from a single group of individuals. *Homo sapiens* remained an insignificant group until some time under a hundred thousand years ago when deployment commenced and man was on his way to becoming a new dominant group. Slow spatial spread was followed by physical divergence into subspecies adapted to different climates, the prototypes of the main races of modern man, black, yellow, and white. Despite this typical tendency toward divergence, the subspecies never diverged to the point of becoming fully separate biological species. In fact, divergence gave way to convergence through migrations and this tendency was accelerated after the close of the ice age. "The whole human deployment has become increasingly a single interbreeding unit, instead of an increasing number of non-interbreeding units."[30] Hence the human deployment appears as unique in the evolutionary process.

The same tendency toward convergence following upon initial divergence is also to be seen on the cultural level. Different cultures and cultural traditions have been a distinct feature of human history, but there has been a countertendency operative during the last several centuries especially. Rather than a continuance of the diverging and distinct cultural developments there has been a trend toward increasing cultural interchange and communication. In 1953 Huxley spoke of the "inevitable outline of the future—the emergence of a single world community," one allowing for a "variety-in-unity," or, as it has been called, an "orchestration of cultures." Cultural relativism, characteristic of one school of anthropologists, ignores the "lessons of biology," for there "are standards in human evolution." Advance is a more important biological criterion than mere survival, and the same criterion must be applied to cultures and cultural values. "A progressive culture is one which contains the seeds of its own further transformation and cultures which are not in some way related to the general trends of the human process may be a drag on the advance of humanity as a whole."[31]

"Biology . . . has thus revealed man's place in nature." Man is the highest form of life produced by the evolutionary process and the only form capable of further major advance or progress. Man is now the "main agency for the further evolution of the earth and its inhabitants," and "his destiny is to realize new possibilities for the whole terrestrial sector of the cosmic process, to be the instrument of further evolutionary progress on this planet." The history of biological evolution can give some guidance here, and it is only logical to conclude that man should continue to increase those qualities which have meant progress in his long past, especially those that have given him his position as the latest dominant type: "his properties of reason, imagination and conceptual thought, and his unique capacities of accumulating, organizing, and applying experience through a transmissible culture and set of ideas."[32] Keeping always in mind the "biological fact" that the developed human individual personality is the highest product of the cosmic evolutionary process, one can draw certain conclusions:

> In the longest-term point of view, our aim must be to develop a type of society and culture capable of ever-fresh evolution, one which continually opens the way to new and fuller realizations; in the medium-term point of view we must secure the reproduction and improvement of the psycho-social organism, the maintenance of the frameworks of society and culture and their transmission in time; and in the immediate point of view we must aim at maximum individual fulfillment.[33]

Almost imperceptibly Huxley slips into the use of terms and concepts that have religious overtones and call to mind Toynbee, Sorokin, and others.

> Man is that part of reality in which and through which the cosmic process has become conscious and has begun to comprehend itself. His supreme task is to increase that conscious comprehension, and to apply it as fully as possible to guide the course of events. In other words, his role is to discover his destiny as agent of the evolutionary process, in order to fulfill it more adequately.[34]

Admitting that he has been driven to use language like the language of religion, Huxley believes that "evolutionary humanism is capable of becoming the germ of a new religion."[35]

The Religion of the Future

At the Darwinian Centennial held at the University of Chicago Huxley took part in the panel discussion of social and cultural evolution. Kroeber, who had drawn up the agenda for the discussion, admitted that religion had received very little space in the program, having received mention only in its "organized" form as one of the "critical breakthroughs" in the schematic history of cultural evolution. Kroeber then proceeded to enlarge on this "third revolution" or phase covering the period from 600 B.C. to

A.D. 600, roughly.[36] Huxley was not satisfied with this type of expansion of the religious element in cultural history.

> Each psycho-social grade involves two aspects: the material and insti-
> tutional aspect and the psychological or symbolizing or ideological
> aspect, with ritual and religion, myth and science. Although material
> technological progress is obviously the basis for material advance . . .
> yet to leave out the other aspects is not scientific. . . .[37]

Huxley went on to point out that some religious element accompanied every breakthrough listed in the agenda. Hence the charge that it was "unscientific" to ignore religion in three of the four revolutions listed in man's past.

Interest in religion was not new for Huxley, since the problem of religion had occupied his critical attention throughout his career. Early he came to the conclusion that the religious element in personality and culture was based on phenomenal reality, on facts that science must take into account. Science should admit "the psychological basis of religion as an ultimate fact."

> The only way in which the present split between religion and science
> could be mended, would be through the acceptance by science of the
> fact and value of religion as an organ of evolving man, and the
> acceptance by religion that religions must evolve if they are not to
> become extinct, or at best turn into outgrown living fossils struggling
> to survive in a new and alien environment.[38]

It is easily apparent from this statement that Huxley also views reli-
gion *sub specie evolutionis*, and he finds it extremely difficult to avoid biological terminology in describing the religious phenomenon. "Religions are . . . noetic organs of evolving man." By the term "noetic" Huxley would have us understand the realm of mental activity in the broadest possible sense, ranging from unconscious awareness, in the Freudian sense, to emotional, purely intellectual, spiritual, and aesthetical awareness. Religions operate in this noetic area, though with special functions.

> Their special function concerns . . . [man's] position and role in the
> universe, his relations to the rest of the cosmos, and in particular, his
> attitude to the powers or forces operating in it, including those of his
> own nature: or in the fewest possible words, with his attitude towards
> his destiny.[39]

The absence of any reference to God in this statement of the function of religion is intentional, since Huxley believes this to be an outmoded concept and not necessary for religion.

Religion has evolved along with man, and the "god hypothesis" or "supernaturalist hypothesis" characterizes the highest level reached in most religions. But this hypothesis has reached the limit of its usefulness; "it is no longer adequate to deal with the phenomena."[40]

> Any belief in supernatural creators, rulers, or influences of natural or human process introduces an irreparable split into the universe, and prevents us from grasping its real unity. Any belief in Absolutes, whether the absolute validity of moral commandments, of authority, of revelation, of inner certitude, or of divine inspiration, erects a formidable barrier against progress and the possibility of improvement, moral, rational, or religious. And the all-too-frequent combination of the two constitutes a grave brake on human advance, and, by obfuscating all the major problems of existence, prevents the attainment of a full and comprehensive vision of human destiny.[41]

Huxley is not willing to throw out all religion, at least in his understanding of the term and reality. But another hypothesis must take the place of the god hypothesis, one that squares with scientific fact and yet is religious in the sense that it relates to the problem of human destiny. "Twentieth century man, it is clear, needs a new organ for dealing with destiny, a new system of religious beliefs and attitudes adapted to the new situation in which his societies now have to exist."[42] It is not difficult to surmise what this new vision of human destiny and the new organ of religion will be: evolutionary humanism. The new vision of human destiny comes from evolutionary biology, where it is shown that man's destiny "is to be the agent of the evolutionary process on earth, the instrument for realizing new possibilities for its future." Not only is this man's newly discovered destiny but it is his "sacred duty."

> The religion indicated by our new view of our position in the cosmos must clearly be one centered on the idea of fulfillment. Man's most sacred duty, and at the same time his most glorious opportunity, is to promote the maximum fulfillment of the evolutionary process on this earth; and this includes the fullest realization of his own inherent possibilities.[43]

Inevitably the new religion of evolutionary humanism will become universal.

> Man cannot avoid the process of convergence which makes for the integration of divergent or hostile human groups in a single organic world society and culture. And an integrated world society cannot operate effectively without an integrated common pool of thought and body of ideas.

Science, in Huxley's estimation, has already reached such a level, being unified and universal in principle at least. "It remains for man to unify and universalize his religion."[44] But this is not to be understood in some rigid or static sense. The emerging religion must imitate the openness of science and form part of the open progressive culture which Huxley admires. Man's "emergent religion must therefore learn how to be an open and self-correcting system, like that of his science."[45] Thus religion will attain to freedom and fulfill its proper role in civilization.

> Religion today is imprisoned in a theistic frame of ideas, compelled to operate in the unrealities of a dualistic world. In the unitary Humanist frame it acquires a new look and a new freedom. With the aid of our new vision, it has the opportunity of escaping from the theistic impasse, and of playing its proper role in the real world of unitary existence.

Man is now able to "inject planned purpose" into the course of evolutionary reality, and the desirable direction can be expressed in terms of a truly religious goal, properly and scientifically understood.

> From the specifically religious point of view, the desirable direction of evolution might be defined as the divinization of existence—but for this to have operative significance, we must frame a new definition of "the divine," one free from all connotations of external super-natural beings.[46]

Divinization of man in the evolutionary humanist sense can be the direction taken by evolution, for it is now open to the conscious purpose of its highest product, man. There can be little doubt that Huxley has a faith and a religion, the new evolutionary humanist faith and religion. "My faith is in the possibilities of man."[47]

NOTES

1.   G. Daniel, *The Idea of Prehistory* (Baltimore: Penguin, Pelican ed., 1964), p. 62.

2.   F. Boas, *The Mind of Primitive Man* (New York: Macmillan, 1938), pp. 169, 172. The first edition of this work appeared in 1911.

3.   See V. G. Childe, *What Happened in History* (Baltimore: Penguin, Pelican ed., 1964), p. 292. See also *Man Makes Himself* (New York, New American Library, 1961), p. 187.

4.   V. G. Childe, *Social Evolution* (Cleveland: World Publishing, 1963), pp. 175, 39, 85.

5.   S. Tax (ed.), *Issues in Evolution*, Vol. III of *Evolution after Darwin* (Chicago: University of Chicago Press, 1960), p. 209.

6.   Tax, p. 229. This is not a new position for White; it appeared in *The Science of Culture* (New York: Grove, 1949) and underlies his later work *The*

Evolution of Culture (New York: McGraw-Hill, 1959). Everything, according to White, the cosmos, man, and culture, can be described in terms of matter and energy. Life is a struggle for free energy, and culture is simply the means man uses for carrying on his life process. Hence culture can be described as a thermodynamic system whose essential function is to harness energy. If this is so, then a "basic law" of cultural evolution, or of historical development, can be formulated. Culture advances in tandem with the increase in the amount of energy harnessed and the increase in the efficiency of the means of controlling energy. Technology is the "key" to cultural development and human progress. On the basis of this "law" White detects only two revolutions of note in the whole of the history of man: the agricultural revolution, succeeding a "human-energy" era going back to the beginnings of man; and the power or fuel revolution of the eighteenth century.

7. See Tax, pp. 42, 260.

8. J. Huxley, *Evolution in Action* (New York: New American Library, 1964) [reprint of 1953 ed.], p. 99. This work was published originally by A. D. Peters, London, and Harper & Row, New York.

9. Huxley, *Evolution*, p. 127.

10. J. Huxley, *Religion without Revelation* (New York: New American Library, 1961) [reprint of rev. 1957 ed.], p. 187. This work was published originally by Harper & Row, New York.

11. Huxley, *Religion*, p. 190.

12. J. Huxley (ed.), *The Humanist Frame* (New York: Harper & Row, 1962), p. 18. Published in England by George Allen and Unwin, Ltd., London. This work consists of a series of essays by distinguished scholars and writers, under the editorship of Huxley, with evolutionary humanism as a comprehensive system of thought being the underlying theme. The central essay (pp. 13–48) is by Huxley and is entitled "The Humanist Frame." Other essays of importance for our purpose are M. Ginsberg, "A Humanist View of Progress," pp. 113–128; H. J. Muller, "The Human Future," pp. 401–414; and Aldous Huxley, "Human Potentialities," pp. 417–432.

13. Huxley, *Religion*, pp. 190–191; see also pp. 45–47.

14. Huxley, *Humanist*, p. 42.

15. Huxley, *Evolution*, p. 9.

16. Huxley, *Evolution*, p. 10. On page 31 of this work Huxley observes that in calling evolution "irreversible" he "was referring to the process as a whole" and not to small-scale and short-range changes, which are "fully reversible." He sums up in this way: "though organs once evolved may be reduced or lost, and sometimes small reversals of trend may occur, long-term and large-scale evolution is truly irreversible," p. 32. See Tax, p. 44, for a similar statement by Huxley.

17. See Huxley, *Evolution*, pp. 10–14, and his *Knowledge, Morality and Destiny* (New York: New American Library, 1960) [reprint of 1957 ed.], pp. 38–56.

18. Huxley, *Evolution*, pp. vi–vii.

19. Huxley, *Evolution*, p. 33.

20. Huxley, *Evolution*, pp. 34–35, 36–37.

21. Huxley, *Evolution*, pp. 47–48; see also pp. 37–46.

22. Huxley, *Evolution*, pp. 55, 56, 57.

23. Huxley, *Evolution*, p. 99.

24.   Huxley, *Evolution*, pp. 100–101.

25.   Huxley, *Evolution*, p. 111.

26.   Huxley, *Evolution*, pp. 118–119; see also his *Knowledge, Morality and Destiny*, pp. 56–84.

27.   Huxley, *Evolution*, p. 14; see also his *Knowledge, Morality and Destiny*, pp. 17–37.

28.   Tax, p. 213.

29.   Huxley, *Evolution*, pp. 14, 118, 122–123. Huxley returns to this point time and again; see *Knowledge, Morality and Destiny*, pp. 152–193, and *Essays on Humanism* (New York: Harper & Row, 1964), pp. 241–250, 251–280.

30.   Huxley, *Evolution*, pp. 120–121.

31.   Huxley, *Evolution*, pp. 121–122, 123.

32.   Huxley, *Religion*, p. 193.

33.   Huxley, *Religion*, pp. 194–195. Huxley examines the cultural process in more detail in *Knowledge, Morality and Destiny*, pp. 73–84.

34.   Huxley, *Religion*, p. 209.

35.   Huxley, *Evolution*, p. 132; see also his *Essays on Humanism*, pp. 218–226, and *Knowledge, Morality and Destiny*, pp. 252–283.

36.   Tax, p. 228; see also p. 209.

37.   Tax, p. 231.

38.   Huxley, *Humanist*, pp. 22–23.

39.   Huxley, *Religion*, p. 182.

40.   Huxley, *Religion*, p. 185; see also *Knowledge, Morality and Destiny*, pp. 243–248.

41.   Huxley, *Humanist*, p. 40.

42.   Huxley, *Religion*, p. 188.

43.   Huxley, *Religion*, p. 194.

44.   Huxley, *Religion*, pp. 208–209.

45.   Huxley, *Humanist*, p. 43.

46.   Huxley, *Humanist*, pp. 46–47; see also his *Essays on Humanism*, pp. 218–226.

47.   Huxley, *Religion*, p. 212.

14

CHRISTIAN EVOLUTIONISM:

Teilhard de Chardin

Considerable discussion greeted the posthumous publication in 1955 of Teilhard de Chardin's *Le Phénomène Humain*, the most important work of the French Jesuit scientist. Written in Peking between 1938 and 1940, revised in 1947 and 1948, it was translated into English under the title *The Phenomenon of Man*. The author was a geologist by training and a paleontologist by avocation, having been personally responsible for several significant contributions in the field of human paleontology. The synthesis and vision embodied in the *Phenomenon* attracted the attention not only of fellow-scientists but even more so the close scrutiny of fellow-priests and Catholics. Not all comments were favorable, as was to be expected, since Teilhard had passed with ease over the borders of a number of different natural and social sciences and even appeared within the precincts of philosophy and theology, if only indirectly and unintentionally.[1]

The purpose of the *Phenomenon* is to present man solely according to the view of the scientist, but the "whole phenomenon of man." Teilhard was aware that as soon as one's vision is extended to the whole of man, as his plainly is, it becomes more and more difficult to keep from entering into the provinces of philosophy and theology. Science, philosophy, and religion tend to converge, especially if the object is man in his totality, body and mind. Disavowing any metaphysical or theological preoccupations, Teilhard intends to consider man solely from the scientific and phenomenal aspect; hence he asks that his work be read quite simply as a "scientific treatise."[2] After long centuries during which man looked at

263

nothing but himself, it has finally become possible to take a "scientific view" of man in his place and significance in nature and the physical world. To Teilhard, man appears as "the momentary summit of an anthropogenesis which is itself the crown of a cosmogenesis."[3]

At the foundation of Teilhard's view of man lies an assumed evolutionary point of departure, if not a completely worked out evolutionistic philosophy. Not only does he accept organic evolution as a fact but he is convinced that the evolutionary point of view must be transported from biology into the other natural sciences and then into the sphere of the human and social sciences. Evolutionary thinking is a condition for valid knowledge in all of the sciences, since a process of evolution can be sighted in every area of reality available to scientific and phenomenal investigation. An amazing unity permeates the whole of phenomenal reality, a triple unity, unity of structure, unity of mechanism, and unity of movement. Unity of structure pervades the world of phenomena, and so one must hold that the social phenomenon is the culmination of the biological phenomenon. As for unity of mechanism, mutation, operative in the biological order, is paralleled by invention in the sociocultural order. What Teilhard calls the unity of movement in the world of phenomena can be seen in the "rise and expansion of consciousness," which culminates in man. The laws and conditions of heredity were responsible for this movement in the biological order, but now cultural acquisition and transmission carry on the same movement.[4]

None of these insights appears to be very much different from those of Julian Huxley, yet very significant differences appear in the Teilhardian synthesis as the theme of the phenomenon of man is developed in the broadest possible context. Not only is the evolutionary point of view extended backwards to the beginnings of the cosmos but Teilhard projects it forward into the future with equal vigor.[5] We shall follow Teilhard as he makes his way through the universe in pursuit of the phenomenon of man.

Cosmogenesis and the Evolution of Matter

The Stuff of the Universe

It is not possible to speak of the phenomenon of man without taking into consideration the material elements of the human organism. If one traces the very fibers of the human as far back as possible in the direction of their beginnings, they tend to disappear, blending with the elemental stuff of the universe. To the eyes of Teilhard the stuff of the universe displays three facets, those of plurality, unity, and energy. A bewildering multiplicity or plurality, a fundamental unity or identity of the minute elements, and a prodigious capacity for action and interaction, these are the basic features of elemental matter.[6] In addition, the totality of matter constitutes a system, the interconnected system of the universe. Furthermore, this system of the cosmos forms a whole, that is, a single figure or structure. Finally, Teilhard is convinced that the cosmos as a whole has a limited or quantified supply of energy.[7]

Science still has more to say about the nature of the cosmos. Physics, following in the path of all the sciences, has become a "history," for even its most extensive object, the cosmos, has a beginning. Cosmogenesis is the term used to describe the cosmos in its temporal and evolutionary dimensions. No doubt we are still ignorant of many aspects of the history of the world, yet we can make some generalizations about it. Two distinct phases can be distinguished in the genesis or appearance of matter, the second phase continuing in the star systems to this day: a first phase, which all at once and once for all gave birth to the atom and its constituents; second, a process of increasing complexity, at least with the molecular level onwards.[8]

Cosmic history, in the sense of the second process enumerated, is still being made on the stars and among the star systems. Evolution of matter proceeds in the direction of large molecules, but only in accord with the laws of energy, the laws of thermodynamics: the principle of the conservation of energy in a closed system, and that of the dissipation of energy or increasing and irreversible entropy in such a system. From the second law it follows that the cosmos must take its place among the realities that are born, grow, and die; the cosmos, not only in its parts but also in its totality, is an object of history. This is the picture of the universe that modern science constructs. But is this all that can be said about the universe from the scientific point of view? Has science stopped too soon, content with the surface or exterior of things only?[9]

The "Within" of Things

Aware of the existence of two radically opposed schools of thought, the materialists concentrating on the externals of things and the spiritualists isolated in their attachment to the inner, immanent activities, Teilhard believed that these two points of view could and must be reconciled in a kind of "phenomenology" or "generalized physics." If science has for its goal one coherent explanation of the phenomenal reality, it must take in the totality of cosmic reality, the "within" as well as the "without" of things. It is necessary to take into account the phenomenon of consciousness, and by reason of the fundamental unity of the universe, this phenom-

enon will be seen to have "cosmic extension." No one can deny that there
is an inner dimension to ourselves, our consciousness. If this is so, it is
thereby certain that a within to things has existed everywhere in nature,
in one form or another, from the beginning. The stuff of the universe
has a within which is co-extensive with the without.[10]

The reason Teilhard offers for the cosmic extension of the within of
things is straightforward. Nothing, no matter how distinctive or different,
could ever come to be in a final state in an evolutionary universe if it had
not already existed in some primitive or primordial way from the very
beginning.[11] If this is true, then we need not be surprised that Teilhard
was convinced that an elemental consciousness and life, the within of
things, could be traced as far back as one could see in the direction of
origins.[12]

From a consideration of the connections between the within and
without of things Teilhard comes to his cosmic law of "complexity-
consciousness," which is not meant to express anything like ontological
causality but sheerly an experimental chain of succession in nature. This
law must be able to explain first the invisibility, then the appearance, and
finally the gradual dominance of the within in comparison to the without
of things. To Teilhard it is quite obvious that there is a connection between complexity of structure and the degree of consciousness among
animal organisms of all kinds. If one assumes that consciousness or life
or spontaneity, all roughly equivalent for Teilhard, pertain in one degree
or another to the basic stuff of the universe, then a cosmic law is involved.
Simplicity of structure and degree of consciousness vary in inverse ratio
to one another. The more complex the organism or structure, the higher
the level of consciousness that is associated. The less complex or the
simpler the structure, the lower the degree of consciousness.[13]

The final question that Teilhard investigates with regard to the
dynamic relations between the within and without of things concerns
energy in the universe. Science has confined itself in the past to describing
material or physical energies in mechanistic terms, ignoring spiritual
energy, or the energy of the soul. This procedure is unscientific in Teilhard's view, for the existence of psychic or spiritual energy is so well
established that the whole of ethics or morals is built on it. There must
be a single energy operating in the universe, Teilhard believes, and that
energy is psychical. It has two distinct components, one which Teilhard
calls tangential and the other which he labels radial energy.[14] Tangential
energy represents energy as generally understood by science and appears
to be operative only with regard to the conservation of things. Radial
energy, on the other hand, is the dynamism that assures the progressive
evolution in certain parts of the cosmos along lines of growing complexity
and consciousness.

Evolution on Earth

The only place in the universe where one is able to study the evolution of matter in its "ultimate phases" is on the earth, and one should start with the without of this evolution and then proceed to the within. Assuming the establishment from the beginning of various zones of elemental matter enveloping the earth called the barysphere, lithosphere, hydrosphere, and the atmosphere, from this point on geochemistry develops progressively in two directions, the zones of inorganic and organic chemistry. The first direction taken by the elements, and the more common one, is toward the crystalline state, the crystallizing world of the minerals. The minerals followed a path that rather shortly came to a dead end, for by their very structure they were unfitted for further growth. No doubt combinations or aggregations of sorts may be produced in the mineral world by simple juxtaposition of atoms or relatively simple atomic groups in geometric patterns, but, as in the case of a crystal, these are not properly speaking "centered" units. There was still another direction open for the elements, one in which the organization of elements resulting was not so simple nor so stable, the world of the organic compounds. Due to the initial advance toward the crystalline state, and to the other more usual sources of energy, surplus energy was available on the surface of the earth, and this free energy effected a process of self-synthesis. Thus was the "polymerizing world" of organic compounds constituted, the second progressive direction of geochemistry. At this stage, rather than a mere juxtaposition of atoms or atomic groups, one comes upon a combination of molecules that form ever-larger and more complex units. Whatever the disproportion between the mineral and organic worlds of elements, inorganic and organic chemistry can only be "two inseparable facets of one and the same telluric operation."[15]

Reconstruction of the development of the within of the elements is not so simple a matter. One thing is certain, Teilhard believes, and that is that some elementary consciousness is bound up with the basic elements of the earth. The very fact of the individualization of our planet confirms this view for Teilhard. The real problem is to explain the emergence of life and consciousness from this "prelife." No sooner is this prelife enclosed in the budding matter of the earth than it emerges under the impulse of the synthesizing forces present. This is fully in accord with the cosmic law of complexity-consciousness. If it is assumed that prelife somehow already existed in the atom and that radial energy is compelling and assisting at the birth of ever-greater complexity among the elements, the development of large molecules is what one would expect to happen. This growing synthesis remains dependent on what is called involution, a double involution, the coiling up of the molecule on itself and the coiling up of the earth on itself.[16]

Biogenesis and the Biosphere

A superficial glance at the extreme forms of the mineral world and the world of life gives the impression of two vastly different areas of reality. However, for some time the scientist has been unable to draw a clear line between living protoplasm and inanimate proteins on the level of the very big molecular aggregates. Something of the same problem arises in trying to distinguish between plant and animal on the unicellular level. We have here one compelling reason for the Teilhardian postulation of prelife in the elements of the universe. "Everything," Teilhard wrote, "in some extremely attenuated extension of itself, has existed from the very first." Nevertheless, a firm belief in the "cosmic embryogenesis" of every being in no way invalidates the reality of its historic birth. The advent of life could not be the result of some simple continuous process. One must postulate at this particular moment of evolution on earth a threshold, the beginning of a new plane of existence.[17]

The Transit to Life

Life seen from the outside properly begins with the cell, which is "the natural granule of life" in the same way as the atom is for elemental matter. Yet it must have its roots in the inorganic world, for the cell, as everything else in an evolutionary universe, cannot be understood unless it is situated in a process with roots in the past and branches in the future.[18] Looking backward, one sees the cell merging with the world of chemical structures, converging on the molecule. Advances in biochemistry seem to confirm the existence of certain molecular aggregates, such as the viruses, which reduce the gap between protoplasm and mineral matter considerably. No doubt the viruses cannot be considered cells, but certain properties normally associated with cells are already present. Thus between the cellular zone and the molecular zone the "mega-molecular" zone must be inserted. In addition, if one assumes, as Teilhard does, that space and time are organically connected, then the existence and distribution in space of mega-molecules presupposes and expresses a duration, an era of sublife. An era of the mega-molecules must be interpolated in the series of ages that measure the past of our planet. Granted such a period, it was inevitable that something very new should be produced. A critical point or threshold must conclude and close the era of the mega-molecule. This is precisely what happened with the appearance of the first cells.[19]

Because the apparition of the cell took place at the extreme limits of the microscopic and infinitesimal, there is no chance of ever finding any trace of this development in the past. Accomplished millions upon millions of years ago, the transformation of mega-molecules remains a mysterious process. Something that can be said about the temporal aspect of this transformation is that naturalists are becoming ever more convinced that the genesis of life belongs to the category of absolutely unique events that are never repeated. Just as nuclei and electrons were formed once and once only in the cosmos, so protoplasm was formed once and once only on earth, or so Teilhard believes. This view is supported by the "deep organic likeness" that stamps all living creatures from bacteria to mankind, and it also explains why there has since been no such thing as spontaneous generation.[20]

It may be impossible to fix any absolute point in time for the advent of life in the form of the cell, but certain revolutionary differences from lower elements and their combinations are plain enough in the cell. The principle of cellular organization is itself something of a mystery, but the extraordinary complexity of cellular structure and the fixity of its fundamental type are evident to the biochemist. The stuff of the universe reappears once again in the cell, but it has reached a higher rung of complexity. If this is so, one can expect, in virtue of the cosmic law of complexity-consciousness, an advance in the within also, that is, in consciousness.

A decisive step in the progress of consciousness on earth must have taken place with the cellular revolution. How can one explain the development from the preconsciousness inherent in prelife to the consciousness, however elementary, of the cell? It must be recognized, Teilhard holds, that the degree of "interiority" of a cosmic element can vary to the point at which it rises suddenly on another level. A critical change in the structural arrangement of the elements of itself effects a change in the nature of the state of consciousness associated. Consciousness not only increases with an increasing synthesis of matter but a qualitative change in the state of consciousness occurs with a marked change in the inner arrangement of the elements. In this case the change is from preconsciousness to a true, if elemental, consciousness in the cell.[21]

The Expansion of Life

Time and again in speaking of the beginnings and expanse of life over the face of the earth Teilhard refers to the biosphere. By this is meant the unity of living matter, forming a single tissue, so to speak, and its universality, comparable to the four concentric layers of the earth, the barysphere, lithosphere, hydrosphere, and atmosphere.[22] Left to such ordinary devices as reproduction, for instance, life or the biosphere would have spread over the earth, but always on the same level. The phenomenon called "controlled activity" intervened at this point, one example of which is the Mendelian mutation. More than mere duplication is assured in the reproduction of organisms, for additions accrue to the biological stock whose sum increases in a predetermined direction. The law of "controlled complication" involved in this process is known to biologists as orthogenesis. Under the impulse of this process life rises toward forms that are more and more improbable. Without orthogenesis life would have merely spread over the earth, but with it there is an advance, an ascent of life that is more and more unlikely and yet understandable.[23]

Life not only spreads and advances but it "ramifies," that is, splits quite spontaneously into natural units that can be graded in an hierarchical order.[24] Advancing life presents neither a chaotic line nor a continuous one, but one that is at once divergent and arranged in the usual biological tiers, the classes, orders, families, genera, species, and so on.

The Rise of Consciousness

Not only is organic evolution a biological fact but it also has a "privileged axis," a direction or goal. Admittedly, the great majority of biologists would deny the assertion that life is going anywhere at the end of its transformations, but they have not used the right approach. One must take into account both the within and the without of things. In order to prove a direction and goal for evolution the thing to do is to select from all the combinations or arrangements tried out by life those that are organically associated with a perceptible variation in the psychism of the organisms possessing it. If animal forms are classified "by their degree of cerebralization," then an order appears automatically. Coherence of this degree could not be the result of chance. Providing a direction of eminent coherence and intelligibility for evolution, it thereby proves that evolution has a direction and goal, or so Teilhard is convinced.[25]

An accurate natural history of the world should follow the within developing; no longer purely an interlocking succession of structural types replacing one another, it would demonstrate "an ascension of inner sap," an "immense ramification of psychism." It may not be possible in the present state of knowledge to realize this project fully, but one can plot the rough outline of the course by using the index of nervous systems and size of brains that are intimately connected with the rise of consciousness. Such a reconstruction would make clear that the mammals form the dominant branch of the tree of life, that the primates are its leading offshoot, and that the anthropoids are the bud in which this offshoot ends up. Here is the precise orientation and privileged axis of evolution, according to Teilhard, but it is not yet the end. An event of another order, a "metamorphosis," is going to crown this long period of synthesis. "Thought is born."[26]

Noogenesis and the Noosphere

To the positivistically inclined scientist man is a most mysterious and even disconcerting object. As science of this leaning reconstructs man, he is an animal so much like others that he can be grouped with them in the same superfamily by the zoologist. This picture of man neglects an essential feature, even an entire dimension of the universe, the within. Man's natural position in the universe can be assessed only if both the within and the without of things are considered. By means of this approach it has been possible to appreciate the direction of the evolutionary movement, and it can serve also to reconcile the "insignificance" as well as the "supreme importance" of the phenomenon of man.

Hominization

The central phenomenon serving to distinguish man from the highest animal is reflection. In man and in man only life becomes a "center," a unity conscious of itself and of its own intimate structure. No doubt it can be said that the animal knows, but it cannot know that it knows, while this is precisely what man is able to do in reflection. Man not only knows but he knows that he knows, and knows himself in the process. The phenomenon of reflection separates man from the animal by an abyss or a threshold which it cannot cross. It is true that the story of life is a movement toward consciousness, and that toward the top of the series the very borders of intelligence are reached. Nevertheless, it is quite certain that the highest animal is not an intelligent being capable of reflection, for it does not and has not in the past developed any culture nor transmitted any heritage other than biological. The change from animal instinct and knowledge to the reflection and thought of man is not simply a change in the degree of consciousness but a change of "nature." This is precisely what one should have expected to find in the ascent of life and consciousness, a transformation in depth rather than an indefinite and continuous advance along the same line.[27]

Transformation of the ascending line of consciousness to a new and qualitatively different level of reflective thought cannot even be imagined, but that access to thought must be represented as a threshold that had to be crossed at a "single stride." By this process the individual of the species became a person, and the species ceased to be purely an anonymous whole bearing exclusively the promises of the future in itself. The movement toward individualization was also operative in the lower orders of organisms. The more each species or phylum became impregnated with "psychism," the more it tended to "granulate." The animal grew in value in relation to the species as a whole, but with the phenomenon of man the process leaped to the level of "personalization."[28] "The cell has become someone."

This is not to be understood as if the whole interest of evolution shifts from life as a whole to isolated individuals, but that it has acquired another dimension. One must consider the "hominization" of the species as well as the "hominization" of the individual. The human person does not exhaust in himself the potentialities of his species. In addition to the developing of reflection in the individual, there is something else to be considered, cultural accumulation and transmission. Cultural accumulation ends up by translating itself into an augmentation of consciousness, the very core of evolution. Hominization is not only the instantaneous leap from instinct to thought in the individual but also the progressive "spiritualization" through human civilization of all the forces of the universe caught up in man's nature.[29]

The awakening of thought and reflection effected a transformation that affects the state of the entire planet. A new era dawned on the earth with reflection, the era of "noogenesis," "the engendering and subsequent development of all the stages of the mind." Together with the birth of a new era, the appearance of thought bore within itself a new world, the "noosphere," "the thinking layer," which since its emergence at the end of the Tertiary period has spread over and above the world of plants and animals.[30]

Ramifying Phases

"Man came silently into the world." This expressive formula sums up all our knowledge about the advent of prehistoric man, the first phase in the deployment of the noosphere. When the paleontologist and prehistoric archaeologist first catch sight of man, certified by the presence of stone instruments, he already sprawls all over the old world from the Cape of Good Hope to Peking. To the scientist, Teilhard believes, the first human could only be viewed as a group rather than an individual and his infancy had to be rated as spanning thousands of years rather than a few. Nevertheless, this group represents the "thickening" and successful deployment of "one solitary stem," since "all human lines join up genetically, but at the bottom, at the very point of reflection."[31] Science, according to Teilhard, comes out decisively in favor of monophyletism as opposed to several biological stems crossing the threshold of reflection.[32]

Two ramifying phases can be reconstructed in the deployment of the noosphere, that of the prehominids and that of the Neanderthaloids. Fossil remains of the prehominids indicate to the paleoanthropologist that anatomically we are on the human side of the line, though there is also present a downward convergence toward "the simian world." Morphologically considered, the prehominids represent a rung between modern man and the anthropoids; they are also an evolutionary stage in the development of modern man, being a type through which modern man must have passed in the course of his evolution, though the prehominids left no direct descendants.

In the opinion of Teilhard the prehominids did cross the threshold of reflection and are in the full sense of the word "intelligent beings," though far from the level of modern man. Proof for this estimation is to be found in the use of fire and the working of stone tools associated with remains of some of the prehominids. One remarkable feature about the prehominids is the multiplicity of genera and species, even in a relatively confined area; this phenomenon justifies the naming of the prehominids as a ramifying phase in the deployment of the noosphere.[33]

The second ramifying phase in the prehistory of man is associated with the Neanderthaloids. After the Lower Quaternary period the curtain falls on the story of man, and when it is lifted, some sixty thousand years or so ago, in Teilhard's estimate the prehominids have disappeared and the Neanderthaloids have taken their place. At this stage in the evolution of man we find both progress in number and progress in hominization. The new humanity is much better represented by fossil remains than that of the prehominids, not only because it is more recent but also because of the effects of multiplication of numbers. If one could have some doubts about the humanity of the prehominids, no such doubts can be welcomed concerning the Neanderthaloids. Indisputable cases of burial certify the presence of true humans, though not precisely the same as us.[34] Progress in hominization may be evident among the Neanderthaloids, but they still manifest a considerable diversity of form and type among themselves. Hence the group of the Neanderthaloids represents the second ramifying phase in the expansion of the noosphere, one quite familiar to the biologist, a typical example of zoological ramification.[35]

The remainder of Teilhard's discussion of the prehistory, history, and future of man can be listed under the concept of convergence. No doubt ramifications are still possible, but never again on the purely biological level after the appearance of *Homo sapiens*. Hence the rest of the story of life represents one continuing phase of convergence, but Teilhard finds certain turning points in this story.

The *Homo Sapiens* Complex

The initial phase of convergence of the noosphere begins with the sudden appearance of *Homo sapiens* replacing the Neanderthaloid groups in the archaeological record. Rather than a continuation of the Neanderthaloids, *Homo sapiens* is a newcomer and stems from an autonomous line of evolution, though it is quite likely that he passed through a prehominid and Neanderthaloid phase. Appearing some thirty thousand years ago, in Teilhard's estimate, the man found on the face of the earth at the end of the Quaternary era is already modern man and "in every way." What is also surprising is the absence of a typical ramification of *Homo sapiens* into different species. Along with the same general bodily features as modern humanity, one can discern the outlines of contemporary racial distinction already present, yet different species of men did not result. The pace of hominization has also quickened. Most of the groping intelligence of the Neanderthaloid groups seems to have been exhausted in their efforts to survive. But with *Homo sapiens* it is assuredly "liberated thought which explodes, still warm, on the walls of caves." The artistry of the caves leaves no doubt at all about the creative capacity of their intelligence.[36]

Homo sapiens is in the fullest sense the same man as present-day humans, though admittedly not yet on our level of culture. There has been no measurable variation or increased perfection in the human brain from his time to ours. This anatomical fact presents something of a problem. According to the law of complexity-consciousness, it is the size and perfection of the brain by which the principal impulse of evolution can be charted among the higher living forms. If there is no appreciable difference between our brain and that of *Homo sapiens*, it would seem that evolution has ceased. Teilhard acknowledges the difficulty and admits, though without prejudice to what may be developing ever so slowly in the nervous system as yet, that evolution has gone beyond anatomy and transformed itself in the process.[37] This means that the story of evolution must be pursued on a different level than before; it is now a story of developing consciousness, of new thresholds in reflection and thought.

The Neolithic Metamorphosis

This phase of the convergence of the noosphere is not one of biological development but of cultural developments and geographical expansion. According to Teilhard, the Neolithic age is of critical importance among all the epochs of the past, for in it civilization was born. Economic or technological criteria are not prominent in the Teilhardian estimation of turning points in the history of man but rather the degree of social development, or "socialization." The Neolithic period was a decisive period of socialization as compared with the initial lengthy period of the *Homo sapiens* complex. After a time long enough for the domestication of animals and plants on which we still live today, we find sedentary and socially organized men in place of the nomadic hunters. Cultural accumulation and cultural transmission developed rapidly. Tradition, collective memory, and historical consciousness appeared. With this phenomenon the noosphere began to turn in on itself and encircle the globe. By the end of this period the world was practically covered with men. Hence it is also a period of geographical expansion, but the principal element is the converging tendency on the psychic level manifested in increasing socialization, cultural accumulation, transmission, and exchange.

The Rise of the West

The long period of conventional history since the Neolithic era up to the end of the eighteenth century is designated by Teilhard as an age of "prolongations" of Neolithic innovations culminating in the rise of the Western world and civilization. Almost the whole of the period investigated in detail by the ordinary historian and whose synthetic description by Toynbee demanded ten volumes is here described as nothing but a continuation of the Neolithic era.[38]

However that may be, Teilhard's extraordinarily brief account of this period of human history is a continuation of the accent on "psychical" factors, which since Neolithic times have outweighed the ever-dwindling "somatic" factors. Most important in the story of man at this time are the phenomena of confluence, assimilation, and a degree of synthesis on the psychic level. These forms of convergence are especially manifest in the rise and spread of the ancient civilizations. The conflict between and the gradual harmonization of these grand "psychosomatic currents" are the essential elements of history.[39]

The story is quickly told. The Mayan and Polynesian centers of civilization soon met their respective fates, while China settled into a state of rigidity and India lost itself in speculation and detachment. Step by step we are driven to the more Western zones, where in the course of a few thousand years "a happy blend" resulted in which reason could be harnessed to facts and religion to reason. Mesopotamia, Egypt, Greece, Rome, one after the other crumbled, but it is more scientific to recognize, yet once again, beneath these successive oscillations, the "great spiral life" thrusting up, following the master line of its evolution. An increasingly organized cosmic consciousness is handed on from generation to generation and becomes ever more luminous in the process. During historical times the "principal axis" of anthropogenesis has passed through the Western world, culminating in Western European civilization. The point is easily substantiated, since all peoples of today "to remain human or to become more so" are inexorably led to formulate their hopes and problems in the very same terms in which the West has expressed them.[40]

Evolution Becomes Conscious of Itself

At this very moment, Teilhard believed, we are passing through an age of transition, having finally thrown off the last vestiges of the Neolithic era. Since the end of the eighteenth century the course of history and of evolution began to change. Economic changes, industrial changes, social changes, especially the awakening of the masses, all of these are symptoms of the different world we live in. Life is taking a step, a decisive step, in us and in our environment. After the long maturation and apparent immobility of the agricultural centuries, a critical change of the noosphere has taken place. If it is true that beneath a change of age lies a change of thought, then some new intuition or awakening lies at the base of the critical change which has made us so different in four or five generations from our ancestors. Modern man has become conscious of the grand movement in which he is caught up. Man now knows that he is nothing other than evolution become conscious of itself, to use Julian Huxley's apt expression. "The consciousness of each of us is evolution looking at itself and reflecting."[41] Consciousness advanced to a plane of new dimensions, the most "prodigious event" recorded by history since the threshold of reflection was crossed.

Evolutionary thinking is what distinguishes modern man from all of his predecessors; he is unable to view anything, even himself, except in an evolutionary light. Evolutionary thinking, however, is also the root of modern man's anxiety and uneasiness. Simply to know that evolution has been directed toward the rise and expansion of consciousness is not sufficient for the hopes of man. Is there a reasonable and suitable outcome to evolution? What should the future of evolution and the future of man, really the same thing, be like? Pessimism and optimism are the choices facing modern man, and there is no middle ground between them.

In support of the optimistic side of the dilemma, Teilhard believed there were reasonable grounds for an "act of faith." The patterns from evolutionary processes in the past give us every indication of a favorable outcome in the future. In the face of high improbability evolution has almost miraculously brought human consciousness into existence. There can be little or no risk in following its lines into the future to the very end. The success of the past is evolution's pledge for the future.[42]

The Future of Man

Two doctrines of progress for the man of the future must be avoided at the outset: extreme individualism and racism. Both are forms of isolation, of the individual or of the group, and both find some justification in the methods pursued by evolution in the past, especially among living organisms. Nevertheless, they are deceptions, ignoring an essential phenomenon, "the natural confluence of grains of thought," and disfiguring the true contours of the noosphere, especially convergence.

Collective Convergence

Two phenomena of coalescence or convergence essential to any forecast of man's future on earth must be kept in mind. The first is the plain fact of the limited spherical contours of our planet joined with the geographical and numerical expansion of man over the earth to the point where we come to constitute an almost solid mass of "hominized substance." The other phenomenon of convergence is the biological truth that mankind is a single, interbreeding species.[43] These two phenomena have led to unification, but why should there be unification in the world, and what is its purpose?

Unification of mankind, or its convergence, becomes intelligible if we see it as the natural culmination of a cosmic process of organization which has remained constant since the beginnings of our planet. From the organic compounds to the cell, from the cell to the metazoa, and now at the level of thought on a planetary scale, one sees unification and synthesis occurring simultaneously with new levels of living unity. There is no way of coherently or scientifically grouping this immense succession of facts, Teilhard believed, except "as a gigantic psycho-biological operation, a sort of mega-synthesis." Consequently, any doctrine of isolation is false and against nature. The outcome of the world, the gates of the future, the entry into the "super-human," these are not the privilege of a selected few only, nor of any chosen people exclusively. Rather, the future lies open to the collective advance of all humanity, in which each individual can share and also find fulfillment.[44]

There are two possible ways in which one can picture the future of mankind in its unified and collective dimension: as a common power and act of knowing and doing or as an "organic super-aggregation" of persons. The first alternative, according to Teilhard, is deficient, failing to give to each and every individual its final value by grouping them in the unity of an organized whole. It is the second alternative that must be chosen, one already intimated in the concept of mega-synthesis. Mega-synthesis is best described as a harmonic union of consciousnesses, a sort of "superconsciousness" in which a single, unanimous act of reflection by all of humanity would cover the whole of the earth. The analogy of the past leads one inevitably to project such a future for mankind.

This is by no means the whole of the picture of mankind's future. Accumulating in the noosphere is free energy, manifested particularly in the consequences of technological improvements, and increasing complexity, where peoples and civilizations can develop further only in togetherness. Here, as we know, are the two perennial signs of a leap forward of the radial, that is, a new phase in the genesis of mind and consciousness.[45]

Omega Point and Convergence of the Person

If it is admitted that evolution is an ascent toward consciousness, then it should culminate forward in some sort of supreme consciousness, or so Teilhard thought. Such a supreme consciousness must contain in the highest degree what is the perfection of our consciousness, "hyper-reflection," or "hyper-personalization." Because the universe has given birth to consciousness, it must somewhere ahead focus on a point which Teilhard calls Omega. This point must have the capacity to reconcile all the lines of converging consciousness in itself. Hence there would be no radical opposition between the trend toward collective convergence, which can be assumed to have as its object the Universal, and an equally associated convergence of each person, whose object should be the Personal. In fact, these movements tend in the same direction, culminating simultaneously in Omega point, which is at once Universal and Personal, indeed "Hyper-Personal."[46]

Two extremes must be avoided here, one obliterating the distinction between persons in the ultimate convergence on Omega, the other identifying Omega with the ultimate convergence. Omega, if it is to be truly Omega, must insure the very centers of our consciousness, our personalities. The "concentration" of a conscious universe must reassemble in itself all consciousness as well as all the conscious, each particular consciousness remaining aware and conscious of itself even at the very end of the operation. In truth, each particular consciousness must become more itself and thus more clearly distinct from others the closer it unites with them in Omega. Nor is Omega to be understood simply as ourselves born of personal convergence. Omega can only be a distinct individual center whose presence radiates at the very heart and core of a harmonious communion of distinct human centers.[47]

Only a form of psychic interactivity that is of an "intercentric" nature could possibly effect such a synthesis of personal centers, and this activity is love. Love is not peculiar to man, for it is a general property of life, pertaining to the within of the stuff of the universe and intimately associated with radial energy impelling growing consciousness and unity. On the human plane love manifests itself in various ways, in sexual passion, in parental instinct, in social solidarity, and so on. But at its highest level love alone is capable of uniting living beings in such a way so as to complete and fulfill them, for it alone takes them and joins them by what is deepest in themselves. This is a fact of everyday experience. Love achieves what is thought to be contradictory, the feat of "personalizing by totalizing," and this is precisely what is expected of ultimate convergence, the reconciliation of the collective with the personal, of the whole with the part, of unity with multitude. Even the supremely intellectual act of science, in comparison with love, achieves only superficial contact between persons. Abstract and impersonal to a degree, science is not capable of personalizing, though the totalizing feature may not be absent.

All of this means that love must eventually develop to the point of embracing all men and all the earth and cosmos. No doubt this seems to fly in the face of fact and seems an impossibility. Love of a man for his wife, his children, his friends, his country seems to exhaust the natural forms of love and man's capacity for love. Yet this view ignores the most fundamental form of love, a natural love, deep in the heart and bound up with all reality, having a cosmic affinity and cosmic direction. Cosmic and universal love is not only possible to man, it is the only thoroughly valid and final form that human love should take.[48]

Universal love of this compass, in the opinion of Teilhard, can be realized only if there is some reality, some source of love and object of love at the summit of the world which radiates as an existing and present reality, evoking that mysterious intercentric relationship we call love. An impersonal collectivity like communism is essentially unlovable, and so are the positivist substitutions of civilization, humanity, and so on. To be supremely attractive to our love, Omega must be supremely present. To satisfy the ultimate requirements of our love, Omega must be independent of the ultimate collapse of evolutionary forces. No doubt Omega is discovered by us at the end of the whole process of evolution, the very culmination of the movement of synthesis and convergence. Yet under the evolutionary aspect Omega still only reveals a part of itself. Encountered as the last term of the series, it is equally outside of every series. It crowns, closes, and transcends all at once. Transcendence, along with autonomy, actuality, and irreversibility, are the attributes of the Teilhardian Omega.[49]

Love focused on Omega, which draws it onward, escapes from the entropy of the universe, and does so increasingly. Only tangential energy goes on dissipating itself in accord with the laws of thermodynamics.

Radial energy, and love ultimately, run counter to this tendency of the tangential, and in man are eventually liberated completely. Hence, a universe, well defined in its outcome, goes on building itself above our heads in the inverse direction of matter, which vanishes. No longer is it to be presumed that the universe is a repository and conservator of mechanical energies, but of persons. Yet not in isolation, for the noosphere will reach its ultimate point of convergence collectively only, and then at the end of the world.[50]

The Ultimate Earth

It is inevitable that a noogenesis ascending irreversibly toward Omega through the strictly limited cycle of a geogenesis must ultimately issue in some break between the two movements. One is forced to contemplate the end of all life on our globe, the death of the planet, the ultimate phase of the phenomenon of man. However the end may come about, it cannot anticipate the reaching of the goal by man, for the hopes for the future of the noosphere are concentrated exclusively upon him as such. There must be a secret compact between the infinite and the infinitesimal to support to the very end the consciousness that has emerged between the two. Relying on this concert of cosmic forces, one can hold only that man will attain his goal. What should be expected, then, is not a halt or detour in any way but an ultimate progression coming at its "biologically appointed hour."[51]

Science assures us that between our modern earth and the ultimate earth there lies an immense period during which there will be an acceleration of the forces of evolution along the lines of the human. Success of this project, really the only acceptable assumption, will take place in a collective and spiritual form. Since man's arrival on earth evolutionary pressures seem to have dropped in all the branches of the tree of life except the human, and there one finds no appreciable bodily changes, or if so they are amenable to human control. Evolution is occupied elsewhere, in a richer and more complex domain, constructing in concert with all of humanity the noospheric mind. This process is already well underway, since a collective consciousness taking in the whole of humanity has been developing for some time.

Judging from the present condition of the noosphere, Teilhard is willing to hazard some predictions about the paths along which evolution in its advanced state is apt to move. Three principal routes stand out: organization of research, concentration of research on the subject of man, and the conjunction of science and religion. We need not delay over the first two, for it is in the third line of advance, the coordination of science and religion, that Teilhard's originality lies. Science cannot go to its natural limits without introducing elements of mysticism or being influenced by religious belief or faith, Teilhard believed. As soon as science passes beyond analytic investigations to synthesis, it is at once led to think in terms of the future and of the totality of things. When this is done science has outstripped itself, for as man turns toward the summit, the totality and the future, he cannot help being concerned with religion. Only in the mutual cooperation of science and religion can complete knowledge be had of the past and of the future of evolution. Synthesis again, without elimination or radical dualism, is Teilhard's proposal for the association of science and religion.[52]

Finally, one must contemplate the end of the world. One possibility for the final convergence is some sort of unanimity throughout the noosphere, a period when disease and hunger have been conquered or greatly reduced by science and all hatred and conflict have disappeared in the warmth of the love of Omega. In this view the final convergence will take place in peace. But there is another possibility, more in accord with traditional apocalyptic thinking. It may be that evil will continue to prosper along with the good and attain some radically new form in the end. Man may choose to focus collectively on himself and his attributes rather than reach out toward Omega. Neither hypothesis leads us to expect indefinite progress, as this is contradicted by the fundamental converging characteristic of noogenesis.[53]

The Christian Phenomenon

If the reconstruction of evolution and the phenomenon of man offered by Teilhard is valid, then Omega, whose actuality and presence are an intimate, crowning feature of the process, must somehow be manifesting itself. If Omega is already in existence and operative at the very core of the noosphere, then some traces of its presence should be manifest here and now. Some excess of personal, extrahuman energy should be perceptible if one looks carefully in the noosphere. As a convinced Catholic, Teilhard believes that the answer to such an inquiry lies in the Christian phenomenon. One should not ignore the Christian fact, for it occupies a prominent place among the realities of this world. The confirmation we need to have of a universe dominated by energies of a personal rather than mechanical nature is to be found in the Christian reality, its belief in an incarnate and personal God, its novel and universal love, its ever-present capacity for growth.

Recast in evolutionary and biological terminology, the Christian phenomenon appears to the naturalist as a "phylum" of love. By reason of its rootedness in the past coupled with ceaseless developments, the Christian fact exhibits the characteristics of a phylum. In addition, because of its tendency toward a synthesis based on love, the Christian phenomenon progresses precisely in the direction presumed for the leading branch of biogenesis. Finally, and most important, the ascending phylum of Christianity implies essentially the consciousness of being in actual and vital relation with a spiritual and transcendent personal point of universal convergence, that is, with Christ-Omega. Only Christianity has the capacity of reconciling universalism and personalism, of bringing together in one vital act of communion the person and the All.[54]

In another work Teilhard reflects on still other points of mutual support and harmony between Christian doctrine and evolutionary theory. Fundamental to Christian doctrine is the belief that the human individual cannot perfect himself or be truly Christian except in and through the "organic unification" of all men in Christ, in the mystical body of Christ. "To this mystical super-organism, joined in grace and charity, we have now added a mysterious equivalent organism born of biology: the Noospheric human unity gradually achieved by the totalising and centrating effect of reflection." To the phases of the evolutionary process, to cosmogenesis, to biogenesis, to noogenesis, the Christian adds a final, overarching phase, that of "Christogenesis." "The Christian believer can illumine and further the genesis of the universe around him in the form of a Christogenesis." The ascending force of Christianity fits so well with the process of cosmogenesis, interlocks so neatly with the process of hominization, that Teilhard can pose this question. Is not "the critical point of maturation envisaged by science simply the physical condition and experimental aspect of the critical point of the Parousia postulated and awaited in the name of Revelation?" Traditional Christian eschatology with its expectation of the second coming of Christ meshes so well with the Teilhardian estimate of the end of the evolutionary process that both events tend to coincide in time.

Hence, Teilhard goes on to speak of another intuition taking shape in human consciousness. "Born of the psychic combination of two kinds of faith—in the transcendent action of a personal God and the innate perfectibility of a world in progress—it is an impulse, or better, a spirit of love that is truly evolutionary."[55] There can be no doubt that Teilhard was convinced that Christian evolutionism is the only answer to every legitimate demand that the scientist, especially of the humanistic-evolutionistic variety as Julian Huxley, can make of any religion of the future. "Can we not say that Christianity fulfills all the conditions we are entitled to expect from a religion of the future?"[56]

NOTES

1. The literature on Teilhard de Chardin is too extensive for reference here, but several works in English can be listed: C. Trestamont, *Pierre Teilhard de Chardin: His Thought* (Baltimore: Helicon Press, Inc., 1959); R. F. Francoeur (ed.), *The World of Teilhard* (Baltimore: Helicon Press, Inc., 1961); O. Rabut, *Teilhard de Chardin: A Critical Study* (New York: Sheed and Ward, Inc., 1961); C. Cuenot, *Teilhard de Chardin* (Baltimore: Helicon Press, Inc., 1965); P. Smulders, *The Design of Teilhard de Chardin* (Westminster, Md.: Newman Press, 1967).

2. Teilhard de Chardin, *The Phenomenon of Man*, trans. B. Wall (New York: Harper & Row, 1961), Preface, p. 29.

3. Teilhard, *Phenomenon*, Foreword, p. 34.

4. See Teilhard, *Phenomenon*, Book III, ch. III, pp. 217–225, and Preface, p. 30.

5. Teilhard, *Phenomenon*, Foreword, p. 34.

6. Teilhard, *Phenomenon*, Book I, ch. I, pp. 39–43.

7. See Teilhard, *Phenomenon*, Book I, pp. 43–46.

8. Teilhard, *Phenomenon*, Book I, p. 49; see also pp. 47–48.

9. Teilhard, *Phenomenon*, Book I, pp. 50–52.

10. Teilhard, *Phenomenon*, Book I, ch. II, pp. 53–56.

11. Teilhard, *Phenomenon*, Book I, ch. III, p. 71.

12. Teilhard, *Phenomenon*, Book I, ch. II, p. 57.

13. Teilhard, *Phenomenon*, Book I, pp. 60–61, and Postscript, p. 300.

14. Teilhard, *Phenomenon*, Book I, ch. II, pp. 63–65. The English translation, for some unknown reason, preferred to render *psychique* from the French original as "physical." We give the normal translation of "psychical."

15. See Teilhard, *Phenomenon*, Book I, ch. III, pp. 68–71.

16. Teilhard, *Phenomenon*, Book I, pp. 72–73.

17. Teilhard, *Phenomenon*, Book II, ch. I, pp. 77–79.

18. Teilhard, *Phenomenon*, Book II, p. 80.

19. See Teilhard, *Phenomenon*, Book II, pp. 84–86.

20. See Teilhard, *Phenomenon*, Book II, pp. 100, 102.

21. See Teilhard, *Phenomenon*, Book II, p. 89.

22. See Teilhard, *Phenomenon*, Book II, ch. II, p. 112; ch. I, pp. 94–96; Book III, ch. I, p. 181.

23. See Teilhard, *Phenomenon*, Book II, pp. 108–109.

24. Teilhard, *Phenomenon*, Book II, p. 113.

25. Teilhard, *Phenomenon*, Book II, ch. III, pp. 142–146.

26. Teilhard, *Phenomenon*, Book II, p. 159, 160; see also pp. 147–159.

27. Teilhard, *Phenomenon*, Book III, ch. I, pp. 165, 166, 168.

28. Teilhard, *Phenomenon*, Book III, pp. 172, 173.

29. Teilhard, *Phenomenon*, Book III, pp. 178, 180.

30. Teilhard, *Phenomenon*, Book III, pp. 180, 181, 182. Several articles in Teilhard's *The Future of Man* (New York: 1964) can be consulted for fuller discussion of the noosphere and related concepts: "A Great Event Foreshadowed:

The Planetization of Mankind," pp. 124–139; "The Formation of the Noosphere," pp. 155–184; "The Human Rebound of Evolution and Its Consequences," pp. 196–213.

31.   Teilhard, *Phenomenon*, Book III, pp. 185–188.

32.   Teilhard, *Phenomenon*, Book III, p. 188, n. 1.

33.   Teilhard, *Phenomenon*, Book III, ch. II, p. 196; see also pp. 190–196.

34.   Teilhard, *Phenomenon*, Book III, pp. 196–197.

35.   Teilhard, *Phenomenon*, Book III, p. 198.

36.   Teilhard, *Phenomenon*, Book III, pp. 199, 200, 201.

37.   Teilhard, *Phenomenon*, Book III, p. 202.

38.   Teilhard, *Phenomenon*, Book III, p. 205.

39.   Teilhard, *Phenomenon*, Book III, pp. 207, 208.

40.   Teilhard, *Phenomenon*, Book III, pp. 210, 211; see also pp. 208–210.

41.   Teilhard, *Phenomenon*, Book III, ch. III, pp. 213, 214, 220.

42.   Teilhard, *Phenomenon*, Book III, pp. 232–233. The optimism of *The Phenomenon of Man* is not a new position for Teilhard, since it dates back to the year 1920 and even earlier. Consult the many articles in *The Future of Man*, pp. 11–81, that are explicitly concerned with the doctrine of progress.

43.   See Teilhard, *Phenomenon*, Book IV, ch. I, pp. 238–242.

44.   Teilhard, *Phenomenon*, Book IV, pp. 243, 244.

45.   Teilhard, *Phenomenon*, Book IV, pp. 248, 250, 251, 252.

46.   Teilhard, *Phenomenon*, Book IV, ch. II, pp. 258, 259, 260.

47.   Teilhard, *Phenomenon*, Book IV, pp. 261, 262.

48.   Teilhard, *Phenomenon*, Book IV, pp. 263, 264, 265, 266.

49.   Teilhard, *Phenomenon*, Book IV, pp. 267, 270.

50.   Teilhard, *Phenomenon*, Book IV, pp. 271–272.

51.   Teilhard, *Phenomenon*, Book IV, ch. III, pp. 273, 276.

52.   Teilhard, *Phenomenon*, Book IV, pp. 277, 278, 284, 285.

53.   Teilhard, *Phenomenon*, Book IV, pp. 288, 289. This is the only mention of evil in the *Phenomenon* except for an appendix (pp. 309–311), added in 1948.

    Teilhard develops his futuristic theme in articles gathered in *The Future of Man*. Especially worthwhile are the later articles, beginning with "The Directions and Conditions of the Future," p. 227 f.

54.   Teilhard, *Phenomenon*, Epilogue, pp. 291, 292, 298.

55.   Teilhard, *The Future of Man*, pp. 223–224.

56.   Teilhard, *Phenomenon*, Epilogue, pp. 297–298. The notion of a main axis of evolution receives a more complete exposition in "Turmoil or Genesis?" in *The Future of Man*, pp. 214–226.

SUMMARY

            It can be claimed fairly enough that the speculative philosophy of history did not enter on an entirely new phase with the views expressed in this section. In some instances the theory of history is only a by-product of more scientific interests. In every case the theories advanced are either a renewal of or an expansion of views expressed a century or so ago. V. Gordon Childe, for example, did not hide a consistent use of a modernized Marxist model of the historical process for his reconstruction of the past of prehistoric man. Leslie White relied on the Comtean law of three stages for his understanding of the intellectual progress of man, while at the base of all his theorizing lies a mechanistic conception of reality which recalls the Spencerian view, if only on a reduced scale. An updated Darwinian biological evolution is the centerpiece of the syntheses of Huxley and Teilhard, and even the grand sweep of the Teilhardian vision is not new. Spencer, and even Herder in his own way, had been there before.

    The whole question of the speculative philosophy of history had been reopened by the work of Spengler, Toynbee, and Sorokin. On the whole, and with the necessary qualifications, they offered a conception of the historical process that was a cyclical and rhythmical view of the courses of the great cultures and civilizations of the past. History manifested a movement in its principal subject, the great literate civilizations, which, if not exactly repetitive, was recurrent and rhythmical. While cross-cultural diffusion, borrowing, and even accumulation of a sort was admitted by the moderates of this group, the truly great moments of progress were seen to be encased in the larger rhythms of the course of a civilization as a whole. The implications of this reading of the past are clear: an indefinite or interminable progress and future could not be held out as a realistic hope for Western civilization as if it were unique and somehow exempt from what had every appearance of being a regularity of the past.

From all sides the critics attacked these theories, especially the professional historians. "All these large syntheses of history are vitiated by an insufficient appreciation of the infinite complexity, of the many-sidedness, of the irreducible variety of the life of mankind in all of its aspects which is after all the stuff of which history is made."[1] These words of Pieter Geyl, an eminent Dutch historian, were an indictment of the theories proposed by Spengler, Toynbee, and Sorokin. As a working historian, Geyl could be expected to advert to the bewildering variety of historical entities, their continuing growth and transformation, as well as the ocean of data available for many periods and areas and its scarcity for others. Facts were selected by these theorists to certify a theory or compelling vision which was brought to the historical process and not found there. All this criticism and more was leveled at those who confined their investigations and theories to the conventional period of history beginning with the first appearance of civilizations some five to six thousand years ago.

Quite another brand of criticism was offered by the authors reviewed in Part Four. They do not delay over the criticisms of the historians but launch an attack from another quarter. Theories of history springing from the conventional period of history alone were bound to be too cramped and shortsighted for universal validity or truth. One must take the long view and encompass the whole history of man. For a prehistoric archaeologist such as Childe and a cultural anthropologist such as White this meant that a million or more years must be added to the conventional period of history. Prehistory, as it is called, must be joined with history if the historical development of humanity is to be assessed in true perspective. At the same time, it was held, because of the nature of the evidence from preliterate times, the objective and scientific methods practiced by the natural historian could be pressed into service.

As we know, this was not the end of the mergers suggested. If man and his past were to be seen in the truest perspective of all, the broadest possible view must be taken. Natural history as well as prehistory must be linked with history in the estimation of Huxley and Teilhard de Chardin. Science must be called in to illuminate the problems of the speculative philosophy of history. The history of man only prolongs on another plane the history of life, beginning perhaps some 2500 million years ago. Life, in its turn, is but an elevated phase of the history of matter, beginning, on one theory, at the very least some 6500 million years before the emergence of life. Man is the most "modern" enterprise

---

[1] P. Geyl, *Debates with Historians* (New York: Meridian Books, 1958), 162.

of life, which is itself a late "medieval" product of a remarkably endowed matter. On such a time scale one would have thought that civilizations and even man himself would be lost to sight. This may be true of civilizations, but science demonstrates, or so Teilhard believed, that a line of progress runs through this unimaginable length of time from matter to life to man, where it has finally become conscious of itself. Huxley explicitly joins Teilhard in this view at the point when life begins, and both feel that anthropocentrism, or humanism, is scientifically justified.

Except for one large critical area, the syntheses of Huxley and Teilhard seem remarkably alike to the layman's eyes. Both insist on the unity of the cosmos and the continuity in natural processes, which are interrelated as elements of a single universal evolutionary process. Each postulates a basic world-stuff endowed with mental as well as material capacities from which man himself ultimately derives through a progressive and creative evolutionary drive. Both hold that the evolutionary dynamic has settled in man, where it has finally become conscious of itself through the work of Darwin and others. Further, they believe that the individual human personality is the highest product of the evolutionary process as a whole. To secure certain progress, all that man has to do is walk along the path that the evolutionary process has taken and in the direction toward which it points. From a teleonomic or unconscious and blindly directed process of natural selection in the past, evolution has become, and can become much more so, a teleological or consciously purposeful process in the mind and planning of man. It is at this point that Teilhard and Huxley begin to part company. Only the latter would have accepted the last point without qualification.

Huxley gives a masterful and classic synthesis of organic evolution and with it a sketch of the whole of human history *sub specie evolutionis*. Ultimately, natural selection is the only effective agency of organic evolution by which the accidents of mutation over a long period of time are converted into biological improvement. Over a period of 2500 million years it has brought off not only biological improvement in all the main properties of life but a line of advance passing from group to group which should be called biological progress. Biological progress culminated in the attainment of true speech and conceptual thinking in man. Since that time purely biological progress has ceased, and another evolutionary process has largely taken over in the area of psychosocial phenomena and human history. Human history is only a recent if very special outgrowth of biological evolution. Approached from this angle it can be studied as an over-all unitary process after the fashion of bioevolution, which escapes detection if attention is riveted on civilizations and the last five or six thousand years.

With the emergence of modern man, after the long period of progressive humanization among proto-men, there has been a growing tendency toward convergence on both the physical and cultural sides which is unique in the evolutionary process. On the physical side, despite an initial tendency toward divergence into subspecies, there has been increasing racial convergence, especially since the end of the ice age. The same phenomenon can be charted on the cultural side as well: following an initial divergence into separate and distinct cultures, there has been a rapidly increasing cultural convergence during the last few centuries. A world community with a world civilization is in the offing, but wise use must be made of the lessons from organic evolution if progress is to continue. Advance is more important than pure survival, a dynamic openness to the future of more value than a static and perhaps deadly overspecialization for the present. Hence the world community of the future must allow for variety in unity, becoming an orchestration of cultures, which will contain the seeds of its own transformation. Always open to evolutionary advance and novelty, the future world community must develop those human faculties that enabled man to attain his position as the latest dominant biological type. It should be remembered that human personality was the final outcome of the evolutionary dynamic on the biological plane and that the full development of personality is the goal of evolution become conscious of itself. To this end all cultural activities must keep pace with evolutionary consciousness on pain of becoming extinct or fossilized. The world-wide population explosion must be contained with appropriate scientific measures if man himself is not to become biologically inferior. Man's destiny is to be the agent and instrument of the evolutionary process on earth. Once this has been seen, it will be admitted that the "god-hypothesis" is outdated and that evolutionary humanism is the only religion that can possibly keep abreast of the scientific evolutionary consciousness.

Teilhard has a different view of the matter. Evolution from the beginning is primarily of a psychic or spiritual nature. Everything in the Teilhard universe originated from an arrangement of a few elements and transforms itself according to a cosmic law of increasing complexification. Imbedded in the basic world-stuff is a drive that impels it from the simple to the more complex. This drive, or "radial energy," springs from an inner dimension of all cosmic matter, the "within" or "conscious," though at different levels of intensity. Development of this inner dimension is outwardly accompanied by a better and more complex material framework. One can trace the growing intensity of the conscious right up to man principally through the accompanying material complexity. Everything in the world, including man, has existed in a lesser form since the beginning of time. This is Teilhard's cosmic embryogenesis. At a crucial moment in time the historical appearance of new entities takes place because of the radial energy that is driving cosmic matter toward ever-increasing centralization and complexity.

One threshold was crossed on earth when life emerged in the cell with an increase of the synthetic character of matter, which was accompanied by a higher level of consciousness. Natural selection and chance mutations are not the ultimate explanation of the progressive development of life, as Huxley believed. The appearance of higher living forms is due once again to the upward striving of the inner dimension of matter, which is now living. All living things, the biosphere, seek a new plane of life and consciousness. Evolution has a definite direction, as it is still pursuing the development of the psychic or spiritual. All at once, perhaps a million years or so ago, another even greater threshold was crossed. Like an arrow shot out from one line of exclusively fitting biological progress, man was suddenly and silently on earth. The biosphere had entered a new order of the noosphere. In man the conscious became self-conscious and self-knowing. Man was not only an individual of a new species but someone, a person. He is the peak toward which all biological striving has been aiming, as the evolutionary pressures in the tree of life have waned since his appearance. Not only that, he is also the summit and crown of cosmological matter. The whole of the cosmos cooperated in the birth of man and on earth is summed up in him.

Evolution did not cease with the emergence of man and the noosphere. From the start evolution aimed at reflective thought, but consciousness must continue to expand and ascend in man's mind until another peak is reached. Man's past, prehistoric as well as historic, can be seen as two decisive steps toward this objective. One step in the development of the noosphere began as long ago as the Neolithic revolution and it continues today at a stupendously accelerated rate: the increasing convergence and unification of mankind, accompanying a geographical expansion encompassing the whole of the earth, which consists in the tendency to form one single world-wide society of mankind. Bound together today by elements of Western civilization, this single humanity is beginning to think and act more and more as a cohesive unit. Decisive as this long step may be, there is still a deeper, more internal, noospheric consciousness that is finally bursting forth from the depths of externally converging mankind: evolution has become conscious of itself in man. Man is beginning to recognize and to become conscious of the grand movement that is carrying him along. Yet increasing socialization and growing evolutionary consciousness are not sufficient for the demands of the Teilhardian evolutionary dynamic.

Evolution must culminate in the highest degree of the conscious. The future evolution of man must follow the same lines that evolution has taken in the past and be consummated by an ultimate convergence at once fully personal and social around one point. This is Teilhard's Omega point. The ultimate convergence will mark the end of the ascent of humanity, since Omega is the cosmic focal point on which the noosphere has been plainly converging since the Neolithic metamorphosis. Omega point is not only a future goal of humanity but also a present radiating center of attraction around which the evolving noosphere is increasingly concentrating. This centripetal movement springs from the love of man, which is the inner evolutionary driving force of the within or conscious on the human plane. Only love is able to effect the final "Hyper-Personal" state of consciousness in which the personal and social are not sacrificed one to the other but each is fulfilled in a higher synthesis. Only a supremely conscious center much like ourselves, that is, a person, can call forth our deepest love and hope to fulfill it. Hence the noosphere mounts irresistably toward a personal Omega point. The final convergence of humanity on Omega point will coincide with the end of the world and of the phenomenon of man in accord with the dictates of the second law of thermodynamics.

This is not all. Thermodynamics and its laws apply only to mechanical or tangential energy and not to the energy of love, which is the highest form of the radial. Love focused on Omega constantly escapes the entropy of the universe and at the death of the individual is completely liberated from the confines of the tangential. The cosmos is a conservatory of persons, not of mechanical energies. Since the beginning evolution has been directed toward the conscious in man, and his total death would render it not only meaningless but absurd. Once the universe admitted thought, it no longer could be completely transitory but must emerge into the absolute. Another universe is in process of being built up whose completion will coincide with the final terrestrial convergence on Omega point and the end of the earth. Omega point, for Teilhard, is Christ the Son of God become man. The fully conscious way to Christ is through traditional Christian belief and religion. Once the Christian faith is accepted, it will be recognized that God the creator is Alpha point.

index

291

Huxley, Julian (Cont'd)
  theory of history, 248–260, 261–
    262
    analogies between psychosocial
      and biological evolution, 254
    biological evolution, 251–254
    biological improvement, 252–253
    biological progress, 253
    evolutionary humanism as only
      scientific hypothesis, 259
    evolutionary humanism as reli-
      gion of future, 248, 259–160
    God-hypothesis outmoded, 258–
      259
    history sub specie evolutionis,
      254
    humanism scientific fact, 248
    monistic evolutionary hypothesis,
      249–251
    mystery of existence, 250
    natural selection, 251–252
    psychosocial evolution, 254–257
    religion of the future, 257–260
    religion sub specie evolutionis,
      258
    self creation, 249
    single evolutionary process, 250–
      251
    single world stuff, 249–250
    teleonomic and teleological evo-
      lution, 255
    uniqueness of human deploy-
      ment, 255–256

Idea (theory) of progress, 21, 22, 23,
  24, 25, 27, 28, 29, 34, 35, 35–36,
  37, 64–65, 73, 85–86, 151, 165–
  166, 246
Idealistic logic, 125–127
Idiographic method, 97–98, 100
Iggers, C. G., 102
Individual, human (person), 58–59,
  83, 114–116, 121, 232, 233, 248,
  271–272, 277–280, 287, 288
Inductive method, 220, 237
Inside and outside of human events,
  143–144
Intuition, 207, 209, 218, 237–238
Irrational factuality of history, 118
Islam, 194, 195
Israel, 8
Italian Renaissance, 18

Jerusalem, 8
Jews, the, 22–23, 217
Joachim of Fiore, 18
Judgment of nations, 15, 46–47
Jung, C., 196

Kahn, S. J., 102
Kant, Immanuel, 28–31, 36–37, 38,
  65, 104, 105, 106
  theory of history, 28–31, 36–37
    halfway house of universal his-
      tory, 30–31
    Idea and universal history, 29
    league of free nations, 30
    progress as presupposition, 29,
      37
    teleological conception, 29
    unsocial sociability, 29–30
Kardiner, A., 232
Keyes, G. L., 16
Kierkegaard, S., 59
Klibansky, R., 101, 103, 155
Kluback, W., 119, 120, 122, 219
Kluckhohn, C., 232, 233, 241
Knox, T. M., 154
Kroeber, Alfred, 167, 220–231, 231–
  234, 235, 236, 237, 238, 239, 240,
  241, 245, 257
  theory of history, 220–231, 231–
    234
    autonomy of cultural, 222–224
    civilization as superstyle, 229
    comparative study of civiliza-
      tions, 224–231
    concept of culture, 232
    concept of style, 225–228
    culture and civilization, 233
    culture-patterns, 223–224
    delineation of civilizations, 224–
      225
    extension of style, 226, 228–229
    future of western civilization,
      231
    human nature and cultural rela-
      tivism, 233
    inductive method, 220
    life-history and civilizations, 230–
      231
    life-history and style, 227
    notion and causality, 232–233
    perception of styles, 227–228
    properties of style, 226–227